Logic and the Art of Memory

*This translation is dedicated to Judith
(the 'Thou' to my 'I'), and
to our children Leah and Lauren, Jonathan and Christopher*

PAOLO ROSSI

Logic and the Art of Memory

The Quest for a Universal Language

Translated with an Introduction by
Stephen Clucas

The University of Chicago Press

The University of Chicago Press, Chicago 60637

The Athlone Press, London SE1 7NX

Translation © 2000 by The Athlone Press and
The University of Chicago

Printed in Great Britain

First published in Italy 1983 by Società editrice il Mulino, Bologna, as
CLAVIS UNIVERSALIS: ARTI DELLA MEMORIA E LOGICA
COMBINATORIA DA LULLO A LEIBNIZ
© 1983 Società editrice il Mulino

09 08 07 06 05 04 03 02 01 00   1 2   3 4 5

ISBN: 0-226-72826-9 (cloth)

Library of Congress Cataloging-in-Publication Data

Rossi, Paolo, 1923–
   [Clavis universalis. English]
   Logic and the art of memory: the quest for a universal language/
Paolo Rossi; translated with an introduction by Stephen Clucas.
      p. cm.
   Includes bibliographical references and index.
   ISBN 0-226-72826-9 (alk. paper)
      1. Logic, Modern—History. 2. Memory (Philosophy)—History.
   3. Language, Universal—History. I. Title.

   BC38 .R6713 2000
   160—dc21

                                                        00-029873

This book is printed on acid free paper.

Contents

Translator's Introduction

In an 'advice' on the education of a nobleman written for his son in 1594, Henry Percy, ninth earl of Northumberland (1564–1632) described a discipline which he called 'Vniuersell Grammer'. This 'Grammer' was completely unrelated to grammar as it was taught in the Elizabethan universities, but is described by Percy as 'a necessary means to expresse our knowledges to others, or to the deliuery of them to posterite by record'. This doctrine did not treat 'those rules vulgarly taught, for the attaining any receaued language', but was rather

> sutche a doctrine generall, as discouereth amongest the whole variete of means sensible, the best wayes to signefy the conceipts of our minds, to others in present or futur, at hand, or any remote distance possible, and in any tyme giuen that is possible, either indifferently to all, or with purpose to somme certain, and in all cases, either of necessite, or discretion. In this doctrine the rules and conditions of languische and caracterisme in his hieght ar generally deliuered, cutting of[f] all equiuocations and sinonymies whiche vulgar tongs ar to mutche pestered with all, and the very route of most of our errors, and controuersyes in opinion, together with the grounds of all occultations, cyphrings, discyphrings &c.[1]

Combining what appears to modern eyes to be an early form of cryptography (in so far as it deals with 'occultations, cyphrings [and] discyphrings') with a quasi-Baconian interest in 'caracterisme' (a general consideration of the functions of symbolic characters or forms of notation) as a means of optimizing human communication, and minimizing the ambiguities of natural language, Percy's short-lived renaissance 'doctrine', or discipline, in many ways confounds modern attempts to situate it, and has universalizing aspirations which seem foreign to modern notions of system or rationality.

In the early years of the seventeenth century Percy's pensioner, the natural philosopher Walter Warner (1562–1643) also entertained hopes of achieving a total knowledge by means of optimizing linguistic communication through symbolic notation, so that 'every singular man may be possessed of all . . . the phenomenes and notions of all the men of the vniuers'.[2] In a series of untitled reflections on the topic of *veritatis conceptio* (a series of definitions, axioms and propositions relating to the ways in which the concepts of intellectual truth are formed in the mind) Warner sketches the outlines of a 'general science' (*scientia generalis*).[3] The various sciences, he argued, could be distributed, ordered and constructed into a single corpus (*in vnum quasi scientiæ corpus ordinatim dispositæ et constructæ*).[4] Nature, he says, is like a language written in different characters (*sunt rerum in natura differentiæ totidem conficiendi sint distinctè differentes caracteres*). The mind has a faculty – *conceptio* – whose task it is to record the signature of these characters in the mind (*facultatis conceptiuæ . . . qua res ipsa per signaturam suam concipitur actus est*).[5] By means of an 'imaginative onomasticon' (*imaginariam . . . onomasticam*) or 'universal alphabet' (*alphabeto vniuersali*) one could order these concepts in such a way that there would be a perfect congruence, without homonymy or synonymy, between the signifier and the thing signified (*significationis cum rebus significantis adæquata congruentia absque omni homonimia aut synonima*).[6] Truth is an 'adequation, conformity or congruence between the concept and the thing conceived, or the intellect and the thing intellectualized' (*adequatio seu conformatio seu congruentia conceptus cum re conceptâ siue intellectus cum re intellectâ*).[7] Falsehood is an incongruence (*incongruentia*) between them.[8] The general science, by beginning with the simplest forms of intellectual truth (*conceptio immediata*) and building up to mediated propositions, and complex notions, would necessarily arrive at universally true knowledge.

Renaissance projects for maximizing (or totalizing) human knowledge, like Percy's 'universal grammar' and Warner's 'general science' (which reached their full expression in the schemes for a 'universal' or 'artificial' language devised by English philosophers in the 1650s and 1660s) can only be understood within the context of a tradition which fused the mediaeval notion of the *ars artium*, which reached its apogee in the *ars magna* of Ramon Lull, mnemotechnics, emblematics, cryptology, the cabala and other symbolic modes of communication. This complex and diverse tradition is the subject of Paolo Rossi's *Clavis universalis*. Drawing together a number of disciplines and practices which have previously been fragmented and dispersed across a number of distinct modern historiographical provinces, Rossi's work reveals them as moments in a recognisible tradition, a community of ideas and shared concepts which linked together various European intellectual milieux. This book is of profound importance for intellectual historians of the early modern period, in its insistence on the need to recontextualize a number of key problems in the science, philosophy and linguistics of the period in relation to a tradition which until relatively recently has been ignored, misunderstood or trivialized.

Rossi's book is also important for its refusal to marginalize the 'logico-encyclopaedic' and mnemotechnical traditions. These traditions, as Rossi points out, were a vital and living intellectual presence in early modern Europe and played a vital role in the rise of early modern science and logic. This point is driven home particularly in the fifth and eighth chapters, where Rossi reappraises the work of Bacon, Descartes and Leibniz in the light of the sixteenth and seventeenth-century developments of the mediaeval *ars combinatoria*. His recontexualization of 'scientific' figures such as Bacon and Descartes in the light of the encyclopaedic tradition preempted many of the more recent critical and sceptical revisions of earlier historiographical accounts of the 'rise of science', which had tended to occlude some of the more characteristically renaissance inflections of the 'new science' in order to produce a 'cleaner', Kuhnian revolutionary narrative of the emergence of modern science. Rossi's 'retroactive' reading of Leibniz (placing him at the 'end' of a Renaissance intellectual tradition rather than reading him 'forwards' as an innovative precursor of modern formal logic who broke decisively with the traditions of the past) gives a clearer sense of the ultimate intellectual trajectory of the tradition, and problematizes the history of logic by placing some of Leibniz's key themes in the context of earlier developments in the occult sciences and metaphysics. Above all Rossi's work shows us how a body of ideas developed not simply as an abstract set of intellectual forms, but as the vehicles of cultural meaning. If, as Mary Carruthers has persuasively argued, 'mediaeval culture was fundamentally memorial, to the same profound degree that modern culture in the West is documentary',[9] Rossi's book is proof that this 'memorial culture' persisted into the age of the printed book, and was still a vestigial presence in the early years of the European Enlightenment.

Rossi has not been alone in redrawing the attention of the scholarly community to the art of memory and the Lullist tradition, however, and (as his own generous 1983 dedication freely acknowledges) Frances Yates's *Art of Memory* is a work which is still justifiably considered to be a milestone in the study of the mnemotechnic tradition in mediaeval and Renaissance Europe. Rossi's book has, however, a number of advantages over Yates's work, which places too much emphasis, perhaps, on the role of Giordano Bruno in the tradition (five of the book's seventeen chapters are devoted to Brunian mnemotechnics) and Yates, as Rossi himself notes, is sometimes prone to exaggeration and selective vision in her single-minded construction of a Renaissance 'Hermetic tradition'.[10] Rossi's intellectual history is less rhetorically persuasive and has less narrative force, but is more cautious and versatile, and weaves together the complicated threads of this tradition (or traditions) with more attention to the details of the historical fabric. Yates, for instance, is far less interested than Rossi in the crucial German pedagogical developments of these ideas,[11] and their connections with the later seventeeth-century schemes for a universal language, and largely neglects the connections between mnemotechnics and natural magic and medicine.

Since *Clavis universalis* was first published in 1960 there has been a host of developments in the various fields of intellectual history relevant to the complex of themes dealt with in the book. Rossi's preface to the second edition in 1983 indicates a number of these. To these I would like to add a selection of my own, most of which have been published since 1983.

Probably the most significant recent work on what Rossi calls the 'logico-encyclopaedic tendency'[12] in early modern culture is Wilhelm Schmidt-Biggemann's *Topica universalis* (1983).[13] A survey conceived on the same grand scale as the books of Rossi and Yates, Schmidt-Biggemann's book complements both studies in its focus on aspects of the tradition which they neglected: Schmidt-Biggemann deals with the dialectics and topical logic of Rudolph Agricola, and the commonplace tradition,[14] and concepts of method within the Aristotelian tradition (with a particular focus on the works of Giacomo Zabarella) and the logical systems of Bartholomaeus Keckermann and Clemens Timpler, but he also extends his study to cover the 'afterlife' of the encyclopaedic tradition: the 'polyhistories' of the eighteenth century.[15] Schmidt-Biggemann places the encyclopaedic tradition in the larger context of the 'history of systems' (*Geschichte von Systemen*), and attends to the period-specific nature of particular conceptions of order and system, seeing the particular cluster of 'systematic models' which go under the names of encylopaedism, polyhistory, polymathy, *scientia universalis*, and *mathesis universalis* as characteristic of early seventeenth-century thought.[16]

There have also been significant developments in some of the subfields which Rossi draws together in this book. In the field of mediaeval mnemotechnics the two immensely rich works of Mary Carruthers – *The Book of Memory* (1990)[17] and *The Craft of Thought* (1998)[18] – with their stress on the cultural significance and impact of techniques and practices of memorization as an 'orthopraxis' have immeasurably deepened our understanding of the mnemotechnical developments of the long Middle Ages. As Carruthers has shown, mediaeval practitioners thought of memory as 'a universal thinking machine', and this idea was destined to have a significant influence on sixteenth-century philosophers, whose encyclopaedic aspirations had been given additional impetus by the 'neoplatonic renaissance' of the late fifteenth century. Lullism (and especially, as Rossi points out, the version of Lullism bequeathed to the sixteenth century by Pico della Mirandola)[19] played a vital part in this development of the idea of a 'thinking machine'. Lullian scholarship which in the early part of the twentieth century was largely the preserve of mediaeval specialists, and had become rather internalist, and disinclined to address the later reception and developments of Lullism in the sixteenth and seventeenth centuries, has begun to address the role of Lullism in later intellectual cultures. Paola Zambelli's study of the Pseudo-Lullian *De auditu kabbalistico*, is exemplary in this respect, and the recent publication of a facsimile edition of the monumental Zetzner edition of Lull and his sixteenth-century commentators,[20] and Anthony Bonner's accessible translations of Lullian works,[21] will no doubt contribute to a renewed interest in this key area of the logico-encyclopaedic tradition.

Amongst the many contributions to the study of early modern mnemotechnics in the past two decades, I would like to single out a recent collection of essays edited by Wolfgang Neuber and Joerg Jochen Berns, *Ars memorativa: zur kulturgeschichtlichen Bedeutung der Gedaechtniskunst 1400–1750* (1993);[22] this collection of essays, ranging from mnemonic bibles of the late mediaeval period to Jakob Bernouillis's *Ars conjectandi*, from Robert Fludd's *Theatrum memoriae*, to Giambattista Vico's *Nuova scienza*, is very much in the spirit of Rossi's *Clavis* (which is a pervasive citational presence throughout the work) in its commitment to the idea of the art of memory and *scientia universalis* as paradigmatic instances of the internal complexity of early modern intellectual culture.[23]

In the field of universal language there have been significant contributions by Gerhard Strasser, *Lingua universalis: Kryptologie und Theorie der Universalsprachen im 16. und 17. Jahrhundert*,[24] and Umberto Eco, whose recent study of universal language, *Ricerca della lingua perfetta nella cultura europea*,[25] has reawakened interest in a subject which has long been the sole province of historians of linguistics. Another work which has introduced encyclopaedic themes to a wider scholarly audience (including intellectual historians and historians of science) is Ann Blair's *The Theater of Nature. Jean Bodin and Renaissance Science* (1997). With its 'fine-grained analysis' of Bodin's *Universae naturae theatrum* (1596), Blair's book, whilst attempting to reconstruct 'what it meant to "do physics" for Jean Bodin and various near contemporaries',[26] draws out the wider significance of a variety of trends in natural history and encyclopaedism in the late Renaissance, and their implications for the structures of Renaissance thought. Blair's discussion of 'theatrical metaphors' in the Renaissance,[27] could usefully be read alongside chapter three of the present work, while her broad-ranging discussions of the 'problem of order' and its connections to pedagogy, classification, commonplaces and dialectical argumentation, resonate with Rossi's treatment of order and arrangement across various disciplines.

Rossi's discussions of dialectics, the relationship between logic and rhetoric, and Renaissance concepts of 'method', can now be supplemented by the studies of Cesare Vasoli, *La dialettica e la retorica dell'umanesimo. 'Invenzione' e 'metodo' nella cultura del XV e XVI secolo* (1968),[28] and Lisa Jardine, whose book on Baconian method and dialectic, *Francis Bacon: Discovery and the Art of Discourse* (1974),[29] makes similar connections between the new habits of thought introduced by Agricolan dialectics and the development of 'scientific method'.

Although it predates Rossi's book, Walter J. Ong's *Ramus, Method, and the Decay of Dialogue*, published in 1958, is also a vitally important book for understanding the development of 'method' and logic in the late sixteenth century, and its elaboration of the role of 'spatialization' of mental constructs in the late sixteenth century merits further attention.[30]

The themes of Rossi's chapter on the 'imaginative logic' of Giordano Bruno, which (together with Cesare Vasoli's 1958 essay on Brunian mnemotechnics)[31] marked one of the first serious attempts to assess Bruno's Lullian and mnemotechnical works in the context of the Lullian revival and the 'occultization' of the art of memory of the sixteenth century, have been warmly embraced by Brunian scholars. Particularly significant in this respect are Leen Spruit's meticulous and thorough account of Bruno's theories of knowledge, *Il problema della conoscenza in Giordano Bruno*, which includes detailed analyses of the Lullian and mnemotechnical works,[32] and Rita Sturlese's reappraisals of Yates's reading of Bruno's mnemotechnics as a form of Ficinian talismanic magic.[33] Wolfgang Wildgen's recent semiotic approach to Brunian mnemotechnics[34] with its rigorous analysis of the functions of Bruno's complex mnemonic diagrams has also made an important contribution to our further understanding of this relatively neglected area of Brunian studies.

As this brief survey will have made clear, scholarship on the intertwined themes of Lullism, encyclopaedism, mnemotechnics, universal languages, and rhetorical and dialectical concepts of 'method' and 'order' has been a pan-European preoccupation, and I hope that this translation of Rossi's important contribution to this field will stimulate new research on these traditions in the English-speaking world. I would also like to express the hope that translations of the important studies of Wilhelm Schmidt-Biggemann and Cesare Vasoli mentioned above (together with Giovanni Crapulli's little-known, but excellent 1969 study *Mathesis universalis*)[35] will follow shortly – the availability of these works in English would be an enormous help in the consolidation and extension of this area of intellectual historical research in the Anglo-American scholarly world.

My acknowledgements are mercifully brief. I would simply like to thank Peter Forshaw (*ponas unum Petrum quem tu cognoscas qui sit tuus amicus!*) for his meticulous reading of the final draft of the translation, and for his help with some of the Latin translations. In accordance with the well-worn academic convention I will, of course, take full responsibility for any remaining errors.

Stephen Clucas
Birkbeck College, University of London

Preface

The term *clavis universalis* was used in the sixteenth and seventeenth centuries to designate a method or general science which would enable man to see beyond the veil of phenomenal appearances, or the 'shadows of ideas', and grasp the ideal and essential structure of reality. Deciphering the alphabet of the world; reading the signs imprinted by the divine mind in the book of nature; discovering the correspondence between the original forms of the universe and the structures of human thought; constructing a perfect language capable of eliminating all equivocations and putting us in direct contact with things and essences rather than signs; the construction of total encyclopaedias and ordered classifications which would be the true 'mirrors' of cosmic harmony – these were the objectives of the numerous defenders, apologists and expositors of Lullism and artificial memory between the fourteenth and seventeenth centuries. They formulated systematic rules for improving the memory, compiled grandiose encyclopaedias and complicated 'theatres of the world', sought to reduce the complexities of human thought to a primordial 'alphabet' of simple notions, and harboured pansophic aspirations and hopes for a universal reformation and pacification of human-kind. These approaches, projects, and themes were widely disseminated in the early modern period, and exercised a decisive influence on the development of logic and rhetoric, and led to a thorough investigation of the problem of language and memory, and questions concerning 'topics', taxonomic classification, signs, hieroglyphs, symbols and images.

It is undoubtedly difficult for the modern reader to understand the enormous influence which this phenomenon exercised on both the culture and philosophy of this period. Nevertheless the fact remains that entire generations of scholars from the early Renaissance to the age of Leibniz devoted themselves to elaborating the rules of discourse, argumentation and persuasion, establishing rules for the art of memory, and to studying the circular figures and complex combinatorial rules of the *ars magna* of Ramon Lull. It is probably no bad thing that the techniques of artificial memory and combinatorial logic have disappeared from European culture; but it is a bad thing that historians have believed (and still believe) that they can understand the controversies, discussions and theories of the early modern period, when they remove them from the vital historical context of these techniques. Anyone who deals with sixteenth-century culture, for example, who has not understood the significance of the connections between logic and rhetoric, and believes that they can trace the history of one without bothering in the least with the history of the other, has, in fact, reached barren conclusions. To suggest, as many scholars have, that the hugely popular works of this tradition were 'insignificant' is, in the final analysis, simply a glib way of avoiding a difficult historical problem: that of *accounting for* the popularity of these books, and the motives which prompted philosophers such as Henricus Cornelius Agrippa, Giordano Bruno, Francis Bacon, René Descartes and Gottfried Leibniz, educational reformers like Johann Alsted and Jan Comenius, and scientists like Robert Boyle or John Ray to take these discussions seriously, to evaluate their function and significance, and to adapt them to different and more complex philosophical ends.

Unless one wants to reject the Latin writings of Giordano Bruno, various chapters of Bacon's *De augmentis scientiarum*, parts of the early works of Descartes, and half of the shorter works of Leibniz from intellectual history as nothing more than 'mistakes' or 'illusions' of the past, unless one wants to marginalize the cultural significance of thinkers like Alsted and Comenius, it is necessary to understand that the intellectual world of seventeenth-century culture (let alone that of earlier periods) is utterly different from that of the post-Enlightenment. Enlightenment rationalism signalled a decisive change in European culture: a series of problems which had inspired logical, rhetorical and linguistic theorists for centuries were expunged for ever. Denuded of their traditional meaning and significance, these problems came to be associated with the foolish, superstitious and impious pursuits of astrology, magic and alchemy – relics of mediaeval darkness, feebly persisting in the age of the new science. Many historians (influenced by the tendentious historiographical narratives formulated by enlightenment thinkers in the course of fierce ideological struggles) have neglected some of the most important aspects of baroque culture. Bruno's interests in the *ars combinatoria* and mnemotechnics, for example, were dismissed by these historians as 'curiosities and eccentricities' – they ignored the fact that Ramus, Bacon and Leibniz saw memory as one of the primary divisions of the new logic; they refused to acknowledge that Bacon's inductive logic and tabular method, and Descartes's doctrine of enumeration, arose out of a specific historical milieu, and made specific references to works and discussions which had been circulating in European cultural circles for more than a hundred years. Comenius was seen simply as a modern educationalist and Leibniz as a theorist of formal logic. They ignored the complex nexus of themes connecting the cabala, ideographic writing, the discovery of 'real characters', the art of memory, the image of the 'tree of the sciences', 'mathesis', universal languages, 'method' (understood as a miraculous key to the universe and a general science), and talked instead of a generic and mysterious entity called 'Platonism', which they deemed to be omnipresent, a shadowy backdrop or hazy landscape, stretching behind the works of major and minor thinkers of the period.

This book arose out of an attempt to shed some light on this 'background' and to sketch in some of the general and particular features of this 'landscape'. In order to do this I have analysed a representative selection of the relevant printed and manuscript sources, and have attempted to trace the dissemination of these works, and their influence on the 'philosophy' (and especially the logic) of some of the great modern philosophers.

The function, significance and aims of the arts of memory and combinatorial logic were variously configured between the fifteenth and seventeenth centuries. The rules of the venerated art, repeated over the centuries, acquired different meanings in different milieux: what had seemed to many during the fifteenth century to be a neutral technique for use in persuasive discourse ended up as the instrument of ambitious projects of reform, laden with metaphysical significance, and associated with the themes of the cabala, mystical exemplarism and pansophia. In this respect, there is an overwhelming difference between the texts of the *ars predicandi* and *ars memoriae* of the fourteenth century and the texts of Bruno and Camillo in the sixteenth. An instrument designed with practical rhetorical puposes in mind becomes (after the encounter with the

Lullist tradition) a search for a 'code' which would allow one to penetrate into the innermost secrets of reality, and to infinitely extend man's potential. Ramus, Bacon and Descartes also profoundly changed the meanings of traditional problems when they included the doctrines of artificial memory within the framework of a doctrine of 'method' or logic, or made use of the idea of the 'chain' (*catena*) or 'tree of the sciences' (*arbor scientiarum*). The artificial memory of the ancients (driven by new imperatives and profoundly transfigured) entered into modern logic, bringing with it the themes of 'universal language' and 'general' or 'primary' science. But in spite of these changes and transformations in the mnemotechnical tradition, there is a surprising continuity of ideas and discussions between the fourteenth and the last years of the seventeenth century. The continuity of this tradition was pan-European, as we can see from the wide dissemination of a vast number of texts and the many common ideas which circulated in particular groups. In the course of the eighteenth century the texts of Pietro da Ravenna and Cornelius Gemma, Johann Alsted and Pedro Gregoire, Lambert Schenkel and Cosma Rosselli, Johann Bisterfeld and John Wilkins, which had been studied, read and annotated by Bruno, Bacon, Descartes, Comenius and Leibniz *were eliminated from European culture*. Even Lullism, which had been one of the fundamental components of the intellectual cultures of early modern France, Germany and Italy, and one of the most popular and academically respected philosophical 'sects' of the period, became, in the second half of the eighteenth century, the sole province of the melancholy, old-fashioned and provincial scholar. The theme of 'artificial memory' suffered a similar fate: begun by Cicero and Quintilian in classical antiquity, and taken up by Albertus Magnus and Thomas Aquinas (who considered it essential to the exercise of the Christian virtue of prudence) and later cultivated by Lull, Bacon and Leibniz, the art of memory was relegated to the margins of culture, ending up alongside works of anthroposophy and spiritualism in the libraries of occultists.

It was probably Leibniz, who had steered the themes of Lullism and artificial memory towards those of a logical 'calculus' and mathematical symbolism, who sounded the death knell of the 'symbols' (understood as 'animated pictures produced by the imagination') which had filled the pages of rhetorical, philosophical and pedagogical texts for over three centuries. With Leibniz, and his works, an entire world disappeared: not only a certain way of understanding the function of images and symbols, but also a way of understanding the function of logic and its relation to metaphysics. When Arthur Collier published his *Clavis universalis* in 1713,[1] the idea of a 'universal key', which had previously been laden with great significance, had lost all meaning, had become a mere convention with no real bearing on the contents of the work. Collier rejected the 'archaic' aspects of Leibniz's work and dismissed Lullian exemplarism, the 'extravagant ideas' of the cabalists, the 'vain dreams' of *pansophia*, and with them the whole encyclopaedic ethos of the preceding two centuries. The projects for a universal character and logical symbolism which had begun, before Leibniz, in the works of John Wilkins and George Dalgarno, were also held in contempt by eighteenth-century rationalism – with historically important consequences. It was no coincidence that Immanuel Kant, almost a century after the publication of the *Dissertatio de arte combinatoria*, radically opposed the idea that compound ideas could be represented by means of combinations of signs and compared Leibniz's characteristic to the inconclusive dreams of the alchemists.

Leibniz's fame in the eighteenth century rested on his reputation as a theologian and a speculative metaphysician, and the *Theodicy* and his discussions on the problem of evil were seen as his greatest achievements. As William Barber (who has studied Leibniz's reception in late seventeenth and eighteenth century French culture) has rightly pointed out, the advent of empiricism 'swept Leibniz . . . into the class of the outmoded exponents of *a priori* systems'.[2] It was two hundred years before Leibniz's logic was taken up again, by Augustus de Morgan and George Boole. At the beginning of the present century, Leibniz's contributions to logic were re-evaluated by Ogden and Richard in their history of logic, *The Meaning of Meaning* (London, 1923). The development of formal logic in the nineteenth century, and the establishment of symbolic logic as a science, was the result of a 'growing awareness that it was a deductive technique independent of the presuppositions of any general worldview' (Barone), and was achieved by systematically ridding it of 'all ontological-metaphysical preoccupations' (Preti). As Husserl had previously noted, modern formal logic arose 'not from philosophical reflections on the significance and necessity of *mathesis universalis*, but from the need for a deductive theoretical technique of mathematics'.

The acknowledgement of Leibniz's 'brilliant anticipations' of modern logic thus went hand in hand with the recognition of formal logic as a respectable philosophical discipline. But Leibniz's logic (like that of Descartes and Bacon before him) emerged out of a milieu which was radically different from that of modern logic. The 'anticipations' or 'precedents' of modern logic which Farrington, Beck and Russell found in Bacon, Descartes and Leibniz, are doubtless of the greatest importance, and any research which helps to make them useful for contemporary scholarship is not only legitimate but ought to be strongly supported. It is, however, equally important to be aware of the differences between early modern scholars and their modern counterparts, to insist on their distinctness and otherness: it is important to clear up the ambiguities surrounding early modern culture, to try to understand the 'hazy background' against which the portraits of our illustrious forerunners have been painted. As Alistair Crombie recently said, in the context of a discussion of the 'precedents' in the work of Galileo: 'It is part of the philosophical enlightenment provided by the history of science to discover that the thought of great innovators whose effectiveness we admire was organised on a pattern in many ways so utterly different to our own.' [3]

Anyone who is familiar with Renaissance scholarship will clearly see the debt which this book owes to the work of Eugenio Garin on the culture of the fifteenth, sixteenth and seventeenth centuries, and – in so far as it deals with the 'continuity' of ideas between the fifteenth and seventeenth centuries – to the work of Delio Cantimori. I wish in addition to express my gratitude to Padre Miguel Batllori of the Istituto Storico della Compagnia di Gesu, to Professor François Secret, Mrs G. Compagnia of the Warburg Institute, to my friends Paola Zambelli and Cesare Vasoli who have given me advice, sent me publications, and provided me with many useful references to relevant articles and studies. Thanks also to Dr Luigi Quattrocchi of the Istituto Italiano in Hamburg who procured me some photographs of Leibnizian manuscripts, and the editorial board of *Rivista critica di storia della filosofia* who allowed me to reproduce those parts of this book which have previously appeared as articles in that journal.

Paolo Rossi
University of Milan, February 1960

Preface to the Second Edition

The art of memory and combinatory logic undoubtedly belong to the category of intellectual fossils. The *ars combinatoria*, which flourished between the fourteenth and sixteenth centuries, finally disappeared in the late seventeenth century, transformed beyond all recognition by the symbolic logic of Leibniz. The 'art of memory' which had been 'invented' by Simonides was absorbed into the encyclopaedias, taxonomies and methods of the seventeenth century and virtually disappeared as a distinct technique. It survives today in the form of advertisements for 'increasing the powers of memory' in the back pages of daily newspapers and Mondadori detective thrillers where we find the same marvellous promises (sometimes using virtually the same words) as those made in the prefaces of fifteenth and sixteenth-century works on the *ars memorativa*. History is always full of surprises. Harry Loraine, who in 1965 claimed to have 'the most phenomenal memory of the century', boasted of having taught no fewer than 250,000 readers (in the USA) how to 'enrich their minds' with thousands of things, facts, faces and names by means of a mnemonic system based on images. In 1968 one of the leading contemporary scientific authorities on the brain, the Russian Alexander R. Luria, who as far as we know had neither read the *ars memorativa*, nor any of the studies on it, published *The Mind of a Mnemonist*, in which he describes a contemporary case of prodigious memory based (as Frances Yates has observed) on the classical principles of mnemotechnics.

Even the study of fossils, as we know, can teach us many things – and not only about the past. It can teach us how ideas which were once vital and living can become culturally extinct, and how the present can carry the past within it, without anybody being aware of it. Historians usually prefer to vaunt the noble origins of the historical present, and they do not restrict themselves to simply 'misunderstanding' the past, but tend to construct imaginative genealogies which eliminate the 'undesirable elements' from the portrait gallery of their forefathers – leaving out those who kept the less commendable company of magi, cabalists, pansophists and the constructors of memory theatres and secret alphabets. In this century historians of science and logic have begun to pay attention to these 'unseemly' and arrogant forefathers who believed that their wisdom was 'as ancient as the world'. But by connecting the characterism of Leibniz directly to classical or late mediaeval logic, or by seeing the taxonomy of Linnaeus as directly descended from Pliny, they have occluded a series of obstructive presences, producing a genealogy in which one finds no extinct species or skeletons in the closet. Reduced to a sort of 'round table' of professors of formal logic or zoologists, the past created by these historians serves only to confirm the truth of the present, a private reserve in which it is very easy to hunt for 'examples': and in the process history loses both its importance and its theoretical substance. Historical reality ceases to be an obstacle to the omnipotence of epistemology, and the dialogue between past and present becomes simple and unproblematic. In this kind of history there is no 'innovation', but simply an unquestioned historiographical continuity which is not grounded on a philosophy of history, but on the presumed existence of an imaginary community of non-existent 'specialists'.

In her book *The Art of Memory* (London, 1966), Frances Yates made two important points which are worth re-emphasizing here.The first concerns the vital importance of mnemotechnics in the ancient world, when scholars did not have the luxury of paper for taking notes, or typing up orations, talks or lectures, and were unable to enjoy the benefits of the printed word. Yates saw the 'interior sight' and 'visual memorization' which allowed the practitioners of the art to pass from the visual (places and images) to the verbal, as something 'mysterious', as a 'faculty' possessed by the ancients which has been irremediably lost by the modern world. Yates's views here, as elsewhere, were a little exaggerated, perhaps, and she tended to push her arguments too far in an 'occultist' or 'Jungian' direction, but it is nonetheless true that the disappearance of the art of memory as a distinct technique between the seventeenth and eighteenth centuries has resulted, in more recent times, in cultural formations in which the faculty of memory has been increasingly attenuated. It must also be added that between the end of the nineteen sixties and the mid-seventies educational theory has gone so far as to suggest a necessary opposition between memory and culture, and has emphasized the deleterious, harmful and repressive character of all forms of mnemonic learning.

The second point emphasized by Yates relates to the historical 'marginality' of mnemotechnics. Ignoring the fact that it was a 'marginal subject, not recognized as belonging to any of the normal disciplines, having been omitted because it was no one's business' she sought to prove that it was 'everyone's business': the history of the organization of memory, she argued, 'touches at vital points on the history of religion and ethics, of philosophy, and psychology, of art and literature, [and even] of scientific method'.[1]

Yates's arguments about marginalization have a general relevance, which can easily be extended from the art of memory to the entire complex of themes treated in this book. Consider the question of universal and artificial languages in the seventeenth century, for instance. Historians of linguistics, philosophy and science have tended to work in isolation on this problem, making no attempts to establish a dialogue. Madeleine David, whose important study of the problem of writing in the sixteenth and seventeenth centuries, *Le Débat sur les écritures et l'hiéroglyphe au XVIIe et XVIIIe siècles* (Paris, 1965)[2] writes as if Giambattista Vico had never existed and makes only a passing reference to the name of Jan Amos Comenius (perhaps because he was by profession a 'pedagogue'?) who had a decisive influence on precisely the kinds of debates which she has studied with such great care. Paul Cornelius, who has written a useful book on the appearance of artificial languages in the literature of imaginary voyages – *Languages in Seventeenth and Eighteenth-Century Imaginary Voyages* (Geneva, 1965) – writes as if Yates's studies on Lullism and the art of memory (which are extremely relevant to his field of research) had not been published. James Knowlson's 1965 article 'The idea of gesture as a universal language'[3] completely detaches his treatment of the literature on gestures employed in the language of deaf-mutes from the context of the related problems of *notae* or 'real characters'. Maurice Crosland's study of the language of chemistry – *Historical Studies in the Language of Chemistry* (London, 1962) 'describes a series of controversies between alchemists and chemists rather than analysing the 'linguistic' problems of which these chemists 'as natural philosophers – were neither ignorant nor indifferent.

Anyone who is even slightly familiar with the works of Francis

Bacon or Giambattista Vico know that the discussions concerning gestural and symbolic language in the seventeenth and eighteenth centuries are inextricably bound up with the debate on Egyptian hieroglyphs understood as a form of writing capable of expressing things and notions directly (without the intermediary of the alphabet and words). One of the best books available on the European reception of hieroglyphs is that of Erik Iversen (an eminent Egyptologist): *The Myth of Egypt and its Hieroglyphs in the European Tradition* (Copenhagen, 1961). But Iversen has systematically excluded from his work all authors who are not 'Egyptologists' in the strict sense of the word: that is to say, scholars who are specifically concerned with the civilization and modes of life of the ancient Egyptians. Consequently, he eliminates from his book not only Giovanni Battista della Porta and John Wilkins, but also Francis Bacon and Giambattista Vico. The works of important figures in the debate, such as William Warburton, however, are virtually incomprehensible if they are removed from the context of the linguistic debates of the seventeenth and eighteenth centuries which were not intended to prepare the ground for the future discoveries of Champollion or (for that matter) for the edification of twentieth-century professors of Egyptology.

Given this situation it should come as no surprise to learn that a linguist like Noam Chomsky – in his *Cartesian Linguistics: A Chapter in the History of Rationalist Thought* (New York, 1966) 'when praising the achievements of pre-eighteenth-century historical linguistics, and the study of universal languages in particular, mentions only the work of Couturat and Leau, apparently oblivious to the two dozen or more works on this subject which have been published since 1903.

More recently, Michel Foucault has exercised his effervescent intelligence on the subject of artificial or universal languages. Foucault's approach is, of course, very different from that of the other kinds of scholars working in this field. His work has none of the prejudices deriving from the disciplinary territorialization of scholarship, or from the supposed disinterestedness of the history of ideas. The historiography of Foucault (which has been accurately characterized as 'stochastic') proceeds on the basis of three assumptions: 1) the analyses of authors and works in the specialized disciplines are a form of misinformation; 2) studies in any language other than French on these authors or works must be totally misinformed; and 3) the texts themselves are used exclusively as cues or occasions for the 'grand general interpretations' which (*a proposito* Foucault) even Levi-Strauss has spoken of ironically.

Foucault's central thesis regarding the fields of knowledge in the sixteenth and seventeenth centuries in *Les Mots et les choses* (Paris, 1966) can be summarized in a few words: the 'natural history' of the early modern period is not a *philosophy of life*, but a *theory of words*. When Foucault explicitly states 'the theory of natural history cannot be dissociated from that of language'[4] it is difficult not to agree and, despite what we have just said in the preceding paragraph, one must give Foucault some credit for having forcefully argued the necessity of this linkage and for pointing out the foolishness of insisting too rigidly on disciplinary boundaries between forms of knowledge which only gained their autonomy in later historical epochs. But Foucault is oversimplifying the issue to the point where it seems fantastical. Foucault becomes engrossed by what he sees as the mysterious and fascinating symmetries and correspondences between the early modern theories of natural history and language, although (in his view) there has been no 'communication of concepts', no 'exchange of methods', no 'transference of models' between these two spheres of knowledge. How then can one explain their proximity? Foucault has no doubts. With the enthusiasm of a seventeenth-century numerologist, he immediately leaps to the conclusion that there is a structural identity and secret correspondence between the two forms of knowledge. This structural identity, Foucault argues, rests upon 'a sort of historical *a priori* which . . . in a given period, delimits in the totality of experience a field of knowledge, [and] defines the mode of being of the objects that appear in that field'.[5]

Foucault (as Kepler once remarked of Fludd) 'finds delight in things wrapped in obscurity' and doubtless considers empirical explanations to be banal. The difference between his method, with its flashes of brilliant intuition (which are often mere repetitions of previous observations made by Bachelard) and the work of intellectual historians (with whom he is constantly at polemical odds) is the difference between writing poetry and John Ray's cataloguing of the plants of Scotland. However, it should be noted that his invocation of a 'historical *a priori*' is, in this instance, completely gratuitous. He *does not know* that the *Character pro notitia linguarum universalis* (Frankfurt, 1661) was written by a professor of medicine from whom Stahl claims to have derived the idea of *phlogiston*; he *does not know* that Becher published a book entitled *Schema materialum pro laboratorio portabili, sive Tripus hermeticus fatidicus pandens oracula chymica* (Frankfurt, 1689) and that, in his alchemical symbology, *just as in his theory of language*, he identifies the characters of the symbols with those of the objects symbolized. Foucault frequently refers to the 'linguistic' texts of Wilkins and the 'botanical' texts of John Ray, but he *does not know* that this structural correspondence is the result of an empirical 'communication of concepts' and a documentable 'exchange of methods'. The judgement of Sartre on this type of work is worth recalling at this point: 'after he has demonstrated the impossibility of historical reflection', Sartre says, Foucault 'replaces the cinema with a magic lantern, movement with a succession of immobile images.'[6]

Oddly enough, universal languages and memory have been poorly served by Louis Couturat's countrymen. In his study of 'Western logocentrism', *Of Grammatology*, Jacques Derrida investigated William Warburton's use of the term 'veils' in his *Essay on Egyptian Hieroglyphs* to reveal what he calls a 'surprising aperture in the logic of materialism',[7] and Jacques le Goff's article on 'memory' in the *Encylopaedia Einaudi*,[8] while it is not guilty of Derrida's intellectual narcissism, is inaccurate, dilettantish and uninformed.

This book was first published, by Ricciardi, in 1960. If, after twenty three years, I were to consider a radical (but certainly untimely) reworking of this book, I would certainly want to take account of a number of works in different fields published in the intervening period. To limit myself only to a few examples: the studies on Lull and Lullism by Eusebio Colomer (1961),[9] Eberhard W. Platzeck (1962),[10] Paola Zambelli (1965)[11] and especially Jocelyn Hillgarth (1971).[12] Other works worth considering are Liselotte Dieckmann's study on the history of hieroglyphic symbols (1969);[13] the studies of Cesare Vasoli (1968) on rhetoric and dialectic in the Renaissance,[14] Charles Webster's book on Samuel Hartlib and the diffusion of Comenius's thought in England (1970)[15] and Leroy E. Loemker's study of the encyclopaedists of Herborn (1961).[16] Among the important recent contributions to Leibniz studies I would single out the work of Albert Heinekamp (1972)[17] and Massimo Mugnai (1976),[18] and in the field of seventeenth-century linguistics, the works of Lia Formigari (1970)[19] and Hans Aarsleff (1964 and 1982).[20] David Knight's study of biological classification (1981)[21] also contains relevant material. I should also refer readers to my subsequent work on themes relating to those of the present volume: 'The legacy of Ramon Lull in sixteenth-century thought', *Mediaeval and Renaissance Studies*, 5 (1961), pp. 182–213; the chapters on 'Lingue universali, classificazioni, nomenclature' and 'Linguisti d'oggi e filosofi del Seicento' in my book *Aspetti della rivoluzione scientifica* (1970);[22] the chapters entitled 'La religione dei geroglifici e le origini della scrittura' and 'Note alla Scienza Nuova' in *Le sterminate antichità: studi vichiani* (1969);[23] and my forthcoming essay 'The nomenclatures in the XVIIth century' (to appear in *History and Philosophy of the Life Sciences*).[24]

The present edition has been extensively revised both in terms of style and presentation. Many of the quotations (except those drawn from manuscript sources) have been translated into Italian, and I have corrected some errors in the footnotes. I have also substantially reduced the number of 'Appendices'. I should like to take this opportunity to note that Frances Yates has identified two additional manuscript versions of Ramon Lull's *Liber ad memoriam confirmandam* (see Appendix I): these are Rome, Vaticana MS Lat. 5347, ff. 68–74 and Monaco, MS 10593, ff. 218–21.

In 1960 when this book was first published Frances A.Yates published her important essays on Ramon Lull (which have now been collected in a single volume entitled *Lull and Bruno: Collected Essays*)[25] and her study on the 'Ciceronian' art of memory (of which I have made extensive use in this book). Her admirable work of synthesis, *The Art of Memory*, was published in 1966 and (as she acknowledges in her preface) was conceived along 'quite different lines' from those of the present volume.[26] In two conferences at the Warburg Institute (then unknown to me) in 1952 and 1955, Yates addressed herself to the mnemotechnical system of Giordano Bruno's *De umbris idearum* and Giulio Camillo's *L'idea del teatro*. Later she read the section of my 1957 book on Francis Bacon which dealt with the *ministratio ad memoriam*.[27]

In 1960 I sent her a copy of this book which makes use of her studies on artificial memory but, to some extent, inevitably encroached on a field of study on which she had been working for many years with exceptional passion (a field, incidentally, which was little studied at that time). Dame Frances Yates was not only a scholar of the highest level, she was also an extraordinary person. I have always been very grateful to her for her many and repeated acknowledgements of my work. It is not, however, for this reason, but because I cannot forget the unexpected and sincere enthusiasm with which, in those far off days, she welcomed my 'encroach-ment', that I dedicate this second edition of the *Clavis universalis* to her memory.

Paolo Rossi
University of Florence, March 1983

CHAPTER ONE

The Power of Images and the Places of Memory

1. HUMANIST POLEMICS AGAINST THE 'PRESCRIPTIONS' OF MEMORY

In one of the fundamental works of modern philosophy, written in the midst of the Enlightenment, David Hume, in his discussion of common sense and memory argued that while the defects of common sense could not be remedied by art or invention, the defects of memory 'both in the field of business and the field of studies' could be minimized or eliminated altogether. Suggesting that 'method', 'diligence' and 'writing' could be used to aid a weak memory, he wrote:

> We scarcely ever hear a short memory given as a reason for a man's failure in any undertaking. But in ancient times, when no man could make a figure without the talent of speaking, and when the audience were too delicate to bear such crude, undigested harangues as our extemporary orators offer to public assemblies; the faculty of memory was then of the utmost consequence, and was accordingly much more valued than at present.[1]

Hume, who confessed to having 'secretly devoured' the works of Cicero in the formative years of his intellectual development, was well aware of the historical existence of a technique or art of memory which, as this passage shows, owed its existence to the flourishing of a civilization which gave an important place to the techniques of discourse, and to a world in which rhetoric was part of a living culture. At the time when Hume wrote the passage quoted above, works dedicated to setting out the rules of 'artificial memory' had all but vanished from the European cultural scene, and had been relegated to the level of intellectual curiosities. This was not the result of a declining interest in the arts of discourse, or the diminishing numbers of refined and discerning listeners. The widespread dissemination of the printed book (and thus of repertories, dictionaries, bibliographies and encyclopaedias), and the progressive development of new logical methods (from Ramus to Bacon, from Descartes to the logicians of Port Royal) had dealt a mortal blow to the popularity and credibility of the mnemotechnical works which, during the fifteenth and sixteenth centuries and in the first decades of the seventeenth, had literally invaded Europe.

It is only by taking into account the widespread popularity of mnemotechnics, not only in literary and philosophical circles, but also in schools, universities and pedagogical programmes, that we can begin to understand the vehemence of the many criticisms and satires which were levelled against it in the Renaissance. Henricus Cornelius Agrippa, for example, in the tenth chapter of his *De vanitate scientiarum*, which deals with the *ars memorativa*, launched a violent attack against what he called the scholarly 'scoundrels' (*nebulones*) of the universities, who imposed the study of artificial memory on their students, and extorted money from the gullible who found the novelty of the art appealing. Agrippa considered the exhibition of mnemonic capacity to be a 'puerile thing', which was often accompanied by 'displays of turpitude and impudence.' These scoundrels 'displayed all their goods outside their doors', he said, while 'inside their houses were completely empty'. While he cites Simonides, Cicero, Quintilian, Seneca, Petrarch and Pietro da Ravenna as the greatest theorists of the memorative art, he draws his readers' attention to two major drawbacks of the art: firstly, artificial memory does not function effectively unless the natural memory is already robust, and secondly, he disapproved of the art's employment of 'monstrous' images and burdensome formulae which impeded rather than helped the memory. The exponents of artificial memory, Agrippa concluded, would drive those who are not content with the natural confines of memory insane with their art.[2]

Ten years later, in his pedagogical manual *De ratione studii*, Desiderius Erasmus (an anti-Ciceronian and a critic of rhetorical abuses) launched an even fiercer attack on the pseudo-Ciceronian method of 'places and images' (*loci et imagines*) which, he said, impaired and corrupted the natural memory.[3] In a more ironic vein, Montaigne (another critic of humanist pedantry) attacked mnemotechnical literature by emphasizing the deficiency of his own memory (with a coarseness which derives from the particular cultural situation in which he was writing):

> There is nobody less suited than I am to start talking about memory. I can hardly find a trace of it in myself. I doubt if there is any other memory in the world as grotesquely faulty as mine is! . . . I may be a man of fairly wide reading, but I retain nothing.[4]

Montaigne, like Erasmus, questioned the Renaissance pedagogical assumption that memory and knowledge were coidentical: 'knowledge in the memory is not knowledge,' he says, 'it is simply the conservation of the knowledge of others.'[5] Montaigne criticized the pedagogical use of artificial memory in favour of a more spontaneous and organic form of learning: pupils should not be required to learn the words of their class texts by rote, but rather to give an account of their meaning and substance. The effects of education should be visible in a pupil's conduct, he argued, rather than in their aptitude for memory. Just as we would not consider the stomach to be functioning correctly if it failed to alter the form and structure of the food we eat, so we should expect the mind to perform a similar function.[6] This is not simply a *general* defence of the freedom of thought against dogmatic teaching methods – the similarity between Montaigne's polemics and a modern teacher's criticisms of the purely factual knowledge of students who learn their lessons by rote is purely superficial. Montaigne had a more specific set of objectives in mind:

> In my part of the world they actually say a man 'has no memory' to mean that he is stupid. When I complain that my memory is defective they either correct me or disbelieve me, as though I were accusing myself of being daft. They see no difference between memory and intelligence. That makes my case worse than it is. But they do me wrong: Experience shows us that it is almost the contrary: an outstanding memory is often associated with weak judgement . . . It is written of Curio the orator that after he had announced that he could divide his speech into three parts or four, or had stated the number of his arguments or reasons, he would often forget one of them or add one or two

more. I have always taken care not to fall into that trap, loathing all such promises and outlines: not simply out of distrust for my memory but because that style is too donnish.[7]

Despite the protests of Erasmus and Montaigne, the 'prescriptions' which they criticized so vehemently were destined to become increasingly popular and widespread during the sixteenth and seventeenth centuries. In the mid-seventeenth century Wolfgang Ratke protested (using similar arguments to those of the great humanists) against the teaching of mnemonics and mnemotechnic exercises in schools.[8] Even towards the end of the century, the 'Ciceronians' (who had somehow survived the criticisms of Erasmus, Montaigne and the Ramist and Cartesian crises) won continued support, in the field of pedagogy as well as rhetoric, for the utility of artificial memory. The vast number of treatises on the *ars memorativa* which were recycled in d'Assigny's *Art of Memory*[9] (which was dedicated in 1697 to 'young students of both universities') were not simply the product of an outmoded grammatical pedantry: one finds in it a final rehearsal of that 'panmethodism' which had been a vital component of sixteenth-century intellectual culture. Physiognomy, the temperament, the passions, the proportions of the human body, discourse, poetry, natural observations, the art of government and military strategy: in the sixteenth century all of these areas of study had been codified and reduced into 'arts'. This period has justifiably been called 'the age of manuals', and it was a century which was 'inexhaustible in its search for normative principles of general and perennial value, which would then be reduced into commodious didactic schemes'.[10] While it is impossible to make a direct connection between these codifications, with their emphasis on 'topics' and 'universal theatres', and the idea of 'method' in the seventeenth century,[11] it is clear that they indicate an increasingly urgent need for an 'art' which could be a key to reality, a universal art able to resolve all problems at a single blow, a 'meta-technique' which would render all particular techniques redundant.

The idea of an art of remembering and thinking which was developed in a 'mechanical' way acquired a renewed impetus when, between the middle of the sixteenth century and the middle of the seventeenth, there was a confluence of three separate traditions of the art of memory: 1) those inspired by Cicero, Quintilian and the

Ad Herennium; 2) those deriving from Aristotle's *De memoria et reminiscentia*, together with the commentaries of Albertus Magnus, Thomas Aquinas and Averroes; and 3) those directly connected to the *Ars magna* of Ramon Lull. The time was right for the development of a conceptual mechanism which, once it was set in motion, could 'work' by itself, in a way which was relatively independent of the work of the individual, until one arrived at a 'total knowledge', which would enable man to read the great book of the universe. The profound influence that this idea exercised on modern philosophy can be seen in the 'machine' which Bacon intended to construct with his new logical method; in the 'wondrous invention' (*mirabile inventum*) which Descartes sought (before he turned to analytical geometry), in the works of Lull and Agrippa; in the pansophical works of Comenius, which were to be the 'carriers of universal light'; or in the miraculous key of Leibniz's 'universal character'.

The ancient Lullian dream of an art which was both logical and metaphysical,[12] because (unlike traditional logic) it dealt with 'primary intentions', and demonstrated the correspondence between the rhythms of thought and reality, and revealed, through mental combinations, the true meaning of real relationships, found renewed expression, in the Renaissance period, in the tortuous mnemotechnical works of Giordano Bruno. It was no coincidence that, in addition to reading the works of Lull, Bruno turned his attention to a little treatise on memory by Pietro da Ravenna,[13] which he had discovered in his youth, a work heavily influenced by 'rhetorical' and 'Ciceronian' ideas on memory. When Bruno dealt with 'imaginative links' in his *De umbris idearum* (i.e. the connections between images and figures and letters) he presupposed a structural unity between logical and psychological mechanisms which would enable the field of knowledge to be infinitely extended, and facilitate the development of a new system of logico-rhetorical invention (*inventio*) which was one of the ultimate objectives of his philosophy. Bruno's mnemotechnical works combined the techniques of the Lullian art with the memory arts based on images and places, which he derived from ancient rhetorical texts and more recent Renaissance treatises on artificial memory.

When we read the vigorous polemics against the art of memory (like those of Ratke, Erasmus, Montaigne or Agrippa) it is difficult not to sympathize with their criticisms, which reject the pedantic

schemes, verbosity and rigid dogmatism of the educational establishment in the name of greater spontaneity and intellectual freedom. But this does not alter the fact that these 'dogmatic' ideas
(both Ciceronian and Lullian) had a profound influence on the formation of a new intellectual culture, which prepared the ground for
the development of new logical methods, from those of Francis
Bacon to those of Gottfried Leibniz. The treatises on artificial
memory were at the centre of a complex of discussions and problems: developments in the arts of discourse and techniques of persuasion, attempts at constructing encyclopaedias of knowledge, the
controversies surrounding the Ramist and Lullist methods, works
on magic, medicine and physiognomy: a range of questions which
concerned not just rhetorical theorists, but philosophers, logicians,
occult scientists, physicians and encyclopaedists of different kinds.

The 'strangeness' of the Renaissance mnemotechnical literature
is partly a result of its being involved on the one hand with the
problems of logic and rhetoric, and on the other with the revival of
Lullism, and the construction of artificial languages, as well as its
association with the ambiguous, magical or occult atmosphere
which attended the resurgence of interest in the *Ars magna*. These
discussions on the art of memory exercised a particular influence
on two of the fundamental problems of the philosophical culture of
the seventeenth century: that of method or inventive logic, and that
of the systematic classification of the sciences or the construction of
an encyclopaedia of knowledge.

2 THE CLASSICAL AND MEDIAEVAL SOURCES OF THE *ARS MEMORATIVA*

'Men have invented many different arts to aid and strengthen the
work of nature', wrote the anonymous author of a fifteenth-century treatise on memory,

> and recognizing the weakness of the memory, and the fragility of
> human nature, they devised an art whereby one could remem-
> ber many more things than would be possible if one relied solely
> on natural means. It was for this reason that writing was invented
> and later (when they realized that it was not always possible to
> carry our writings around with us, and because writing is not

always possible) around the time of Simonides and Democritus the art of artificial memory was invented.

This comparison of the mnemonic art with other techniques which supplement our natural abilities is not, as we shall see, without significance. But when one examines the treatises of the *ars memorativa* composed between the mid-fourteenth and the seventeenth centuries, one is struck by more than just the repetition of this comparison: one also finds recurrent references to Aristotelian psychology, to the great Latin manuals of rhetoric, to the works on memory and the commentaries of Albertus Magnus and Thomas Aquinas. In many cases these treatises do no more than expound, comment upon, and amplify the rules, doctrines and precepts which had been devised many centuries before in ancient Greece and Rome, reaching the writers of the fourteenth century and the Renaissance through the work of the great scholastic teachers of the Middle Ages. It will be useful here to outline briefly the themes of the most important of these sources.

(a) Aristotle's De memoria et reminiscentia
Although Aristotle's treatise on memory, the *De memoria et reminiscentia*, was intended to be a general treatise on psychology, and not simply a dissertation on mnemotechnics, this work nonetheless contains a number of ideas which were destined to bear significant fruit in later centuries, when they were put to use by those whose primary concern was the development of mnemonic techniques. The mnemotechnical theorists made substantial use of the following Aristotelian doctrines: 1) The idea that the presence of the image or fantasm (φάντασμα) is necessary for the functioning of memory (μνήμη). This necessity of the image (which is seen as a weakened form of sensation) is attributed to the fact that there are close links between memory and both the imagination (φαντασία αἰσθητική) and sensation. 2) The idea that recollection or reflexive memory, or the actualization of stored memories (ἀνάμνησις), is facilitated by *order* and *regularity*, as, for example, in the case of mathematics, where it is difficult to remember things which are presented in a disordered and confused way. 3) The formulation of a law of association according to which images and ideas are associated on the basis of similarity, opposition or contiguity. In an influential passage of the *De memoria* (II, 452a, 12–15) Aristotle stated: 'Sometimes the

memory seems to proceed from places (τόποι). The reason for this is that man passes rapidly from one step to the next, for example from milk to whiteness, from whiteness to air, from air to humidity, from humidity to a memory of autumn, supposing that one sought to remember this season.' Aristotle also referred to the use of images in *De anima* (III, 3, 427b, 14–20): 'It is clear that the imagination is something distinct from sensation and thought. . . . It is in our power when we use it, and it can in fact be used to bring something before our eyes, as it is by those who use memory-places and fabricate images (ἐν τοῖς μνημονικοῖς τιθέμενοι καὶ εἰδωλοποιοῦντες), while sensation does not depend on our will.'[14]

(b) Cicero's De oratore (II, 86–8)

In Cicero's *De oratore* memory is dealt with as one of the five necessary parts of an orator's technique. First Cicero relates an anecdote concerning the poet Simonides, who was 'said to be the first to have set forth the art of memory' (*primum ferunt artem memoriae protulisse*). Simonides had been able to identify the bodies of the guests at a banquet, after the ceiling of the banquet-hall collapsed, mutilating them beyond recognition, by remembering the place (*locum*) that each of them had occupied at the table. Cicero goes on to discuss the expedience (based on the presupposition that order is good for the memory) of choosing 'places' (*loci*), and making images which correspond to the facts or concepts one wishes to discuss, and *arranging these images in the places*. The order in which they were arranged would enable one to recall the facts. The art of memory, Cicero argued, was analogous to the process of writing: the places have the same function as a wax tablet, while the images function like the letters which are written on it. Images are used because visual memories are more persistent than other kinds of memory, and because the 'memory-places' themselves are necessarily visual. There ought to be many places, Cicero says, which should be clear, distinct and disposed at regular intervals (*modicis intervallis*). The images will be more effective if they are fashioned so as to be more striking to the imaginative faculties.

(c) Quintilian's De institutione oratoria (XI, 2)

While he had some reservations about the usefulness of mnemotechnics, Quintilian (who began his exposition in *De insti-*

tutione oratoria with the same anecdote about Simonides) presented a broader and much more detailed treatment of the topic than Cicero. Quintilian dwelt at length, for example, on the construction of the 'places' for the artificial memory: in order to achieve effective results, he says, one should select a particular building, arranging the various images in the the same order as the places to be found in the various rooms of the building. 'Mentally visiting the building' (which could be a public building, or the bastions of a city, or a day divided into various periods, or an imaginary edifice) it would be possible to 'pick up' the various images (and thus bring to mind the facts or concepts which they represent) from the various places in which they have been 'stored'.

(d) *The* Rhetorica ad C. Herennium *(III, 16–24)*

In this anonymous text (which mediaeval scholars attributed to Cicero, calling it the *rhetorica nova* or *secunda* in order to distinguish it from the *de inventione* or *rhetorica vetus*), we find the same rules and precepts as we have found in Cicero and Quintilian. The distinction between natural and artificial memory is here clearly formulated:

> There are, then, two kinds of memory: one natural, and the other the product of art. The natural memory is that memory which is embedded in our minds, born simultaneously with thought. The artificial memory is that memory which is strengthened by a kind of training and system of discipline.[15]

Amongst the list of suitable 'places', which must be numerous in order to accommodate the many things which we need to remember, we find: 'a house, a colonnade, a corner, an arch, and other similar things'.[16] Images, which are the 'forms' (*formae*) or 'notes' (*notae*) or 'likenesses' (*simulacra*) of the things which we wish to remember, are arranged in the places (*loci*):

> [in the same way in which] those who know the letters of the alphabet can thereby write out what is dictated to them, and read aloud what they have written, likewise those who have learnt mnemonics can set in memory-places what they have heard, and from these memory-places deliver it by memory. [17]

While images are variable and erasable, the places of memory must be fixed and arranged in an orderly manner – this enables one mentally to recall images from any point: from the beginning, the middle or the end of an order or list of things.[18]

(e) Albertus Magnus's De bono *(IV, 2) and commentary on the* De memoria et reminiscentia; *Thomas Aquinas's* Summa theologiae *(II, ii, 49) and commentary on the* De memoria et reminiscentia

The discussions of memory in Albertus's *De bono* and the *Summa theologiae* of Aquinas[19] are explicitly derived from Aristotelian and pseudo-Ciceronian sources. For Albertus 'the best art is that which Cicero has left us'; the precepts of mnemotechnics, he says, are useful for both ethics and rhetoric, and the memory of things which concern life and justice is twofold – natural and artificial: 'It is natural memory which helps us easily to remember things we have known or done in the past. Artificial memory is that memory which is constructed by means of the arrangement of *places* and images.' As in all the other arts, perfection in the art of memory is attained naturally, and since in our actions 'we are directed from the past towards the present and the future, and not vice versa', memory is presented, along with intelligence (*intelligentia*) and providence (*providentia*) as one of the three components of the virtue of Prudence. As Frances Yates has convincingly argued,[20] the source of Albertus's and Aquinas's conception of memory as part of Prudence was Cicero's *De inventione*, and since Cicero had distinguished, in his 'second rhetoric' (i.e. the *Rhetorica ad Herennium*), between natural memory and the 'artificial memory' which uses 'places and images', that distinction and the rules applying to artificial memory found their way into Albertus's and Aquinas's discussion of memory, and assumed a position of central importance. The breadth and detail of Albertus's discussion attests to the profound influence of 'Ciceronian' mnemotechnics on his work: virtually all of the precepts of the *Rhetorica ad Herennium* are meticulously examined in the *De bono*. Let it suffice, by way of an example, to note here the passage in which Albertus refers to the 'unusual' character which memory-images ought to possess:

That which is extraordinary impresses the memory better than the ordinary. For this reason, as Aristotle affirms, the first philosophers composed poetry, because fables, which are composed of marvellous things, leave a greater impression on the memory.

The quotation from Aristotle here is particularly significant: these works by Albertus and Aquinas attempt to synthesize the Aristotelian and 'Ciceronian' accounts of memory. This is particularly evident in Aquinas's treatment of this theme in his *Summa theologiae*. Beginning with the identification of memory as a part of prudence, Aquinas goes on to compare the idea that prudence can be augmented and perfected 'either by practice or by grace' (*ex exercitio vel gratia*) with the idea that memory can be perfected by means of art. The four rules of artificial memory cited by Aquinas are those regarding 1) the use of images, 2) the order which facilitates the passage from one concept to another, or from the concept to the image, 3) the need for careful consideration when constructing 'memory-places', and 4) the need for frequent repetition in order to conserve thoughts in the memory. The first and the third of these rules derive from the *Rhetorica ad Herennium*, while the second and fourth are drawn from Aristotle's *De memoria et reminiscentia*. In his commentary on the *De memoria*, however, he omits the first rule, while the third is adapted to the needs of the Aristotelian text by neglecting to mention the construction of 'memory-places' (*loci*).[21]

3 THE *ARS MEMORATIVA* AND THE *ARS PREDICANDI* IN THE FOURTEENTH CENTURY

In treatises on the *ars memorativa* composed between the fourteenth and seventeenth centuries, in addition to citations from Aristotle, Cicero, Pseudo-Cicero, Quintilian, Albertus and Aquinas, we also find references to Plato (especially to *Timaeus* IV, 26b, which refers to the greater mnemonic capacity of adolescents), Seneca (who in his discussion of the memory of kindnesses received in *De beneficiis* III, 2–5, touches on the themes of the 'frequency' and 'order' of memory-acts), St Augustine (the passages on memory in *Confessions* X, 8 and the brief references in *De Trinitate*, IX, 6). This summary list of 'authorities' suffices by itself to show how the treatises of the *ars memorativa*, which were so widely disseminated in Europe after the fourteenth century, were the products of an ancient and uninterrupted tradition. This tradition was developed in different ways and in different spheres of knowledge: while Aristotle's work on memory dealt primarily with questions connected with the problem of sensation (mediaeval commentaries on the *de memoria et reminiscentia* were often coupled with commentaries on the *De sensu et sensato*), the imagination and the relationship between the sensitive and intellective soul, the texts of Cicero, Quintilian and Pseudo-Cicero were almost exclusively concerned with rhetorical questions, and so treated the art of memory as a *technique* whose tasks and problems were strictly functional, designed to meet the particular needs of the orator.

From the *De rhetorica* of Alcuin, to John of Salisbury's attempt to revive the ideals of *eloquentia*, to the *Speculum maius* of Vincent of Beauvais, all the great works of mediaeval rhetoric took their primary impetus from the texts of Cicero.[22] For this reason, as it has been correctly suggested, one can speak of 'scholastic rhetoric' only if one eliminates from the term 'scholastic' all reference to the 'authority' of Aristotle. In Albertus and Aquinas the two lines along which the treatment of memory was to be developed in the course of the Middle Ages (the 'speculative' line and the 'technical' line) appear closely linked for the first time. For the two great masters of the scholastic tradition the rational psychology of Aristotle provided a framework within which the mnemotechnical art (which found its highest expression in the *rhetorica secunda* of Cicero) was to be incorporated and justified. As Yates has shown,[23] the strictly rationalistic basis of the mnemotechnics of Albertus and Aquinas was, at least in part, an attempt to rid the art of memory of the magical-occult influence of the *ars notoria*, and to expunge the magical conception of the art of memory as a 'perfect art' or key of universal reality. In the *ars notoria* (as some later Renaissance texts confirm) the art of memory appeared to be closely linked with the idea of a secret art or 'perfect science' (*scientia perfecta*) by means of which one could attain 'the understanding of all the sciences and natural arts' (*ad omnium scientiarum et naturalium artium cognitionem*) through a combination of conventional mnemotechnical rules with formulaic invocations, mystical figures and magical prayers.[24]

One thing at least is clear – the synthesis of Aristotelian and Ciceronian doctrines inaugurated by the two great Dominicans was an example which many later writers on the mnemonic art followed. This path is clearly taken, for example, by the Dominican

Bartolomeo da San Concordio (d. 1347). In the chapter of his *Gli ammaestramenti degli antichi* where he deals with 'those things which are helpful for attaining a good memory', after citing the *Rhetorica ad Herennium*, the *Timaeus*, the *De memoria* and the second book of Aristotle's *Rhetorica* and Horace's *Ars poetica*, Bartolomeo quotes extensively from Aquinas's commentary on the *De memoria* and from the 'second part of the second book' of the *Summa theologiae*: 'A man must choose appropriate likenesses for the things which he wishes to remember, but not conventional ones; because unusual things are more marvellous to us . . . It is also appropriate for us to consider the things which one wants to remember in a particular order so that remembering one thing leads us to another.' The reference to the Ciceronian doctrine of *loci* and *imagines* is even more explicit: 'Images and similitudes of those things which we want to memorize must be lodged in certain places.' The eight 'precepts' prescribed by Bartolomeo (1. beginning in boyhood; 2. concentrating closely; 3. frequent repetition; 4. ordering; 5. starting from the beginning; 6. selecting appropriate likenesses; 7. not overloading the memory with too many things; 8. using verses and rhymes) are a synthesis of the advice given in the various texts to which he refers.[25]

Another fourteenth-century vernacular treatise on artificial memory which has been mistakenly attributed to Bartolomeo derives its ideas (despite the fact that the author twice declares that he is 'departing from Cicero') almost exclusively from the *Rhetorica ad Herennium*. In addition to the definitions of the memory-place ('a thing capable of containing in itself any other thing') and the memory-image ('the representation of those things which we wish to retain in the mind') we also find in this short work the Pseudo-Ciceronian distinction between natural and artificial memory-places (the one made 'by the hand of nature' and the other 'by the hand of man') and the rules concerning the construction of memory-places, and the symbolic character of images:

> It is also necessary to indicate the image with a sign which is appropriate to the purpose for which it has been made, for example a crown is appropriate for the image of a king and a shield for the image of a knight . . . It is also necessary when fashioning the image of something that the actions depicted should be peculiar and appropriate to the thing represented, as it

is fitting to give a lion an image which is courageous . . . So we see always that it is advisable to place the images in places as one places letters on the page.[26]

These directions concerning the relationship between memory-places and images which are derived from the *Rhetorica ad Herennium* remained fundamental axioms of the 'art' for the next three hundred years, and appear in many other fourteenth-century texts. In a fourteenth-century treatise compiled by 'Peter of Prague' in the early fifteenth century, for example, we find the following definition: 'The art of memory is divided into two parts: places and images. Places are not different from images to the extent that the images are fixed in them, just as images are drawn on paper . . . thus the places are like matter, and images are like form',[27] and we also find, with slight variations, most of the rules prescribed in Bartolomeo's treatise. Evidence for the diffusion of *ars memorativa* in fourteenth-century Dominican circles, in addition to the texts already cited, can be found in the connection which is often made between the *ars memoriae* and the *ars predicandi*. Lodovico Dolce, who was one of the foremost sixteenth-century translators and popularizers of Latin rhetorical and mnemotechnical works, referred in 1562[28] to the *Summa de exemplis et similitudinibus* of Fra Giovanni Gorini di San Gemigniano (d. 1323)[29] as one of the principal texts of the mnemonic art and included Gorini's name, along with Cicero and Pietro da Ravenna, in a list of the founders of the art. In Gorini's work – which was recommended to its readers as being 'most useful to preachers, to help them frame whatever arguments they wish to present' – analogies between vices and virtues and celestial bodies and terrestrial motions provided the basis for a method of constructing images which was designed to enable preachers to produce orderly expositions, which would also capture the imaginations of their listeners. In addition to practical aims of this kind, there was a genuine interest in developing memorative techniques amongst the exponents of that 'science which deals with the artificial form of preaching' (*scientia quae tradit formam artificialiter praedicandi*),[30] which was widely diffused in the fourteenth century.[31] In the unique mediaeval cultural product which is the *ars predicandi* the practical aims of rhetorical persuasion, and the need to construct images able to provoke controllable emotions, were combined with more general reflections on order and method as

instruments for impressing both the contents and the form of orations in the memory.

4 TECHNIQUES OF MEMORY IN THE FIFTEENTH CENTURY

In many of the mnemotechnical treatises of the fifteenth century
the speculative dimension which was so characteristic of the discussions of Albertus, Aquinas and Fra Bartolomeo seems to have
been largely abandoned in favour of more practical considerations.
The *Artificialis memoriae regulae* of Iacopo Ragone da Vicenza (composed in 1434 and compiled in various manuscript collections),[32]
for example, is almost exclusively concerned with a detailed examination of the techniques for establishing suitable memory-places:

> By your command, renowned Prince, and on your behalf, I have
> reduced the rules of artificial memory, as we practised it in for-
> mer times, into a book, imitated not only from the many true
> words and wise sayings of Marcus Tullius Cicero, [but also] from
> other most worthy philosophers who have written most knowl-
> edgeably of this art . . . As Cicero taught, and as Thomas Aquinas
> also attests, artificial memory is achieved by means of two things:
> namely, places and images. They considered it necessary for
> places and things to be conjoined in order and retained together
> in the memory, thus as Saint Thomas said, 'he who wishes to
> hold anything in the memory ought to arrange his thoughts in
> order, so that once one thing has been remembered it is easy to
> proceed to another.' This was also maintained by Aristotle, in
> whose book *De memoria* it is written: 'We remember things by
> means of places. Therefore it is necessary to have places so that
> appropriate images can be fashioned and displayed in them.' But
> we must choose images which are fitted to our intentions, as
> Thomas maintained, saying: 'A man ought to choose convenient
> similitudes for those things which he wants to remember.'[33]

After referring briefly to Ciceronian and Thomistic sources,
Ragone goes on to discuss the characteristics of 'local' memory in
a much more articulate way than the authors whom he cites:

> Memory-places are quite different from images: memory-places

are not corners of a room, as some believe, but fixed images on which delible images are written like letters on paper: memory-places are like matter, whereas images are like forms. The difference between them is the same as the difference between the fixed and the non-fixed. This art moreover is divided into a hundred memory-places, and this exhaustiveness makes it extremely useful. Although, if it pleased your Highness, you could easily invent more memory-places for the same purpose by imitating the ones I have given you here. Not only should one make a mental note of these places and keep them firmly in the mind by means of a good method, but one should do so with the utmost diligence and application, so that you will promptly be able to repeat any number of quotations both forwards and backwards. If you neglect to do this, however, everything you have attempted will have been in vain. It is expedient therefore, to link the method and the memory-places together, only you must ensure that the distance between them is neither too short nor too long, but a moderate distance – six, eight or ten feet or so, depending on the size of the room. Neither should they be too bright nor too dark, but moderately lit. The reason for this is that memory-places which are too wide or narrow, too bright or too dark hinder the searching power of the imagination, and impede the memory by dispersing or crowding together the things which are represented in them, just as one's eyes get tired from reading if the letters are very irregular and badly written or too cramped. Indeed the size of the memory-places is extremely important, so that the number of places is capacious enough to house the images, because thought dislikes a lack of order – it's no use trying to put a horse in a hole where a spider's built his web, it won't fit. But you will find the size of these memory-places is dealt with separately in the next section immediately below.[34]

The memory-places must be arranged so that they may be read quickly and easily: their size and the distance between them should be based on psychological observations. Having made these observations, and having taken account of the particular associations between the various things to be remembered, one then chooses a 'building' in which the memory-places (and the images) are to be gathered together:

One should also avoid choosing memory-places which are too populous, such as streets or churches, since too much familiarity or the representation of extraneous things will cause confusion and the images which appear in the mind will be confused rather than clear, which is most highly to be guarded against, because if you locate a memory-place in an open space and you put the likeness of some thing in it, when you wish to remember something concerning the place and the likeness, the comings and goings of passers-by, and the hustle and bustle of the crowds might throw your thoughts into confusion. Therefore one must ensure that one has a house which is completely empty and unfurnished, and take care not to use monks' cells or the houses of strangers for memory-places because they are too similar to each other, and if you cannot differentiate between them, you might get confused. Choose a house in which there are twenty rooms, halls, kitchens, staircases, and the greater the difference between these places, the better. Make sure that these rooms and their contents are neither too large nor too small, select any five equidistant places in these rooms which (as we said before) are no more than about six, eight or ten feet apart. And begin as follows, always proceeding towards the left or towards the right, whichever is more appropriate for the layout of the house, so that you do not have to double-back on yourself. So let your memory-places follow the order of the house as it appears in reality, so that the imprinting [of memory images] may more easily be done according to a natural order.[35]

Another anonymous manuscript author, who most probably belongs to the same period and cultural milieu, lingers in equally painstaking detail over the 'material' characteristics of the memory places (size, brightness, non-uniformity etc.), and on the choice and function of images.[36]

Concerning the order of memory-places. With regard to the understanding and order of memory-places you should know that the place in artificial memory is like paper in writing, because when a man writes something down on paper because he wants to remember it, the paper does not change. Memory-places too should be immovable, that is to say they should be decided once and for all, and never changed or altered like paper. Then one forms images of the things or names which one wishes to remember in these memory-places, just as things are written on paper when a man wishes to remember them. *Concerning the form of places*. The memory-places should be constructed in such a way that they are neither too small nor too large, so that one should not, for example, choose a house or a field or a whole staircase as a memory-place. Nor, as I have said, should one choose a place which is too small, such as a small stone or a hole and so on. This is because the human intellect cannot concentrate on things which are too large or too small, for so the image vanishes. For this reason you should choose medium-sized places, that is, places with clearly-defined boundaries, and not too dark. Neither must you choose a location for your memory-places which is too solitary, such as a desert or a forest, nor a place which is too populous, but an average kind of place, which is neither too populous nor too desolate. Take care you know the aforementioned places well and that you arrange them according to the quinary number, that is by fives. The memory-places ought not to be dissimilar, so for example, one could use a house for the first place, a colonnade for the second, a corner for the third, the foot of the stairs for the fourth, and the head of the stairs for the fifth. On the fifth or tenth place you should put [the image of] a golden hand or an emperor. Let this emperor be well dressed (imperially dressed in fact) or use something else which is either wonderful or appalling, so that you will be able to remember it better. That is enough about the form of memory-places. Now however let us consider the images which are to be put in the aforementioned memory-places. *Concerning the images*. Images are like writing and places like paper. Let us say that you wish to remember [a number of] proper or common names or Greek words, or other words whose meanings you do not know, for messages or arguments or for other occasions. First let us consider the memorizing of proper names. First you should put images in appropriate places, as follows: if you wish to remember a rich man who is called Peter, immediately place [the image of] a Peter whom you know, who may be your friend or enemy, or someone with whom you are acquainted, and let this Peter be doing or saying something ridiculous or unusual in this memory-place . . . In a second memory-place put an Albert whom you know, as before (that is to say, this Albert should be doing something unusual or appalling, such as hanging himself).

If you want to remember your horse's name, put the image of an enormous white horse in the third place, and let it be trampling your friend or enemy with the hooves of its front or hind legs, or doing something similar, as we said before.[37]

From reading these texts we can get a fairly clear idea of how the 'Ciceronian' *ars memorativa* functioned (I say 'Ciceronian' because the mnemotechnical arts of the Lullists and the Aristotelians used very different procedures). In order to practise the mnemonic art one must first establish a formal structure which can be used to remember any series of things or names (*res aut verba*). This formal structure – usually called a 'chart' (*carta*) or 'outline' (*forma*) – is reusable and is constructed arbitrarily: one chooses a locality (a building, portico or church, for example) which can be real or imaginary, and establishes within it a certain number of *memory-places*. The arbitrary or conventional character of these choices is limited by a certain number of rules concerning 1) the characteristics of the locality and its memory-places (spaciousness, solitude, brightness etc.) and 2) the order of the memory-places. The capacity of the formal structure governed the number of things one could remember: a locality with a hundred *loci*, for example, could only be used to remember a hundred names or objects: a great deal of time was devoted to the problem of the 'multiplication of places' (*multiplicatio locorum*) or progressive enlargement of the structure.

This formal structure lent itself to being 'refilled' with mental contents of various kinds (*imagines delebiles*, either 'matter' or 'writing'). To 'refill' the structure one selected images which symbolized the things or terms which one wanted to remember in a striking and durable way. There were rules also concerning the 'arbitrariness', 'monstrosity' or 'strangeness' of memory images and the relationship between the image and the things which one wished to memorize. The images were disposed 'provisionally' into places (in order to remember a particular series of names or things). Mentally running through the chosen locality or fabricated structure (in a semi-automatic way), one could gain immediate access – through recalling the images and the suggestions evoked by them – to the terms or things belonging to the series which one wanted to remember. Given the fixed structure of the memory-places, the terms and things could be extracted in any order one desired.

The treatises we are concerned with devote a considerable amount of space to the problem of the arrangement of memory-places (*dispositio locorum*) and that of image-formation. The majority of fifteenth and sixteenth-century treatises insist on precisely this kind of codification.[38] The almost exlusively 'technical' character of these treatises explains their uniformity. The authors who deal with the *ars memorativa* present themselves not as 'inventors' of the art, but as 'expositors': they limit themselves to transmitting a set of pre-existing rules, seeking merely to expound them in an accessible way and, if possible, to integrate or improve them. Naturally, the reduction of the rules to a formulaic scheme[39] made the art easier to construct and to learn. It is helpful to remember the 'technical' character of these treatises when considering the purposes for which they were written. In the fifteenth century the 'Ciceronian' art of memory was seen as an instrument useful for a variety of activities, albeit rather speculative and lacking in specific aims. The small manuscript treatise of Guardi (or Girardi?,)[40] 'a distinguished doctor of arts and teacher of medicine' (*eximii doctoris artium et medicinae magistri*), for example, claimed to instruct its readers in the memorization of substantial and accidental terms, textual authorities (*auctoritates*), everyday speeches, the contents of letters, collections and books of history, scientific and philosophical discourses and arguments, and foreign poetry and linguistic terms. The method for remembering messages, testimonies and arguments is handled in all the treatises, although in some cases as an extension of the rules governing mnemotechnics for the purpose of winning debates.[41]

Because of its origins in practical rhetoric the *ars memorativa* was often presented as a useful tool for those who were employed in civil activities. The *Congestorius artificiosae memoriae*[42] of Romberch, for example, a text which was widely read throughout sixteenth-century Europe, addressed itself to theologians, preachers, professors, jurists, physicians, judges, procurators, notaries, philosophers, professors of the liberal arts, ambassadors and merchants.

5 THE *PHOENIX* OF PIETRO DA RAVENNA

While it seems difficult to believe that texts of this kind could be considered useful, numerous contemporary accounts attest to the considerable achievements of mnemotechnical theorists. The celebrated Pietro da Ravenna (Pietro Tommai), author of a small treatise on artificial memory published in Venice in 1491,[43] who was later to be an important influence on the works of Bruno, claimed to have devised more than a hundred thousand memory-places, so that he could surpass anyone in the knowledge of sacred scriptures and the law. 'When I left my country', he wrote, 'to visit as a pilgrim the cities of Italy, I can truly say *omnia mea mecum porto* [I carry everything I own with me], but I kept on constructing more and more memory-places.'[44] When he was barely ten years old Pietro, in the presence of his jurisprudence teacher Alessandro Tartagni da Imola in the University of Pavia, is reputed to have recited from memory the whole text of the civil law (*totum codicem iuris civilis*) including both text and glosses, and to have been able to repeat the lectures of his teacher verbatim. Later, in Padua, he amazed the Chapter of regular canons by reciting from memory sermons he had only heard once. In page after page in which the desire to provoke admiration in his readers is combined with shrewd self-promotion Pietro speaks of his prodigious abilities: 'My witness is the University of Padua: every day I read, without a book, my lectures in Canon law, just as if I had the book before my eyes; I remember the text and the glosses without omitting a single word . . . Using nineteen letters of the alphabet I have arranged twenty thousand passages of canon and civil law and, in the same order, seven thousand passages of the holy scriptures, a thousand verses of Ovid . . . two hundred sentences of Cicero, three hundred of the philosophers, and the greater part of the work of Valerius Maximus.'[45]

A more impartial testimony is offered by Eleonora d'Aragon, who called the whole city of Ferrara to witness the prodigious memory of Ravenna,[46] or Bonifacio del Monferrato who, after having witnessed his extraordinary powers, recommended him warmly to the King, to princes, to 'magnifici capitani' and to noble Italians.

The great fame which this singular figure enjoyed in Italy and throughout Europe was not on account of his (by no means negligible) legal scholarship, but rather because he presented himself as a living example of the validity of an art in which many scholars had invested their hopes and aspirations. As Professor of Law at Bologna, Ferrara, Pavia, Pistoia and Padua, Pietro Tommai doubtless contributed to the increasing interest in the *ars memorativa* throughout Italy. Sought after by Doge Agostino Barbarigio da Bugislao Duke of Pomerania and by Frederick of Saxony, Pietro saw the gates of the University of Wittenberg opening before him, around 1497. After having refused an invitation from the King of Denmark, he went to Cologne, and from there, after accusations of incorrect behaviour (*scholares itali non poterant vivere sine meretricibus*), was constrained to return to Italy. Pietro's notoriety had important consequences: his *Phoenix seu artificiosa memoria* exercised a significant influence on all subsequent mnemotechnic works. Most of the Italian and German theorists of the sixteenth and seventeenth centuries owed a considerable debt to the work of Ravenna. The diffusion of his work can be traced through its publication history: first printed in Venice, the *Phoenix* was then republished in Vienna, Vicenza, Cologne, and eventually translated into English (around the middle of the sixteenth century) from an earlier French edition. This one example should suffice to show how, by the end of the sixteenth century and the first decade of the seventeenth century, the interest in 'local memory' had begun to spread beyond the borders of Italy.[47]

The work of Ravenna seems to have been constructed according to the rules of the 'Ciceronian' tradition. Pietro, however, concentrated more on the function of images than on the rules concerning the choice of memory-places. To make the art of memory effective, he argued, one needed to understand the things which excited and stimulated the imagination:

> I usually fill my memory-places with the images of beautiful women, which excite my memory . . . and believe me: when I use beautiful women as memory images, I find it much easier to arrange and repeat the notions which I have entrusted to those places. You now have a most useful secret of artificial memory, a secret which I have (through modesty) long remained silent about: if you wish to remember quickly, dispose the images of the most beautiful virgins into memory places; the memory is marvellously excited by images of women . . . This precept is useless to those who dislike women and they will find it very difficult to gather the fruits of this art. I hope chaste and religious men will pardon me: I cannot pass over in silence a rule which has earned me much praise and honour on account of my abilities in the art, because I wish, with all my heart, to leave excellent successors behind me.[48]

6 NATURE AND ART

Works like those of Romberch and Pietro da Ravenna had, as I have said, eminently 'practical' aims: they addressed themselves to philosophers only if, as physicians, notaries, or jurists, they were employed in worldly tasks. Even in these treatises, however, there are themes (such as the use of images for example) which have close links with other areas of Renaissance culture, and themes (such as the relationship between art and nature) which were debated at length in more specifically philosophical spheres.

'Local memory is an art by which we can remember easily and in an orderly way, many things of which – using our natural powers – we could not have such a ready or distinct memory', maintains the author of MS Urb. Lat. 1743.[49] This topic, which has its origins in the texts of Cicero and Quintilian, recurs frequently with significant emphases. The anonymous author of MS Lat. 274 in the Bibliotheca Marciana[50] likened his mnemonic art to that of the ancient inventors of the technique, feeling it necessary to place the art under the legendary patronage of Democritus,[51] who is presented as the expositor of the extraordinary difficulties and 'obscurities' of the *Rhetorica ad Herennium*:

The artificial memory art, O reverend father, is that art by which a man is able to remember many more things than he can by means of natural memory. You ought to know that nature is assisted by being joined with art, just as a ship is helped in crossing the sea, because it cannot pass over the seas by means of the power and means of nature, but only by means of the power and means of art; thus the philosophers call art the assistant of nature. Likewise men have invented various arts to help them deal with different aspects of nature, so because man's memory is naturally weak, he invented an art to help nature or memory so that he was able, through the power of art, to remember many things which he would not otherwise be able to remember by means of natural memory and although they invented writing they could not remember everything that they had written. Some time after this, they realized that they could not carry everything they had written around with them, and the things they needed to remember were not always available in written form, and so they invented a subtler art so that they were able to remember many things without any kind of writing, and this art they called artifical memory. This art was first invented in Athens by the most eloquent philosopher Democritus. And although various philosophers have striven to explain this art, it was done best and most subtly by the aforementioned philosopher Democritus, who was the original inventor of the art. And although Tullius, the most perfect orator, dealt with this art in his book of rhetoric he considered it so obscure and subtle that he believed that no one should practise it unless they had been taught the art in Democritus's manner, or they had been aided by divine grace.[52]

7 The art of memory, Aristotelianism and medicine

Other fifteenth-century works seem to have emerged from a very different cultural atmosphere, addressing 'psychological' and 'philosophical' rather than rhetorical themes, in which the influence of Aristotelian and Thomist ideas were more predominant than those of the 'Ciceronian' rhetorical tradition. One finds in these treatises various attempts to extract some rules for artificial memory directly from the texts of Aristotle. A typical example of this is the *De nutrienda memoria* published in Naples in 1476, in which Domenico De Carpanis sets out to present the doctrines developed by Aristotle in the *De memoria et reminiscentia* 'seasoned with the salt of the holy doctor Thomas Aquinas'.[53]

The 'common sense' (*sensus communis*) seems to de Carpanis to be like a gigantic forest in which the images created by the five senses are accumulated. The intellect acts on this 'chaos' in three ways: first, it becomes conscious of the images, then it connects them in a specific order, and thirdly it connects similar things and deposits them in the 'coffers of the memory' (*archa memoriae*). When one recites things from memory, the intellect, 'as if taking food from a larder, utters the words by means of the ruminating teeth of the intellect'.[54] Memory, in its turn, operates on two levels: at the level of sense and at the level of intellect. The sensitive memory is strictly connected to the body and can remember 'only corporeal things'; the intellective memory, on the contrary, is 'the repository of eternal species'. Alongside the principal theses of Aristotle, the author almost always places passages drawn from the eleventh book of Augustine's *De Trinitate*: the Aristotelian doctrine of the corporeal character of the contents of the sensitive memory is thus placed alongside the passage from Augustine on the memory of sheep which, after feeding, return to the sheepfold; the Augustinian thesis of the identity between memory, intellect and will is cited to confirm the intellective character of one of the two parts into which the memory is subdivided. Also the doctrine of 'aids' (*adminicula*) for the memory reappears, influenced by the context of its Thomistic source (it appears in passages dealing with order and repetition).[55] De Carpanis also uses the notions of 'similitude' (*similitudo*) and 'contrariety' (*contrarietas*). Without mentioning the art of 'local memory', the author manages to derive 'Ciceronian' rules from Aristotelian psychological texts.[56]

A similar attempt can be found in the *De omnibus ingeniis augendae memoriae* of the physician, historian and poet Giammichele Alberto da Carrara which was published in Bologna in 1481.[57] Here too the observations of Aristotle on order, on the passage from like to like, and on *contrarietas* are interpreted as 'rules' for the *ars memorativa*.[58] But Carrara's work is particularly significant because, in addition to these Aristotelian derivations, and the propounding of a particular type of 'local memory' (based on the subdivision of animals' bodies into five parts)[59] it demonstrates the close connection in the Aristotelian tradition between the art of memory and medicine. Referring closely to the works of Galen and Avicenna, Carrara deals firstly with the problem of the localization of the memory before moving on to discuss the principal illnesses which obstruct the use of the memory. After pausing to expound a series of rules concerning food, drink, sleep and exercise he concludes with a list of remedies. This idea of a 'therapeutics of memory', which had previously appeared in the *Regimen aphoristicum* of Arnaldo da Villanova, and was widespread in mediaeval medicine, also appears in the work of Matteolo da Perugia who published, around this time, a short work on mnemonic medicine.[60] In both works there are frequent references to Avicenna: Carrara's claim that humidity is an obstacle to memory, for example, is to be found in earlier Arabic medical texts.[61] Unlike Matteolo and other texts of this kind, however, Carrara's treatise was based on extensive reading. In addition to the classical works on memory, he also cites Galen, Boethius, Hugh of St Victor, Scotus and Averroes.

8 THE CONSTRUCTION OF IMAGES

Through contact with the medical tradition and with some of the theses of Aristotelianism, the late fifteenth-century writer on *ars memoriae* came into contact with ideas which were neither merely 'technical' nor 'rhetorical'. When, in the mid-sixteenth century, the Lullist tradition and the rhetorical *ars reminiscendi* converged, the technical 'Ciceronian' treatises came to play a specific role. The art of *loci* and *imagines*, despite its apparent neutrality and timelessness, was connected to renaissance culture in numerous ways. Only by bearing these connections in mind is it possible to understand the fascination that these often dry and banal texts exercised on thinkers such as Bruno and Agrippa. If one reflects on the importance of signs, *imprese* and allegories in renaissance culture, or the Ficinian texts on 'symbols and poetic figures which conceal divine mysteries, and considers the significance of the taste for allegories and 'symbolic forms' in the writings of Cristoforo Landino, Lorenzo Valla, Pico della Mirandola and Angelo Poliziano (and, much later, Giordano Bruno), one cannot fail to become aware of the resonance that the art of memory (in so far as it involves the construction of *images*) was destined to have in an age which loved to clothe ideas in sensible forms, which delighted in intellectual discussions about personifications such as Fever and Fortune, which saw hieroglyphs as a means to conceal truth from the vulgar, which loved 'alphabets' and iconologies, and considered 'reality' to be something which was gradually revealed through signs, 'fables' and images.[62]

In a characteristic and justly famous text, Alciati, while speaking of 'an art of inventing and devising symbols', discussed at length the differences between *schemata*, *imagines* and *symbola*.[63] Eighty years later, in an equally famous book, Cesare Ripa presented a 'description of the images of the virtues, vices, emotions and human passions, celestial bodies, the world and its parts', announcing that his book (which is truly 'the key to sixteenth- and seventeenth-century allegory') should be used 'in order to represent by means of their proper symbols everything which can be found in human thought'.[64] For the word 'memory' we find the representation of a 'woman with two faces, dressed in black, who holds a pen in her right hand and a book in her left': the two faces signify that memory embraces 'all things past, and through the rule of prudence, all things which will happen in the future'; the book and the pen, symbols of reading and writing, 'show that, as it is said, the memory can be perfected through use'.[65] In a manual of iconology, composed in the last years of the sixteenth century, we find the ancient ideas about practice and writing as aids to the memory (two centuries later Hume spoke of 'diligence' and 'writing'), as well as echoes of the discussions on memory and 'prudence' which had enthused Albertus Magnus and Thomas Aquinas.[66] But the idea of a sensible representation of 'things' and 'words' and the 'personification' of concepts which inspired Ripa (and many others after him), was undoubtedly closely connected to the part of mnemotechnic theory which dealt with the construction of images.

The orthodox tradition of the *ars memorativa* is not lacking in statements which show an awareness of the problem of images. Many pages of Iacobo Publicio's *Oratoriae artis epitoma* (Venice, 1482)[67] are useful for understanding the links between memory-images and those of iconology. Pure intentions (*intentiones simplices*), Publicio says, are 'spiritual' and so cannot be conveyed by means of corporeal similitudes, and disappear quickly from the memory. Images have the task of fixing ideas, words and concepts in the mind through a striking gesture or a cruel face, or the visible appearances of stupor, sadness or severity. Sadness and solitude could be used as symbols of old age, carefree happiness could symbolise youth, voracity could be expressed by the wolf, timidity by the hare, scales were a symbol of justice, Hercules's club was a symbol of strength, the astrolabe a symbol of astrology. But when constructing images one should turn above all to the works of the poets Virgil and Ovid. Their representations of concepts such as Fame, Envy and Sleep can be used in the 'arrangement into places' (*collocatio in locis*) of the memory art which uses rare and notable images.[68]

Symbols and images are useful for remembering things: even when the idea of 'the disposition of images into places' was abandoned, the idea of symbols and images as aids to the memory persisted. The *Istoria universale provata con monumenti e figurata con simboli degli antichi*, published in 1697 by Francesco Bianchini, was to 'combine the ease and facility of learning and comprehending with the stability of ordering and remembering';[69] the 'picture set out in the frontispiece' of Giambattista Vico's *Scienza nuova* was to be used by the reader 'in order to conceive the idea of this work before

reading it, and to consign it more easily to the memory'.[70]
Memory was 'the mother of the Muses' for Vico, as for Hobbes:

> This decaying sense, when we would express the thing itself . . .
> we call *Imagination* . . . But when we would express the *decay*,
> and signifie that the Sense is fading, old and past, it is called
> *Memory*. So that *Imagination* and *Memory*, are but one thing,
> which for divers considerations hath divers names.[71]

This Hobbesian distinction clearly articulates what was to
become a recurrent theme throughout the seventeenth century.

CHAPTER TWO

Encyclopaedism and Combinatoria in the Sixteenth Century

1 THE RENAISSANCE OF LULLISM

The sixteenth century saw rapid developments in two major areas relevant to the cultural milieu we are investigating. The first of these was the wide dissemination in England, Germany and France of the tradition of local memory stemming from Cicero, Quintilian, the *Rhetorica ad Herennium* and Thomas Aquinas, which received its fullest treatment at the end of the fifteenth century in the work of Pietro da Ravenna. The second was the interaction between this tradition and that of the *logica combinatoria* which reached its pinnacle in the works of Ramon Lull. Between the mid-fifteenth century and the mid-sixteenth century, Nicolaus Cusanus, Cardinal Bessarion, Pico della Mirandola, Lefèvre d'Etaples, Charles de Bovelles and later Bernardo Lavinheta, Henricus Cornelius Agrippa and Giordano Bruno disseminated and commented on the works of Lull dealing with the *ars magna* and *combinatoria*, and initiated what was to become an intellectual obsession in European culture. The full significance of these figures and their adherence to a set of ideas which are completely alien to a post-Cartesian and post-Galilean mentality has been misunderstood both by interpreters who have seen the *ars magna* as a kind of historical precursor of symbolic logic, and by those who have preferred to dismiss, with facile irony, the 'strangeness' of many of the most significant thinkers of this important period of western culture.

An interest in the cabala and hieroglyphic writing, artificial and universal languages, the search for the primary constitutive principles of all possible knowledge, the art of memory and a preoccupation with logic understood as a 'key' to the hidden secrets of reality: all these themes were connected to the revival of Lullism in the Renaissance. This inextricable complex of themes, familiar to those who have studied the philosophical texts of the sixteenth and seventeenth centuries – from Agrippa to Fludd, from Gassendi to Henry More – is vital for a clear understanding of that mysterious phenomenon known as 'Renaissance Platonism'.

Many of the themes which make up this complex had significant repercussions for a series of problems which are traditionally considered to be of central importance to philosophy and science: the Baconian and Viconian theory of 'signs', 'images' and 'language'; the Baconian and Cartesian discussions of the 'tree of the sciences' and the 'faculties'; the polemics on the importance of dialectic and its relation to rhetoric, and those concerning 'topics' and the problem of 'method'; and finally those natural philosophical treatises which dealt with the 'logical structure' of material reality, the 'alphabet of nature' and the 'characters' impressed by God in the cosmos. It is unnecessary to go into the background of these ideas here, but we should bear in mind that for a fuller understanding of some of these questions it would be useful to examine the sixteenth-century diffusion of Lullism and its relations to the preceding tradition of the art of memory.

2 AGRIPPA AND THE *ARS MAGNA*

In the opening years of the sixteenth century, in a dedicatory letter prefixed to his commentary on the *Ars brevis* of Ramon Lull, Cornelius Agrippa[1] gives a thumbnail sketch of the diffusion of Lullism in European culture: Pedro Dagui and his disciple Janer are celebrated in Italy, he notes, and the teachings of Fernando da Cordoba were famous throughout the European schools; Lefèvre d'Etaples and Bovillus in Paris had been devoted to Lull; and the Canterio brothers[2] had shown the marvellous possibilities of the art not only to France and Germany, but also to Italy. In addition to paying his respects to the great teachers of Lullism, Agrippa also discussed the scope and meaning of Lullian *combinatoria*, and the reasons for its superiority and its efficacy. The art, he said, has nothing to do with the 'vulgar', it does not deal with particular objects and for this reason it is the queen of all the arts, and an easy and reliable guide to all the sciences and all doctrines. The *ars inventiva* is characterized by its 'generality' and 'certainty'; aided only by the art, without any prior knowledge, men would be able to eliminate all possibility of error and find 'the knowledge and the truth of all knowable things.' The 'arguments' of the art were infallible and irrefutable; all particular discourses and principles of the particular sciences could be universalized and illuminated by means of the art, because it contained and included every science – the task of the art was the ordering of all knowledge.[3]

In this preface Agrippa, who many years later (in his *De vanitate scientiarum*) wrote a ferocious critique of the Lullian technique,[4] emphasized two fundamental principles which were characteristic of the Renaissance perception of Lullism. Firstly it was considered to be the most general and universal science, which because it dealt with certain principles and infallible demonstrations could be used to determine an absolute criterion of truth. Secondly, because it was considered to be the science of sciences, the art provided the means for an exact and rational ordering of all knowable things, whose various aspects could (by means of successive subsumptions from the particular to the general) be adduced and verified by the art.

The young Agrippa had done no more than expound, in a clear and vigorous fashion, ideas which already enjoyed a wide currency in sixteenth-century thought. He was not the first to insist upon the 'inventive' capacity of the art and its 'encyclopaedic' aims. The theme of logic understood as a 'key' to universal reality, as a discourse concerning itself not with other discourses but with the articulations of the real world, were already to be found, in fact, in the texts of Lull and his followers, together with the aspiration toward a universal ordering of the sciences and their concepts which would correspond to the order of the cosmos itself. It would be possible to speak, to this extent, of a 'logico-encyclopaedic tendency' in Lullian thought itself. It is a central and dominant motif both in the 'mystical' and the 'polemical-rationalist' aspects of the art.[5] The learning of the rules of the art and the ordinate classification of concepts presupposes the construction of a mnemonic system. It is presented as an integral part of encyclopaedic logic. In order to clarify this idea, it might be useful at this point to outline briefly some of the primary characteristics of the Lullist problematic, as they appear in the works of Lull and in those of the later Lullian tradition.

3 ART, LOGIC AND COSMOLOGY IN THE LULLIAN TRADITION

In the texts of Lull the combinatorial art is presented as a 'logic' which is also at the same time a 'metaphysics' (*ista ars est logica et metaphysica*), but is different from both of them, 'in the way of considering its object' and 'as regards its principles'. While metaphysics considers entities external to the soul 'from the point of view of their being' and logic considers them according to the being which they have in the soul, the art – supreme among all the sciences – considers entities in both ways at once.[6] Unlike logic, which deals with second intentions, the art deals with first intentions; while logic is 'an unstable and unsteady science' (*scientia instabilis sive labilis*), the art is 'permanent and stable' (*permanens et stabilis*). By means of the art it is possible to discover the 'true law' (*vera lex*) which is inaccessible to logic. A month's practice in the art would enable one not only to trace the common principles of all the sciences, but also to achieve greater results than those possible through studying logic for a whole year.[7] A prior acquaintance with traditional logic and natural philosophy were, however, considered a useful preparation for the acquisition of the art: 'A man who has a good intellect and diligence and understands logic and natural things can apprehend this science in two months: one month for the theory and another month for the practice.'[8]

The Lullian art was presented then, as inextricably bound up with the understanding of the objects which constitute the world. Unlike formal logic it deals with things, and not with words alone. It is concerned with the structure of the world, and not just the structure of discourses. An exemplaristic metaphysics or universal symbolism is at the root of this technique which claims to be able to speak simultaneously of logic and metaphysics, and claims to set out not only the rules which are the bases of all discourses, but the rules according to which reality is structured. The primary characteristics of the *ars combinatoria*: the breaking down of compound concepts into simple and irreducible notions, the use of letters and symbols to represent simple notions, the mechanization of conceptual combination by means of movable figures or diagrams, the idea of a perfect and artificial language (superior to common language and the technical languages of particular sciences), and the identification of the art with a kind of conceptual mechanism which, once constructed, is absolutely independent of subject matter, have led intellectual historians, from Bäumker to Gilson, to compare the *combinatoria* (not without some justification) to modern formal logic.[9] Unlike some of the less cautious historians, however, both Bäumker and Gilson have taken account of the influence of metaphysical exemplarism and symbolism on Lull's thought. Lull considered God and the 'divine dignities' to be the archetypes of reality, and he saw the entire universe as a gigantic ensemble of symbols which had their ultimate reference outside the physical world of appearances in the structure of divine being: 'the similitudes of divine nature are impressed in every creature according to their ability to receive them, which varies according to their proximity to the superior level, which is man, so that every creature carries, to a greater or lesser extent, the mark of its Maker within itself.'[10]

Lull's idea of the 'trees of the sciences' (expounded in his *Arbre de sciencia*), cannot be understood simply as an example of the formal classification of knowledge: Lull believed that the 'trees' of the art corresponded to the profound reality of things, which the philosopher could discover by reflecting on the symbolic significance of the various parts of the tree. The eighteen 'roots' of the first trees, for example, which represent the real world of creatures, correspond to the principles of the art. In this way, as Carreras y Artau has correctly observed,[11] the 'roots' or real foundations of things, the principles of the art, and the 'divine dignities' appear, in Lullian terminology, to be absolutely interchangeable terms.

The close links between the art and the theory of the elements have been clearly demonstrated by Frances Yates in her essay on 'The art of Ramon Lull'.[12] The traditional 'logical approach' to the Lullian doctrine (the work of Karl Prantl, for example) is shown by Yates to be partial and insufficient. Her close study of the unpublished *Tractatus novus de astronomia* of 1297 has not only revealed the significance of the application of the rules of the art to astrology, but has also explained why in the various works of Lull the nine divine principles (whose 'influences' were identified in the *Tractatus de astronomia* with those of the signs of the zodiac and the planets) constitute the basis of the universal applicability of the art to the study of medicine, law, astrology, theology and – in the *Liber de lumine* – to the study of light.

Lullian exemplarism allows us to see the art as a kind of cosmology. This is clearly demonstrated, for example, in one of the

earliest texts of European Lullism to which Yates's work has
redrawn our attention. Tomas le Myésier, author of the *Electorium
Reimundi* composed in Arras in 1325,[13] was a personal friend and
enthusiastic disciple of Lull. In a kind of grand compilation, he
sought to present the essential characteristics of the doctrine of his
teacher. He saw the art's primary function as being the defence of
the Christian faith against the Averroists and as a means to lead all
men to understand the divine truth and holy mysteries. In this
expository or introductory preface of the work, Myésier presents
the art as closely linked to cosmology: the circle of the universe,
whose graphic representation is accurately described by the author,
comprises the angelic sphere around which rotates the *primum
mobile*, the empyrean, the crystalline, the sphere of the fixed stars
and the seven spheres of the planets. The earth (on which is
depicted a tree, an animal and a man) is surrounded by the spheres
of water, air and fire. Each of these nine divisions of the universe
corresponds to one of the nine letters of the Lullian alphabet
(BCDEFGHIK) in its double significance as absolute and relative
predicate, although, according to Lull, some of the significances of
these letters change according to the different spheres to which
they are applied.[14]

The *Electorium* of Myésier is not an isolated case: the presence of
cosmological references in the extensive Lullian literature of late
fourteenth-century Europe is documentable. In many texts from
this period an adherence to (or at least a strong sympathy for)
Lullism is combined with the idea of a necessary relationship
between the construction of an art which is indifferently applicable
to all branches of knowledge and the fashioning of a hierarchical
and unitary image of the universe. One of the greatest European
philosophers to be influenced by Lullist themes, Nicolaus Cusanus,
emphasized exemplarism and the divine dignities as the foundation
of the art. 'This', wrote Cusanus, 'is the first foundation of the art:
all the things which God created and made, were created and made
in the likeness of his dignities.'[15] Cusanus, like Lull, considered the
principles of the combinatory art – goodness, magnitude, eternity,
power, wisdom, will, virtue, truth and glory (*bonitas, magnitudo,
aeternitas, potestas, sapientia, voluntas, virtus, veritas, gloria*) – to be 'the
principles of being and of understanding' (*principia essendi et
cognoscendi*). Exemplaristic metaphysics is a guarantee of infallibility
for a logic which deals directly with reality rather than with dis-

course. While he implicitly criticizes Gerson and proposes a terminological reform of the Lullian art, Cusanus in his postil to the *Ars
magna* seems to accept the substance of Lull's teachings:

> The names of the aforesaid principles are unusual for philoso-
> phers, but nonetheless these principles, made up by the inventor
> of that art, signify true things. Therefore, given that there is
> nothing mute in reality because of our affirmation and negation
> . . . and all which is true is consonant with the truth . . . the
> aforesaid art cannot be refuted [as Gerson wishes] because of the
> impropriety of its terms. But rather in order that it accord with
> the other sciences, it must conform to their terms.[16]

Even more closely linked to the 'exemplaristic' approach of
Lullism is the Cusanian doctrine of the ascent and descent of the
intellect according to which it is possible to elevate oneself to an
understanding of God ascending from the likeness of the divine
perfections impressed in his creatures, and descending from the
understanding of divine being and its attributes to the understanding of reality which is the mirror of that perfection.[17]

In the *Liber de ascensu et descensu intellectus*, composed by Lull in
Montpellier in 1304, Lull deals at length with the idea of the
reconstruction (in the human intellect) of the divine archetype
which presided over the material creation, by searching for analogies and signs in the physical world (an idea later taken up and
developed by Cusanus). Through the description of the complicated ladder of being, from stones to plants, through animals to
man, through the angels to God, this theme came to be identified
with the other well-known theme of the minute reconstruction or
'encyclopaedia' of the cosmic hierarchies. This same cosmological
approach is also found in the *Liber creaturarum* of Raimundo Sibiuda
(Sabunde, Sebond) who was influential on Cusanus, Lèfevre
d'Etaples, Bovelles and Montaigne. The *Liber* was composed
between 1434 and 1436, the same years in which Cusanus was pas-
sionately reading and transcribing the texts of Lull. We find here
not only the doctrine of the ascent and descent of the intellect, and
the idea of the art as the 'root, origin and foundation of all the sciences' which would allow the practitioner to achieve miraculous
results in a very short time ('one learns more in a month with this
science than in one hundred years studying the *doctores*'), but also

the image of a 'ladder of nature' (*scala naturae*), whose various steps are retained in the memory and represented by means of figures:

> This is the first and radical and fundamental premise of this science: considering these steps in themselves, and planting and rooting them in the mind and constructing figures as they really occur in nature.[18]

The ordered succession of steps on the ladder offers us a hierarchical and organic image of the universe: the first level comprises things which exist but do not live or feel or understand (minerals and metals, the heavens and celestial bodies, artificial objects); the second level includes things which live, but are deprived of feeling and understanding (plants); the third includes animals, which both live and feel; and the fourth level is where man resides, who lives, feels and understands. Man, as the microcosm, summarizes the properties of the universe in himself, and is the living image of God.

4 THE *ARBOR SCIENTIAE* AND THE ENCYCLOPAEDIA IN THE SIXTEENTH CENTURY

In the *Arbre de sciencia*, composed in Rome in 1295, the 'tree' diagrams are presented as a means to 'popularize' the art and make it easier to learn. In this work the encyclopaedia is presented as an integral part of Lull's projected total reform of knowledge. The basis of the encyclopaedia, which is divided into sixteen trees, is the idea of the coincidence of the unity of knowledge and the unity of the cosmos.

A suggestive illustration in the Ambrosian manuscript which contains the Catalan version of Lull's work[19] shows the philosopher and a monk at the foot of the 'tree of the sciences'. Lull turned to the monk (a figure which appears at Lull's side in all the illustrations of the various trees) for comfort after his missionary plan, which included the propagation of the art, had met with a frosty welcome from Boniface VIII. It was a monk (Lull says in his preface) who had counselled him to present the great art in a new form. The eighteen roots of the tree of the sciences comprise the nine transcendent principles (or 'divine dignities') and nine relative principles of the art: difference, concord, contrariety, beginning, middle, end, majority, equality, and minority (*differentia, concordantia, contrarietas, principium, medium, finis, maioritas, aequalitas, minoritas*). The tree is subdivided into sixteen branches, each of which corresponds to one of the trees in the 'forest' of the sciences: the 'elemental tree' (*arbor elementalis*), the 'vegetal tree' (*arbor vegetalis*) which comprises botany and the application of botany to medicine, the 'sensual tree' (*arbor sensualis*) which concerns sensible and sentient beings and animals, the 'imaginary tree' (*arbor imaginalis*) which deals with the mental entities which are similitudes of real entities drawn from the preceding trees, the 'human tree' (*arbor humanalis*), the 'moral tree' (*arbor moralis*) which handles ethics and the doctrine of the vices and virtues), the 'imperial tree' (*arbor imperialis*) which is connected to the *arbor moralis*, and is concerned with the 'government of a prince' (*regimen principis*) and politics, the 'apostolic tree' (*arbor apostolicalis*) which deals with ecclesiastical government and the hierarchy of the church, the 'celestial tree' (*arbor celestialis*) which deals with astronomy and astrology, the 'angelic tree' (*arbor angelicalis*) which deals with angels and angelic helps, the 'eternal tree' (*arbor eviternalis*) which deals with immortality, the after life, hell and paradise, the 'maternal tree' (*arbor maternalis*) and the 'Christian tree' (*arbor christianalis*) which deal with mariology and christology, the 'divine tree' (*arbor divinalis*) which deals with theology, divine dignities, the substance and person of God, divine perfections and productions. The 'tree of examples' (*arbor exemplificalis*) in which the contents of the preceding trees are expounded allegorically and the 'tree of questions' (*arbor quaestionalis*) in which four thousand questions referring to the preceding trees are proposed, are presented as auxiliary to the main *corpus* of the encyclopaedia.

The unity of being is guaranteed by the fact that the absolute and relative principles of the art are the common roots of physical and intellectual reality. On these roots (symbolized by the nine letters of the Lullian alphabet) we can place either the *arbor elementalis*, whose branches indicate the four simple elements of physics, and whose leaves symbolize the accidents of corporeal things, and whose fruits refer to individual substances such as gold or stone, or the *arbor humanalis* which draws together both the human faculties and 'natural habits', and the 'artificial habits', or mechanical and liberal arts.

The Lullian image of the tree of the sciences, which was later taken up by Francis Bacon and René Descartes, was destined to be a popular idea, but the most persistent Lullian influence on European thought was the aspiration towards an organic and unitary corpus of knowledge and a systematic classification of reality. There were obviously other sources and cultural milieux from which this idea emerged, but Lefèvre d'Etaples and Charles de Bovelles, Pierre Grégoire and Valerio de Valeriis, Johann Alsted and Gottfried Leibniz referred specifically to the texts of Lull and the Lullists when discussing this theme. In the 'pansophic ideal' which dominated seventeenth-century culture there was an insistence both on the necessity of possessing total knowledge, and on the existence of a single law, key or language which would enable one to read the alphabet impressed by the Creator in material things. For the pansophists the real world and the world of knowledge formed a unified and harmonious whole and shared an identical structure. We will return to the pansophic texts of the seventeenth century later; for the moment we will dwell briefly on some of the sixteenth-century texts in which we find a coherent expression of these aspects of the Lullian inheritance.

The *In rhetoricam isagoge* was published in Paris in 1515 by Remigio Rufo Candido d'Aquitania, at the insistence of his friend Bernardo de Lavinheta, one of the most famous Lullists of the time. Attributed to Lull, and republished in the editions of the works of Lull by Zetzner, it is clearly a pseudo-Lullian work: there are frequent references to Cicero and Quintilian, to Platonic dialogues, to mythology and to Greek and Roman history. It is a text composed almost certainly between the end of the fifteenth and the beginning of the sixteenth century, which came to be considered an authentic work of Lull. The work itself is a curious mixture of rhetoric, cosmology and encyclopaedic aspirations. In the preface addressed by Rufo to his disciples, the brothers Antonio and Francesco Boher, the encyclopaedic aim of the work is presented as closely linked to the needs of the orator:

Through the counsel and inspiration of our friend Bernardo de Lavinheta, the most studious scholar of Lull, we bring to light this *Rhetorica*, so that the image of all the sciences can be admired and contemplated in this book as in a very clear mirror. It is necessary that the orator should have knowledge of everything, and master with diligence the whole world of the sciences, which has been called the 'encyclopaedia'. For this reason the author wishes to include, briefly and concisely, all those things which are relevant to the comprehension of each science.[20]

In this pseudo-Lullian text there is no shortage, naturally, of the occult colouring characteristic of Renaissance magical and alchemico-Lullian literature:

> From darkness emerges light. One who emerges on a mountain summit surrounded by cloud and mist, makes the darkness his hiding-place. Those who want to learn the method of speaking need to achieve it through silence. Like the silence of Pythagoras.

After a summary reference to the 'subjects' (*subiecta*) of the Lullian art (*Deus, angelus, coelum, homo, imaginativa, sensitiva, vegetativa, elementativa, instrumentativa*) and to the logical predicaments (*praedicamenta*), there follows a lengthy series of synoptic tables in which all knowledge is accumulated and expounded according to a strict order. The consideration of the 'imaginative subject' (*subiecta imaginativa*), for example, is transformed into a classification of animals, the various parts of the human body, and types of human beings, subdivided according to the four elements:

> Among men, some are:

> Terrestrial: such as farmers and miners.
> Aquatic: such as sailors and fishermen.
> Airy: such as acrobats and comedians.
> Fiery: such as blacksmiths and giants.

Likewise under the *subiectum* 'angel' we find the hierarchy of angels (*hierarchica angelorum*), while the treatment of predicates gives place to a classification of the various types of historical narrative and dialectic demonstration, the various parts of rhetoric, the partitions of ethics, the types of virtue, and the various mechanical and liberal arts: agriculture, stock-rearing, hunting, stage-craft, cooking, manual labour, philosophy, music, geometry, mathematics and medicine.

Still more typical of this type of rhetorico-encyclopaedic treatise is the *De arte cyclognomica* (1569) of Cornelius Gemma, astronomer and professor of medicine at Lyons, author of a text on the comet

of 1577, and a book on prodigies and the monsters of nature.[22]
Gemma's work is primarily concerned with medicine, but he sets
out to unify and harmonize the methods of Hippocrates, Plato,
Galen and Aristotle, and to found a universal method valid for
medicine as well as for all the other arts and sciences. The method
is subdivided by Gemma into three parts because the understanding is directed towards the comprehension of things past, the study
of things present, and the divination of the future. In the first part
we have 'memory and its artificial method', in the second 'science
and the method of proceeding in it' and in the third 'prediction and
its method'. Seeking a *via compendiosa* for truth, Gemma insists at
length on the essential function of symbolic representations, Lullian
circles, and images in a method which consists of an ordered classification of all the elements of reality.[23] The major part of his work
is dedicated to a meticulous, ordered listing of natural and super-
natural elements and the faculties. It is devised as a total encyclopaedia in which the themes of Hermetic and Pythagorean
wisdom are dominant. In the section entitled 'The Pythagorean
quaternary throughout the seven orders of the world distributed in
equal proportions' (*Quaternio pytagoricus per mundi septenos ordines
pari proportione distributos*),[24] matter, qualities, the spirit, and the soul
are divided according to whether they belong to the intelligible,
celestial, ethereal or sublunary world, and whether they pertain to
animate things, man or the State. The table in which these partitions are represented has the task of showing the secret correspondences between each of the elements, and clarifying the way in
which the senses or the imagination, the reason (*ratio*) or rational
soul (*mens*) are linked to the totality of the universe, to the celestial
bodies, to the heat present in animate beings, to ethereal spirits, to
the intelligences which preside over the motions of the stars etc.
This is also the purpose both of the diagrammatic representation of
the soul which sets out the fifty-one faculties of man,[25] and of the
figure of the three ladders, each of which is a tabular representation
of the parts of metaphysics, physics and logic. These tables also pur-
port to show the aims of these three sciences, the relationship
between the various parts of the single disciplines, and the order in
which every part ought to be placed in relation to the universal
order.[26]

Underlying the fantastic classifications, and the strange figures
which fill Gemma's text, behind the unconditional adherence to

the hermetic tradition, is the presupposition of the unity of knowledge, which is seen as a mirror of the unity of the cosmos: 'by
means of the idea itself of divine virtue, the reasons of all things are
reflected in each of the particles of the world'. This principle – as
Gemma himself explicitly states – constitutes the first foundation of
the whole art.[27]

A work which emerges from a similar set of concerns – despite
a fundamental difference in tone due to its predominantly logical
orientation – is the work of Pierre Grégoire of Toulouse, which
was first published in Lyons between 1583 and 1587. The title itself
is indicative: *Syntaxes artis mirabilis in libros septem digestae per quas de
omni re proposita, multis et prope infinitis rationibus disputari aut tractari,
omniumque summaria cognitio haberi potest* [A systematic treatise of the
wondrous art, digested into seven books, through which one can
learn how to dispute and expound an almost infinite number of
arguments concerning any proposition, and how to summarize
them all'].[28] In addition to the usual theme of an art capable of discovering the axioms common to all the sciences and of elaborating
absolute criteria of certainty, we find many of the same problems
here which had already been confronted by Agrippa and Lavinheta
in the same period. But the text of Grégoire was not a simple
'commentary' on the Lullian art. Unlike the commentators, after
referring to Lull and the principal theorists of universal syntax, he
elaborates a true encyclopaedia of the sciences not unworthy of
being compared (at least in terms of volume and extent) to Bacon's
De augmentis scientiarum. It is founded on a 'mirror of the arts'
(*speculum artis*), in which he presents both the 'methods of investigating, examining, disputing and answering' and the classes or 'little rooms' (*cellulas*) to which all knowledge must be referred. The
reference to the absolute and relative principles of the *ars magna* is
explicit, but just as interesting, if not more, are the pages in which
the aspiration to encyclopaedic and universal knowledge is linked
to a faith in a substantial intercommunicability between all the sciences. As always happens in these texts, the unity of knowledge is
converted into another unity which corresponds to it, the unity of
the cosmos:

> Since, as Cicero says, there is nothing sweeter than to know and
> to investigate everything, I have reached the conclusion that the
> particular precepts of the individual sciences, which are distinct

one from another, can be collected in a single general art by means of which they can become mutually reciprocal. In all things it is always possible to trace a single genus in which species agree and participate, despite the fact that they might differ in some properties; consequently it is clear that, once the genus is fully understood, the notion of species is understood more easily, just as we understand the division of a river into its tributaries once we have followed the river from its source and seen the places where the river divides. In the same way it does not seem impossible or absurd that the diverse works of the different arts can be realized by means of a single instrument . . . Thus all particular natural bodies are composed of different mixtures of the four elements, and all animals and plants participate in a unique vegetative force by which they grow, and all the different senses are contained in a single body, and corporeal and incorporeal things coexist in man, who consists of soul and body, and heaven itself includes all inferior things harmoniously within itself, moving and ordering things with a single motion, in a single sphere, with a single influence.

The foundation of a 'unified science' is associated, once again, with a Platonic-Pythagorean or 'magical' conception of reality understood as a living unity. The extension of the art or single method to all disciplines and to all branches of knowledge is possible by virtue of a metaphysical presupposition: that of a cosmos which reflects the ideas of the mind which presided over its creation:

And finally all things are created and governed by the sole mind of God, all the light of the stars participates in the light of the sun, and all virtues participate in justice . . . God and man coexist in a single hypostasis: in our Lord Jesus Christ. And since this is how things are . . . doubtless the mind and reason of man can extend itself to all the arts, where they are guided by an excellent general method of knowing and understanding . . . To each of the particular sciences belong the notions – or universal preludes – by means of which the art and one's ability can be easily strengthened.[28]

At the end of the sixteenth century the aristocratic Venetian Valerio de Valeriis reached similar conclusions in his *Opus aureum* (published in 1589), which took up, in a modified and integrated form, the Lullian project of the *arbor scientiarum*. In de Valeriis, the problem of the tree of the sciences is presented as closely linked to the formulation of the rules of the *combinatoria*:

> The work is divided into four parts. In the first we deal with the information necessary for understanding the 'trees'. In the second we show the fourteen trees on which the understanding of all entities depends. In the third part we show in what way the general art of Raimondo [i.e. Lull] can be adapted to this task, teaching how to multiply concepts and arguments almost to infinity . . . mixing roots with roots, roots with forms, trees with trees, and the rules with all these and many other ways.[29]

The interpretation of the 'figures' of the art given in the fourth part seem to have been profoundly influenced by Agrippa's commentary on the Lullian art and, most probably, the theories of Giordano Bruno which, between 1582 and 1588, were published in his Lullist and mnemotechnical works. In addition to Agrippa and Bruno, de Valeriis makes many references to Scotus and Scotism,[30] and introduces a doctrine of absolute and relative predicates. The need for a 'golden art' (*arte aurea*) arises in every case, including this one, from a recognition of the pluralistic, 'chaotic' character of the intellectual world, the poverty of human understanding, and the need for a 'singular and marvellous artifice' (*singulare ac mirabile artificium*) which would make it possible to contemplate the order behind the chaotic appearances of the cosmos, and to enable men, after infinite labours, to 'repose perpetually and securely in the shadow of the trees of science'.[31] For de Valeriis too, the roots of the trees coincide with the principles of the art, while the order itself of the succession of the various principles is presented as dependent on 'nature'. The 'ladder of nature' (*scala naturae*) is invoked, for example, in connection with the problematic application of the roots (or principles) of the art to the *subiecta*:

> In the uniform application of these roots to the *subiecta* one must use the greatest diligence . . . It is necessary to observe the ladder of nature and all that which, on the inferior level, denotes a perfection deprived of imperfection, ought to be attributed to

the superior level. The operation attributed to stones (which occupy an inferior level) must be attributed to plants, which occupy the second level of the ladder of nature . . . That which involves an imperfection, if it agrees with the inferior level, should not be attributed to a superior: from which it follows that *contrarietas* and *minoritas* cannot be attributed to God, even if they are applicable to inferior things. The divine Lull orders the ladder of nature according to nine subjects and fourteen trees . . . One who desires to know many things in all disciplines should form this ladder.[32]

The works of Grégoire and de Valeriis are typical: from treatments of this kind the idea of a 'universal syntax' drew fresh nourishment and renewed force, and with it the idea of a key to the mysteries of the ideal and the real and a criterion for the construction of a complete encyclopaedia of the sciences. From Lull to the end of the sixteenth century, and then from Alsted to Leibniz, the conviction persisted that the Lullian art, or cabala, or the 'golden' or combinatorial art, or 'general science', coincided with the metaphysical discovery of the ideal fabric of reality.

5 THE MEMORATIVE TECHNIQUE IN THE WRITINGS OF RAMON LULL

The problem of a rapid and easy acquisition of the rules of the art and the order in which the notions were to be arranged in the 'encyclopaedia' was presented in the works of Lull and the Lullists, not as a marginal or secondary problem, but a constitutive and essential one. The rotating figures, the trees, the synoptic tables and the classifications, were presented in these texts as instruments which could transform an ignorant and unlettered youth into a wise man (whose abilities to understand and to act would be far greater than those who had been trained in traditional logic and philosophy) in an extraordinarily brief time (authors vary in their estimates between a month and two years). It is natural then, that the memorative technique (or, in Lullian terms, *confirmatio memoriae*) should be seen as closely linked to the *combinatoria*.

Throughout the seventeenth century it was customary to use the terms 'artificial memory' (*artificium mnemonicum*), 'mnemonic system' (*systema mnemonicum*) and 'memorative logic' (*logica memorativa*) to denote both large-scale cosmological-encyclopaedic works and straightforward manuals of combinatorial techniques. Johann Heinrich Alsted, who presented his encyclopaedia as a 'mnemonic system of the liberal arts and all the faculties' (*artium liberalium et facultatum omnium systema mnemonicum*) and Stanislaus Mink who in 1648 called his exposition and revision of the Lullian *ars magna* a 'mnemonic logic' (*logica mnemonica*), were drawing on a tradition which had its roots in sixteenth-century European Lullism, and the works of Lull himself.

In the prologue to his *Logica nova*, written in Catalan in Genoa in 1303 and translated into Latin in Montpellier in the following year, Lull outlined his programme for the application of the principles of his 'general art' to logic (considered as a particular art and discipline) and distinguished his new logic from the traditional one, insisting on the ease with which his compendious logic could be acquired and remembered:

> In order to avoid the prolixity and weakness [of traditional logic] we have invented (with God's help) a new and compendious logic which can be acquired without too much difficulty and labour, which can be completely and totally conserved in the memory and remembered with extreme ease.[33]

Lull frequently insisted upon the necessity of learning the principles of his art mnemonically.[34] His works were not simply 'instruction manuals' on how to practise the Lullian art: all the 'technical' elements of the art (the figures, the trees, the verses) had an explicitly mnemonic function.[35] In the verses of his 'Application of the General Art' (*Aplicaciò de l'art general*), a didactic poem of 1301 which expounds in popular form the advantages deriving from the application of the art to the various sciences, Lull insists on the miraculous brevity of his combinatorial art and how quick and easy it is to learn and retain:

> Que mostrem la aplicaciò
> Del Art general en cascuna
> Que a totes està comuna
> E per elles poden haver
> En breu de temps et retener.[36]

[We reveal the application
Of the general Art to each branch of science,
    So that it will be common to all,
And through this art they will be able to acquire them
    Quickly and retain them in the memory.]

Lull turned his attention to the problem of memory and the *ars memorativa* in his earliest writings. In the 'Book of Divine Contemplation' (*Libre de contemplació en Dèu*) of 1272, he proposed the construction of three great arts, corresponding to the tripartite division of the 'virtues' or 'powers' of the rational soul (i.e. memory, intellect and will). The 'inventive art' (*ars inventiva*), the 'amorous art' (*ars amativa*) and the 'art of memory' (*ars memorativa*)[37] were connected to the 'tree of science' (*arbor scientiae*), the 'tree of love' (*arbor amoris*) and the 'tree of remembrance' (*arbor reminiscentiae*) respectively. The *Ars inventiva* (1289), the *Ars amativa* (1290), the *Arbre de sciencia* (1295) and the *Arbre de filosofia d'amor* (1298), represent the partial realization of this project. In 1290 he wrote the *Arbre de filosofia desiderat*: the art of that which is 'desired', and in the course of this work he partially realizes his long-projected art of memory. Moving through the 'tree of philosophy' (*l'arbre de filosofia*), and following its complex structure, it was possible, Lull believed, to attain a true understanding of things, to learn how to love only good things, and artificially to remember things past. The trunk is the 'being' from which the 'branches' and 'flowers' (which simultaneously represent the nine principles and nine predicates of the art) derive. The letters *b* to *k* designate the eighteen 'flower-principles' of the *ars magna*, the letters *l* to *u* designate the eighteen 'branch-principles'. The structure of the tree is as follows:

FLOWERS			TRUNK	BRANCHES		
b. goodness	difference	power	BEING	God	creature	l.
c. magnitude	concordance	object	BEING	real	fantastic	m.
d. duration	contrariety	memory	BEING	genus	species	n.
e. power	beginning	intention	BEING	moving	motile	o.
f. wisdom	middle	point	BEING	unity	plurality	p
g. will	end	void	BEING	abstract	concrete	q.
h. virtue	majority	work	BEING	intensity	extension.	r.
i truth	equality	justice	BEING	similarity	dissimilarity	s.
k. glory	minority	order	BEING	generation	corruption	u.

Using the inventive-expository technique, which he developed at greater length in the *ars brevis* and the *ars magna*, in this work Lull once again describes the circular figures or 'wheels' (*rotae*) of the art, and gives definitions of the principles, the ten rules, the propositions and questions. The memorative technique is based on the systematic application of *d* (memory) to each of the branches symbolised by *l*, *m*, *n* etc. From this application nine combinations are derived – *dl*, *dm*, *dn* etc. Through these combinations specific aspects of the artificial memory are realized, each of which has a different function. In addition to the 'rules' of the ancient and mediaeval treatises on memory, we find here references to 'concordance' (*concordantia*), 'contrariety' (*contrarietas*) and 'difference' (*differentia*) derived from the combinations *dp* (memory–unity/plurality) and *ds* (memory–similarity/dissimilarity) and the subordination of the particular to the general, derived from the combination *dn* (memory–genus/species). Lull here uses the rudimentary associative psychology which he derived, directly or indirectly, from Aristotelian works.

The rules of memory found in the *Arbre de filosofia desiderat* have been treated at length by Carreras y Artau,[38] so we will concentrate instead on some of Lull's unpublished works which have not previously been examined in any detail. Let us consider first of all the *Liber de memoria* which was composed in Montpellier in February 1304 and survives in two manuscript versions.[39] In this text, which is presented by the author as the realization of a long-standing project,[40] Lull makes reference to a 'tree', the 'tree of memory' (*arbor memoriae*), which was not listed among the sixteen trees of the *Arbre de sciencia* of 1295. In the *arbor memoriae* nine types of memory are listed each of which corresponds to one of the nine relative principles, and one of the nine *quaestiones*. The treatise begins thus:

> A man was passing through a wood wondering why knowledge is difficult to acquire but easy to forget, and it seemed to him that it was because of a defect of memory, due to a misunderstanding of its essence, and its natural operations or conditions, and for this reason he decided to write this book about memory, so that memory and those things which pertain to it might be properly understood. The subject of this book is the general art, and we intend to use this art to investigate memory and its rules and principles . . . Memory is a thing whose essential and innate property is to memorize. This book is divided into three parts.

The first is about the tree of memory and about the conditions and principles of the general art with its rules and definitions. The second part concerns the flowers of memory, and the rules and principles of this general art as it is applied to memory. The third part is about questions concerning memory and their answers. First of all let us speak of the first part. The tree of memory spreads its branches and is divided into nine flowers.

The first flower is *b*, and *b* signifies 'goodness', difference, receptive memory and the question 'whether?'; the second flower is *c* and *c* signifies magnitude, concordance, remissive memory and 'what?'; *d* signifies duration, contrariety, conservative memory and 'from which?'; *e* signifies power or beginning, active memory and 'why?'; *f* signifies wisdom, middle, discrete memory and 'how much?'; *g* signifies will, end, multiplicative memory and 'with what kind?'; *h* signifies virtue, majority, significative memory and 'when?'; *i* signifies truth, equality, terminative memory and 'where?'; *k* signifies glory, minority, combinatorial memory and 'how?' and 'with what?'. In this art it is necessary to know this alphabet by heart.[41]

By referring to the tables and figures of the *Ars brevis* and the *Ars magna*, and correcting and emending the manuscript in two or three places,[42] it is possible to reconstruct how Lull intended to apply the *ars generalis* to the specific field of memory. The structure of the Lullian *combinatoria* appears in this case to be as follows:

ABSOLUTE PRINCIPLES	RELATIVE PRINCIPLES	SUBIECTA: MEMORY	QUAESTIONES
b.bonitas	differentia	receptiva	utrum
c. magnitudo	concordantia	remissiva	quid
d. duratio	contrarietas	conservativa	quo
e. potestas	principium	activa	[quare]
f. sapientia	medium	discretiva	quantum
g. voluntas	finis	multiplicativa	quando
h. virtus	maioritas	significativa	quale
i. [veritas]	aequalitas	terminativa	ubi
k. gloria	minoritas	complexionativa	quomodo et cum quo

This is not the place to enter into a detailed explanation of the complexities involved in the application of the *ars generalis* to the *subiectum* of memory. For a technical exposition of this kind one can turn to Eberhard Platzeck's account of the techniques and procedures of the combinatorial art.[43] It will be sufficient for our purposes to select a passage which is particularly indicative of the type of problems to which Lull turned his attention. In the following passage Lull deals with the problem of the relationship between the memorative faculty and the body, and with the problem of the passage from the general to the particular in order to lay the foundations for a memorative technique:

> Memory is located in a place, as stated in rule *i* in the third part . . . and it is in place accidentally [*per accidens*] and not in itself [*per se*]. This is because it is bound to the body, since memory in itself is not locatable because it does not have a surface but is in the place in which the body is, and as the body is changeable from one place to another, so is the memory in itself [*per se*]. Memory moves objects from one place to another but does not change itself – it changes its operations, objectively receiving species which are similitudes of places which it combines and multiplies and therefore because it is conditioned by place, the practitioner of the art must use it by means of place. Thus if he wishes to remember something consigned to oblivion, let him think about the place where the thing was; firstly according to genus, as in which city; then according to species, as in which district; then in particular, as in which house, whether it was in the hall or the kitchen, and many other things in a similar fashion. Through such a discourse memory will multiply itself.[44]

Despite the fact that Lull's concern here is clearly with the process of the successive determination of particulars – in his terminology the 'handling of the descent from the general to the particular' (*tractatio de generali ad specialia postea descendens*) – it is difficult not to hear in this passage a distant echo of the discussions concerning the selection of memory-places in 'Ciceronian' mnemotechnics. Lull's examples (the city, the street, the house, the room, the kitchen) are virtually identical to those recommended by the 'Ciceronians'. Some elements of this tradition must have entered into Lull's philosophy via the works of St Augustine.[45] The precise relationship between Lull's memorative techniques and the

Ciceronian tradition is extremely tenuous and difficult to determine. It would be a mistake, however, to continue to interpret the Lullian art solely as a preliminary stage in the development of 'formal logic' and to undervalue the influence of the Augustinian thematic (which sees the distinction between memory, intellect and will as a symbolic expression of the persons of the Trinity) on his works. In fact, as Frances Yates has noted, the Lullian art seems to have been conceived as an image or similitude of the Holy Trinity. In its fullest form it consists of three modes or aspects: the first (which is realized by means of the combinatoria or 'new logic') works through the intellect; the second (related to Lull's mystical writings) works by means of the will; the third concerns memory and transforms the whole art into a vast mnemotechnical system.[46]

The influence of Augustine on Lull's philosophy is well documented. In addition to the numerous passages of the *Liber de contemplaciò* and of the *Arbre de filosofia desiderat* noted by Carreras y Artau, I would like to single out, as particularly symptomatic, the 'Book of Divine Memory' (*Liber de divina memoria*)[47] written in Messina in March 1313. In this work the topic of memory, as in Augustine, is subordinated to theological purposes. Here is the beginning of the treatise as it appears in the Ambrosian manuscript:

> God, with your mercy, here begins the book about your memory. Since we do not have as much knowledge about divine memory as we do about divine intellect and will, we decided to investigate divine memory so that we might know as much about it as we know about divine intellect and will, and so increase our knowledge of God . . . Concerning the division of this book: this book is divided into five parts. In the first part we shall deal with the memory of man, in the second part we shall investigate divine memory through divine intellect, in the third part divine will, in the fourth part the divine trinity, and in the fifth and final part we shall deal with divine reasons . . . Human memory is the power with which man contemplates those things which are past and in order to make this clear we offer this example. The imaginative power does not act (that is to say does not imagine) at the same time as the sensitive power attains its object, and because of this it is able to have an experience of this object wherever it pleases; likewise when a man is in the act of thinking or imagining an object, the memory is not able to

remember that object because the intellect and will impede the action of the memory, because intellect apprehends the object, and will loves or hates it, and this shows us that memory is a power in itself contrary to those who say that memory is not a power in itself but is rooted in the intellect and that together they are one power, which is an error as has been declared above.[48]

In addition to the works on memory of 1304 and 1313 to which we have already referred, there is a third unpublished work on memory – the 'Book on the Strengthening of the Memory' (*Liber ad memoriam confirmandam*) – composed in Pisa in 1308 during a stay at the convent of San Domenico.[49] The treatise opens with a statement of the aims of the *confirmatio memoriae* ('the reason for which we have composed the present treatise is to show a better way of strengthening man's memory which is weak and fallen') and continues with a distinction between the three natural powers of the soul – 'capacity' (*capacitas*), 'memory' (*memoria*) and 'discrimination' (*discretio*) – each of which can be perfected by means of a particular technique. Each of the three natural powers has a corresponding 'artificial power' which can be acquired by means of the art. The function and task of the art is to create a method of learning and transmission of knowledge which will not fatigue the young for no purpose:

> Firstly this method is useful for anyone involved in scholarly studies, so that they may easily learn the way to increase their knowledge, without their efforts being in vain – so that their labours may be transformed into repose and their sweat into glory. It is especially suitable for teaching young boys because it does not weigh down the body, but allows them to climb quickly (with unencumbered bodies and happy minds) to the summit of the sciences, without excessive hardship. For there are many who, like beasts, pursue the study of letters with a great deal of physical effort, and without the skilful exercise of their intellects. Their bodies are worn out from lack of sleep, and all their efforts are unprofitable. This method, however, is a proper and easy way for a virtuous student to attain the treasury of knowledge and relieves him of the oppressive burden of these efforts.[50]

The art appears here as a means to free pupils from vain and cumbersome pedagogical techniques: the theme of an 'artificial' strengthening of the natural powers of the soul is linked to the Franciscan notion of 'spiritual felicity'. The 'capacity' (*capacitas*) of the memory can be perfected through attention and the orderly partition of arguments.

He then makes some specific observations on the perfecting of memory itself, which are particularly noteworthy, and distinguishes this work from the other Lullian texts on this subject:

> I come therefore to the second thing, namely to memory which, according to the ancients, is either natural, or artificial. Natural memory is that which anyone receives when he is created or generated, [which varies] according to the matter from which he is generated, and the prevailing planetary influences: and thus we see some men have better memories than others, but there is no point speculating about this, since this must be left to the power of God. The other kind of memory is artificial memory, of which there are two kinds. The first kind uses medicines and plasters, and I consider this to be extremely dangerous, since occasionally such medicines are given to men with the wrong disposition, and in unnecessarily high dosages, so that the brain becomes too dry, and we have heard of and seen many who, through a weakness in the brain, have become demented, and this is displeasing to God because someone who is insane is no longer concerned with the grace which God has bestowed upon him. And even if the man does not become insane he never (or very rarely) attains the fruits of knowledge. The other kind of artificial memory is acquired in another way, for anyone can retain a great deal in his memory provided that he constantly repeats it to himself, for, as Alanus says in his parables, the student is just like an ox. For just as the ox eats grass quickly and swallows it without chewing it, and later regurgitates it, and finally, when it is better digested, converts it into flesh and blood: so the student gathers knowledge thoughtlessly and without deliberation, and in order to preserve it, must mull it over in the mind so that it takes root and is habituated in the memory, since what one easily grasps, easily departs and it is just so with memory which, as it is said in the Book of Memory and Reminiscence, is strengthened by frequent repetition.[51]

Three main points need to be emphasized in this passage: firstly we should note the reference to Aristotle's *De memoria et reminiscentia*, a reference which is present both in the Paris and Munich manuscripts, but is omitted from the Ambrosian text (the Paris manuscript also has a mistranscription of 'Aristotelem' in place of 'Alanum') and the insistence on 'repetition' (*reiteratio*) as an essential element in the strengthening of memory. Secondly, the lack of reference to the *arbor memoriae* and the open polemic against 'sinful' attempts to apply medical techniques to memory; thirdly, the distinction (drawn from the 'ancients') between natural memory and artificial memory. What we have here are statements and theses which attempt to establish a connection between the Lullist treatment of memory and other theories which sought to combine rhetorical motifs with Aristotle's treatment of memory in the *De reminiscentia*. While the use of the term *discretio* seems to derive from the Aristotelian concept of 'recollection' (*reminiscentia*), the reference to the 'ancients' seems to suggest the influence (albeit indirect) of the 'Ciceronian' mnemotechnic tradition.

We shall dwell at some length on this text, because it is indicative of an attitude to which Lull specialists have not previously turned their attention: Lull does not apply the rules of the art to the specific field of memory, but places the entire structure of the Lullian *combinatoria* at the service of artificial memory:

For the purpose of reciting long passages from memory I decided to establish some relative terms with which one could give answers concerning all things . . . These in fact are the terms mentioned above: 'what,' 'why,' 'how much' and 'how'. By any one of these you will be able to repeat from memory twenty counter-arguments or whatever facts might have come to you while you were talking, and how admirable it is that you might be able to keep in mind a hundred arguments so that, as the occasion arises, you can recite them well . . . Therefore he who strives to possess knowledge and desires to have universal knowledge of all things, let him work with the utmost diligence through this treatise and he will, without doubt, become more skilled than others . . . Firstly, therefore, using the first term, 'what', you will be able to repeat certain questions or arguments or whatever else you might wish to remember, by emptying the second figure of the things which it contains, by using the second term you will be able to respond or repeat twice as much, by emptying the third figure and multiplying it with the first.[52]

The *Liber ad memoriam confirmandam* has survived in only three late manuscripts from the sixteenth century, which, in addition to numerous errors, have significant variants. The generic reference to *quaestiones*; the continual references to a *Liber septem planetarum*, or 'Book of the seven planets' (which may be a reference to the *Tractatus novus de astronomia* of 1297) in which *capacitas*, *memoria* and *discretio* would be defined; the confused exposition of the techniques of *evacuatio* and *multiplicatio* which had been clearly theorized in the *Ars magna*; the impossibility (because of the divergent readings) of verifying the authenticity of the reference to Aristotle's *De memoria*: these and other elements in the surviving manuscripts should make us cautious in considering this work. The text is undoubtedly authentic, but it has probably been much altered and corrupted. The conclusions regarding Lull's relationship to the Aristotelian and 'Ciceronian' mnemotechnic tradition can be validated only if they can be confirmed by an analysis of the other unpublished works on memory.

In the case of the *Liber ad memoriam confirmandam* there are a few doubts. The case of MS Urb. Lat. 852[53] (which has been erroneously identified as a version of the *Liber de memoria* of 1303) is much clearer. This is clearly a treatise on local memory, composed according to the strictest and most conventional rules of Ciceronian mnemotechnics, and has been falsely attributed to Lull. Here are some passages from it:

Local memory by Ramon Lull. The memory art is carried out in two ways, namely by means of places and images. Places do not differ from images except that places are not corners, as some people think, but certain kinds of fixed images on which delible images are written, as if on paper. Thus places are like matter, and images like form . . . However it is necessary that these places have clear boundaries, and that the distance between them is neither too long nor too short, but a moderate distance, such as five feet or so; neither should it be too bright or too dark but moderately lit . . . You should choose, therefore, if you can, a particular house with twenty-two different and dissimilar rooms . . . and you should always have these places fixed in your mind's eye as they are positioned in the rooms, and you should know how to recite from them backwards and forwards in turn, and know what comes first, what comes second, what comes third and so on . . . If some familiar name is given to you to remember, for example 'John', take a John known to you . . . and you will put [the image of] him in a place.[54]

That a work of this kind, belonging to a very different cultural tradition, could be attributed to the Majorcan philosopher is not without significance. In the sixteenth century, when orthodox Lullists were developing the *combinatoria* for purely mnemonic purposes, there was a cross-fertilization between the 'Ciceronian' and Lullian traditions. The results of this cross-fertilization were widely disseminated in the works of Giordano Bruno. But almost sixty years before the appearance of the *De umbris idearum*, *Cantus Circaeus* and *De compendiosa architectura et commento artis Lullii* (all published in Paris in 1582) one of the most famous teachers of European Lullism, and a member of the circle of Lefèvre, attempted a synthesis between the 'Ciceronian' art of memory and the Lullian *combinatoria*.

6 BERNARDO DE LAVINHETA: *COMBINATORIA* AND LOCAL MEMORY.

In 1612 Johann Heinrich Alsted edited Bernardo de Lavinheta's 'Explanation and compendious application of the art of Ramon Lull' (*Explanatio compendiosaque applicatio artis Raymundi Lullii*) for the publisher Lazarus Zetzner[55] who in 1598 had published a definitive collection of Lullian texts and commentaries. The work had first been published in Lyons, almost a century before, in 1523. While Alsted railed in his preface against the 'ridiculous' Aristotelians and the 'inept' Ramists who were persecutors of Lull and Lullism, and intolerant of all intellectual freedom, he nonetheless found it prudent to warn his readers that there were many 'scholastic' or 'papist' elements in the work of Lavinheta: 'He explains the practices of the Lullian philosophy according to his own customs and those of his century, which is to say, in a barbarous and papistical fashion. You must therefore be careful not to dash yourself on these same rocks.' What had inspired Alsted, in spite of its scholastic and Catholic 'barbarism', was Lavinheta's attempt to construct an encyclopaedia of the sciences on the foundations of the Lullian art. The application of the *ars Lullii*, as the title makes clear, concerns logic, rhetoric, physics, mathematics, mechanics, medicine, metaphysics, theology, ethics and jurisprudence.

In his partition and classification of the sciences Lavinheta invokes the Lullian image of the single tree of knowledge, of which the various particular disciplines are different branches. Even though he introduces partitions and distinctions which are very different from those used in the Lullist art (the three branches of the *trivium*, for example), Lavinheta drew a great deal of his work (especially in his logic) from the figures of the *combinatoria*. His intention to use the *ars magna* in order to discover the universal and necessary principles which would unify the entire field of knowledge appears clearly in the section entitled *Introductio in artem Raymundi Lullii*:

> A single general art is needed which has general, primitive and necessary principles, by means of which the principles of the other sciences can be verified and examined . . . The special arts and sciences are too prolix, and the brief life of man demands that the intellect possess some universal instrument.[56]

Lavinheta included in his treatise a tract on cosmology and natural philosophy (in the discussion of the third figure), whole works on medicine (*Hortulus medicus*, *De medicina operativa*, etc.) and observations on the 'art of preaching' (*ars predicandi*) and scriptural interpretation. Lavinheta was thus working in substantially the same milieu as the pseudo-Lullian *Rhetorica* and his work inaugurated a new kind of Lullist encyclopaedism which culminated in the works of Grégoire and de Valeriis in the last years of the sixteenth century.

Lavinheta's course at the Sorbonne marked the triumphant re-entry of Lullism into Paris after the nominalist parenthesis which resulted from the controversy between Pietro d'Ailly and Gerson. When one considers the great influence exerted by Lavinheta's lectures on the scholarly world, and his intense editorial activity in the major European centres, from Paris to Lyons, to Cologne, and his popularity in the seventeenth century, it is clear that his treatment of memory (elaborated in the final section of the *Explanatio*) must have been particularly significant. In these final pages of the *Explanatio*, Lavinheta suggested the possibility of constructing an art which would combine the memorative techniques of Lull and those of Cicero and Quintilian. Lavinheta's definition of natural memory is drawn from Lullian texts and from mediaeval commentaries on Aristotle's *De reminiscentia*:

> Natural memory is that power whose task is to recall things to the mind, an organ which we have already discussed in our treatise on natural philosophy. Natural memory is situated in the occipital lobe in the form of a pyramid, and its power is spiritual. Its task consists in the conservation of the species acquired by means of the intellect and in reinvoking their images (*similitudines*) in the intellect at the command of the will.[57]

His definition of artificial memory is drawn almost verbatim from Lull's unpublished *Liber ad memoriam confirmandam*:

> Artificial memory is twofold: the first part consists in medicines and in poultices which our doctor judges to be very dangerous, because medicines can be taken which are contrary to the disposition of the individual, the excessive heat drying up the brain and can lead in some men to dementia and idiocy.[58]

Introducing a distinction between 'sensible things which are gathered by the senses and intelligible things which are gathered only by the intellect', Lavinheta goes on to distinguish between two types of artificial memory: 'There is a twofold method of artificial memory and the first is much easier than the second', Lavinheta says. The 'easier' method is the familiar 'local' or 'Ciceronian' memory. To remember objects which have been perceived by the senses or have been produced by the imagination, one uses memory-places (*loci*) disposed in a particular order, which are filled with images. For the purposes of this art, Lavinheta says, 'one must establish specific places in a familiar space, such as a church, a monastery, or a house in your city'. We also find here, naturally, the rules governing the order of the memory-places and the arrangement of the images (*similitudines*) in these places.[59] The familiar themes of iconology, which is entrusted with the task of representing and recalling 'intellectual things' to the memory, also reappear in this work. To fix an intellectual concept in our minds – 'Dominus est illuminatio mea et salus mea', for example – we must use emblematic figures:

> One can place in the designated memory-place the solemn image of a well-dressed man who holds a light in one hand, and salt in the other, and although *sale* [salt] and *salute* [health] signify diverse things, because there is a certain likeness in the sound of the two terms, the one can lead us to remember the other.[60]

When one is dealing with intellectual objects, things 'which are remote not only from the senses, but also the imagination', the 'Ciceronian' technique is insufficient. In these cases it is necessary to use a second, more complicated type of artificial memory: the *ars generalis* devised by Lull. Here, Lavinheta maintains (putting the old Ciceronian terminology to a new use), all the possible objects of knowledge can be 'arranged in a few places (*loci*)' and, by means of the principles, figures, rules and *quaestiones* of Lull's art, the practitioner can master the whole field of the knowable.[61]

7 LOGICA MEMORATIVA

For Lavinheta, Lull's *combinatoria* is both a logic and a mnemotechnics. On the one hand it is a 'universal instrument' by means of which all the principles of the particular sciences can be examined; on the other it is an *ars reminiscendi* which has wider applications than Cicero's *ars memoriae*. This combination of Lullian and 'Ciceronian' techniques was widespread in the early sixteenth century. In 1510, thirteen years before the publication of Lavinheta's work, the representatives of the academic body of the university of Cracow met to consider an accusation of sorcery against the Franciscan Thomas Murner, the author of *Logica memorativa, chartiludium logicae sive totius dialecticae memoria*, published in 1509. In this work, in which Murner devised a memory system in which intellectual concepts were represented by plastic symbols, there was a clear Lullian influence.[62] The final report on the case, written by Ioannes de Glogovia, is a fascinating document which, more effectively than a long discussion, gives us a vivid impression of how widespread such ideas had become, even in academic circles, and also helps us to explain the connection (which was particularly prominent in Renaissance German universities) between logic and mnemotechnics:

> I, magister John of Glogau, member of the college of the University of Cracow; bear witness that Father Thomas Murner, a German . . . has constructed for us this *Chartiludium* and perfected it to such an extent that in the space of a month men who are vulgar and ignorant . . . can become erudite and able to remember things, so that there has arisen amongst us a strong suspicion concerning the aforementioned father: that, rather than teaching the precepts of logic, he has transmitted something which has to do with magic.[63]

The idea of a 'memorative logic' (*logica memorativa*) or at least the idea of a substantial affinity between logic and the art of memory, underlies the continued attempts in European intellectual culture, from the early sixteenth century to the time of Leibniz, to use the Lullian art to construct an *ars generalis*, designed to unify the field of knowledge, and a *systema mnemonicum* or encyclopaedia of the sciences. Giordano Bruno's reform of logic and the encyclopaedism of Johann Alsted were, in this respect, part of a common milieu. It was certainly no coincidence that one finds, among the explicit sources of Leibniz's 'characteristic' not only some of the major figures of European Lullism, but also many of the most important works of the *ars reminiscendi*.

It is worth emphasizing one further point in connection with the Cracow case: the accusation of magic which was levelled against Murner was, to some extent, justified. The *logica memorativa*, the *combinatoria*, the *ars inventiva* and the *ars reminiscendi* were often presented as the foundations of a miraculous art, a 'short cut' by which the practitioner could penetrate into the secret recesses of nature. The 'logic' or art of Giordano Bruno, for example, which was clearly influenced by Lullism and the 'art of memory', as well as the cabala, and emblematics, was clearly conceived by its inventor as a form of magic. Pius V, Henri III of France, the Spanish ambassador at the court of Rudolph II and Giovanni Mocenigo all saw Bruno as the inventor and the possessor of a secret art, capable of immeasurably extending man's dominion over nature. This type of 'logic' was only much later freed from the taint of magic. In the *Historia et*

commendatio linguae characteristicae universalis, Leibniz, while distinguishing between 'true' and 'false' cabala, also sought to free the
combinatoria from accusations of magic: 'From the time of
Pythagoras onwards', Leibniz wrote,

> men have been persuaded that the greatest mysteries are hidden
> in numbers, and it is probable that Pythagoras introduced this
> opinion into Greece from the East, along with many other
> things. But ignoring the true key of arcana, the curious have
> fallen into superstition and futility, hence giving rise to a vulgar
> cabala very different from the true one, and there are many
> books full of trifles bearing the false name of 'magic'.[64]

CHAPTER THREE

Theatres of the World

1 SYMBOLISM AND THE ART OF MEMORY

In the late sixteenth century the Lullian *combinatoria* was generally understood to be a mnemonic or memorative logic (*logica memorativa*), which was both an 'art of arts' (*ars artium*) or 'universal instrument' (*instrumentum universale*) which one could use to examine the principles of all the particular sciences, and an art of recollection (*ars reminiscendi*) which was the foundation for a complete mnemotechnical system (*systema mnemonicum*) or encylopaedia of knowledge. The 'Ciceronian' *ars memoriae* and the Lullian *combinatoria* (conceived as a form of mnemotechnics) were seen as the key components in the construction of 'pansophia', or total knowledge. To achieve this total knowledge, in addition to the new logic (which mirrored the structure of the world) one needed an encylopaedia or 'universal theatre' which was its natural complement. The 'new logic' and the 'theatre' presupposed what might be called a 'specular' doctrine of reality, that is to say a belief in the perfect correspondence between words (*termini*) and things (*res*), between logic and ontology.

In the last chapter I attempted to sketch out the broad outlines of the development of the Lullist tradition during the sixteenth century. The complex tradition of 'Ciceronian' rhetorical mnemotechnics also underwent some decisive changes between the last years of the fifteenth century and the first decades of the seventeenth century. These changes did not affect the technical apparatus of the art (which in spite of occasional augmentations remained substantially unchanged), but rather its cultural significance.

The *ars memoriae* which had been esteemed in the fourteenth and fifteenth centuries, as a useful rhetorical device for preachers, or as a technique which could be used by politicians, writers and jurists to improve their public speaking, began in the late sixteenth century to acquire a very different significance. In the mnemotechnical works of Giordano Bruno, for example, it was linked to an exemplaristic and neoplatonic metaphysics and the cabala, and to discussions on the relationship between logic and rhetoric, the ideals of *pansophia* and the universalizing aspirations of Lullism. When it was placed in the context of these new intellectual concerns, the *ars memoriae* took on a metaphysical significance, and was increasingly subordinated to various philosophical agendas. The limpidity of expression and clarity which characterized the treatment of this art in Cicero, Quintilian, Albertus, Aquinas and Pietro da Ravenna gave way in the treatises of the second half of the sixteenth century to a baroque taste for hieroglyphs, alphabets, symbols, images and allegories. The differences between the mnemotechnical works of the fifteenth century, or those of Pietro da Ravenna, and the works of Bruno in the late sixteenth century are overwhelming. In the former we find an attempt to elaborate, on a rational basis, a rhetorical technique based on a study of mental associations; in the latter we find a complex occult symbolism which is seen as a 'veil' concealing a 'secret wisdom', which can only be recovered through the ambiguity of emblems, the allusivity of images, 'seals', and *imprese*. Originally designed as an instrument for practical purposes, the *ars memoriae* became increasingly identified with the search for a magical 'cipher' or 'key' which would allow one to penetrate into the hidden secrets of nature.

Around the middle of the sixteenth century it was not just rhetorical theorists who occupied themselves with the *ars memoriae*: Cornelius Agrippa, Giulio Cesare Camillo, Giovanni–Battista della Porta, Cosma Rosselli and Giordano Bruno considered the rules of memory as instruments to be employed for much wider purposes than those of rhetoric and dialectic. In these authors we find themes from the cabala, Lullism, magic and astrology, the *ars notoria*, Hermetic texts, and references to the works of Pico della Mirandola and Marsilio Ficino. Bruno, an author of commentaries on the works of Lull and an innovator of the *ars memoriae*, believed that the theology of Scotus Erigena, the *combinatoria*, the 'mysteries' of Cusanus, and Paracelsian medicine all derived from a common source. At the time when Bruno was writing (in the 1580s and 90s) these kinds of beliefs had already become commonplace: in 1550, for example, Jacques Gohory had published his *De usu et mysteriis notarum liber* in Paris. Gohorry (Leo Suavius) was a parliamentary advocate and diplomat, a commentator of the works of Paracelsus, translator of Machiavelli's *The Prince* and *Discourses*, and

a scholar of alchemy, botany and musical theory. In his discussion
of signs he referred constantly to the angel magic of Johannes
Trithemius, the Christian cabala, the *Ars notoria*, the works of Pico
and Ficino, the *ars memoriae*, the Lullian *combinatoria* and to the
Teatro del mondo of Giulio Camillo.[1] Gohorry's approach is symptomatic of the sixteenth-century re-evaluation of the *ars memoriae* to
which we referred earlier. But before we begin drawing conclusions, it will be necessary to attempt to trace the wider European
influence of some of the more popular Italian texts of the new art
of memory. The following survey will consider some of the 'theatres of the world' in which the metaphysical themes of the cabala
and encyclopaedism are superimposed on the original mnemonic-
rhetorical intentions of the *ars memoriae*. We shall be paying particular attention to those works in which the themes of the Lullian
combinatoria and the *ars mnemonica* are most obviously combined.

2 THE DIFFUSION OF THE *ARS MEMORIAE* IN ENGLAND AND GERMANY

Having received his instructions from 'Madame Logic', the hero of
Stephen Hawes's allegorical-didactic poem, *The Pastyme of Pleasure*,
continues his ascent into the 'Tower of Doctrine' and enters the
room of 'Dame Rhetoric'. After she has exactly enumerated the
five parts of rhetoric and their connection to the various faculties
of the soul, the learned dame turns to the subject of memory:

> Yf to the orature many a sundry tale
> One after other treatably be tolde
> Than sundry ymages in his closed male
> Eache for a mater he doth than well holde
> Lyke to the tale he doth than so beholde
> And inwarde a recapitulacyon
> Of eche ymage the moralyzacyon
>
> Whiche be the tales he grounded pryvely
> Upon these ymages sygnyfycacyon
> And whan tyme is for hym to specyfy
> All his tales by demonstracyon
> In due ordre maner and reason

Than eche ymage inwarde dyrectly
The oratoure doth take full properly

So is enprynted in his propre mynde
Every tale with hole resemblaunce
By this ymage he dooth his mater fynde
Eche after other withouten varyance
Who to this arte wyll gyve attendaunce
As thereof to knowe the perfytenes
In the poetes scole he must have intres.[2]

In this poem, published in London in 1509, the classical doctrine of rhetoric was formulated in English for the first time. Even though it is orientated towards a 'poetic' use, the reference to the doctrine of *loci* and *imagines* could not be clearer. Hawes's attempt to adapt the terminology of the *Rhetorica ad Herennium* to the particular requirements of the poetic art was not without precedent in England. The *Poetria nova* composed by Goffredo di Vinsauf between 1208 and 1213 was (as Howell has shown) one of the principal sources of Hawes's poem.[3] The importance attributed by Hawes to the *ars reminiscendi* in the formation of the poet, however, is evidence of a substantial re-evaluation of the function played by the *ars memoriae* in the *ars rhetorica*. This same emphasis, which is an index of an upsurge in interest in the techniques of the *ars memoriae*, can also be seen when one compares the third edition (1527) of William Caxton's *Mirrour of the World* with the two preceding editions (1481 and 1491), and with the *Livre de clergie nommé l'ymage du monde* (c.1245) of which the work of Caxton is a more or less faithful translation. In the third edition, in addition to a brief treatment of rhetorical invention, *dispositio*, style and more extensive observations on *pronuntiatio*, we find a detailed exposition of the memorative techniques in which many of the familiar classical themes appear: the comparison between the art and writing, the doctrine of *loci* and *imagines*, and the reference to 'corporeal' images.[4]

The interest in this kind of discussion is directly linked to the rebirth, in English humanism, of the great tradition of classical rhetoric, a renewal which can, in many respects, be associated with rapid changes in English society, the increasing prominence of jurists in the political and cultural arena, religious debates on the efficacy of sermons, and parliamentary controversies. The teaching of rhetoric and the 'method of the transmission of knowledge' occupied a predominant position in the curricula of English schools and universities between the mid-sixteenth and the mid-seventeenth centuries. Leonard Cox's *Plesaunt and Persuadible Art of Rhetorique* was presented in 1532,[5] as a work necessary for advocates, ambassadors, and all those who had need to speak before public assemblies. As the ideal of the courtier and gentleman (who was required to be an expert in both 'courtesy' and politics) became increasingly prominent in English culture there was a corresponding increase in the publication of rhetorical manuals and an intensification of debates concerning 'good manners', and the related problems of 'persuasion', 'tolerance' and civil society. It is only by taking account of this cultural milieu that one can begin to understand the intensity and harshness of the controversies which raged in the last years of the sixteenth century between the Ramists and the embattled defenders of scholastic logic and Ciceronian rhetoric.

Many of the motifs which can be found in the writings of Hawes and Caxton were doubtless drawn from classical and mediaeval sources, but there is also evidence to suggest a direct Italian influence on the development of these ideas in England. In addition to the substantial influence exercised in England by Guglielmo Traversagni da Savona's *Nova rhetorica* (1479), we can also point to the publication, c.1548, of Robert Copland's *An Art of Memory That Otherwise Is Called the Phoenix*, purporting to be a translation of an anonymous French work. This little book was in reality (as Howell has noted) a translation of Pietro da Ravenna's *Phoenix*, as we can see by comparing the following two passages:

And for the foundacion of this first conclusyon I wyll put foure rules. The fyrste is this. The places are the wyndowes set in walles, pyllers and anglets, with other lyke. The II rule is. The places ought nat to be nere togyther not to fare a sonder. The III rule is suche. But it is vayne as me semeth.[6]

Et pro fundamento huius primae conclusionis quatuor regulas pono. Prima est haec: loca sunt fenestrae in parietibus positae, columnae, anguli et quae his similia sunt. Secunda sit regula: loca non debent esse nimium vicina aut nimium distantia. Tertia sit regula vana ut mihi videtur.[7]

Given these precedents, it is not difficult to see how one of the most popular and significant works of sixteenth-century English literary criticism, Thomas Wilson's *Arte of Rhetorique* (1553), could draw on Italian sources to construct a kind of memory-art which both recalls the works of Pietro da Ravenna, and also seems to anticipate, in its use of mythological images, the later mnemotechnical writings of Giordano Bruno:

> As for example, I will make these in my Chamber. A doore, a window, a presse, a bedstead and a Chimney. Now in the doore, I wil set *Cacus* the theefe, or some such notable verlet. In the windowe I will place *Venus*. In the Presse I will put *Apitius* that famous Glutton. In the Bedstead I will set Richard the third King of England, or some notable murtherer. In the Chimney I will place the blacke Smith, or some other notable Traitour.[8]

During the sixteenth century the Ciceronian art of memory was even more widely disseminated in Germany than in England. In Germany one finds not only the usual inclusion of the memorative technique in general treatises on rhetoric, but an increasing number of specialized works. In 1504, for example, a work entitled *Ars memorativa S. Thomae, Ciceronis, Quintiliani, Petri Ravennae* was published, which placed Pietro da Ravenna definitively among the classics of the art. In 1505 Georgius Daripinus Sibutus published an *Ars memorativa* in Cologne and in 1510 Simon Niclaus aus Weida's *Ludus artificialis oblivionis* was published in Leipzig. Ten years later the popular manual of Johannes Romberch, the *Congestorium artificiosae memoriae*, which was modelled on the work of Ravenna, was published in Venice, and later enjoyed great popularity throughout Italy in the translation of Lodovico Dolce.[9] In 1525 Johann Fries published an *Ars memorativa* in Strasburg, where in 1541 and 1568 Walther Riff's *Memoria artificialis* and Johann Menzinger's *Praecepta de naturali memoria confirmanda* were published. Finally, in Wittenberg (which was the publishing centre that popularized the works of Ravenna), Johannes Spangerbergius's *Libellus artificiosae memoriae in usum studiosorum* was published in 1570. Spangerberg's work was extremely popular and was reprinted many times, before being included in Lambert Schenkel's *Gazophylacium* (1610), an anthology of mnemotechnical works which was widely circulated throughout Europe.

The harsh polemic of Cornelius Agrippa against the use and abuse of the mnemonic arts seems more comprehensible when one considers it in the context of this flood of mnemotechnical texts in sixteenth-century Germany. Blaming Cicero, Quintilian, Seneca, Petrarch and Pietro da Ravenna for this 'frenzied madness', Agrippa railed against the art of memory as an ineffective pedagogical technique which was not only burdensome to pupils in the classroom but encouraged 'a puerile glorying in ostentation' rather than helping to instil true wisdom. Agrippa here reformulated, in particularly vigorous and incisive terms, the traditional arguments of the adversaries of mnemotechnics – the same arguments which Bruno was to criticize so vehemently fifty years later:

> Artificial memory would not be able to last for the briefest second without natural memory, and natural memory can, in fact, be blunted by these monstrous images, and a kind of mania or frenzy can be caused because of the tenacity of the memory. The art, by overburdening the natural memory with innumerable images of words and things, can lead those who are not content with the limits imposed upon them by nature to the point of madness.[10]

It was a curious position for Agrippa to adopt, given that this opposition of the laws of nature to the impious presumption of art comes from one of the most fervent and enthusiastic supporters of the Lullian art, from a man who had devoted an enormous amount of energy to reforming and 'perfecting' the complicated structure of the *ars magna*.

Agrippa's *De vanitate* was published in 1530. Two years later, in his *Rhetorices elementa*, one of the greatest Reformation exponents of logic and rhetoric, Philip Melanchthon, assumed a similar position against the *ars memoriae*. Although Melanchthon eschewed the vehement polemical tone of Agrippa he was unequivocal in his denunciation of the traditional techniques for perfecting natural memory:

> Things that have been invented and arranged in an orderly fashion can be expressed by means of words. All art can be subsumed under these three headings. On the other two parts we cannot offer any precepts, since memory can be aided very little by means of art.[11]

In his insistence on the connection between 'reasoning' (*cogitatio*) and 'arrangement' (*dispositio*), and on the role of 'topics' (*topica*) in the ordering of concepts which were jumbled together 'in a great heap' (*in magno acervo*), however, Melanchthon articulates the 'double thesis' of 'order' and 'limitation' on which the doctrine of *loci* (and thus the entire mnemotechnical art) was founded. There is, in fact, a very close connection between topics, understood as a means of ordering concepts, and the art of memory, as Francis Bacon shrewdly observed.[12] We will consider this at greater length in chapter five. What is worth stressing here is the comparatively slight impact of Agrippa and Melanchthon's critiques in German circles. Not only did treatises dedicated to 'Ciceronian' mnemotechnics continue to be circulated in Germany, but after the confluence of the classical and Lullist traditions, there was a resurgence of these kinds of works and, in the seventeenth century, the mnemotechnical tradition involved some of the most important figures of German intellectual life.

3 SPANGERBERGIUS

The *Libellus artificiosae memoriae in usum studiosorum collectus* of Johannes Spangerbergius, published in Wittenberg in 1570,[13] is an excellent example of the vigour with which the themes of artificial memory were circulating in German intellectual circles in the late sixteenth century. The author of this work (which is perhaps the most lucid sixteenth-century exposition of the *ars reminiscendi*) has no pretence to originality: 'I have drawn these brief essays on artificial memory from esteemed authors and have collected them in a compendium.' Presenting the art in catechetical form, Spangerbergius had two primary concerns: to make the art clear and easy to learn, and to give an account of the art which gathered together both the classical sources, and more recent rhetorical and medical works on the subject. It is worth pausing to consider some of Spangerbergius's definitions and rules because they will help us to understand many of the views to be found in the works of Giordano Bruno. In addition to the traditional 'heroes' of memory (Simonides, Themistocles, Cyrus, Cineas and Carneades) the author singles out Cicero, Quintilian and Seneca among the ancients, and Pietro da Ravenna and Cusanus amongst the moderns as the foremost exponents of the art. In Spangerbergius's work the 'Lullist' Cusanus becomes one of the masters of the mnemonic art. The idea that the aims of the *ars Raimundi* coincided with those of the *ars memoriae* was, as we have seen, destined to grow stronger, and works like Spangerbergius's *Libellus* contributed to the high esteem which Lull's *combinatoria* enjoyed in the seventeenth century, and continued to enjoy until the publication of Brucker's *Historia critica philosophia*.

After defining the memory as 'the comprehension, retention and conservation of things which are past' and distinguishing between natural and artificial memory, Spangerbergius immediately attacked those critics of the art who had suggested that it was dependent on the natural perfection or imperfection of memory. Firstly he denies that the unaided natural memory can attain perfection, and secondly he connects the artificial perfectibility of the memory with the greater or lesser perfection of natural gifts. Artificial memory, he argued, was useful both for learning the sciences and for the temporary retention of arguments which is necessary for the poet; it was also useful for the teacher, the orator and the advocate. In addition to the ordinary forgetfulness, caused by the 'corruption' of 'the species of things past', Spangerbergius also identified two types of 'pathological' amnesia: one deriving from the prevalence of the passions, diseases or old age (through 'diminution'), and the other from *ablatio*, or lesion of the cerebral organs. While the forgetfulness caused by corruption could be remedied by the use of the doctrine of *loci* and *imagines*, rhetoric must cede to medicine in the treatment of those kinds of amnesia caused by *diminutio* and *ablatio*. Following in the footsteps of the *Rhetorica ad Herennium* and the *Phoenix* of Pietro da Ravenna, Spangerbergius sets out the doctrine according to the traditional rules. His division of *loci* into three fundamental types, and his enumeration of the ten 'rules' for the construction of images, are drawn largely from the work of Ravenna. The *Phoenix* is also the source for his theory of images – the only original element of the work is his distinction between 'images of things' (*imagines rerum*) and 'images of words' (*imagines vocum*). Spangerbergius divides his work (as Bruno did later) into 'theoretical' and 'practical' sections. The practical section, entitled 'the practice of memory' (*praxis memoriae*) uses the rules of the theoretical section to construct a series of examples and models, designed for specific purposes. Concerned primarily with the construction of mnemonic images, Spangerbergius provided the following dichotomous table of all the possible types of words (*dictiones*):

Every *word*
is either *unfamilar* or
 familiar, it denotes something which is either *invisible* or
  visible, which is either an *accident* or
   a *substance*, which is either
    inanimate
     or *animate*, which
      has either a *common* name
       or a *proper* name.[14]

The first of the six cases is that of 'an unfamiliar word' (*dictio ignota*): in place of the word (the meaning of which is irrelevant) one can substitute, by means of a 'vocal similitude' (*vocalis similitudo*), 'a known word' (*dictio nota*) signifying a visible thing which is similar to the sound of the thing to be remembered (such as using 'palam instrumentum' in place of 'praepositio palam'). In cases where vocal or phonetic similitude is not possible, one can proceed 'by means of inscription' (*per inscriptionem*), that is to say, one substitutes images in a fixed order in place of each of the letters which make up the word. The second case is that of a 'familiar word denoting an invisible thing' (*dictio nota rei invisibili*), for example the word 'justice'; in addition to 'image' (*figmentum*) and 'inscription' (*inscriptio*), it is possible here to use 'comparison' (*comparatio*) and 'similitude' (*similitudo*), employing what we would call the 'laws of association' (e.g. 'black leads us to think of white, an inkpot makes us remember a writer'). The third case is a 'familiar word' (*dictio nota*) concerning a 'visible thing' (*res visibilis*) which is an accident (*accidens*) rather than a substance, e.g. 'snow'. Here one can fashion an image which refers directly to 'the principal subject' (*subiectum principale*) of the word 'such as white stands for snow' etc. The fourth case is that of 'a familiar word' (*dictio nota*) denoting a 'visible thing' (*res visibilis*) which is an 'inanimate substance' (*substantia inanimata*): this can be expressed by means of an image of a person 'who is doing something with this thing'. The fifth case is the 'familiar word' (*dictio nota*) denoting a 'visible thing' (*res visibilis*) which is an 'animate substance' (*substantia animata*) which has a 'common name', e.g. 'farmer': here the image is constructed, according to Ciceronian rules, by substituting the image of a 'known person' for the thing to be remembered. Finally the sixth case is that of a familiar word denoting a visible thing which is an animate substance which has a proper name, e.g. 'St Peter' or 'St Paul'. Here Spangerbergius has recourse to iconology, fashioning the image of a man in particular clothes and particular postures (a man with keys, in the case of St Peter, or a man with a shield in the case of St Paul etc.).

Spangerbergius's system of classification is actually far more sophisticated than this brief summary suggests: he makes fine distinctions, for example, between different types of 'similitude' (*similitudo*) and 'image' (*figmentum*),[15] and we should remember that in actual use the *praxis mnemonica* would be confronted with far more complex cases than the ones he chooses for his examples, which would require the interweaving of various types of *dictio* in the same proposition or discourse. But after all these abstract diagrams, Spangerbergius returns once more to the liveliness of images – the *Libellus* reminds us once again of the close links between the practice of the *ars memorativa* and 'vision', between the doctrine of *loci* and *imagines* and the iconology, symbols and emblems which exercised such a fascination on the sixteenth-century imagination:

> If you want to remember these words: Pietro, whip, dog, pig, water, worm, sand – construct this imaginary connection: Pietro beats a dog with the whip, the dog, irritated by it, bites a pig. The pig, fleeing, breaks a vase at the bottom of which there are worms hidden in the sand.

When we reflect on the prevalence of 'baroque imagery' in late sixteenth-century culture it would be wise to remember the intense visuality of the mnemotechnical works of the period..

4 THE MNEMONIC MEDICINE OF GUGLIELMO GRATAROLO

When we turn from the mnemotechnical works of Spangerbergius to those of the physician and scholar Guglielmo Gratarolo of Bergamo we find ourselves in a very different atmosphere – one permeated by Aristotelianism, magic and occult medicine.[16] Gratarolo, whose life and career has been drawn to the attention of scholars (in very different ways) by the works of Frederic Church and Lynn Thorndike, fled from Bergamo to Basel after his conversion to Protestantism in 1550. His *Opuscula . . . de memoria reparanda, augenda confirmandaque ac de reminiscentia* was first published in Zurich in 1553[17] and was reprinted in Basel in 1554 with a dedication to the Emperor Maximilian. This volume contained, in addition to a treatise on physiognomy and a dissertation on the 'prediction of storms' (*prognostica tempestatum*), a manual on the *ars memoriae*. Translated into French in 1555 and English in 1563,[18] and reprinted again in 1558 it was also included in 1603 in the *Introductiones apotelesmaticae* of Iohannes ab Indagine.[19] As part of Indagine's *Introductiones* (a treatise on mnemonic medicine heavily indebted to the works of Avicenna and Averroes) Gratorolo's little treatise became immensely popular. Although he was deeply interested in magic and alchemy (he edited works by Arnaldo Villanova, Giovanni Rupescissa and a number of pseudo-Lullian works), Gratarolo studiously avoided any reference to the *ars notoria* in his work on memory, referring instead to the works of Albertus Magnus and Averroes on the one hand, and to the *Rhetorica ad Herennium* on the other. Gratarolo also made extensive use of a fifteenth-century treatise on memory, Giovanni Michele da Carrara's *De omnibus ingeniis augendae memoriae* (1481),[20] a fact which Thorndike failed to notice in his discussion of this work.[21] The twenty general precepts of the art presented in the sixth chapter of Gratarolo's work 'The philosophical reasons, rules and precepts concerning memory' (*Philosophica consilia, canones, et reminiscentiae praecepta*) and almost the whole of the seventh chapter were lifted, with minor stylistic changes, from Carrara's work. Compare, for example, the following definition of the four 'motions' of the memory in Carrara and then in Gratarolo:

There are four motions involved in remembering: the motion of the spirit which transports the figures from the cogitative to the memorative faculty; the depiction and fixing of the figures in the memorative faculty itself; the carrying of these figures (by the spirits) from the memorative to the cogitative faculty; and the action of recognition in which remembering properly consists . . . The artificial memory, as Cicero says in the second book of the *Ad Herennium*, consists of *loci* which are like the wax and the tablet, and *imagines* which are like the figures of letters. We are thus able to restore, with the greatest of ease, that which we have received. Cicero thought that one hundred images were sufficient, but the blessed Thomas believed that he could retain more than this.[22]

Here are the corresponding passages in Gratarolo (note the identical references to passages from the *Ad Herennium* and Thomas Aquinas):

> There are four motions involved in remembering: the first is the motion of the spirit which transports the figures and the species from the cogitative to the memorative faculty. The second is the depiction and fixing of the figures in the memory itself. The third is the carrying of these figures (by the spirits) from the memorative to the cogitative or ratiocinative faculty. The fourth is the action of recognizing in which remembering properly consists . . . The artificial memory, as Cicero says in the second book of the *Ad Herennium*, consists of *loci* which are like the wax and the tablet, and *imagines* which are like the figures of letters. We would thus be able to restore, with the greatest of ease, that which we have received . . . . Cicero thought that one hundred images were sufficient, but the blessed Thomas believed that he could retain more than this.[23]

The references to Albertus and Averroes lose much of their significance, of course, when one take account of Gratarolo's use of this source. The only original material in the *Opuscula*, besides a fleeting allusion to the anatomy of Vesalius,[24] are the curious medicinal remedies prescribed for the strengthening of the memory (e.g. 'to aid the memory and the eyes, wash the feet frequently in hot water, in which you have boiled lemon balm, laurel and camomile'). This ransacking of other texts was a widespread activity among the writers of treatises on local memory. In 1562, for example, and then again in 1586, Lodovico Dolce (one of the most prolific polygraphs of the sixteenth century) published in Venice his *Dialogo nel quale si ragiona del modo di accrescere et conservar la memoria*: despite Dolce's pompous presentation of the work, it is nothing more than an Italian translation of the work of Romberch on the same subject.

5 LULLISM AND CABALA IN THE 'THEATRES OF THE WORLD'

There was nothing in Italy, until the works of Giordano Bruno, to compare with Ramus's approach to memory in France. Nonetheless, when we are considering the confused and complicated construction which was Giulio Camillo Delminio's *L'idea del theatro*,[25] we ought to remember the enthusiastic judgement of this work by his contemporaries. Francesco Patrizi, for example, saw the *Theatro* as a successful attempt to 'enlarge' rhetoric and 'extend' it towards logic and ontology: 'Through his mastery of the most rigorous terms of the precepts of the teachers of rhetoric he has enlarged it so that it has spread through all the most spacious places of the theatre of the whole world.' Interweaving hermetic, neoplatonic and cabalistic themes Camillo's rhetoric becomes, as Garin has observed, 'an attempt to make the articulations of oratorical discourse correspond to the fundamental structures of being'. It is hardly surprising that when compared with the great rhetorical texts of the fifteenth century, Camillo's nebulous enterprise appears to be 'a parody of the more rigorous approaches of the Renaissance theorists'.[26] However, even if we were to dismiss the impassioned polemics which this 'parody' provoked, and the enthusiasm of François I, Francesco Patrizi and Bartolomeo Ricci as the vagaries of intellectual fashion, we cannot explain away Camillo's contemporary reputation as part of the history of social customs (*storia del costume*).[27] Although Camillo's idea of a theatre 'in which, by means of the doctrine of places and images, we can hold in the mind and master all human concepts and all the things that are in the entire world',[28] was closely connected to the mnemotechnical tradition, it also anticipated the unprecedented development of the *ars reminiscendi* in the seventeenth century, which (under the influence of cabalistic doctrines) brought together two closely related ideas: that of a 'universal machine' or 'key' to reality, and that of an organic and ordered collection of all intellectual notions and natural phenomena. In Camillo's work the use of images in the art of memory was linked to the ancient magical-alchemical theme of a secret knowledge:[29] 'in our dealings we use images to signify those things which must not be profaned'. Comparing the art of memory to the cabala, Camillo saw it as a means of attaining 'true wisdom'. By making rhetoric a 'mirror of the world' Camillo undermined the conventional uses of both art of memory and rhetoric. In his work the art of memory is no longer simply a rhetorical technique but an instrument of the prophet and the magus:

> Solomon in the ninth book of Proverbs says that wisdom has built itself a house and founded it on seven columns. These columns signify the stability of eternity; we must understand that they are the seven sefiroth of the supercelestial world, the seven measures of the fabric of the celestial and inferior worlds which contain the ideas of all things belonging to the celestial and the inferior world . . . Our highest task is to find order in these seven measures, so that they can be kept sufficiently distinct so that we can uncover their hidden meaning, so that they can strike the memory . . . This high and incomparable arrangement [*collocatione*] can be used not only for conserving the things, words and arts entrusted to them . . . but also to bring us true wisdom, by means of which we will be able to understand things not by their effects, but by their causes.[30]

By replacing the traditional *loci* of Ciceronian mnemotechnics with 'eternal *loci*' which could express 'the eternal nature of all things', Camillo sought to construct a mnemonic system on astrological-cabalistic foundations. His 'amphitheatre' with its seven 'gates' is not presented as a formal structure for ordering oratorical materials. His search for the characters of the seven planets and the 'seven measures of the fabric of the celestial and inferior world in which are contained the ideas of all things celestial and inferior' transformed a treatise on the art of memory into a work of cosmology and metaphysics. In Camillo, as for Bruno later, the 'rhetorical' purposes of the art were subordinated to higher purposes:

> If the ancient orators wanted to arrange the parts of their daily orations they used ephemeral *loci*, because they were dealing with ephemeral things, but since they wanted to commend to us the eternal nature of all things . . . we find eternal *loci* in their orations. Our highest task is to find order in these seven measures . . . But because we want to go beyond these highest measures to those which are higher still, and because they are so distant from our understanding, and have only been glanced at obscurely by the prophets, this would be to try our hand at a thing which is

too difficult, so for this reason we will use the seven planets in their stead . . . but we use them not as limits beyond which we cannot proceed, but as images which to the minds of the wise represent the seven celestial measures.[31]

This transformation of the *loci* of artificial memory into the 'eternal *loci*' of a hermetic wisdom was encouraged by suggestions which Camillo found in various Lullist and Christian-cabalistic texts. That Camillo was familiar with Lullism we know from the personal testimony of Girolamo Ruscelli, who in 1594 recalled that 'Giulio Camillo . . . told me that he had made a long study of this art of Raimondo'. [32] Jacques Gohorry, in his *De usu et mysteriis notarum*, named Camillo as one of the greatest commentators and followers of Lull. When the *Idea del theatro* appeared in 1550, most of the important texts of the Christian cabala had already been published and were being widely circulated throughout Europe: Paulus de Heredia's *Epistola de secretis* (c.1486), Pico's *Heptaplus* and *Conclusiones*, Johannes Reuchlin's *De verbo mirifico* and *De arte cabalistica* (1497–1517), Petrus Galatinus Columna's *De arcanis catholicae veritatis* (1518), Agostini Giustiniani's *Psalterium, Hebreum, Grecum, Arabicum, & Chaldeum, cum tribus latinis interpretationibus & glossis* (1516), the works of Paolo Ricci (1507–15), the *De Harmonia Mundi* of Francesco Giorgio Veneto and the works of Agrippa (1532).

The sixteenth-century fascination for symbolism, allegoresis and mystical exemplarism created the conditions for a synthesis between Lullism and the Christian cabala. In a famous passage Pico had compared the *ars combinatoria* with the most elevated part of natural magic which concerned superior beings in the supercelestial world. Pico saw a close connection between the *alphabetaria revolutio* of Lull and the mysticism of letters and names which is an integral part of the cabala.[33] During the course of the sixteenth century Pico's idea was accepted by many followers of the Christian cabala, and by the end of the century the word 'cabala' was routinely applied to the art of Lull. The comparison was not a superficial one and was not simply a consequence of the ambiguity of the term 'cabala' which – as François Secret has shown 'had diverse meanings in the Renaissance period. Many Christians (especially among the major religious orders of the Catholic church) turned to the cabala for apologetic purposes.[34] The letters and images, figures and combinations of the cabala and Lullism referred to the book of nature which could be read and interpreted by the pious Christian philosopher. In the *Encyclopaedia seu orbis disciplinarum epistemon* of 1559, for example, Paul Skalich developed Pico's ideas on the links between Lullism and the cabala into a full-blown encyclopaedic project.[35] In his 'divine, angelical, philosophical, metaphysical, physical, moral, rational, doctrinal, secret, infernal conclusions' of 1553 he sought to present the image of a unified symbolic universe which, with the aid of cabalistic wisdom, would enable his readers to renew and perfect Lull's miraculous art.

Passing over some of the less important manifestations of the art of memory in the mid-sixteenth century, such as the plagiarized works of Lodovico Dolce and the brief, conventional treatments of memory in Cavalcanti's *Retorica* (1562) and Toscanella's *Retorica di Cicerone ad Erennio ridotta in alberi* (1561),[36] we shall consider instead the less well-known *Ars reminiscendi* of Giovanni Battista della Porta. In addition to the conventional distinction between the medicine of memory and the *ars memorativa*, the traditional classical references, and the usual attempts at synthesizing the Aristotelian-Thomist and the Ciceronian traditions, we find here a new emphasis: the semiotic function of 'hieroglyphs' and 'gestures', a theme which Francis Bacon and Giambattista Vico were later to develop at greater length. Della Porta introduces this topic when he is discussing Ciceronian memory-images: 'those animated pictures which are recalled into the imagination to represent a fact or a word'.[37] When one wishes to devise images for abstract words, such as 'because', 'or', 'much' etc., he says, one should use images from scripture to signify the individual letters of the word. In many cases it is not possible to refer to the 'meaning' of a word when devising a memory-image. It is at this point that he introduces a comparison with hieroglyphs:

> For this we turn to the method of the Egyptians who, because they had no letters with which to represent the concepts in their souls, and so that they could more easily retain the useful speculations of philosophy, began to write with pictures, using the images of quadrupeds, birds, fishes, stones, plants etc. instead of letters. This can be applied to our purposes, since we also want to use images instead of letters in order to depict them in the memory.[38]

Many of the most important intellectual figures of the sixteenth and seventeenth centuries devoted themselves to the problem of hieroglyphic writing and, later, to that of Chinese ideograms. The contemporary trend towards 'Egyptomania' and the fashion for emblems and *imprese* in European culture is symptomatic: to give an idea of the scale of this phenomenon it will suffice simply to list some of the many editions of the *Hieroglyphica* of Horapollo (the Greek manuscript was acquired by Cristoforo de' Buondelmonti in 1419, the Greek text published in Venice in 1505, a Latin version in Paris in 1515, 1521, 1530, 1551, and in Basel in 1534, in Venice in 1538, in Lyons in 1542 and in Rome in 1597) or Pietro Valeriano's treatise, *Hieroglyphica sive de sacris Egyptiorum aliarumque gentium* (Basel and Florence 1556; 1567, 1575 and 1575 in French translation; Latin editions 1579, 1595, 1602 in Lyons, and in Venice in Italian), which – according to Daniel Morhof, writing at the beginning of the eighteenth century – was 'in the hands of many'. The *Emblemata* of Alciati first appeared in 1531 at Basel, and went through over 150 editions, many with commentaries, and was translated into various European languages. One of the first followers of Alciati was the Bolognese Achille Bocchi, a friend of Valeriano whose *Symbolicarum quaestionum libri V* was published in 1555. In 1572 Ruscelli's *Imprese illustri* was published, and in 1603 the extremely influential *Iconologia* of Cesare Ripa. Although these are primarily literary works, it is extremely important when we are tracing the development of philosophical and 'speculative' phenomena such as Lullism and the *ars reminiscendi* to take account of such works because they were an important means of cultural transmission for neoplatonic and cabalistic themes and the hermeneutic methods associated with them.

The fact that non-European civilizations had been able to achieve the systematic representation and communication of concepts by means of hieroglyphs or images instead of the letters of the alphabet not only seemed to confirm the feasibility of the *ars memoriae* and Lullism, but also suggested the possibility of devising a universal language which could be 'read' and 'understood' independently of the differences between contemporary languages, nationalities or historical situations.[39] If we bear in mind that the technique of the *ars memorativa* and the rules of Lullism were presented as independent of particular languages (the 'technique' or 'art' was separate from the formulation of the rules in any specific

language) then we can gain a clearer understanding of the relationship between cultural phenomena as apparently diverse as the art of
memory, the revival of Lullism, iconology, and the contemporary
fascination with hieroglyphs, symbols and emblems.

In the *Thesaurus artificiosae memoriae* of the Florentine Cosma
Rosselli (published in Venice in 1579)[40] we find once again the
admiration for hieroglyphs, as direct expressions not just of letters,
but of concepts ('instead of letters, which in those times had not yet
been invented, the Egyptians used animals and many other objects
to indicate both names and concepts')[41] together with the idea of
the *ars memoriae* as a universal encyclopaedia. The doctrine of *loci*,
originally conceived as having a limited function within rhetoric, is
transformed into an instrument for the description of the elements
of reality. Placing hell, purgatory and paradise among the *loci com-
munia amplissima* the Dominican Rosselli converts his treatise first
into a theological encyclopaedia, then into an extensive and
detailed inventory of the celestial elements, the spheres, the heavens, the empyrean, demons, instruments of the mechanical arts,
artificial figures, natural figures (gems, minerals, plants, animals) and
finally writing and the various alphabets (Hebraic, Arabic,
Chaldaic).

This desire to order the elements of natural and celestial reality
seems to dominate even in the most famous of the 'theatres' of the
late sixteenth century, the *Universae naturae theatrum* published in
Lyons in 1590 by the great jurist and political writer Jean Bodin.[42]
Here we are very far from the atmosphere of Lullism and cabala. In
Bodin we find the demand for rigour and clarity characterististic of
the followers of Ramus: the meticulous division of natural causes,
the elements, meteors, stones, metals, fossils, living beings and
celestial bodies into tables seems to be based on the identification
of method with order and the 'apt arrangement of things' (*apta
rerum dispositio*). But Bodin's *Universae* is also grounded on a firm
belief in the fundamental coherence of the various elements of the
cosmos. The divine majesty of God is revealed in the ordering
work of creation, in which he arranged the chaotically confused
parts of matter into their appropriate places. The task which con-
fronts the wise man is not dissimilar to that which faced God, and
nothing can be more beautiful, useful and convenient than the
patient encyclopaedic ordering which allows man to reproduce,
within permitted limits, the perfection of God's work. Those who

neglect this search – however subtle their reasoning may be – produce vain and deformed knowledge: having mixed tares with their wheat, they have lost the opportunity of making an effective use of their knowledge. The 'theatre' conceived as a coherent and rigorous *dispositio*, on the other hand, allows one to discover 'the indissoluble coherence and complete consensus of the elements of the real' in which everything corresponds to everything else.[43]

The Ramist conception of method exercised a profound influence on the thought of Bodin.[44] Ramus's belief in the identity of *dispositio* and *memoria* explains the similarity between the 'theatre' of Bodin and the laborious encyclopaedias constructed in the course of the sixteenth century by the exponents and theorists of artificial memory.

In the writings of Camillo and Rosselli, the encyclopaedic-descriptive intention, the ambitious project for a total encylcopaedia, had been clearly superimposed on the original intentions of the mnemonic art. During the course of the sixteenth century the summary and concise lists of *loci* and images of the fifteenth-century theorists gradually evolved into complex encyclopaedias. This evolution was not simply the result of the persistence of the mediaeval themes, nor was it simply the result of the renewed interest in the ideas of Lull and the cabala. There was a genuinely new approach to the tradition of the *ars reminiscendi* emerging,[45] which saw the *loci* and *imagines* of the art as a 'mirror' or 'artificial theatre' of reality rather than as a set of rhetorical rules for improving the orator's memory. It was in precisely this way that Giordano Bruno, the passionate exponent of Lullism and magic, intended to use the ancient and modern texts on the art of memory.

CHAPTER FOUR

The Imaginative Logic of
Giordano Bruno

1 THE LULLIAN AND MNEMOTECHNIC WRITINGS OF BRUNO

Many intellectual historians and scholars of the philosophy of
Giordano Bruno have had difficulties with the works which he
wrote between 1582 and 1591 on the *ars combinatoria* and the *ars
reminiscendi*. When confronted with these unfamiliar and seemingly
paradoxical ideas they have tended to be dismissive and even openly
antagonistic. Leo Olschki and Guido de Ruggiero regarded Bruno's
Lullism as 'eccentricities' or 'crude illusions', and Dorothea Singer,
who was otherwise deeply sympathetic to Bruno's philosophy, on
more than one occasion expressed her inability to understand his
interest in the *ars combinatoria*.[1] One finds a very different attitude
towards Bruno's mnemotechnical works amongst those positivist
historians (such as Felice Tocco) who had considered the question
of their relationship to Bruno's other Latin works and to the Italian
dialogues.[2] It is precisely those scholars who have renounced 'rationalist', 'modern' and 'anachronistic' interpretations of Brunian
thought in the name of greater historiographical fidelity who have
been most successful in understanding this part of Bruno's philosophical career: I am thinking here particularly of the work of
Frances Yates, Antonio Corsano, Eugenio Garin and Cesare Vasoli,
who have all tackled the problem of Brunian Lullism and symbolism.[3]

Cesare Vasoli has outlined the importance of this approach to
Bruno's work:

The themes and motifs of Brunian mnemotechnics are essential
for a fuller understanding of Bruno's historical and philosophical
position: his reformist ideals, his hopes of developing practical
methods which would have a profound effect on the intellectual
situation of his times, and his desire to bring about the 'renewal'

of knowledge and religion which he spoke of in the Italian writings . . . We need to be aware of the continuity between the mnemotechnical works which he wrote between 1582 (the presumed date of the lost *Clavis magna*) and 1591 (when he published the *De imaginum signorum et idearum compositione*), and the metaphysical works which developed alongside them. We must try to understand the organic links between his logical-mnemonic techniques and the methods of his philosophical inquiry. For if Bruno strove for so many years to carefully develop and perfect his mnemotechnic doctrine, it was not merely to pander to the intellectual fashions of the times, or to indulge himself in the delusions of practical magic or cabalistic revelation, but rather because he was looking for a method which would help him to convey the central principles of his doctrine in the quickest and most effective way.[4]

Both Corsano and Vasoli have rightly emphasized the importance of the influence of Pietro da Ravenna's writings on memory on the philosophical development of the young Bruno. In a passage of the *Triginta sigillorum explicatio*, Bruno tells his readers that he had encountered the art of Ravenna when he was still an adolescent:

It was this little spark which, fanned by ceaseless meditation, grew into a fire on the highest grounds. From these flames leapt many sparks, and those which found suitable material burst into burning rays of light.[5]

In the great fire started by that little spark many of the peripatetic doctrines on which Bruno 'had been fed and nourished since his youth' were consumed. In place of the deductive procedures of scholastic logic Bruno proposed a gradual approach to the rational faculties via the imagination and memory. He preferred fleeting images to the rigid concatenation of causes, a radical diversity of meanings rather than the reduction of all consciousness to intellect:

It is a foolish discourse which seeks to treat sensible things in the same way as rational and intelligible things. Sensible things are not true in relation to some common universal measure, but in relation to a homogenous, particular, peculiar, variable and mutable measure. I wish to give universal definitions of sensible things in so far as they are sensible, which is the same thing as trying to define intelligible things in sensible terms.[6]

Although Bruno's interest in symbols, hieroglyphs and 'seals', and his desire to give sensible forms to abstract ideas has some affinities with the contemporary literary taste for imagery and emblematic representation, it is impossible to separate this approach from the wider intellectual currents which we have been investigating in previous chapters, in which themes deriving from the texts of Pietro da Ravenna (and other exponents of Ciceronian mnemotechnics) were interwoven with those of Lullism, allegorical symbolism, metaphysical exemplarism, cabalistic literature, pansophic ideals, the dialectical-rhetorical debates of humanism and religious reform.

When placed in the larger context of the Lullist tradition, the themes of the *ars reminiscendi* take on metaphysical significance. In this respect Bruno's appoach is not unlike that of Rosselli and the sixteenth-century constructors of 'world theatres', in which the art of memory is viewed not simply as a rhetorical technique but as an instrument for representing the structure of reality. In this approach the rules of memory, like the techniques of the *ars combinatoria*, are justified through a belief in the full correspondence between symbols and things, between the 'shadows' of the mind and the world of ideas, between the mnemonic 'seals' and the structures of cause and effect in the physical universe. It was this belief which was the principal point of contact between the rhetorical tradition which conceived the memory as 'mirror' or 'theatre' of the world (e.g. Camillo) and reformed Lullism, which avidly embraced the Platonic-exemplaristic presuppositions of Lull's original system. Bruno seems close to the spirit of these rhetoricians and Lullian commentators when he conceived of his mnemotechnical art as a translation of the ideal relations which make up the texture of the universe into sensible and imaginative forms. It was only through the allusivity of images, shadows and 'intricate species', he believed, that these ideal relations could be grasped by the human intellect and submitted to rational analysis.

Just because Bruno (like Lull and his sixteenth-century followers) was involved in what was essentially a metaphysical and exemplaristic project, it does not mean that he was not interested in the 'practical' reform of knowledge. He believed, in fact, that the pedagogical effectiveness of his mnemotechnical art, the rapid communication and diffusion of his ideas, and the reconstruction of an encyclopaedia or total system from the fragmented disciplines would necessarily lead to such practical reforms. Bruno believed that the 'miraculous art' of mnemotechnics would lead to a 'renewal' or reform of knowledge, and bring about an infinite increase in man's capacities, and his dominion over nature. This was certainly the way it was perceived in the Platonic circles of Paris in which, as Frances Yates has shown,[7] Copernicanism and Ramist reformism were circulating alongside more occult scientific interests in subjects such as the cabala and Lullism. Bruno's integration of rhetorical memorative techniques with the Lullist tradition had a lasting influence, not just in French intellectual circles, but also in those of England, Germany and Bohemia. Paris, London, Prague, Wittenberg and Frankfurt were, as we have seen, the publishing centres responsible for the wider dissemination of Lullism, and the *ars reminiscendi* in the sixteenth century – and by the time that Bruno began publishing his mnemotechnical works the intellectual circles of these cities were already familar with works by authors such as Pietro da Ravenna, Charles de Bovelles, Thomas Wilson, Johannes Spangerbergius and Bernardo Lavinheta.[8]

Bruno's *De umbris idearum* is probably the most famous of the three works which he published in Paris in 1582. It was in this work that his attempt to provide 'precise metaphysical reasons' for the technical elements of the art is most clearly visible.[9] The basis of Bruno's particular synthesis of the *ars combinatoria* and the Ciceronian art of memory can be summarized in three theses:

1. The ascent of the soul from darkness to light is achieved by apprehending the shadows of eternal ideas. Through these shadows truth is in some way revealed to the soul, which is the prisoner of the body.

2. The ideas or 'shadows', in which the structure of being is reflected, are perceived by the sensible and imaginative faculties. They appear in the mind as 'phantasms' and 'seals'.

3. Through the artificial retention of the 'chains' (or relations between the 'shadows') in the mind one can reconstruct, by means of a gradual process of purification, the connections which exist between the ideas themselves. The contemplation of

the unity which is hidden in the confused plurality of appearances leads to a rational understanding of ideal relations .

In Bruno, as in the *Syntaxes* of Grégoire and the *Opus aureum* of de Valeriis, the unity of knowledge and the unity of the cosmos are interchangeable concepts:

> Since there is an order and connection in all things, and since the body of the universe is one, and there is one order, one direction, one principle, one end, one beginning of the universe, we must endeavour to proceed (through the egregious operations of the soul, and keeping the ladder of nature before our eyes) from motion and diversity towards rest and unity, by means of inward operations . . . You experience a progress of this kind when you approach distinct unity from confused plurality. This cannot be achieved through the use of universal logic which proceeds from the lowest distinct species towards a confused mean [species] and from these, still more confused, to the supreme species. This consists rather in arranging many unformed parts into a unified whole. Since none of the parts and species of the universe exist separately in themselves or are without order (which exists in the most simple and perfect form in the first mind, irrespective of number) if we connect things to things, uniting them through the reason, what would we not be able to understand, remember or perform? One thing defines all things. The light of beauty in all things is one. One spark flashes out from the multitude of species.[10]

At the very moment in which he begins to 'reform' the Lullian *combinatoria* (by suggesting thirty subjects and predicates instead of the nine proposed by Lull, and by refusing to distinguish between absolute and relative predicates), Bruno begins to introduce (and modify) elements from the Ciceronian tradition. What the Ciceronian tradition calls 'places' (*loci*) and 'images' (*imagines*) he calls 'prime subjects' (*subiecta*) and 'secondary' or proximate subjects' (*adiecta*). The conventional comparison between the mnemotechnical art and writing is then construed in a different way: 'Writing has a prime subject, that is the surface of the paper; it also has a minimal proximate subject, and for its forms it has written characters.'[11] Bruno's works also repeat many of the rules of memory which we have encountered in the mnemotechnical writings of the fifteenth and sixteenth centuries. In the opening paragraphs of his *Ars memoriae* we find the familiar discussions of the relationship between art and nature, and signs and signification, together with the idea of the artificial instrument as a 'productive intellect'. We also find the traditional appeal to the example of Simonides and the precepts concerning the size, distance and brightness of the memory places. Bruno's conception of the memory place, which Tocco considered to be 'too expansive' to have been derived from the Ciceronian tradition, was in fact compiled from many different sources. The idea of using 'animated objects' in order to represent places was not a new one: it can be found, for example, in Michele Alberto da Carrara's fifteenth-century treatise the *De omnibus ingeniis augendae memoriae*.[12]

The influence of this tradition can be seen at work even in the contorted periods and baroque imagery of the *Cantus Circaeus*, published in Paris in 1582. In the second dialogue of the *Cantus* (which was republished with some modifications in London in the following year with the new title of *Recens et completa ars reminiscendi*), he reworked the ideas which he had already handled in *De umbris idearum* in a more accessible manualistic style.[13] In this work Bruno presents the art of memory as a technique by which anyone could improve their natural abilities. The art's principal merit, in fact, was its purely technical and instrumental character:

> It is our intention, with the approval of the divine will, to follow a methodical path, and one which can be procured by art: by means of which one can correct the defects, fortify the weakness, and aid the natural power of memory, so that anyone (as long as they possess adequate powers of reason and a modicum of judgement) can make progress in it, and no-one (excepting the aforementioned proviso) will be excluded from the practice of the art. This art is not as laborious as those of our predecessors (whose inventions have inspired us to greater efforts), and through our daily meditations we have made significant advances in the art, in terms of its ease, certainty, and brevity.[14]

We should not, however, be misled by such statements into thinking that Bruno's art is simply a practical technique. A few lines further on we find a typically Hermetic theme: the necessity of preserving the secrecy of the art:

In *Euthydemus*, Plato exhorts philosophers to keep to themselves things which are arcane and solemn, and to communicate them only to a few worthy ones . . . We ask the same of those who hold these things in their hands: we ask them not to abuse the gift which has been given to them. We ask them to consider that which is represented in the figure of Prometheus who, having revealed the fire of the gods to man, incurred their indignation.[15]

Even more interesting, however, is Bruno's attempt to distinguish the meanings of the terminology used in his art from that of other disciplines. The term *subiectum*, for example, is understood differently from the way it is used in traditional logic or physics. In Bruno's art it is given a 'convenient meaning which is technical or artificial'. It is not the 'subject' of a formal predicate which, in logic, is the counterpart of the predicate, neither is it the 'subject' of substantial, accidental or artificial forms as in Aristotelian physics. Bruno's *subiectum* is 'the subject of imaginative forms, which can be attached or detached, which shifts and changes according to the wishes of the cogitative and imaginative operator'. In the same way the word 'form' (*forma*) is not used as a synonym for 'idea', as it is in Platonic metaphysics, nor as a synonym for 'essence', as it is in Aristotelian metaphysics. It is not the substantial or accidental form which informs matter, as in Aristotelian physics, nor does it designate an 'artificial intention' (*intentio artificialis*) which is 'added to physical things'. Bruno's *forma* is part of a logical discourse, but one which is imaginative, rather than 'rational': 'The term *forma* is taken in its logical sense, but not that of rational logic – but rather that of an imaginative logic, that is to say it is a logical term which is taken in a broader sense.'[16]

This idea of the 'augmentation' of traditional logic, and the development of an 'imaginative logic' (*logica fantastica*) is one of the central motifs of Brunian discourse. If, like Tocco, we were to maintain a rigid distinction between the mnemotechnical and the Lullian works in Bruno's corpus, emphasizing the 'psychological' character of the former and the 'metaphysical' character of the latter,[17] we would be making an artificial distinction between strands which were organically connected in Bruno's philosophy. The originality of Bruno's approach to the rhetorical-mnemotechnical and Lullist traditions resides precisely in his attempt to find a point of convergence or common ground (or rather, a 'synthesis') between the two techniques which had emerged and developed autonomously over a long period. As a reformer of the *ars reminiscendi*, Bruno did not hesitate to supplement the traditional system with the instruments and rules which had been developed by practitioners of the *ars combinatoria*. He launched a vigorous attack against earlier mnemotechnical systems and differentiated his own mnemotechnical doctrines from those of his predecessors in several ways. Firstly, he rejected the conventional distinction between the memory place and the memory image, arguing that there needed to be a real connection (either associative or logical) between *subiectum* and *adiectum*.[18] Secondly, in order to create this real connection, he replaced the lists of household items traditionally recommended by fifteenth-century authors with complex mythological and astrological images (related to his Hermetic interests) which not only enabled him to represent the immediate subject of the image in visual form, but also facilitated the systematic and orderly representation of the complex relationships linking the central subject to all the characters and notions associated with it.[19] Thirdly, he used the rotating figures of the Lullist system as instruments of a system of artificial memory, using the letters of the Latin, Greek and Hebrew alphabets to represent and combine the images or *adiecta* of the art.[20]

The hundred and thirty fundamental memory places (*subiecta*) which can be derived from the various literal combinations are presented as essential components of an artificial memory system, but also as the basic elements of a system of logical relations. For Bruno there was no substantial difference between 'logic' and the 'art of memory'. This *logica memorativa*, which was the ultimate aim of Bruno's aspirations, was also closely connected to his metaphysics. The mnemotechnical art, he said, was 'a certain habit, or vestment of the rational soul which extends from the principle of the animated world down to the principle of life within all singular souls'.[21]

Our examination of the great Renaissance commentaries on the *Ars magna* has already shown us that 1) the *ars combinatoria* began as an attempt to develop a technique of artifical memory, and the 'trees', 'wheels' and tables of the art were conceived as instruments of a memorative logic, and 2) that the idea of a memorative logic was closely related to encyclopaedic interpretations of Lull's 'tree of the sciences' which transformed many Lullian commentaries into true encyclopaedias.[22] Given these facts it is hardly surprising to find that Bruno emphasized the mnemotechnical aspects of Lullism, nor that he believed that it was possible to describe the constitutive elements of the universe using the nine *subiecta* of the art.[23] In the light of these considerations Tocco's claim that a work like the *De progressu et lampade venatoria logicorum* of 1587 was 'a compendium of Aristotelian topics' written completely independently of Bruno's commentaries on the Lullian art hardly seems tenable.[24] His use of the images of the field (*campus*), the tower (*turris*) and the hunter (*venator*), allow us to link this tract on dialectics with the memory treatises of the early 1580s, and the explicit references to 'figures' is consistent with the themes of Lullism.[25] Many of the encyclopaedic works of the sixteenth century (the *In rhetoricam isagoge* of 1515 for example) did not deal solely with the 'internal' workings of the art, and Lullism was often closely linked to cosmological and rhetorical themes.[26] It was thus no coincidence that Bruno concerned himself with the problem of the 'application' of the memory art to rhetoric and physics. In the *Artificium perorandi* (written in Wittenberg in 1587 and published by Alsted in 1610), he attempted to apply Lullian mnemotechnics to different modes of rhetorical discourse, while in the *Figuratio aristotelici physici auditu* of 1586, he set out to translate the central concepts of Aristotelian physics into images. In the London works of 1583 the complex images of the seals were not direct representations of objects to be remembered, but visual representations of the rules of the art itself. Despite the importance of these works,[27] it would be more useful at this point, perhaps, to consider Bruno's attitudes towards Lullism in the *De lampade combinatoria* of 1587. In Bruno's estimation Agrippa had failed to grasp the true significance of the *combinatoria* – he praised the art rather than the works of Lull themselves. While he found the works of Lefèvre and Bovelles worthier of consideration it was only by introducing his own reforms that the *ars magna* would be able to achieve its final fulfilment and reach the highest level of perfection: 'Thus we have completed the art invented by Ramon Lull by defending it from all presumptuous criticisms and by rendering any further additions to it impossible.'[28]

It is important to note that in this brief sketch of the Lullian tradition Bruno also suggests that there had been a common source for the metaphysical theology of Scotus Erigena, the Lullian Art, the 'mysteries' of Nicolaus de Cusa and the medicine of

Paracelsus.[29] The reasons for this congruence seemed quite obvious to Tocco: Bruno saw Lull's works as Neoplatonic, in so far as it sought (by assuming the identity of the real and the ideal) to understand the structures of reality by understanding the relationships between ideas. While it was conceived as a refutation of traditional logic and replaced *topica* and *analytica* with 'images' and 'words', the Brunian art functioned in a very different way from dialectics. Resisting any identification with rhetorical techniques, Bruno's art was designed to enable performance of miraculous deeds and the construction of a total encyclopaedia:

> At certain points some things seem to be appropriate to the art by virtue of their usefulness even respecting natural things: such are the signs, the notes, the characters, the seals. These things give the art its great power by seeming to act outside the limits of nature, above nature, and – if the situation requires it – against nature.[30]

The objective of the art was not simply the re-enforcement of natural memory or the improvement of the intellectual faculties: it would 'clear the way for invention in many faculties.' In the most important of Bruno's works on magic, we also find references to 'seals', signs and figures which, together with gestures and ceremonies, are seen as the basic elements of a mystico–ritual language which opens the way for divine colloquies: 'With a certain kind of god there can be no participation unless it is by means of signs, seals, figures, characters, gestures and other clearly defined ceremonies.'[31] In works like *De magia*, the *Theses de magia* and *Magia mathematica* in which Bruno conceives of magic as a 'governess' and 'mistress' of nature, who is able to understand the secret correspondences between things and to grasp the ultimate formulae of reality, the problems debated in the mnemotechnical and Lullian works are finally resolved.[32] The idea of a unitary universe which is deciphered through symbols here reaches its zenith:

> One single light illuminates everything and one life animates everything . . . To those who ascend higher not only will the unique life of everything, the unique light in everything and the unique goodness be visible because all the senses are one sense, and because all notions are one sole notion, but also because all

things, including notions, sense, light and life are one single essence, one virtue, one operation.[33]

In order to understand Bruno's magic – his attempt to create an art capable of bringing men nearer to religious reform by using themselves as an instrument – it is necessary to analyse the relationship between the Lullian and mnemotechnical aspects of Bruno's work and the better-known philosophical statements of his major works. This examination will also help us to come to a clearer understanding of Bruno's language and style. We would no longer be compelled to see the convulsive rhythms of his Italian prose as the product of 'faith in instinct and excessive spirit' (as one famous literary critic would have it). The task of placing images (*adiecta*) in memory-places (*subiecta*), is that of 'presenting, figuring, denoting, indicating, in order to express and signify as one does in a picture or by writing'. The multiplicity of images must exhaust the implicit and explicit meanings contained in the ideas and form a single unity with them. Behind the recurrent images, the frequent repetitions, and the succession of symbols which give sensible form to intellectual concepts, one can see a specific set of philosophical convictions:

> Philosophers are in a certain manner painters and poets, poets are painters and philosophers, painters are poets and philosophers. True poets, painters and philosophers love each other and are beloved of each other reciprocally: a philosopher is nothing if he is not one who depicts and presents images.[34]

2 THE *ARS COMBINATORIA*, THE *ARS MEMORATIVA* AND NATURAL MAGIC IN THE SEVENTEENTH CENTURY

The search for a 'universal key' which could help one to decipher the 'alphabet of the world', and the idea of an encyclopaedic 'theatre' which would be a mirror of reality were gradually subsumed within the emergent discourse of Renaissance magic. The rules of artificial memory, detached from their original applications in the fields of dialectics, rhetoric and medicine, came to be seen instead as miraculous instruments which could help man to realize the dream of a 'total knowledge' or 'pansophia'.

This was certainly the view of many of the practitioners of *ars memorativa* and Lullism in the first half of the seventeenth century. Between 1617 and 1619 (at the same time as the young Descartes began to express his interest in Lullism and the arts of memory) the works of Johannes Paepp were published in Lyons. One of these works, the *Schenkelius detectus seu memoria artificialis hactenus occultata* was a detailed commentary on Schenkel's *Ars memoriae*, a work which Descartes knew well. In the *Artificiosae memoriae fundamenta* and the *Introductio facilis in praxin artificiosae memoriae*, Paepp set out to expound the Aristotelian, Ciceronian and Thomist doctrines on memory, but he had also patently been influenced by the Lullist tradition, and was familiar with its most significant exponents, from Bruno to Alsted.[35] Following in the footsteps of Alsted, he fiercely criticized the denigrators of the art, and defended the idea of the interdependence of logic and mnemotechnics: while logic was necessary for some of the arts and disciplines, he argued, memory was indispensable for all forms of knowledge.[36] Paepp emphasized the mnemonic function of the Lullist 'wheels',[37] and studied the works of the mediaeval *ars notoria*, and in his account of the mnemotechnical tradition refused to distinguish between 'Ciceronians' and 'Lullists', listing among the founders of the art not only Quintilian and Cicero, but Lull and Gratarolo, Pietro da Ravenna and Romberch, Rosselli and Giordano Bruno, Schenkel and Alsted.[38] A substantial part of his work is devoted to a discussion of the doctrines of Bruno, and (like Bruno) his treatise becomes an inventory of iconographical themes and a series of descriptions of images of the gods.[39] Paepp was more interested in the miraculous effects of the art than in discussing its relationship to rhetoric or the encyclopaedia,[40] and in his view the techniques of the *ars combinatoria* and the *ars reminiscendi* were akin to magical or occult practices: the art of memory could swiftly transform an ignorant youth into a wise man, and give him access to prodigious powers, so that he would quickly earn the admiration of the learned and the rulers of the commonwealth.

In Bruno, as we have seen, Lullism and the *ars reminiscendi* are intimately connected to his occult philosophical ambitions. Tommaso Campanella, who prided himself on his intellectual gifts, presents a similar, although subtly different variation on this theme. Campanella boasted to Cardinal Odoardo Farnese that he could teach natural and moral philosophy, logic, rhetoric, politics, astrology, and medicine using a special method which would teach in one year what it took ten years to learn by ordinary teaching methods. This claim comes up again, together with the same insistence on the possibility of an extraordinary 'facility' of apprehension, in his utopia, the *Città del sole*. By the time they were ten years old the children of Campanella's 'solar city' had 'effortlessly' acquainted themselves with all the sciences, simply by studying the images of the gigantic encyclopaedia which was painted on the sides of the city's six walls.[41] Instead of the words and 'logical' procedures of Lullist encyclopaedism, Campanella's system was based on sensible images. In the lost *De investigatione rerum*, composed between 1587 and 1591, Campanella proposed a dialectic *ex solo sensu* which classified the objects of sense into nine categories 'in such a way that one can argue anything, not only by means of words, as in the method of Ramon Lull, but by means of sensible objects'. The *De sensu rerum et magia* of 1620[42] also proposed a systematic form of knowledge based on the senses and things rather than words. In this work Campanella characterized memory as 'anticipated meaning', criticized the claims of peripatetic medicine, the affirmation that it is possible to operate on the memory using the findings of medicine; and he continually emphasizes the co-identity of memory and imagination. It is easy to see, in view of these convictions, why Campanella was also sympathetic to the idea of 'local memory'. The conclusions of Ciceronian mnemotechnics seemed to corroborate his belief that memory was a 'weakened sense': 'The art of local memory, since it represents ideas in the form of sensible and striking similitudes, shows that memory is a weakened form of sense perception, which is renewed and fortified by these sensations.'

The art of 'local memory' was certainly not lacking in followers in the seventeenth century: in the writings of Johannes Austriacus and Adam Bruxius, Francesco Ravelli and Lambert Schenkel, John Willis and Juan Velasquez de Azevedo[43] we find discussions of the themes and rules of 'classical' mnemotechnics, commentaries on works concerning memory by Aristotle, Cicero, Quintilian, Aquinas and Pietro da Ravenna, together with attempts to combine and synthesize Ciceronian mnemotechnics and Lullian *combinatoria*, the construction of 'memory theatres' and encyclopaedias, the elaboration of new and more complex images, and reflections on the nature of signs, gestures and hieroglyphics. These works helped

popularize and disseminate a set of ideas which were already familiar from the discussions of classical authors. It is worthwhile, however, giving further attention to other kinds of work in which
magic is not simply the cultural context of the arts of memory (as
in the works of Bruno and Campanella), but is their primary justification. In these kinds of works the connections between magical
techniques and artificial memory are explicitly theorized, and the
ars reminiscentia is presented as a form of magic. In the *Magia naturalis* of Wolfgang Hildebrand, published in 1610, for example, artificial memory is simply seen as the application of the magical art to
a particular form of operation.[44]

In his *Regina scientiarum* and *Encyclopaedia*, Pierre Morestel deals
with a wide variety of themes: the art of Lull, he says, is the 'queen
of sciences', it does not concern itself with a particular object, it is
characterized by its generality and certainty. It is a self-sufficient
mode of knowledge, and can help us to find the truth in every
branch of knowledge. In place of the mnemonic art of the ancients,
based on the doctrine of *loci* and *imagines*, Morestel proposes a 'new'
art of memory – the *ars combinatoria* of Ramon Lull. In Morestel's
works Lullism and mnemotechnics are closely associated with the
themes of the cabala, and with the search for a 'universal key'.[45] The
anonymous author of a work entitled *Ars magica*, published in
Frankfurt in 1631, also makes connections between occult philosophy and mnemotechnics (in this case the Aristotelian and medical
mnemonics of Gratarolo), devoting two chapters of his treatise to
memory and the use of astrological images to reinforce it.

In the *Pentagonum philosophicum medicum sive ars nova reminiscentiae*
(1639) of Lazare Meyssonnier – physician to the king of France and
a correspondent of Descartes, an exponent of astrological medicine,
chiromancy and physiognomy – we find the themes of the medicine of memory, combined with those of Lullism and the cabala. In
his *Belle magie ou science de l'esprit* , however, we find not magical
medicine but a 'method for the ordering of the reason' and a 'natural logic for solving all sorts of problems.'[46] We find a similar concern for the discovery of a universal method in the magical-medical
texts of Jean d'Aubry, where he argues the need for a 'science of
sciences' compared to which the particular sciences were merely
shadows. In his outline for a total encyclopaedia he vigorously
argues for the unity of knowledge and on the artificiality of sepa-
rating the disciplines:

In the first three chapters you will see all the knowledge of the world, and the order of all things . . . You will learn in the third chapter that there is only one science, because there is no single science which settles problems without using some kind of divination. This science gives me infallible answers and solutions to everything, as it is the rule of every truth.[47]

Even in the texts of Robert Fludd, probably the most important exponent of hermeticism and cabalist symbolism in the seventeenth century, we find an extensive treatment of the art of memory, which closely follows the conventional rules.[48]

Another thoroughly magical and Hermetic work which concerns itself with mnemotechnical themes is the *Traicté de la memoire artificielle* of Jean Belot, published in Lyons in 1654 as an appendix to his *Familieres instructions pour apprendre les sciences de Chiromancie et Physionomie*.[49] Belot sees the whole of Lull's *ars combinatoria* as a kind of magical 'artificial memory': using the marvellous invention of Ramon Lull, he argued, one can miraculously abbreviate the sciences, and quickly grasp the fundamental principles of every branch of knowledge, which would normally require a lifetime's labour. By revealing the essence of the art which Lull had deliberately concealed in series of enigmas, and by surpassing the doctrines of Bruno, Agrippa, Alsted and Lavinheta, and by making the art accessible to everyone – from preachers to merchants – Belot proposed to combine the *ars combinatoria* and chiromancy, substituting the figures and terms in use in the chiromantic art for the figures of the *ars combinatoria* and the images of Ciceronian mnemotechnics.[50] Despite the pretence of novelty, the 'wheels' which Belot uses in his art appear to have been taken directly from the Lullian commentaries of Agrippa, and there are clear traces of Brunian influence at many points. He derives from Agrippa and Bruno, for example, his arguments concerning the links between dialectic and rhetoric and Lullism and the secret arts – an idea which he discussed at greater length in his *Rhetorique*. The full title of this treatise is, in this respect, quite significant:

The rhetoric, by means of which one can discover that which is proper in oration, and which is disputable by dialectic, according to the subtlety of the Lullist art, and other more secret arts which are contained in one single lesson necessary in every art.[51]

The aims of Belot's 'rhetoric' are seen as identical to those of ancient Jewish wisdom and the doctrines of the cabalists:

That which Antiquity sought with great labour, without how-ever having acquired perfect understanding of it, I give to you in complete form: it is that [wisdom] which the prophets, the Magi, the Rabbis, Cabalists and Masoretes, (and latterly the learned H. C. Agrippa) wanted to acquire.[52]

By equating rhetoric and dialectic and the 'secret arts', and com-bining the *ars combinatoria* with cabala, astrology, magical medicine, and by relating the five parts of rhetoric to cosmological partitions drawn from the Hermetic tradition,[53] Belot – in the mid-seven-teenth century – takes the more influential ideas of Agrippa, Bruno and Camillo to their logical conclusion. The early writings of Belot date back to 1620 : it was at precisely this time that Francis Bacon and René Descartes began to voice serious criticisms of this kind of literature. They were unanimous on one point: used in this way the *ars combinatoria* and arts of memory resulted in vain and fruitless works 'nothing more than fairground tricks to astound and deceive the vulgar crowd, rather than contributions to the progress of sci-ence.

CHAPTER FIVE

Artificial Memory and the New Scientific Method: Ramus, Bacon, Descartes

1 PETRUS RAMUS: 'MEMORY' AS A PART OF LOGIC

The reception of fifteenth-century discussions of the *ars memorativa* in the sixteenth and early seventeenth centuries was not restricted to the exponents of magic and hermeticism. The latter half of the sixteenth century saw the fruition of Ramus's attempt to set the problems of memory and the rules of mnemotechnics in a broader intellectual context, concerned with the reform of methods of invention and the transmission of knowledge. This was a very different milieu: involved with the rigorous treatment of the themes of dialectic and rhetoric, attentive to the themes of logical disputation, and interested in the latest developments in mathematics and geometry. Through these discussions the idea of 'memory aids' exerted a significant influence on the mid-seventeenth-century texts dedicated to the reform of method. Francis Bacon, for example, saw the *ministratio ad memoriam* as a constitutive element of a new scientific method, while Descartes made constant references to a philosophy which would help mitigate the natural infirmity of the memory.

The Ciceronian tradition which, through the works of Ramus, had a Europe-wide influence, as we have seen, underwent its most successful and sensational developments in Italy. In France, one should disregard texts such as Campanus's *Memoria artificialis* and the *Ars memoratiua* of Leporeus (Paris 1515 and 1520),[1] which were merely exhaustive restatements of the work of Ravenna, and concentrate instead on major exponents of logic and rhetoric in this period of French culture. Instead of theorizing the mnemonic art as an autonomous technique, Petrus Ramus[2] was preoccupied with the problematic relationship between memory, dialectics and rhetoric. The primary aim of his reform was to remove memory from the province of rhetoric, to which a secular tradition had assigned it, and to develop it as a constitutive element of dialectic or the new logic.

Ramus liked to present his reform as a return to the teachings of classical philosophy, as a simplification or clarification of that Aristotelian teaching which, he believed, had been corrupted by the terminological confusion of the scholastics and the traditional rhetoric which stemmed from Quintilian. The philosopher who, in a brilliant exercise, intended to demonstrate the falsity of all Aristotle's propositions, also said: 'We preserve the books of the ancients and have recourse to them when it is necessary: we teach the pure and true philosophy which is collected in their books.'[3] He also used Aristotelian texts to provide the foundations for his definitions of the parts of dialectic.[4] He went back to Aristotle too, for the conjunction of philosophy and eloquence which he theorized in a celebrated oration in 1546: 'Aristotle combines the wisdom of intellect with the fecundity of discourse: in his morning strolls he taught philosophy, in his afternoon strolls he taught rhetoric.'[5] To reconstruct the true significance of Aristotle's teaching, to discover the truths present in the Aristotelian texts it was necessary, according to Ramus, to distinguish clearly between the domains of grammar, dialectic and rhetoric: the first deals with problems of etymology, the second with the art of invention and judgement, and the third ought to be limited to dealing with stylistic techniques and delivery, to the ornamentation and transmission of the material produced by dialectics.

Ramus identified what he saw as an error in the history of logic and rhetoric which he felt had distorted the meaning of both disciplines. Aristotle said (and Cicero and the scholastics had agreed) that it was possible to construct two different logics, one valid for the field of *science*, and the other in the realm of *opinion* and *popular discourse*. The first was for the wise, and the second for the vulgar. Ramus rejected this twofold division: there was a single theory of *inventio* and *dispositio*, he argued, which was valid in every field, and for every discourse.[6] The belief in the existence of two logics had led to a hybrid concept derived from Quintilian who not only confused dialectic and rhetoric but had further aggravated the situation by mixing together the themes of rhetoric and those of ethics:

Man is endowed by nature with two general and universal qualities: reason and discourse. The doctrine of the first is dialectic, and that of the second, grammar and rhetoric. Dialectic deals with the general forces of human reason in thinking and the disposition of things; grammar deals with the etymological and syntactical purity of discourse so that one can speak and write correctly. Rhetoric shows us how to adorn discourse with tropes and figures as well as teaching us the dignity of delivery. The other arts are generated by these general and universal instruments . . . Aristotle caused the greatest confusion when he made invention the first part of rhetoric, which is false, because invention (as I have said before) belongs to dialectic . . . Quintilian said that the subject matter of rhetoric was everything which is pertinent to discourse . . . and divided rhetoric into five parts: invention, disposition, elocution, memory and action. It is amazing how ignorant Quintilian was of the nature of dialectic: he confounded dialectic and rhetoric; he did not realize that invention, disposition and memory belong to dialectic, and that rhetoric is concerned only with elocution and action.[7]

Ramus insisted continually on the separation of dialectic from rhetoric. To those who objected that the orator had no choice but to use arguments elaborated by means of dialectic, he retorted that the conjunction of dialectic and rhetoric did not exclude, but required, a separation between the *theory* of dialectic and that of rhetoric:

Geometry, music and astrology cannot be sustained without numbers: these arts must therefore explain numbers and subordinate themselves to their service. The uses of all the arts (as I have often said) are interconnected, but the precepts of individual arts, however, should not be confounded, but should be expounded in separate studies.[8]

According to Ramus, the *artes logicae* comprised both *dialectic* (or logic) and *rhetoric*. The first is articulated into *inventio* and *dispositio*, the second into *elocutio* and *pronuntiatio*. Following Cicero and Quintilian, Ramus identified *dispositio* (i.e. the orderly arrangement of parts) with *iudicium*, or judgement (the second book of the *Dialectica*, known as the *Secunda pars Rami*, deals specifically with *De iudicio et argumentis disponendis*), and brought back into his treatment of *dispositio* those parts of dialectic which deal with axioms or propositions, syllogisms and method:

> There are two parts of logic: topics, for the invention of arguments (that is, as it says in the *Organon*, the principles of the elements) and analytics for their disposition . . . Disposition is the correct placement of the things found . . . and this part is what is properly called judgement, because syllogism is the common rule for judging everything . . . There are two parts to dialectic: invention and disposition. In fact, once you have chosen the question which you wish to discuss, then you can seek the proofs and arguments one after another. Disposing these arguments in order, one explains the question itself.[9]

In an earlier passage the term *memoria* is identified, along with *inventio* and *dispositio*, as one of the constitutive elements of dialectic ('invention, disposition, and memory belong to dialectic; to rhetoric only elocution and action'). For Ramus *memoria* had a very specific task: it was an *instrument for introducing order* into both understanding and discourse. As such it can neither be omitted nor neglected by the orator:

> You say that one ought to consider three things as an orator: the thing said, where it is said, and in what way it is said. The first is comprehended by invention, the second by collocation and the third by elocution and action. But what about memory? You say that it is common to many arts and that for this reason it has been omitted. But in truth, I tell you, invention and disposition are also common to many arts. So why are these recognized and memory despised?[10]

Given this *ordering function* of memory (which was traditionally identified as one of the five 'great arts' of rhetoric) it seems significant that memory was identified with the doctrine of judgement (*iudicium*) which belonged to dialectic or logic. *Dispositio*, *iudicium* and *memoria* became in many Ramist texts interchangeable terms: *iudicium* was allocated the task of placing or arranging the 'things found' (*res inventas*) in a rational order:

We assign invention, disposition and judgement to dialectic with good reason, leaving elocution and action to the orator . . . We define judgement as the doctrine which places the things found and judges this placement relative to the matter proposed: this doctrine is also the doctrine of memory (if it can be disciplined) and it is very true and certain because there is one rule for the two great powers of the soul: judgement and memory . . . Reason has two parts: the invention of arguments and their judgement in disposition . . . and memory is a kind of shadow of disposition . . . therefore these three parts (that is, invention, disposition and memory) belong to the art of dialectic.[11]

Despite the doubts advanced by Ramus concerning the possibility of a discipline of memory as an autonomous art, indeed precisely *because* of these doubts, his conception of method as the *systematic and ordered disposition of notions* absorbs many of the 'rules' of mnemotechnics. The absorption of memory into logic and the identification of the problem of method with that of memory gave rise to the concept of method as a *classification of reality*, a notion which became vitally important to European thought in succeeding centuries. This identification of memory and method, while anticipating the Baconian position half a century later, also brought Ramus close to Melanchthon who in his *Erotemata dialecticae* saw method as

a habit, or science, or art which, by means of a secure method, opens a pathway through inaccessible places and the disorderly confusion of things, so that we can identify and extract matter pertinent to our argument in an orderly fashion.[12]

There are some common aims among the many authors of the Ciceronian and Lullian traditions: the systematic ordering of *notiones* and *argumenta*, the orderly *collocatio* of *loci*, the construction of *encyclopaedias*, the creation of a *topica universalis*. The fact that a young Bohemian scholar Johann â Nostiz could develop a new logic based on the teachings of Lull, Ramus and Giordano Bruno confirms this fundamental unity of intentions.

The works of Ramus, then, emphasized the inclusion of the problem of memory within a wider discourse in which it was seen not just as a useful technique for orators, advocates, and poets, but as concerned with questions pertinent to method and logic. Instead of turning to modern historians of philosophy, who have equivocated endlessly over the significance of the Ramist reform, it may be more instructive for us to turn to the statements of Omar Talon (Audomarus Talaeus), the great theorist of sixteenth-century rhetoric, and Ramus's devoted disciple and collaborator. 'Ramus', he wrote, 'has brought back the theory of *inventio* and *dispositio* and *memoria* to logic (to which it properly belongs).'[13] It is also useful to consider Pierre Gassendi's opinion of Ramus's project:

> Having observed that rhetoric had been commonly divided into five parts: invention, disposition, elocution, memory and action or delivery, he [i.e. Ramus] believed that only two of these were pertinent to rhetoric (that is to say, elocution and action or delivery), and that only two arts were pertinent to logic: invention and disposition. Given that both are useful to memory it could be added to the other two. He subdivided logic or dialectic . . . into two parts: invention and judgement (he preferred this term in fact to disposition). Thus the entire art was encompassed in two books.[14]

The revolutionary impact which his seemingly innocuous reforms had on the history of logic has only recently begun to be realized. In view of the limits of the present work, it is sufficient to note that Ramus's approach signalled a radical change. Bacon and Descartes (and, much later, Leibniz), followed Ramus's lead by attempting to absorb the art of memory into the more general field of logic and method.

2 BACON AND DESCARTES: THE POLEMIC AGAINST THE 'JUGGLERS' OF MEMORY

Francis Bacon published his *Advancement of Learning* in 1605, and the *Novum Organum* (the drafting of which began around 1608) and the *De augmentis scientiarum* in 1620 and 1623 respectively. The *Cogitationes privatae* of Descartes came out in 1619, the *Regulae ad directionem ingenii* were composed between 1619 and 1628, and his *Discourse on Method* was published in 1637. In the same thirty years the French and English philosophers reached remarkably similar conclusions about the *ars combinatoria* and *ars memoriae*.

In the works of Descartes and Bacon[15] there is evidence of a direct knowledge of sixteenth-century works on mnemonics. Bacon often mentions 'collection of loci', 'syntaxes' and 'artificial memory', and makes explicit references to the 'doctrine of loci', the 'collocation of images' and the Lullian 'typocosmia'. Descartes, who makes far fewer explicit references and generally refrains from quotation, nonetheless mentions having read Schenkel's *Ars memorativa*, and often refers to the *ars memoriae* and the role played by 'sensible images' in the representation of intellectual concepts. He also refers to the Lullian idea of the 'chain of the sciences' (*catena scientiarum*), mentions his particular interest in one of Lull's anonymous followers, and asked his friend Isaac Beeckmann about the publication of Agrippa's Lullist works, and discussed with him the significance and potential of the Lullian art. The themes of the *ars memorativa* and *ars combinatoria* seem to have exercised a significant influence on the thought of Bacon and the young Descartes, and some of these themes can be related directly to Bacon's conception of a 'new logic' and Descartes's 'new method' of philosophizing.

More of this later. What I want to emphasize now is the significance of Bacon's and Descartes's critiques of the superficial and magical uses of memorative techniques. The assessments of the Lullist art which we find both in Descartes's letter to Beeckmann in 1619 and the *Discourse on Method*, and in Bacon's *Advancement of Learning* and *De augmentis*, are very significant in this respect. Having endured the idle boasts of an elderly practitioner of the *ars brevis* who claimed that he could speak for a whole hour on any argument whatever and could then go on to speak on the same theme for another twenty hours in different ways, Descartes (although he was deeply interested in the problem) saw this vaunted loquacity as mere bookish erudition, an activity better fitted to stir the admiration of the vulgar, than to the pursuit of truth. This uneasy suspicion on the part of the young Descartes was transformed eighteen years later, in the *Discourse on Method*, into a certainty: the art of Lull, he now argued, was used to speak indiscriminately on things about which one knew nothing – or rather to find truths without understanding them, or simply to transmit truths that were already known:

Yesterday I met an erudite man in a house in Dordrecht, with whom I spoke about the *ars parva* of Lull . . . He was an old man, a bit talkative, and his learning, drawn from books, was more in his mouth than in his brain . . . I got the impression that he spoke more to gain the admiration of the ignorant than to find out the truth . . . His logic, and syllogisms and the greater part of his precepts were used rather to explain to others what they already knew or even, as with the art of Lull, to speak without judgement about things of which he was ignorant, rather than to learn them.[16]

Bacon came to identical conclusions in his text of 1605 (translated into Latin in 1623). The Lullian method, Bacon thought, while it enjoyed great favour amongst certain charlatans, was not worthy of being called a method. He marvelled at this pseudo-scientific ostentation which seemed to him to have been designed simply to make ignorant men appear learned. Based on a chaotic mass of words, the art substituted a superficial knowledge of terms for the effective knowledge of arts. He likened it to a junk shop, where one finds many objects, none of which has any value:

One cannot pass silently over the fact that some individuals, who are more foolish than wise, weary themselves with a method which is unworthy of this name, being in reality a method for imposture, which is only useful for swindlers. This method uses a smattering of science so that an ignoramus can make show of a non-existent erudition. The art of Lull, and the *Typocosmia* which someone has recently invented are arts of this kind. Both consist of an undigested mass of terms from the various arts which are used to make someone who knows the terms sound as if he knows what they mean. A collection of this kind is just like a junk-shop where one finds many old rags, but nothing of any value.[17]

These attacks on the 'ostentation' and 'charlatanism' of the Lullian *ars combinatoria* are of immense historical significance. Both Bacon and Descartes opposed the reduction of the *ars memorativa* to the level of a magical art. While this accusation was not really a new idea (many sixteenth-century commentators made the very same point), what *was* new was the significance that it came to assume in the works of Descartes and Bacon, who were both engaged in a broader polemical attack on the magical–occult tradition. Bacon's judgement in 1623 (which can usefully be compared with that of Descartes in his *Discourse on Method*), seems to echo the opinions of one of the great commentators of Lull, Cornelius Agrippa, who was himself openly sympathetic toward the magical arts:

> It is necessary to warn you of one thing: this art is used more for pomp and the ostentation of knowledge than to procure knowledge: it has in itself more impudence than efficacy.[18]

Until now we have been discussing the *combinatoria*, but it is also worth comparing Descartes's and Bacon's views on the Ciceronian *ars memorativa*. Descartes was not, for example, slow to criticize Schenkel's *De memoria liber* (published in 1595), which he considered to be foolish in the extreme. In addition to the usual rules of the *ars reminiscendi*, Schenkel's work also contains significant references to Aristotelian and Thomist works, and Galenic medicine, and alludes not only to the doctrines of Simonides, Themistocles and Cyrus, but also to Augustine and Pico della Mirandola, Pietro da Ravenna and the Lullist Bernardo de Lavinheta.[19] Schenkel, as far as Descartes was concerned, was a 'charlatan': such 'false arts' were useless to the sciences: what was needed was an art dedicated to the true understanding of causes.[20] Bacon's opinion, although richer in explicit references, is similar to that of Descartes: he did not deny that by cultivating the memory it was possible to achieve miraculous results, nor did he believe (as it was popularly held) that the memorative techniques could have a deleterious effect on the natural memory. The way in which the art had been used appeared to him to be sterile: superficially impressive, but actually vain and useless. It was perfectly possible to memorize a great number of words repeated one after another in the same order as they had been spoken, or to compose a great number of extemporaneous verses on a chosen topic, by means of the education of one's natural faculties. These faculties could, through repeated exercise, be brought to a miraculous facility. But, Bacon suggested, we should take no more account of this than we do of the agility of acrobats or the dexterity of jugglers. 'Amongst the methods and syntaxes of commonplaces which I have seen', he wrote,

> there is none which has any value; the very titles of these treatises show the effects of the schools rather than of the real world; the pedantic subdivisions utilized by their authors do not penetrate into the marrow of things.[21]

3 MNEMOTECHNICS AND LULLISM IN BACON AND DESCARTES

(a) Bacon

Bacon's critique of the mnemonic arts here amount, it cannot be denied, to an outright rejection. However, in the following passage, he also entertains the possibility that it is possible to make a *different* use of the arts of memory than the traditional one. If these arts were used to demonstrate the prodigious level to which a faculty can be made to attain, instead of employing them to charlatanical ends, it might be possible to use them for serious and concrete purposes; it might also be possible to improve and perfect existing techniques of memorization in the light of this new purpose. Memory – he wrote in the same chapter of the *De augmentis* (and this passage is absent from the corresponding chapter of the *Advancement*) – has until now been imperfectly and poorly investigated. There are many works dedicated to the amplification and fortification of the memory, and it might be possible to perfect both the theory and practice of the *ars memorativa* through the elaboration of new precepts.[22] A reformed memorative art with new objectives seemed desirable to Bacon for two reasons: for use in the 'ancient and popular sciences' and for the development of a 'completely new' scientific method of investigating nature. This distinction between the two different functions or fields of application of the *ars memorativa* is formulated theoretically in the *De augmentis*. Here we find again the distinction (dear to all the theorists of mnemotechnics) between 'natural' and 'artificial' memory. Believing that the natural powers of the memory (without the help of ordered tables) are sufficient in the interpretation of nature – Bacon writes – is like maintaining that a man without the aid of writing can solve the calculations of a book of ephemerides. But leaving on one side the *interpretatio naturae*, which is a completely new doctrine, a sound aid to memory can be of the greatest use even in the ancient and popular sciences.[23]

   We will say more about the function of memory-aids (*ministratio ad memoriam*) in Baconian logic and the influence of renaissance mnemotechnic treatises on Bacon's new scientific method (the *interpretatio naturae*) in section four below. For the moment we will restrict ourselves to singling out the influence of Renaissance discussions of artificial memory on Bacon's treatment of traditional logic. Traditional logic, according to Bacon, was still invaluable in the fields of discourse, debate and controversy – that is to say in the field of professional activities and civil life. The other logic – the new, inductive logic is, however, indispensable in the field of man's progressive conquest of the natural world. The first of these two logics, according to Bacon, exists *de facto*; it was created by the Greeks and had then been refined and perfected over many centuries. The second logic, however, is presented as a project or an enterprise which had, as yet, never been attempted. The realization of this project presupposed a radical modification of man's attitude towards nature and, consequently, a change in the definitions of 'philosophy' and 'science'. But in terms of the objectives prescribed for it in traditional philosophy, the old methods of logic are not seen as defective. On this point Bacon is quite clear: if one desires to cultivate and transmit the existing sciences, if one desires to teach men to adhere to pre-existent truths and to make use of them, or if one desires to learn the arts of inventing arguments and prevailing in disputes, the old logic is perfectly functional, even if it is necessary to synthesize and perfect it. Bacon repeatedly emphasized that he was not concerned with popular arts or opinion in his work, nor did he pretend that the new logic could fulfil the purposes for which traditional logic had been constructed. In the *Novum organum* Bacon argued that sciences founded on opinion and probable judgements (in cases, that is to say, where one is concerned not with the true understanding of things, but with the procuring of assent) the use of anticipations and of dialectic was a good thing (*bonus*), even though it was indefensible in the terms of the new logic. The dialectic now in use, he declared in the preface of the *Instauratio magna*, is not absolutely able to 'reach the subtleties of nature' but it can be used effectively in the 'field of civil matters and of arts which concern discourse and opinion'. Only when one wants to triumph over the obscurities of nature, rather than adversaries, attaining certain and demonstrable understanding rather than probable opinions, inventing works rather than arguments, is it necessary to make use of the *interpretatio naturae*, which is radically different from the *anticipatio mentis* or ordinary logic.[24]

In ordinary logic, the memorative techniques play a more specific function. In the fifth chapter of the fifth book of the *De augmentis*, dedicated to *ars retinendi* we find the themes of the Ciceronian *ars memorativa* reappearing: the doctrine of *loci* and *imagines*, the thesis of a necessary connection between images and their places, the necessity of representing concepts sensibly by means of images and emblems. The theme of a topical or systematic collection of *loci* is also resumed in these pages: it is customary to say, wrote Bacon, that the collecting of memory-places can be harmful to knowledge. The labour necessary to create such collections is, on the contrary, extremely worthwhile, because it is impossible to achieve intellectual results without the solid basis of a vast knowledge. The *loci* 'furnish materials for invention and render the judgement more acute, allowing it to concentrate itself on a single point'. The two principal instruments of the art of memory are the 'prenotion' and the 'emblem'. The first has the task of placing limits on research, which could otherwise become infinite – it limits the field of notions and establishes parameters within which the memory can be exercised with facility. Memory has, above all, a need for limitations, and Bacon focused on three primary means – the distributive order of the things to be memorized, the artificial memory-places 'already prepared in anticipation', and verses to be memorized.

In the first place the memory must agree with the pre-established order, secondly it must be placed in specific relation to the memory-places being used, thirdly there ought to be a 'trigger word' which is connected in some way with the verse to be remembered. The memory-places introduce order and coherence into the formulation of images, but the images, in their turn, are easier to construct if one uses emblems. Emblems 'render intellectual things sensible, and since the sensible strikes the memory more forcibly, it is impressed in it with greater ease'. Bacon did not consider emblems to be restricted solely to the specific sphere of memory, but saw them rather as a means of communication in their own right. In addition to emblems, he also recommended the use of *gestures* and *hieroglyphs*, which he saw as functioning in a similar manner: gestures were 'transitory emblems', while hieroglyphs were 'emblems fixed by means of writing'. Gestures are related to hieroglyphs in the same way as spoken language relates to written language; while hieroglyphs (like emblems) always have something in common with the thing signified (*similitudo cum re significato*). 'Real characters' or ideograms were not emblematic: their significance was arbitrarily determined by convention and custom. Real characters, like the letters of the alphabet, are purely conventional, but the former, unlike the latter, refers in a direct way to the thing signified 'representing neither letters nor words, but things or notions.' A book composed of real characters could thus be read and understood by people belonging to different linguistic groups and speaking different languages, provided that the conventional meanings of the various ideograms were established in advance.[25]

Discussions about artificial memory in the Renaissance were connected at various points to contemporary discussions about the nature of gestures and hieroglyphs. Giovanni-Battista della Porta's *Ars reminiscendi* did much to further these investigations into the problematic nature of images. Having defined the image as 'an animated picture which we recall in the imagination in order to represent a fact or word', Porta found himself facing a grave difficulty: it is not possible to construct appropriate images for all words ('some of the words which we want to remember have their images, others do not'). In the case of words which do not signify material things, such as 'because', 'or', 'much' etc., it is necessary to allocate images to written characters: that is, assigning images to the individual letters or groups of letters which make up a word. In other cases it is possible to consider the overall meaning of the word in assigning an image, and he compares this method to the development of the Egyptian hieroglyphs. The Egyptians 'did not have letters with which to write concepts', della Porta says, 'so in order that they could easily recall their philosophical speculations, they replaced writing with pictures, using images of quadrupeds, birds, fishes . . . which we consider to be very useful for our enquiry, because this is what we are seeking to do in using images instead of letters so that we can depict them in the memory'. Other meanings, della Porta continued, can be expressed by means of gestures ('we can likewise express the meanings of some words with gestures'.) Similar conclusions can be found in Rosselli's *Thesaurus artificiosae memoriae* (1579) and in Johannes Austriacus's *De memoria artificiosa libellus* (1610) which, like Bacon, had included gestures and hieroglyphs in the more general category of 'signs'.[26]

Bacon's views on memory, then, appear to have been profoundly influenced by earlier discussions of the nature of signs and images. But Bacon's debt to the Renaissance tradition of the *ars memorativa* is seen most clearly in the *Novum organum* (II, 26), where he uses the 'techniques' developed by the theorists of artificial memory, but also augments them with new rules and new psychological insights of his own:

The object of our inquiry is memory, or that which excites and aids the memory. Things which aid the memory include: order or distribution, and topics or 'places' in artificial memory (which may either be places in the proper sense of the word, such as a door, a corner, a window and so on) or familiar and known persons, or anything you like (provided they be placed in a certain order), such as animals, vegetables etc. Words, letters, characters and historical persons can also be used for this purpose, although some of these are more appropriate and convenient than others. Such artificial places are wonderful aids to the memory, and raise it far above its natural powers. In the same way, verse is more easily learned and remembered than prose. From these three instances, viz., order, artificial places and verse, a single memory-aid can be constructed. And this kind of memory art may properly be called *the interruption of infinity*. For when we try to recollect or remember something, if we have no prenotion or perception of what we are seeking, we seek and toil and wander aimlessly, as if in infinite space. Whereas, if we have a particular prenotion, infinity is at once interrupted, and the memory has a more restricted space to range over. Now in the three aforementioned instances the prenotion is clear and certain. In the first place it must be something which suits the order; in the second it must be an image which bears some relation or conformity to the places fixed; in the third, it must consist of words which are appropriate to the verse; and thus infinity is interrupted. Another instance will give us another kind of memory-aid: whatever connects intellectual conceptions with sensible images (which is the most frequently used method in mnemonics) assists the memory. Another instance will give us a third kind of memory-aid: things which make their impression on the mind by way of a strong passion (by inspiring fear, admiration, shame, delight etc.) assist the memory. Another instance will give us a fourth kind of memory-aid: things which are imprinted when the mind is clear and not preoccupied (either before or after the impression), such as the things we learn in childhood, or the things we think of before going to sleep, or things that happen for the first time, remain longest in the memory.

Less explicit, and thus more difficult to determine, are Bacon's links with the Lullian tradition. Bacon mentions Lull only once, in a phrase which (as we have seen) seems to have been openly critical. Nevertheless, some themes of Bacon's philosophy are related to the Lullian idea of 'universal syntaxes'. In his presentation of the project of a universal science or 'prime philosophy or wisdom' (*scientia universalis, philosophia prima sive sapientia*) which is distinct from traditional metaphysics in book three of the *De augmentis*, for example, Bacon makes use of the Lullian image of the *arbor scientiarum*. The prime philosophy is seen as a 'generalized physics founded on natural history', which seeks to determine forms on the one hand, and final causes on the other. Prime philosophy concerns the 'common root' of the tree of the sciences, which precedes the partition and subdivision of the various branches of knowledge. The axioms which are common to many sciences are not reducible to simple similitudes: they refer to to the signs and vestiges of nature:

> The precept followed by musicians, of passing from harsh and dissonant harmonies to sweet and consonant harmonies, is this not just as true for the emotions? And does not the rule governing the falling cadence not correspond to the rhetorical rule for thwarting expectations? . . . Do not the organs of the senses not perhaps have an affinity with instruments of reflection: the eye to the mirror, the ear to a narrow, concave instrument? These are not similitudes, as it might seem to men of limited understanding, but the signs and traces of nature which are imprinted in diverse matter and subjects.[27]

Through the organic collection of axioms, whose absence Bacon laments, it would be possible to bring to light the unity of nature.

Bacon's harsh criticisms of the 'jugglers' of memory, then, is not an attack on the memorative techniques *per se*, but on *the attempts to reduce them to the level of occult and magical arts*. Placed in the service of the more serious objectives of rhetoric and logic, the *ars memorativa* still had a function in the new encyclopaedia of the sciences. Like the *ars generalis* of the Lullian tradition, the Baconian project of a *scientia universalis, mater reliquarum scientiarum* aimed to uncover the unity of knowledge which has its foundation and justification in the immanent unity of the world.

(b) Descartes

There has been much fruitful and insightful discussion of the images and symbols in Descartes's texts, although the terms of these discussions have not always been historically appropriate. One universally acclaimed Descartes scholar, for example, has related the passages of Descartes's *Olympica*, which concern the representation of 'spiritual things' by means of sensible bodies, to 'some Aristotelian philosophical idea which is not discussed'. Another scholar, commenting on these same passages, who claimed to be seeking 'the profound and interior resonance' of Descartes's words, has seen them as the expression of a man 'who is in search of pure inspiration'. A third, pondering on the reasons for Descartes's image of the 'tree of the sciences', saw it as an image of a living reality, relating it to the 'circulation of life present in the tree itself'.[28] If we abandon the attempt to unearth the 'interior resonances' of Descartes's texts, and consider them instead in the light of the texts of sixteenth-century encyclopaedists, it is possible (although achieving more modest results) to illuminate some of the more obscure texts of the young Descartes and to give more precise meanings to many of his statements and observations.

One thing is immediately noticeable about Descartes's 'condemnation' of the arts of memory: like Bacon's, it is much less severe than appears at first sight. In a passage written between 1619 and 1620, commenting upon and criticizing the *ars memorativa* of Lambert Schenkel, Descartes appears to accept the terminology and the conceptual framework of the problem of memory as it is set out in 'Ciceronian' treatises. Not only does he attribute to the imagination the same function which is attributed to it by the theorists of artificial memory, but he also recognizes that artificial memory can be an effective instrument. He contrasts Schenkel's *ars memorativa* to a 'true art of memory' whose fundamental rules he outlines as follows:

> Having carefully considered the useful nonsense of Lambert Schenkel (in his book *De arte memoriae*), you would think that you could easily grasp with the imagination everything which I have discovered: by means of the reduction of things to their causes. And because all causes can ultimately be reduced to one cause, it is clear that the sciences have no need of memory. If one comprehends one of the causes, thanks to the impression of the first cause, all the vanished images of the other causes can be reconstituted in the brain. This is the true art of memory: in

complete contrast with the art of that muddlehead. Not because his art is ineffective, but because it is not based on the correct order, and wastes paper which could be employed for better purposes. The correct order consists in this: that the images formed should be reciprocally dependent upon each other. I have thought out another method: from interconnected images one can obtain new images which are common to each individual image, or at least from all of the connected images one could obtain a single image related to them all. And one should not just consider the nearest image when composing a new image, but also the others in the series, so that the fifth is connected to the first by means of a stake driven into the ground, the image in the middle by means of the ladder by which they descend, the second by means of an arrow fired towards it, the third in some analogous way, according to a true or fictitious means of signification.[29]

Descartes was obviously influenced in this project for a new memorative technique by some of the traditional precepts of the *ars reminiscendi*. Descartes's real interest in the art of memory (which cannot be dismissed as simple intellectual curiosity) is also evident in some entries from his diary headed *Cogitationes privatae*. In these pages we find one of the favourite themes of the mnemotechnical treatises on artificial memory: the use of corporeal and sensible images for the representation of abstract concepts or 'spiritual things':

As the imagination uses figures to conceive of bodies, so the intellect uses sensible bodies, like the wind and light, for representing spiritual things . . . Sensible things can help us to conceive of Olympian things: the wind signifies the spirit, motion and time signify life, light signifies understanding, heat signifies love, and sudden activity signifies the creation.[30]

The fact that Descartes in his later years completely rejected the use of symbols in philosophy does not negate, for the historian, the task of tracing the 'obscure' thematic origins of a philosophy which claimed to found itself on rational clarity and discrimination. At the time he was devising this new memorative technique, Descartes seems to have privileged imaginative and poetic discourse over the rational discourses of philosophy and reason. Like many of the 'magi' of the sixteenth century he delighted in the construction of 'automata' and 'shadow gardens'. He was familiar with the Lullian commentaries of Agrippa, and was interested in the *ordo locorum* in dialectics.[31] Like the Lullist commentators before him, he insisted on the unity and harmony of the cosmos: 'One active force, love, charity and harmony, is present in all things . . . Every corporeal form acts by means of harmony.'[32] This is not just a youthful concession to philosophical fashion. Many years later, after he had read Comenius's *Pansophiae Prodromus*, Descartes still insisted (although he rejected Comenius's plan as impracticable) on the strict analogy between human understanding ('unique, simple, continual, reducibile to a few principles') and a 'unified, simple and continuous nature', of which the understanding is a 'picture' or 'mirror':

> God is one, and has created nature from a few principles and elements, so that it is unified, simple and continuous, everywhere coherent and consistent with itself. From these few principles an almost infinite number of things can be generated which nonetheless are all distinct, and have a certain order and hierarchy in the three kingdoms – mineral, vegetable and animal. The understanding of these things, like the unique creator himself and his unique creation (nature), must be unique, simple, continuous, uninterrupted, based on a few principles (in fact, on a unique principle of principles) from which all things are derived, down to the individual connections, deduced according to the wisest order. Thus our contemplation of universal things and of individual things is similar to a picture or mirror which represents with absolute precision the image of the universe and its parts.[33]

However one chooses to interpret the meaning of this passage, it is clear that the programme of the young Descartes – a man who had not yet 'taken a decision on the foundations of physics' - seems very close to those of the Lullian 'syntaxes' and 'encyclopaedias' of the late sixteenth century. He assumes that there is a profound unity concealed beneath the apparent multiplicity of the sciences, a law of connection, a common logic which unites them. Once the individual sciences are 'unmasked', it is possible to construct a *catena scientiarum*, which would enable the individual sciences to be remembered as easily as remembering a series of numbers:

At the moment the sciences are masked, take away that mask, and they will appear in all their beauty. To one who sees the chain of the sciences it will be no more difficult to remember the sciences than to remember a series of numbers.[34]

The problem of the encyclopaedia appears here, once again, to be inextricable from the question of memory. The same terms and concepts are attributed to Descartes in Nicholas Poisson's *Commentaires ou remarques sur la Méthode de R. Descartes*:

> There is a bond which makes it so that one truth cannot be found without uncovering another, and one needs only to find the beginning of the thread in order to reach another without interruption. These, more or less, are the words of Descartes, which I have read in one of his manuscript fragments: all the sciences are concatenated and one cannot master one to perfection without the others following spontaneously and thus the entire encyclopaedia is learnt all together.[35]

In the first of the *Regulae*, Descartes says that the subsistent connection between the individual sciences is so strict that it is easier to learn all of the sciences together than to separate one of them from the others. The bonds of conjunction and reciprocal dependence between the sciences, make it impossible to choose a particular science if one is interested in attaining truth:

> It is necessary to believe that the sciences are all connected in some way between themselves so that it is much easier to learn them together than to separate one of them from the others. One who seriously wishes to search for the truth ought not to choose a single science: all of them are conjoined and are reciprocally dependent on one another.[36]

If we turn from Descartes to the texts of seventeenth-century Lullism, we find a very different intellectual atmosphere: one permeated by magic and occultism, aiming at the discovery of a universal medicine and the construction of a total encyclopaedia, full of references to the Hermetic tradition. We also find, however, the same insistence on the *catena scientiarum*, on the apparent multiplicity of the sciences, and the correspondence between ordered knowledge and the harmonic order of nature which we find in the Descartes texts we have cited. The physician and magus Jean d'Aubry, who was a follower and translator of Lull, while he defended himself from the accusation of having practised magic, made use of the idea of the *catena scientiarum*, drawing on Pico's cabbalistic commentary on the creation:

> The parts of knowledge (which the foolish and the ignorant call sciences) are chained together one to another so that it is not possible to understand the smallest part without having a full understanding of the whole. This is shown to us by Pico della Mirandola's *Heptaplus* which deals with the days of the creation, and Paolo Veneto's *Armonia del mondo*.[37]

The study of the connections between Descartes's project of an 'entirely new science'[38] and his interest in the mathematization of physics (evident in his letter to Beeckmann in 1618) is beyond the scope of the present work. The similarities between Descartes's ideas and the passages we have cited from contemporary Lullists demonstrates, however, the reductive character of the repeated attempts to identify the Cartesian *mathesis universalis* as a simple extension of the mathematical method to all fields of knowledge.[39] The *scientia nova*, Descartes said, must 'contain the first rudiments of human reason and bring out the truth from any subject'; it is the source of all human understanding. The Cartesian project (like that of Bacon) had its origins in a particular historical milieu: the Lullist encyclopaedism which had been absorbed by sixteenth-century culture and reached its apogee in the seventeenth century. In the Lullist commentaries of Agrippa, in the *Syntaxes* of Grégoire, in the *Opus aureum* of de Valeriis, in the *Explanatio* of Lavinheta, and later in the *Regina scientiarum* of Morestel and in the writings of d'Aubry, there was a search for a 'unique instrument' common to all sciences, a single 'key' or 'wisdom' capable of guaranteeing absolute certainty and absolute truth and furnishing infallible solutions, which could function as a rule for every possible form of knowledge. The direct or indirect knowledge which Bacon and Descartes had of these widely disseminated texts (which were translated and republished many times in the principal cultural centres of Europe) brought the image of the *arbor scientiarum* into cultural prominence once more. This milieu was behind their search for a *sapientia* or *sci-*

entia universalis, the mother, source and common root of every branch of knowledge – although in their hands this search was destined to undergo a profound philosophical reorientation:

> The partitions of the sciences are not like different lines which meet at an angle, but like the branches of a tree which join together in the trunk (which, before it subdivided into branches, was straight and continuous). It is therefore necessary, before dealing with the first partition, to found a universal science which is the mother of all the others, which can be seen as a common thoroughfare among the pathways of knowledge, before the road separates and becomes distinct. We give this science the name of prime philosophy or wisdom.[40]

> Whoever has carefully considered my mode of thought, can easily see that I am not dealing with common mathematics, but that I expound another kind of discipline of which [figures and numbers] are the vestments rather than the parts. Such a discipline ought in fact to contain the first rudiments of human reason and ought to be extended to the truths of all subjects. To speak frankly, I am persuaded that it is more important than any other thought which can be humanly transmitted, being the source of all the others . . . Thus all philosophy is like a tree, where the roots are metaphysics, the trunk physics, and the branches which issue from the trunk are all the other sciences.[41]

4. MEMORATIVE TECHNIQUES AND THE NEW LOGIC.

(a) Memory-aids in the Baconian method: tables, topics and induction
When viewed in the context of the Ramist conception of memory as part of dialectic, Bacon's classification of logic in the *Advancement of Learning* of 1605 and in the *De augmentis scientiarum* of 1623 takes on a particular significance. According to Bacon logic was divided into four principal parts, the 'intellectual arts'. This four-part division is based on the ends and aims of human endeavour. Man *finds* what he has been looking for, *judges* what he has found, *retains* what he has judged and *transmits* what he has retained. These four tasks are the subject of four arts:

1. The art of inquiry or invention
2. The art of examination or judgement
3. The art of custody or memory
4. The art of elocution or tradition[42]

Bacon's classification combines the traditional partitions of rhetoric, and Ramus's distinction between dialectic and rhetoric. He departs from both of them in giving the term 'invention' a much wider significance than the traditional one which distinguishes between the invention of arguments and inventions in the sciences and arts. In this last area, Bacon notices the greatest deficiencies: while traditional logic is more than sufficient for the invention of arguments, allowing men to invent new arts (and thus to dominate nature) a reform of scientific method was necessary, in order to provide the understanding with a new organ or instrument.[43] The *interpretatio naturae* or the 'new induction', theorized by Bacon in the second book of the *Novum organum* is thus only one of the two parts of the art of invention which is, in its turn, one of the four parts into which Baconian logic is subdivided.

The reform of scientific induction is thus only a part of the general restauration of knowledge which Bacon wanted to realize. When discussing 'ancient and popular sciences' or 'ordinary logic' Bacon had sought (as we have seen) to clarify the role of memory and the memorative arts in the part of the *ars inveniendi* which is limited to inventing arguments for the purpose of persuasion, but he also related the problem of the *ars memorativa* and the function of memory to the *interpretatio naturae*, the new logic of scientific enquiry.

Although Bacon insisted in his *Delineatio* on the absolute distinction between ordinary logic and the logic of science, his discussion of the *ministratio ad memoriam* (which he saw as an integral and constitutive part of the new scientific method) raises problems which are quite similar to those experienced in the 'arts of discourse' or 'ordinary logic'. In the invention of arguments, the difficulties arise from the multiplicity of *terms* and arguments. In scientific works and scientific method, the difficulties arise from an infinite multiplicity of *facts*. The doctrine of the 'memory-aids', developed in his *Delineatio* and later reprised in the *Novum organum*, is a simple adaptation of the rules governing the invention, memorization and arrangement of arguments to the exigencies of scientific discourse.

The invention of arguments and construction of coherent and persuasive discourses, required, Bacon suggested, 1) the setting-out of an extensive collection of arguments (*promptuaria*), and 2) the establishment of rules for the limitation of the field of investigation and for determining the parameters of a specific and limited field of discourse (*topica*). The role of the art of memory was to elaborate a technique (using prenotions, emblems, order, *loci*, verses, writing, etc.) by which one could achieve these two aims.

Bacon adopted a similar approach to scientific method, or what he calls 'the interpretation of nature' (*interpretatio naturae*):

> The memory-aids perform the following function: they help one to draw up a particular history whose parts are disposed in a particular order from the immense multitude of particular facts and from the mass of general natural history. The order of the particular history makes it easier for the intellect to work on the materials and execute its proper functions . . . Firstly, the things to be investigated for a given problem should be set out in the same way that one sets out *topica*. Secondly, one should arrange and subdivide the material into *tables* . . . Thirdly, one should set out how, and at which moment, the research will be integrated and the preceding pages or tables transposed into new tables . . . The *ministratio ad memoriam* therefore consists of three doctrines: the invention of *loci*, the method of tabulation and the method of beginning the research.[44]

Unaided memory, he says in the *Delineatio*, is not only incapable of grasping the immense variety of facts, but is not even able to indicate the specific facts which are necessary for a particular investigation. Prior to general natural history (which corresponds to the *promptuaria*, or indiscriminate collection of facts, in rhetoric) one needs rules for determining the field of research and for ordering the contents of this field. In order to remedy the natural debility of memory and to enable it to function as an instrument of understanding we need a *topica* (or collection of *loci*) which allows us to identify the facts which we need to examine in a given inquiry, and *tabulae* which help us to order the facts so that the intellect is not faced with a chaotic and confused reality, but an organized one.

Many thinkers, from Ramus to Melanchthon, from Pietro da Ravenna to Rosselli, from Romberch to Gratarolo, had addressed themselves to the problems of the *topica* and artificial memory, stressing the function of *loci* as a means of delimiting and ordering fields of research. Melanchthon, for example, (although we could have cited many other authors in his place) said that *loci*

> teach us where to look for the matter we are seeking, and how to select things from a great mass of material. The *loci* of invention (*loci inventionis*), whether in dialectics or rhetoric, do not direct us towards the matter one needs, but teach us how to select the matter from the information one has already accumulated.[45]

The *Partis instaurationis secundae delineatio* came out around 1607, but in his later works Bacon became even more explicit. In the *Novum organum* (II, X), for example, he said: 'Natural and experimental history is so diverse and scattered that the intellect is confounded and almost fragmented unless it is reduced into some fit order. It is therefore necessary to use tables and *coordinationes instantiarum* so that the intellect can operate on them.'[46] The famous Baconian *tabulae* are seen as an integral part of the *ministratio ad memoriam* in the *Novum organum*. These tables have a precise function: the organization and ordering of the contents of the natural histories. Once the material has been organized into the three *tabulae* the intellect possesses an ordered series of facts, it is no longer 'almost fragmented'. This method was later developed into what Bacon called the 'new induction'.

Bacon's conception of the inductive process doubtless had its beginnings in the doctrine of the *tabulae*. The *tabulae* are constructed so as to reduce the chaotic multiplicity of physical facts into an ordered arrangement so that the intellect can follow the connections between its various parts. In this sense, the compilation of the *tabulae* are the product of Bacon's enduring interest in the idea of the 'invention of natural *loci*'. The first sustained attempt by Bacon to lay down the basis for the invention of natural *loci* and develop a method of tabulation was in 1607–8 and it was no coincidence that, at this point in his work, Bacon used the words *topica* and *tabulae* (or *chartae*) as synonyms. In the *Cogitata et visa* of 1607 he explained the function of the tables in the following way:

> After a long and difficult meditation, the first thing which one must do is set out the tables of invention, that is, the forms for a

legitimate investigation of clearly defined arguments, which is to say a particular matter ordered appropriately for the work of the intellect. And this will be virtually an exemplar or visible description of the work to be realized.[47]

The following year, in the *Commentarius solutus*, there is a brief note which reads: 'The finishing of the three tables, de motu, de calore et frigore, de sono.' If we look at the notes of the *Commentarius* we find a list of natural *loci* regrouped in different *chartae*.[48] The three short works which were written in this period have a similar structure, and represent the first attempt at realizing the programme set out in the *Cogitata et visa* and in the *Commentarius solutus*: the *Inquisitio legitima de motu*, the *Sequela chartarum sive inquisitio legitima de calore et frigore*, and the *Historia et inquisitio prima de sono et auditu*.[49]

In the preface to the first of these three works, Bacon revealed the essential function of the *topica* and the tables, and distinguishes between two different types of table: those which collect together the most evident facts and refer to a particular object of research (*machina intellectus inferior seu sequela chartarum ad apparentiam primam*) and those which have the more important task of aiding the intellect to understand 'that which is hidden', penetrating into the 'form' of things (*machina intellectus superior sive sequela chartarum ad apparentiam secundam*). The nineteen tables listed by Bacon in the *Inquisitio legitima de motu* constitute a *topica* or 'provisional systematization' which permit one to pass on to the tables of the second group. The latter (the *machina superior*) are the *tabulae presentiae, absentiae, graduum* of the *Novum organum*.[50]

The image of the universe as a 'labyrinth' or 'forest', the belief that the architecture of the world 'is full of ambiguous paths, false appearances ('signs, knots and complicated and intricate spirals')[51] radically conditions the Baconian doctrine of method. One of the tasks – if not the fundamental task – of method is, for Bacon, the introduction of order into the chaos of reality. Thus in the *Delineatio* of 1607 we find the following significant admission: '[the truth] emerges more easily from falsehood than from confusion.' It was the elimination of confusion which, in this work, was seen as one of the primary functions of memory-aids.[52]

Eliminating confusion, supplying the deficits of factual understanding, collecting 'certain instances' – for Bacon these appear to have been the essential tasks of the method of the interpretation of nature. Compared to these tasks, the tables themselves appear to him to be no more than simple examples of an immense work which was still to be realized ('neither are the tables we have made perfect, they are only examples').[53] The draft of a logic of scientific method which Bacon had been working on since he wrote the *Valerius terminus* was suddenly interrupted because he had become convinced that the construction of 'perfect tables' was the decisive element in the foundation of a new form of knowledge. The construction of natural histories, the organized collection of facts, the delimitation of different fields of inquiry, the drawing up of a series of lists of natural *loci* pertaining to a specific field , or 'particular histories' (*historiae particulares*): these tasks suddenly seemed to Bacon to be of such pressing importance that it was worth interrupting the drafting of the *Novum organum* and putting aside the new 'logical instrument' which he had been working on for many years.[54]

The ordered collection of materials, the construction of an organized encyclopaedia of all the natural facts collected in the particular histories, the preparation of a collection of facts or 'general history' which was able to furnish new materials for the particular histories (*Sylva sylvarum*): all these projects seemed to Bacon, at least towards the end of his career, to be the most important of his inquiries directed towards the perfecting of scientific methodology. Every one of the particular histories which Bacon laboured over anxiously after 1620 (his project comprised one hundred and thirty such histories) responded to a double exigency: to eliminate traditional opinions and to start afresh with a field of certain facts. Having arranged these facts within particular fields he would then proceed to an ordered collection. If one leaves aside general considerations and proceeds to a direct reading of these Baconian 'histories', it is clear that they are presented as 'collections of natural *loci*' and that they represent an attempt to complete the work of collection begun in the *Inquisitio legitima de motu*, in the *Inquisitio de calore et frigore*, and in the *Historia et inquisitio prima de sono et auditu*.

In his substitution of a collection of natural *loci* for the collection of rhetorical *loci*, his unconventional use of the art of memory, and his conception of the *tabulae* as a means of ordering reality in which the memory prepares an 'organized reality' for the operations of the intellect, Bacon had introduced into his logic of scientific knowledge, some of the typical elements of the rhetorical-dialectical tradition. His 'new' logic (although he probably would not have believed it) was very similar to Ramus's or Melanchthon's approaches to dialectic, which they saw as an instrument for the orderly arrangement of notions. Melanchthon, it will be remembered, defined method as an art which opens up a pathway 'through inaccessible places and the confusion of things' (*per loca invia et per rerum confusionem*) by ordering and arranging the 'things pertinent to the question in hand' (*res ad propositum pertinentes*), while Ramus defined *dispositio* (which he identified with *iudicium* and *memoria*) as the 'apt arrangement of things which have been found' (*apta rerum inventarum collocatio*). Despite the many differences between dialectic and the Baconian concept of scientific method, there are also some striking similarities: for Bacon 'method is a means of ordering and classifying the elements of natural reality'. The doctrine of *ministratio ad memoriam* had, in this respect, exercized a decisive influence on Bacon's construction of a new logic and his formulation of a new scientific method.[55]

(b) Memory-aids and the doctrine of enumeration in Descartes's Regulae
Quotations of Renaissance treatises on artificial memory can be found not only in Descartes's early manuscript fragments, but also in his later writings, such as the *Regulae*. When, in rule XVI of the *Regulae*, Descartes sees writing as an art devised to remedy the natural debility of the memory, and speaks of the intellect as 'being aided by the images depicted in the fancy', he is repeating in traditional terms common places which can be found in almost all the Ciceronian mnemotechnical works, as can be seen by comparing the following two passages, the first from Descartes's *Regulae* and the second from a typical sixteenth-century treatise on the art of memory:

> It is worthwhile remembering all the other dimensions, so that they can be recalled easily whenever they are required. The memory appears to be naturally disposed to this end. But since it is often weak and imperfect . . . the art of writing was opportunely invented. By this means we can confidently . . . write down on paper all that we wish to recall.[56]

> Men invented various arts to aid nature in different ways. And since the memory of man is naturally weak, they sought to find

some art to aid nature or memory . . . and in this way they invented writing.[57]

Bacon referred to this same tradition in his *De augmentis*:

Writing is clearly an aid to memory and it is generally said that memory, deprived of this aid, is weak when confronted with extensive tasks, which can be recalled in no other way than writing.[58]

In the complex methodology of Descartes's *Regulae* the recourse to 'corporeal images', or symbols, or writing, acquires a particular meaning. Writing, and 'representation on paper' free the mind from the debilities of memory, so that the imagination and intelligence are free to concentrate on the ideas at hand. We represent on paper those things which we want to remember, but which do not require our constant attention, and so do not need to be memorized. In this way we can avoid memorization diverting part of our available intelligence from the cognition of the present object. This mnemonic function is entrusted to arbitrarily chosen signs or symbols (a, b, c etc. for the known, and A, B, C for those which are unknown): these should be 'very brief', Descartes says, so that 'after having looked over things individually, we can run through them again swiftly in our thoughts, so that considering all of them together, we can accomplish far more than we would ordinarily expect'.[59]

In Cartesian thought the problem of 'notation'[60] or writing, and the connected issue of memory-aids,[61] becomes enmeshed with the problem of intuition and the 'continuous and uninterrupted motion of thought' which is deduction. In *Regulae* III, Descartes clarifies the reasons for the copresence of intuition and another 'way of understanding which comes about through deduction'.

Intuition (which for Descartes is 'a mental concept which is both distinct and self-evident') in so far as it excludes every possibility of doubt, is required not only for single propositions ('everyone can intuit that he exists, that he thinks, that a triangle is delimited by three lines' etc.), but also for any kind of *discourse*. For example, we know that $2 + 2 = 4$ and that $3 + 1 = 4$. Not only can we intuit that $2 + 2 = 4$ and that $3 + 1 = 4$, but we can also intuit that the third proposition (i.e. that they are *both* equal to four) is concluded necessarily from the first two.[62] Deduction, in principle, is reduced to intuition. There is however, no correspondent *factual* reducibility to this reducibility *in principle*: for here one must introduce a different term, that of deduction. Many things are known with certainty despite the fact that they are not evident in themselves: a truth, which is not self-evident in itself, can in fact be the necessary consequence of an uninterrupted chain of self-evident truths along which our mind passes in a continuous motion of thought. Every stage of this motion, every 'link in the chain' is grasped by means of an immediate intuition, but the conclusion (that is to say the necessary connection between the first and last links of the chain) is not present to the mind in the same self-evident way which characterizes intellectual intuition. We 'know' that the last link of the chain is linked to the first; we do not see, however, at a single glance, all the intermediate links upon which the connection depends: we are limited therefore to passing along them successively and *remembering* that the single links, from the first to the last, are attached one to another. The distinction between *intuitus* and *deductio* is conceived as a movement or a succession which is completely absent from *intuitus*. The actual self-evidence which is present in intuition is not necessary for deduction: deduction, to a certain extent, derives its certainty from memory.[63]

In the case of deductions which are not particularly complex, or 'short chains', natural memory is sufficient. Where the 'chains' are too long for our intuitive capacities to cope with, and the deductions correspondingly more complex, Descartes declared that it was necessary to 'aid the natural infirmity of the memory' (*memoriae infirmitati succurrendum esse*). The understanding of a necessary connection between the first and the last link of the chain recalls the deduction of the last link: to deduce it one passes 'with a continual and uninterrupted motion of thought' from link to link. If a single link is overlooked the deduction will be impossible or illegitimate. In this way memory comes to one's aid:

> Deduction is sometimes executed by means of a long concatenation of consequences which, when we come to them, do not easily remind us of the whole path which has lead us to that point: for this one must aid the weakness of memory through a continual movement of thought.[64]

This process, which Descartes called 'enumeration' or 'induction' (*enumeratio sive inductio*), is precisely the 'aid' to memory to which he refers. The aims of this *ministratio ad memoriam* (to use the Baconian term) is to increase the speed of deduction so that the role of memory is reduced to a minimum (although not completely eliminated) by granting to a set of cognitions too complex to be grasped in a single intuition the immediate self-evidence which is the privilege of the intuitive capacity:

> If by means of different operations I have understood the relationship between A and B, between B and C, then C and D, and finally between D and E, I do not see the relation between A and E, nor can I obtain it with exactness from the previously understood relations if I do not remember them all. For this I have to run through them a number of times with a kind of movement of the imagination which intuits the single relations and transfers them together into other intuitions. By this means I can learn to pass from the first to the last with such celerity that – hardly leaving anything in the memory – I seem to intuit the whole ensemble. In this manner, while aiding the memory, one can also mitigate the slowness of the intellect and to some extent enlarge its capacity.[65]

It is possible to reveal even more significant points of contact between Descartes's *Regulae* and the tradition of the *ars memorativa*. Leslie Beck, who has worked on the methodology of the *Regulae*, has clearly (and I think correctly) distinguished between two senses of the term 'enumeration' in Descartes.[66] When Descartes refers to 'enumeration' in the *Discourse* he means either 'complete enumerations' (*denombrements entiers*) or 'general reviews' (*revues générales*). The Latin translation of the *Discourse*, revised by Descartes himself, makes this distinction even clearer: the expression 'denombrements entiers' is translated as *singula enumerare*, and 'revues générales' by *omnia circumspicere*.[67] Despite this apparently clear distinction between the two different functions of enumeration, the fact remains that Descartes seems to have used this term to designate two separate things: 1) the memory-aid which is necessary for particularly complex deductions or excessively long 'chains', and 2) the ordering of the conditions on which the solution of a particular problem depends and the preliminary ordering of data prior to research which seeks to 'isolate' and determine the nature of the problem itself.

> Enumeration or induction is a diligent and accurate research into everything which concerns a proposed question, so that it can be concluded with certainty and evidence that nothing has been unjustly omitted.[68]

The function attributed to *enumeratio* here seems quite different from that to which we have previously referred. Here *enumerare* means 'to proceed towards a classification' (which is normally worked out before the deductive process) 'with a view to the determination and limitation of problems'. It involves, as Beck has correctly pointed out, a 'preparatory marking-out of the field of knowledge in which a proposed investigation of some particular problem is presently to take place'.[69]

Beck, who (like other interpreters of Descartes) is almost exclusively concerned with the formal structure of the Cartesian method and the relations between Descartes's various writings,[70] does not notice the affinity between Descartes's concept of 'enumeration' and Bacon's *topica* (which is also presented as a memory-aid). Bacon considered the primary function of memory-aids to be the construction of rules for delimiting the 'infinite field' of human understanding, and thus determining a specific and limited field of knowledge:

> From the immense multitude of facts a particular history is extracted, whose parts are disposed in an orderly manner . . . In the first place we set out which things need to be investigated for a given problem, which is similar to a topic; in the second place we set out the order into which they are to be disposed and subdivided.[71]

Enumeration as an aid to memory has, for Descartes, the function of arranging a 'complete and accurate inquiry into a proposed question'. Once a problem or question had been isolated and determined (which, as we have seen, was the task which the rhetorical tradition entrusted to *loci*) one should, according to Bacon, proceed to ordination: a subdivision and classification of the material pertinent to the proposed question. Descartes takes a similar view of this procedure:

No man's life would be long enough for a full consideration of the proposed question. But if all the materials are disposed in the best possible order, so that they are reduced as far as possible to determinate classes, one can deal with one of these classes, or something from each of them, or at least be certain that one was not needlessly repeating one's efforts. It is one of the greatest benefits of a well-established order, that one can quickly and easily perform many tasks which, at first glance, appear to be immense.[72]

It is not my intention to examine here the differences between Baconian induction and Descartes's *inductio* or *enumeratio*. Despite the obvious differences between the systems of these two 'founders' of modern philosophy, I would like to emphasize the presence and persistence of themes drawn from ancient and early modern discussions of artifical memory. The influence of these discussions can be seen not only in Bacon and Descartes's interest in the problems of mnemotechnics, and in their use of the image of the *arbor scientiarum* and their projects for a *sapientia* or *scientia universalis*, but also in their discussions concerning the use of 'memory-aids'. We are not dealing here with the remnants of a venerable tradition, the last vestiges of an unimportant and historically insignificant literary genre; nor are we dealing with concessions to an outmoded intellectual fashion. In Bacon's *Interpretatio naturae* and Descartes's *Regulae ad directionem ingenii* we find theses which have been drawn directly from the rhetorical tradition of the *ars memorativa*: the isolation of a question by means of a preliminary classification of its constitutive elements; the vital and indispensable role of order and arrangement in such classifications; the use of ordered and 'artificial' classifications as a necessary remedy for the insufficiency and infirmity of natural memory. Like Ramus before them, Bacon and Descartes had included a theory of memory-aids as part of their logical methods, and saw a technique for strengthening memory to be indispensable both for the formulation and the functioning of their new logic or method.

In the works of Ramus, Bacon and Descartes the ancient problem of artificial memory, which had been a passionate concern of physicians, philosophers, rhetoricians, encyclopaedists and natural magicians for over three centuries, entered (albeit profoundly transformed) the field of modern logic. Through the influence of

Baconian thought (together with the encyclopaedic works of Alsted and Comenius) on the linguistic investigations which developed in England in the second half of the seventeenth century, the problem of artificial memory survived to exert a significant influence on the various projects for the construction of total dictionaries, perfect languages and universal encyclopaedias in the 1650s and 1660s. In the Lullist tradition the connections between memory, logic and the encyclopaedia were insisted upon at some length. 'If order is the mother of memory', Alsted wrote, 'then logic is the art of memory.' It is perhaps worth noting that when he began his project for a universal character, Leibniz turned – not to Bacon, Alsted and Comenius – but to Ramon Lull and his Renaissance commentators and made substantial use of many of the influential texts of the *ars memorativa*.

CHAPTER SIX
Encyclopaedism and Pansophia

1 THE UNIVERSAL MNEMONIC SYSTEM: JOHANN HEINRICH ALSTED

The encyclopaedic ideal which dominated seventeenth-century culture from Bacon to Leibniz found its clearest expression in the vast enterprise of Johann Heinrich Alsted (1588–1638) – the teacher of Comenius at Herborn, editor of the mnemonic works of Giordano Bruno, a follower of Lull and Ramus, and a pedagogical reformer. Beneath the bewildering superabundance of quotations and ostentatious erudition, and the chaotic mixture of logical, rhetorical, physical and medicinal themes, we find a number of important ideas rehearsed in his numerous treatises and manuals, culminating with the great *Systema mnemonicum* – ideas which were destined to exercise a decisive influence on the development of the pansophic ideal and encyclopaedism in the early seventeenth century .

For Alsted, the reformation of the techniques for transmitting knowledge and the systematic classification of all manual and intellectual activities played a vital role in the development of a new 'system' of the sciences, which would unify the principles of all the disciplines in a single corpus. By means of the encyclopaedia, which would reveal the systematic nature of knowledge, it would be possible to construct a new method, and develop a new, more rational, form of pedagogy.[1] Alsted's adherence to the Lullian ideal and his insistence on the value of memory as a technique for the encyclopaedic ordination of notions can only be understood as a function of this project. In order to find a 'compendious method' (*via compendiosa*) which would lead mankind towards a total knowledge, Alsted believed, one must devote oneself to the three major logics of the past: those of Aristotle, Lull and Ramus. These thinkers had turned men away from their 'brutish and cyclopic' state and led them 'towards the more amenable pastures of science'.

Despite their differences, Alsted believed that the three philosophers had a common aim and method, and that their doctrines
could, and should, be reconciled.[2] In the *Panacea philosophica seu . .
. de armonia philosophiae aristotelicae lullianae et rameae*[3] of 1610 Alsted
attempted to reconcile the three methods of Aristotle, Lull and
Ramus by painstakingly collating passages from their works. This
same preoccupation was central to his *Clavis artis lullianae* of 1609.
In the third chapter of that work, 'Of the three logical sects which
are flourishing today' (*De tribus sectis logicorum hodie vigentibus*),
Alsted turned his attention to the state of contemporary logical
studies. Having briefly outlined the tenets of Aristotelian logic, and
examined the works of Melanchthon, Goclenius, Scaliger,
Zabarella, Piccolomini and Suarez, Alsted laments the lack of
vigour amongst German Lullists and contrasts the sad situation of
German logic – fraught with controversies between Aristotelians
and Ramists – to the flowering of Lullian studies in Spain, France
and Italy. The commentaries on Lull by Agrippa and Bruno,
Grégoire and de Valeriis, he argued, had obscured rather than clarified the complexities of the *ars combinatoria*, aggravating the technical difficulties of Lullism by adding their own imaginative
embellishments to Lull's techniques. In order to revive the fortunes
of Lullism, Alsted believed, it was necessary to turn back to the
work of Pico della Mirandola, Bernardo da Lavinheta, Fernando de
Cordoba, Lefèvre d'Etaples, Charles de Bovelles and the Canterio
brothers, and to resume the great project of Lull beginning from
new foundations: creating a universal science which – like Ariadne's
thread – would be the criterion of truth for all forms of knowledge.
This *ars generalis*, which Alsted continually compared to the cabala,
was to be achieved through identifying the 'general terms' and
'general principles' of all the particular sciences which would lead
gradually to the discovery of the 'common' terms and principles
underlying all knowledge.[4]

Alsted believed, then, that there were universal axioms and principles which are common to all the sciences. The arts and sciences
seem, at first glance, to be like a disordered and chaotic forest, but
behind this chaos we can vaguely discern the outlines of a hidden
order. The rigid distinctions between the sciences are only provisional: on closer inspection the tangled undergrowth of the forest
reveals itself to be the orderly ramifications of a single common tree
of knowledge, from which the branches of the particular sciences

and arts diverge according to a rational order. In order to construct a new universal method one needed to restore order, coherence and system to the chaos, advancing courageously into the forest of knowledge, explaining the orderly structure of the branches, and discovering the trunk and roots which they share in common.

In Alsted's philosophy the problem of method is reduced essentially to that of the ordination of notions and the systematic classification of the world and human knowledge. Logic, which is the instrument of method,[8] is thus primarily concerned with ordering and classifying:

> The only logic is the art of memory. There is no mnemotechnics besides logic. Ramon Lull was aware of this when he said, in his little book *De auditu kabbalistico*, that 'method is not just for the exercise of the human intellect, but also provides us with a remedy for forgetfulness'. If order is the mother of memory, then logic is the art of memory. Dealing with order is, in fact, the task of logic.[5]

The encyclopaedia is thus presented as a *Systema mnemonicum*, and logic is seen both as a 'direction of the intellect' (*directio intellectus*) and a 'confirmation of the memory' (*confirmatio memoriae*).[6] In this way Alsted attempted to reconcile Ramist dialectic and Lullian *combinatoria*. In the *Systema mnemonicum duplex* of 1610, for example, he introduced Lullian elements into his treatment of the fundamental principles of Ramist dialectic, arguing that: 'The first law is that of homogeneity, the second is coordination . . . [and] the third law is called the law of transition.'[7] While Alsted's encyclopaedia brought together aspects of the Lullian tradition, Ramist influences, and echoes of the scholarly discussions concerning the art of 'local memory',[8] ultimately he was more interested in pedagogical than in logical reform. He believed that the organization of education, schools and teaching methods ought to correspond, point by point, to the systematic order of the encyclopaedia. As Pierre Bayle was later to note,[9] Alsted's primary aim in systematizing the arts and the sciences was to work towards a unitary knowledge capable of liberating mankind. Alsted's pupil Comenius subsequently took up his mentor's ideals, and disseminated his message across the length and breadth of Europe.[10]

2 Pansophia and the *Magna didactica*: Comenius

Pansophia involved the search for a universal method, logic and language which would allow man to understand and control nature through the possession of a universal wisdom. In Comenius's proposal for a pansophic reformation we find elements not only of the teachings of Francis Bacon and Johann Alsted, Wolfgang Ratke and Johann Valentin Andreae, but also many themes derived from the traditions of the *ars memorativa* and Lullist encyclopaedism.[11] Whilst sketching out the fundamental outlines of his philsophy in the *Conatuum pansophicorum dilucidatio*, Comenius identified the authors that had preceded him in his task, and the works which had comforted and inspired him. Since antiquity, he said, many famous men had attempted 'the collocation of all human knowledge' (*complexum totius eruditionis*). Aristotle had proposed three laws that he considered necessary for the achievement of human omniscience: 'the universality of principles, the true method of order, and the infallible certainty of truth'. Those modern scholars – Comenius continues – who are authors of encyclopaedias, polymathy, syntaxes, theatres of wisdom, panurgias, great restaurations and pancosmias, have all returned to these three basic laws. The titles to which Comenius alludes here are works known to us: the writings of de Valeriis and Grégoire, Camillo and Patrizi, which are significantly compared to the *Instauratio magna* of Francis Bacon. Comenius repeats the solemn motto of Seneca: 'Much has been done by those before us, but they have not finished the work; much remains, and much will remain, to be done; not even in a thousand centuries will it be impossible for somebody to add something else.' In his plans to realize 'a universal work', Comenius was consciously following in the footsteps of the encyclopaedic tradition. Like his predecessors, he claimed that his encyclopaedia was not just for the use of the learned, but for all Christian people. Once he had realized his projected pansophia, which was to be '[the] solid compendium of universal learning, the shining torch of the intellect, the fixed precepts of the truth of things, the certain collection of the circumstances of life and ultimately the blessed ladder to God himself',[12] Comenius believed that the destiny of the human race would be changed irrevocably.

Comenius's continual references to theatres, syntaxes, and encyclopaedias would, in itself, be sufficient proof of an effective continuity of themes and interests, between the major exponents of Lullist encyclopaedism and the theorists of pansophia. But in addition to this we can also point to the even more significant (although less well-known) fact that Comenius was influenced by some of the major theorists of the *ars memorativa* which (after 1550) had become closely associated with the revival of Lullism. A full account of the context in which Comenius developed his pansophic attempt to ground the totality of knowledge on 'figures' and 'vision' would require a detailed knowledge of the numerous discussions of the mnemonic function of images in the late sixteenth and early seventeenth century. Comenius characterized the first part of his *Orbis sensualium pictus* as 'the picture and nomenclature of all the principal things in the world and all the principal actions of life'. The reality of things, Comenius argued, had to be intuited and seen through images.[13] The foundations of correct teaching, which should be 'full and solid' rather than abstract and scholastic, 'clear, distinct and articulated like the fingers of the hand', rather than obscure and confused, depended upon the 'correct presentation of sensible things to the senses'. A true education of the mind depended on the correct use of images, the senses and memory. Images played a vital role in Comenius's pedagogical theory: he regarded them as 'the likenesses of all the things in the entire world, to which (within appropriate limits) all invisible things will be reducible'. Taking up the central motif of Campanella's *Città del sole*, Comenius comes to the following significant conclusions:

> Our ends can be achieved by displaying pictorial summaries of all the textbooks of each class on the walls of the schoolroom. In this way numerous texts can be represented concisely by means of illustrations, portraits and reliefs, which will give daily exercise to the senses and the memories of the students. We know from the ancients that Hippocrates secretly copied the laws of medicine on the walls of the Temple of Aesculapius, and God did the same when he filled the great Theatre of the World with pictures, statues and images as living representations of his wisdom.

This was not just a generalized rehearsal of commonplace themes, however. Comenius's 'philosophical alphabet' was designed to replace the pedagogical use of the *syllabary* (in which letters were reproduced beside images of animals 'cuius vocem litera imitatur')[14] which Comenius condemned as a 'vexatious torture of the intellect'. The 'philosophical alphabet' was, in fact, closely modelled (with only slight differences) on the 'mnemonic alphabets' found in numerous fifteenth and sixteenth-century treatises on the *ars reminiscendi*. We can find references to the same technique of reinforcing memory (which Comenius used extensively in his *De sermonis latini studio* of 1644) in the *Theatrum sapientiae*, together with allusions to 'theatres of the world' and the cabala. Because of the worthiness of the objects it contains, Comenius said, the *Theatrum* ought to be given the more solemn name of *Templum*. The temple of Christian pansophia was to be constructed according to divine ideas, precepts and laws, and would be consecrated to all the nations of the world: it would be an 'ordered arrangement' of the intellectual faculties, the objects produced by natural power in the visible world, man and the products of human intelligence, the inner reality of man, God and the angelic powers and the products of true wisdom. When reading these pages of Comenius, it is difficult not to be reminded of the complex emblematic constructions of de Valeriis and Camillo, and the grand surveys of universal reality presented in the *Thesaurus memoriae* of Rosselli.[15]

Comenius's project of a 'total encyclopaedia' is also linked to Lullism, discussions of the 'chain of the sciences' (*catena scientiarum*), and to the various projects for a unitary science or universal art which were so common in the sixteenth century. The object of wisdom, Comenius wrote in the *Pansophiae prodromus* of 1639, was at various times attributed to philosophy, medicine, theology, law; it was conceived as the object of a particular science; identified with a partial vision which obstructed any attempt at reaching a totality, or comprehending the unity of the world. Through a total vision, reading the great book of the universe, and by means of a gradual progression from the encyclopaedia of sensible species (*orbis sensualis*) one could attain the encyclopaedia of intellectual species (*orbis intellectualis*), a unitary vision which was the highest aim of knowledge, which could never be achieved through the accumulation of partial accounts.[16] All the attempts to attain unity through the enumeration and collection of particular solutions and techniques were doomed to failure. They either result in vast, useless lists which try – through a 'collection of minutiae' - to exhaust the totality of words and things, or highly ordered encyclopaedias which are more like elegant, linked chains than a machine capable of functioning in an autonomous and coherent fashion.[17] Such collections were like orderly piles of timber arranged with great care and patience, rather than the living tree of the sciences, whose leaves, branches and fruit draw nourishment and vigour from their roots. It was only possible to give life to the tree of knowledge through a totalizing unitary vision: 'I speak of the pansophia which is the living image of the universe, which in every direction is coherent in itself, growing and fructiferous' (*Pansophiam dico, quae sit viva universi imago, sibi ipsi undique cohaerans, seipsam undique vegetans, seipsam undique fructu appellens*). To these useless, pedantic lists of words and things he contrasts the 'storehouse of universal knowledge' (*promptuarium universalis eruditionis*), the book of pansophia: here the chaos and obscurity of exhaustive compilations are replaced by compendiousness, clarity and the rejection of all obscurity, by identifying the 'perpetual connection between causes and effects' (*perpetua connexio causarum et effectuum*), and following the 'continual flow of ordered series from beginning to end' (*ordinis continuo fluentis series a principio ad finem*).[18]

Although Comenius was highly critical of his Lullist predecessors and wrote polemical refutations of their works, the Comenian encyclopaedia was not (in so far as it achieved its original objectives) substantially different from the Lullian 'encyclopaedias' of the sixteenth century, and there was a considerable amount of common ground between them. This becomes clearer when we look at Comenius's treatment of some characteristic problems: 1) the relationship between logic and the encyclopaedia, 2) the correspondence between the universe of signs and the universe of things, 3) the encyclopaedia as a 'mirror' of the unity of the world (which is ordered according to the harmony of the divine laws), and lastly, 4) the encyclopaedia as a 'universal key' giving access to that unity and harmony.

On each of these points Comenius's position is clear. The vocabulary of the *Janua linguarum* ought to be coidentical with the encyclopaedia (*januam linguarum et encyclopaediam debere esse idem*) and is presented as a 'key to the human intellect' (*intellectus humani clavis*), which is like reading the divine alphabet impressed in things. The principal benefits of this new method were the rigorous ordering of notions and the unitary and hierarchical images of the universe, which made it possible to refer every notion to its genus and species, 'so that whatever one says about any particular thing, at the same time one says everything which it is possible to say about it' (*ut quicquid de ulla re dicendum est, simul et semel de omnibus dicatur de quibus dici potest*); the entire encyclopaedia seems to be founded on a reduced number of 'axioms' or of 'propositions which are true in themselves, not demonstrated out of previous statements, but illustrated by examples' (*sententiae per se fide dignae, non demonstrandae per priora, sed illustrandae solum exemplis*); the world of knowledge is structured like the 'chains' of reasoning used in mathematics:

> The solution is to structure the arts and sciences in such a way that whenever one moves from things known towards the unknown, one proceeds slowly and gradually, like following links in a chain; every link is connected to the one before it . . . Just as when a theorem or a problem is demonstrated in mathematics one is led to certain knowledge and effects . . . so in pansophia, having demonstrated one part of the universal doctrine, certainty and infallibility will be consequent upon it.[19]

The infinite variety of notions and things is then reducible to a limited number of 'axioms' or 'principles'. This reducibility (which makes the construction of the book of *pansophia* possible) is based on some familiar presuppositions: that there is a total correspondence between the structure of discourse and the structure of the world, and that the same underlying principles (*rationes rerum*) are present in God, Nature and in the Encyclopaedia. These underlying principles are identical: in God they are 'archetypal' (*ut in Archetypo*), in nature they are 'ectypic' (*ut in Ectypo*) and in the encyclopaedia they are 'antitypical' (*ut in Antitypo*).[20] Despite the fact that many philosophers were sceptical about the possibility of finding a 'universal key', Comenius insisted that the world was reducible to a few fundamental elements, and that there was a strict correspondence between the material creation and the structures of the intellect, imagination and language:

> The things outside of the intellect seem almost infinite, although they are not, because the world (the stupendous work of God) basically consists of a limited number of elements and forms and because all this has been thought out by means of the

[encyclopaedic] art, it can be reduced to determinate genera and principal points. Since there is a correpondence between things and their concepts, and between the images of concepts and words, and since in particular things there are fundamental principles from which other principles follow, I thought that it would be possible to teach these fundamental principles which are found equally in things, concepts and discourse. It also occurred to me that chemists have found out how to liberate the essences or spirits of things from superfluous matter, so that they can concentrate an enormous quantity of mineral or vegetal power into a single drop and that this drop had a greater medicinal efficacy than the mineral and vegetal body from which it was extracted. Might it not be possible (I thought) by gathering together and concentrating the precepts of wisdom scattered across the wide fields of the sciences, to take them from there (where they are lying alone) and sow them far and wide? We must not dismiss this idea through doubt, because every act of doubt is a blasphemy against God.[21]

By identifying the fundamental principles and essences, and setting them up as a faithful mirror of nature, the encyclopaedic art reveals the profound harmony which binds the universe together:

God, who is the source of all harmony, makes all things harmonically . . . Musicians define harmony as the pleasing consonance of many voices and such, in truth, is the harmonious concert between the eternal virtues which exist in God, and the virtues created in nature, and those expressed in the art. There is a harmony between God, nature, and the [encyclopaedic] art, and it is a divine harmony. The [encyclopaedic] art is the image of nature.[22]

This belief underpinned Comenius's faith in the possibility of universal salvation, and his conviction that, by means of pansophia, it would be possible to bring to an end the wars, quarrels, and disagreements which until then had dominated the world.[23]

3 ENCYCLOPAEDISM AND COMBINATORIA IN THE SEVENTEENTH CENTURY

As we can now see, the Lullist tradition had a considerable influence on some of the greatest representatives of European culture. Bacon, Descartes, Alsted, Comenius and, some time later, Leibniz, developed a number of themes present in the Lullist encyclopaedic tradition and incorporated them within a wider debate concerning the nature of logic, the function of philosophy, and the relationship between the sciences and educational reform. In many of the works published by the followers and commentators of Lull in the course of the seventeenth century we find a tedious rehearsal of traditional motifs, an insistence on themes that had become common places, and a pedantic repetition of the rules of the *ars combinatoria*. Discussions of the encyclopaedia, and the links between the transmission of knowledge, method and language were now developed at a higher level, in different intellectual contexts. It is worth giving an account of these traditional encyclopaedic texts (many of which were admired by important thinkers) not just to draw attention to the active presence of what was an extremely influential tradition, but also in order to reflect on some of the characteristic imperatives of seventeenth-century culture.

We have already discussed the projects for the unification of the sciences found in the works of Morestel, Meyssonnier and Jean d'Aubry, but there are other, perhaps more significant, examples, which are worth discussing. In 1632 in Paris, R. L. de Vassi – a counsellor to the King – published his *Le Fondement de l'artifice universel*.[24] This book, despite the marvellous promises and claims in its dedicatory letter, is in fact merely an anthology of partially translated extracts from the works of Lull. What is significant about the work, however, is that the work of Lull is presented as an appropriate instrument for the methical ordering of the sciences and the realization of the encyclopaedia. In a situation which de Vassi himself considered to be less than favourable to Lullian studies ('the artificial practice of Doctor Lull', he says 'has been forgotten by the majority of people and is commonly rejected by the learned community'), it is interesting to see that the texts of the *ars combinatoria* can be seen here playing a prominent part in one of the most significant debates of the time. One finds a similar attitude also in the writings of Janius Caecilius Frey (d. 1631), whose works were well known to Leibniz. Frey was physician to the Queen Mother in France and author (in addition to writings on medicine and physiognomy) of a compendium of Aristotelian philosophy and of a treatise entitled, *Via ad divas scientias artesque, linguaram notitiam, sermones extemporaneos nova et expeditissima.*[25] In the posthumous edition of his works[26] we find, besides his usual interests in rhetoric and language, logic (*via ad scientias*) and the encyclopaedia (*scientiae et artes omnes ordine distributae et desumptae*), an attempt to reduce all the sciences to general axioms and principles (*axiomata philosophica*) and discussions of methods for the ordering of research. Frey rehearsed the rules of the 'Ciceronian' art of memory and – following in the footsteps of Lavinheta – incorporated them into his theoretical exposition of the *ars combinandi.*

> Rational philosophy comprises logic, dialectic and the mnemonic art. Dialectic provides the matter and arguments for disputation. Logic provides us with the forms of argumentation. Dialectic can be Lullist, peripatetic or Ramist.[27]

The construction of a system of scientific axiomatics (the reduction of all the fundamental terms of particular sciences according to the principles of a reformed *combinatoria*), and the determination of the relationships between the various branches of knowledge are also the central themes of Ivo de Paris's complex *Digestum sapientiae* (c.1648) and of the *Commento all'arte lulliana* of Julius Pacius, pupil of Zabarella who fled to Geneva, and became professor at Heidelberg and Padua.[28] This last text, compiled by one of the most acute and renowned translators and commentators of Aristotle's *Organon*, by a man who was not only a famous logician, but also a renowned jurist, is worth a detailed discussion in its own right. But for our present purposes, it is more useful to turn our attention instead to a work published in 1659 which had an immediate impact on Europe and enjoyed great popularity afterwards: the *Pharus scientiarum* of the Spaniard Sebastian Izquierdo.[29] Aristotle, Cicero, Quintilian and Lull – Izquierdo wrote – had laboured for centuries over the construction of a universal art or 'science of sciences'. This ancient aspiration towards a 'logica prima' which can, like a beacon, guide the course of navigators in the sea of wisdom, had found its modern counterparts in the *Sintaxis* of Pierre Grégoire, the *Digestum* of Ivo de Paris, the *Cyclognomica* of Cornelius Gemma and Francis Bacon's *Novum organum*. To complete the work which had been begun by these authors, Izquierdo insisted, it was necessary to understand three things: 1) the encyclopaedia (which the ancients called *scientia circularis* or *orbicularis*) is not simply an aggregate of all the particular sciences, but is a special science (*in speciale quadam scientia consistere*) which comprehends all sciences in itself, including the principles of the special or universal science itself; 2) the 'partial' logic of Aristotle had to be replaced by an 'integrated' logic which included not just an *ars intelligendi* (which perfects the intellect) but also an *ars memorandi*, which aids the memory, and an *ars experiendi*, which is used to increase the capacity of the imagination and the external senses; 3) metaphysics ought to proceed with absolute mathematical rigour according to the model of the mathematical sciences: 'If metaphysicians had reasoned demonstratively, beginning (in the manner of mathematicians) from self-evident principles, the greater part of metaphysics would have been constructed already.' These Cartesian suggestions are made more explicit, when Izquierdo (after having criticized the art of Lull for its 'barbarous' terminology, the insufficiency of its binary and ternary combinations, and its inability to descend from universal terms to particulars) identifies *combinatoria* with the *calculus*. Only the mathematization of the *ars combinandi*, Izquierdo argues, would enable us to create that unique instrument of all the sciences 'by means of which the edifice of science can be constructed and can grow infinitely'.

The idea of bringing the *Ars magna* closer to the procedures of mathematics, and developing the *ars combinatoria* into a kind of 'calculus' was to be taken up and developed later by Leibniz. But when the young Leibniz turned to the 'new' *combinatoria* he was not (as many have believed) putting forward an innovative and original idea. We can find the same ideas clearly formulated, for example, in the writings of the ostentatious Jesuit Athanasius Kircher,[30] renowned in his own time for his miraculous abilities in physics, archaeology, philology, Egyptology, and the history and theory of language, and author – amongst other things – of the celebrated *Mundus subterraneus* and an equally famous treatise on the mysteries of numbers.[31] If we are to understand this cultural milieu, it is important that we remember that this desire for the 'mathematization' of the combinatorial art, the exaltation of the *combinatoria* of Diophantus (*Diophantus nobilis mathematici ars combinatoria*) and its reconciliation with the *combinatoria* of Lull, was present not only in the writings of logicians such as Izquierdo, but in the works of a man like Kircher, who was profoundly concerned with the themes of the Hermetic tradition and gnostic wisdom: with magic, the cabala and numerological speculations on the 'mystery of numbers' (*misteria numerorum*). Despite his rhetorical tirades on the value of the experimental method and the defence of the new science, Kircher believed in occult qualities, in 'sympathies and antipathies', and in the powers of the imagination, reaffirmed the theory of spontaneous generation, and was convinced of the existence of subterranean demons. In short, Kircher constantly emphasized the 'miraculous' and 'marvellous' aspects of reality. When the emperor Ferdinand III, during the fierce controversies sparked off in Germany by the publication of Izquierdo's *Pharus scientiarum*, appealed to the doctrine of Kircher, because it was informed by a sense of the real utility of the Lullian art and the possibility of its greater simplification, the German Jesuit set to work on a complicated reform which extensively remodelled Izquierdo's book.[32] While he addressed some of the criticisms of his predecessor, Kircher's work focused primarily on his prevalent interests: the construction of images and allegories, the elaboration of figures and symbols, and the mysteries of the alphabet.

In the last decades of the seventeenth century, particularly in the work of the Jesuits,[33] Lullism was still associated with an atmosphere of Hermeticism and magic – traditions which had now become problematic and ambiguous. In the farraginous writings of another Jesuit, Fr. Caspar Knittel at the end of the seventeenth century, we find only a tedious exposition of the rules of the *combinatoria* and a monotonous repetition of the theses of Kircher.[34] In the early years of the eighteenth century, the great scholar and 'polyhistor' Daniel Morhof was deeply critical of these reforms, and this kind of magical-philosophical work: 'Knittel's reform consists only in the invention of new alphabets, using different letters; it seems to me a very poor thing.'[35]

4 The philosophical alphabet of Johann Heinrich Bisterfeld

An 'alphabet' of a completely different kind was the subject of the work of Johann Heinrich Bisterfeld, who in the 1650s had projected a 'philosophical alphabet' based on the collection and ordering of all the technical terms and definitions employed by each of the sciences into accurate tables.[36] In creating these tables, and searching for perfect definitions, Bisterfeld hoped to achieve the encyclopaedia, that 'pictorial amphitheatre of the world' (*pictum mundi amphitheatrum*) which is 'the most orderly articulation of all the sciences' (*ordinatissima compages omnium disciplinarum*).[37] Rather than concerning himself with logic and method (understood as the regulation of the intellect and the remediation of the natural infirmity of memory respectively), Bisterfeld emphasized the decisive importance of what he calls 'logical practice' (*praxis logica*), which is an 'artificial conjunction' (*artificiosa coniunctio*) of the terms of logic and those of the encyclopaedia, a mixture of the instruments of logic with the idea of a universal encyclopaedia. The basis of his method was the identification of the transcendental terms 'which are the prime roots of the universal encyclopaedia'. Both analysis (the reduction of a discourse or text to its simple terms) and genesis (or 'combination of simple elements') begin with these transcendental terms. Like ascending the steps of a ladder one can then arrive at that 'art of definition' (*artificium definiendi*) which permits the exact definition of all the terms of the encyclopaedia and a resolution of all the terms into primary terms.[38]

The definitions, which are the 'keys and patterns' (*claves et normae*) of the *praxis logica*, are the foundations of the whole edifice: 'The more man knows solidly, the more he can define' (*Tantum scit homo solide quantum scit definire*): to achieve exact definitions of real and intellectual entities, separate and collective entities (the *entia positiva* and *entia privationis*) it is necessary in the first place to have a dictionary (*nomenclatura*) of terms drawn from the various discourses of the particular disciplines. On the basis of this dictionary one could construct tables which would be 'representations of the whole world and the whole encyclopaedia' (*totius mundi totiusque encyclopaediae repraesentiones*). By means of the tables one could discover the homogeneous, subordinate and coordinate terms. The construction of a 'primitive table' (*tabula primitiva*) comprehending the terms common to all the separate tables, or the greater part of the sciences, would lead to the comprehension of the harmony of the sciences which, Bisterfeld tells us, is both the 'basis and the key' (*basis et clavis*) of the practice of logic:[39]

The harmony of the sciences is the basis and the key of the practice of logic. This harmony is that most sweet agreement which
ensures not only that all the sciences are consonant one with
another, but also ensures that the parts of each science accord
with themselves: and this harmony is so profound that the wisest men believe that henceforth there will no longer be sciences,
but only one single science, or rather that the body and system
of all the sciences is singular.[40]

In order to realize this unified system, to discover the transcendental terms into which all other terms are analytically reducible,
Bisterfeld considered a minute and accurate enumeration of all
things and notions as indispensable. The 'theatre of the world', with
its tables representing all the things which the human mind can discuss, was also held to be fundamental to the art, logic or 'science of
sciences':

> The transcendental terms are the prime roots of the universal
> encyclopaedia which is the orderly collection of all the disci-
> plines or a pictorial amphitheatre of the world . . . The universal
> art of definition teaches us how to accurately find and evaluate
> the definitions of all the terms of the universal encyclopaedia . . .
> The universal tables constitute the noblest alphabet of all the dis-
> ciplines. These ought to contain everything and represent all the
> things which the human mind can discuss, and he who has the
> most thorough knowledge of the tables has the firmest grasp of
> the seeds of science. These are the best-equipped workshops for
> every kind of thought and bring before our eyes all that which is
> around us, and that which we can discuss. From these tables
> we can recover all themes, all arguments, all syllogisms, all
> methods.[41]

CHAPTER SEVEN

The Construction of a
Universal Language

1 BACONIAN GROUPS IN ENGLAND: PROJECTS FOR A UNIVERSAL
LANGUAGE

At the beginning of his *Essay towards a Real Character*, published in
London under the auspices of the Royal Society in 1668,[1] in which
John Wilkins set out the fundamental outlines of his project for a
'philosophical', 'perfect' or 'universal' language, he referred his
readers to those parts of the *Advancement of Learning* (and of the *De
augmentis scientiarum*) in which Bacon had explained the differences
between hieroglyphs and 'real characters'. Hieroglyphs, Bacon
maintained, in so far as they were emblems, 'always have something
in common with the thing signified' (*semper cum re significata aliquid
similitudinis habere*); while real characters were 'not at all emblematic' (*nihil habent ex emblemate*), but artificially constructed characters, whose significance depended only on a custom or usage which
was arbitrarily established (*ad placitum*) and agreed upon 'as though
by a silent pact' (*tanquam pacto tacito recepti*). The letters of the
Roman alphabet are conventional, Bacon reminded his readers, but
real characters (unlike their alphabetic counterparts) would 'represent not just letters or words, but things and notions' (*nec literas nec
verba, sed res et notiones exprimunt*). Bacon was aware that the
ideogrammatic written languages of China and the Far East
(*provinciis ultimi Orientis*) were already using 'real' rather than 'nominal' characters – that is to say characters which represented things
and concepts, rather than letters and words. Using these characters,
he said, people who spoke different languages (once they had established the meanings of the characters by convention) could communicate with each other through writing. A book written in these
characters could thus be read and understood by anyone in their
own language. Bacon was aware that to invent a written language
of this kind would require a great number of characters: to function

efficiently, he said, 'there ought to be as many [characters] as there are radical words' (*tot enim esse debent, quot sunt vocabula radicalia*).[2]

Many English logicians and linguists in the second half of the seventeenth century dedicated themselves to the task of creating an artificial language which would eliminate the confusions and imperfections of natural languages, replacing conventional words with symbols which would directly represent 'things', rather than sounds.[3] In 1652 Francis Lodowick's *The Groundwork or Foundation Laid (or so Intended) for the Framing of a New Perfect Language* was published in London; in 1653 Thomas Urquhart (1611–60), the translator of Rabelais, published his *Logopandecteision, or an Introduction to the Universal Language*; four years later Cave Beck published *The Universal Character by Which all Nations may Understand One Another's Conceptions;* the *Tables of the Universal Character* and the *Ars Signorum, vulgo character universalis et lingua philosophica* of George Dalgarno (1626–87) were published in London in 1657 and 1661 respectively; finally, in 1668, John Wilkins (1614–72) published the aforementioned *Essay towards a Real Character and a Philosophical Language*.

In order to understand the significance of these works (and others like them) and their historical function, and to understand the cultural atmosphere which produced them, and the reasons for their contemporary success and influence, one must take account of three major historical phenomena which are characteristic of the intellectual life of mid-seventeenth-century England: 1) firstly, the profound influence exercised in England by the work of Bacon and by the 'Baconian' groups of the Royal Society, who were engaged in a fierce war against the rhetoric of late humanism and a passionate defence of the new science; 2) secondly, the great 'revolution' which followed the advent of 'experimental philosophy' and mathematical physics – a revolution which was not simply 'intellectual', because it changed not only ideas (culture, literature and modes of thought), but also academic and scientific institutions, education and lifestyles; 3) thirdly and finally, the profound influence exerted on the philosophical, political and religious culture of seventeenth-century England by the work, teaching, utopianism and aspirations of Jan Amos Comenius.

Let us begin then with Bacon, because his statements about *real characters*, and his approach to the problem of language, were presupposed (implicitly or explicitly) in all of the subsequent treatises on universal language. In his influential work on the 'materialistic' character of Bacon's linguistic theories, Richard Foster Jones pointed out the profound influence exercised by Baconian theories on the 'stylistic revolution' in Restoration prose, in both the secular sphere (works on history, natural philosophy and politics) and the religious (especially in books of moral edification, sermons and prayers).[4] Foster-Jones has spoken of 'Bacon's antipathy towards language'. In reality it seems to be something more than simply an 'antipathy' – Bacon's approach is founded on the conviction that language, like other products of the human spirit, is (or can be) an *obstacle* to the comprehension of reality, a barrier which is *placed in between* man and real facts or the laws of nature. In order to 'get closer to things', it was necessary, in Bacon's view, to reject those terms which do not correspond to real things, and to learn to construct words which do correspond to the effective reality of things. The 'idols' *(idola)* which are imposed on the intellect through words, Bacon says in the sixtieth aphorism of the *Novum organum*, are of two kinds: either they are names of things which do not exist, or they are the names of things which exist, but are confused, ill-defined and *abstracted from things* in an arbitrary and partial way. The first category refers to fantastical concepts or theories ('Fortune', the '*primum mobile*' etc.) which can be dispelled by logical refutation. The second category is more problematic, because one is dealing with an inexpert or imperfect 'abstraction of things' which has resulted in the prevalence of confused concepts.

These statements allow us to clarify Bacon's position regarding language: concepts ought to be abstracted correctly from things, and correspond to them; where the concept has been constructed in a vague or imprecise manner the word assigned to the concept reflects this vagueness and imprecision. The words assigned to things, in their turn, influence the intellect: the words which denote vague concepts 'turn and reflect their force back against the intellect' *(verba vim suam super intellectum retorqueant et reflectant)* and impede the search for precise concepts. In this way words 'reflect their rays and their images within the mind, and are not only harmful to communication, but also to the judgement of the intellect'. When one attempts to make words correspond better to nature, through more accurate observation or better abstraction, 'the words rebel', and give rise to sterile controversies which concern language and words rather than the reality of things. For this reason Bacon does not seem to have set much store by attempts to achieve precise definitions of the type used by mathematicians: 'When dealing with natural and material things', Bacon said, '*definitions can never remedy this evil*, because definitions themselves consist of words, and words generate other words.'

This was an extremely significant conclusion, and his critical account of the use of the term 'humid' (developed in the *Novum organum*) may help us come to a clearer understanding of this view of the relationship between language and knowledge. The equivocal nature of the term 'humid', Bacon suggested, depends on the equivocal nature of the *concept* of 'humidity', which was used to denote a number of different states which had been 'abstracted superficially, and without the necessary checks, only from the properties of water, and from other commonly occurring liquids'. Confronted with this variety of meanings, Bacon did not try to give a definition which fixed the semantic field of of the term 'humid', which would have predetermined the possible uses of that term and limited its meaning, but tried instead to develop a concept (based on 'a study of particular cases, and their series and order'), which would resolve the diversity of states into a unity, and so become a criterion for explaining the reasons for this diversity. The validity of this criterion, however, would necessarily depend on the extent to which the new concept *corresponded to the reality of things*. It becomes apparent from this how Bacon was able to see 'concept' and 'word' as synonymous or coidentical: i.e. for Bacon weak concepts were 'the bad and inept imposition of words' (*mala et inepta verborum impositio*), or 'words arbitrarily abstracted from things' (*nomina temere a rebus abstracta*), although this emphasis is somewhat at odds with the conventionalist emphasis of his account of language use. In sum: Bacon was unwilling to accept a theory which identified the truth of a proposition with the logical coherence of the terms which make up that proposition: in the Baconian method, one is continually brought back to things, sensible qualities, and the properties of bodies. The 'materialistic' inspiration of this conception of language becomes explicit when Bacon drew up a kind of 'scale' (*graduatoria*) in which he ranked the 'different levels of aberration and error present in words'. The least defective kinds of terms are those denoting common *substances* (chalk, mud etc.); more defective are those terms which denote *actions* (generating, corrupting etc.); the most defective are the terms used to denote *qualities* (heavy, light, dense, etc.).[5]

Opposing 'things' to 'words', Bacon insisted on the need for a language which referred to the operations or forces present in nature, whilst at the same time emphasizing the philosophical dangers inherent in the use of language. He believed that all or many of these dangers could be eliminated by the developement of an artificial language, composed of symbols for all of the 'radical words'. But it is also important to remember that Bacon was one of the leading proponents of *anti-Ciceronianism*. He preferred brief aphorisms to the bulky periods of the followers of Cicero, maintaining the need to return to an 'Attic' or 'Senecan' style. He preferred expressivity and clarity, and the 'grave' and 'sententious' brevity of the stoics, to rhetorical ornamentation, stylistic flourishes, analogies or metaphors. Bacon polemicized against the verbal disputations of the scholastics, and opposing the language used in the universities, he argued in favour of a style which was brief and essential, precise and plain, able to put man back into contact with the world, after many centuries of 'voluntary blindness'.[6]

In the writings of Bacon's followers and admirers, and in the works of many of the greatest defenders of the new science we find many of Bacon's linguistic views energetically reaffirmed. A few examples will suffice. In his *Academiarum examen* (London, 1653) John Webster, a chaplain in the Parliamentary army, and a fervent upholder of the Baconian philosophy, launched a violent attack on the rhetoric and oratory which 'serve for adornation, and are as it were the outward dress, and attire of more solid sciences'; rejecting grammatical studies, which he saw as an impediment to real progress in knowledge, he insisted on the need for '*Hieroglyphical, Emblematical, Symbolical* and *Cryptographical* learning', which would help overcome the confusions and imperfections of natural languages.[7] In his *Considerations Touching the Style of the Holy Scriptures* (written in 1653 and published in 1651) Robert Boyle (who had long been interested in the idea of an artificial language) expressed a strong distaste for unnecessary stylistic ornamentation. In an autobiographical essay Boyle contrasted his passion for experimental philosophy and the real understanding of things, with his aversion to the study of languages, inveighing against the ambiguity and 'licentiousness' of scientific terms which he considered to be detrimental to the progress of true philosophy: 'My propensity and value for learning', he wrote, 'gave me [. . .] much aversion and contempt for the empty study of words.'[8]

Another fervent Baconian, Joshua Childrey, also reflected upon the damage which is inflicted upon science by the confusion of natural languages. In his *Britannia baconica* (London 1660), he declared his intention to 'tell [his] tale as plainly as might be', so that he might 'be understood of all, and that I might not disfigure the face of Truth by daubing it over with the paint of Language'.[9] Meanwhile Thomas Sprat, whose *History of the Royal Society* (1667) reflected the opinions of many of his colleagues, severely condemned the use of metaphors, verbosity of expression, and the continual mutability of natural languages, as evils from which men of science ought to be liberated.[10] Defending the Royal Society from the attacks of Henry Stubbs who had dared to assail 'all true-hearted virtuous, intelligent Disciples of our Lord *Bacon*', George Thomson wrote in 1671:

'Tis *Works*, not *Words*; *Things*, not *Thinking*; *Pyrotechnie*, not *Philologie*; Operation, not meerly *Speculation*: must justifie us Physicians. Forbear then hereafter to be so wrongfully Satyrical against our noble Experimentators, who questionless are enterd on the right way of detecting the Truth of things.[11]

2 LINGUISTIC SYMBOLS AND MATHEMATICAL SYMBOLS.

The works which set out to construct a 'philosophical' or 'perfect' language found a favourable reception in this new cultural climate. Clearly, given the need for clarity and rigour, new developments in mathematical studies helped foster these projects for a symbolic language, but it would be futile to maintain that the universal languages *depended* on – or historically *derived* from – these developments. The rigorous demonstrations and widespread employment of symbolic notation in mathematics, however, reinforced the idea that it was possible for scientists to reduce their style to a 'mathematical simplicity' of the kind espoused by the Baconian Thomas Sprat in his *History of the Royal Society*. The Society, Sprat observed, had made a constant Resolution to reject all the amplifications, digressions and swellings of style: to return back to the primitive purity, and shortness, when men deliverd so many *things*, almost in an equall number of *words*. They have exacted from all their members, a close, naked, natural way of speaking; positive expressions; clear senses; a native easiness: bringing all things as near the Mathematicall plainness as they can: and preferring the language of Artizans, Countrymen, and Merchants, before that of Wits, or Scholars.[12]

This tendency was even more explicit amongst those thinkers who were directly influenced by Thomas Hobbes, who defined 'terms' as symbols of relations and quantity, and saw language as a kind of 'calculus'. The views of Seth Ward – professor of astronomy at Oxford – are typical in this respect. He saw the 'Symbolicall' writing which had been 'invented by *Vieta*, advanced by *Harriot*, perfected by Mr *Oughtred* and *Des Cartes*', as the best remedy for the excessive verbosity of mathematics. This principle, Ward suggested, could be extended to language as a whole, so that 'Symboles might be found for every *thing* and *notion*', so that the confusions and equivocations of natural languages would be eliminated. With 'the helpe of Logick and Mathematicks' all discourses could be 'resolved in sentences', and these sentences into words, and – since words are 'either simple notions or [. . .] resolvable into simple notions – once you had discovered the simplest concepts and assigned symbols to them, it would be possible to develop a rigorous, demonstrative discourse which would reveal 'the natures of things':

> Such a language as this (where every word were a definition and contain'd the nature of the thing) might not unjustly be termed a naturall Language, and would afford that which the *Cabalists* and *Rosycrucians* have vainely sought for in the Hebrew, And in the names of things assigned by Adam.[13]

Some time after 1650, William Petty, a member of the Royal Society and the great pioneer of political economics, also began work on a universal language, which, he said, was composed of characters 'incomparably easier to use than actual letters', and a 'Dictionary of sensible words' which was designed to furnish the terminology necessary for a Hobbesian mechanism. 'The Dictionary I have often mentioned', he wrote in a letter to Southwell, ' was intended to translate all the words used in argument and important matters into words that are *signa rerum et motuum*.'[14] Robert Boyle, in a letter of March 1647 also saw the translinguistic character of mathematical symbols as proof of the possibility of constructing a language composed of real characters:

> If the design of the Real Character take effect, it will in good part make amends for what their pride lost them at the tower of Babel. And truly, since our arithmetical characters are understood by all the nations of *Europe* [. . .] I conceive no impossibility that opposes the doing that in words that we see already done in numbers.[15]

The practitioners of algebra and mathematics themselves were also involved in these discussions on language, writing and symbols. In the writings of the mathematician John Wallis, for example, the treatment of algebraic characters and *notae* are presented as part of a more general discussion of signs, ciphers and writing. Keenly interested in the historical development of algebra Wallis emphasized, in the pages of his *De algebra,* the advantages which William Oughtred's *characteres* or *notae compendiosae* had over the unwieldy form of notation used by Viète. In his *Mathesis universalis* of 1657 there are numerous references to the problem of writing in general and occult writing in particular. In *De loquela siue sonorum formatione*, the preface to his *Grammatica linguae anglicanae*, Wilkins reflected at some length on questions relating to grammar and the production of sounds. Finally in the *De algebra* we find, in addition to a ferocious attack on the mathematical incompetence of Hobbes and his 'vile paralogisms', a lengthy chapter extolling the advantages for the mathematician of mnemotechnical techniques for strengthening the memory.[16]

3 THE COMENIAN GROUPS: UNIVERSAL LANGUAGE AND UNIVERSAL CHRISTIANITY.

The influence of Comenius's teaching on the projects for a universal language has been meticulously documented.[17] No book dedicated to the idea of a universal language had appeared in England before Comenius's visit to London in 1641; after that year numerous works devoted to the topic appeared in print. It was no coincidence: Samuel Hartlib, who corresponded with Comenius for many years, and was seen by his contemporaries as Comenius's principal defender and popularizer in England, was a fervent supporter and editor of works on the universal language. In 1646 Hartlib published the work of Francis Lodowick (*A Common Writing*); he encouraged numerous attempts to create a vocabulary of essential terms, and wrote to Robert Boyle about these issues; he also contributed to the publication of George Dalgarno's *Ars signorum*. We find explicit references to Comenius in the writings of Henry Edmundson (his *Lingua linguarum* of 1655)[18] and John Webster (the *Academiarum examen*, published in 1654), while John Wilkins, the most famous and celebrated of the theorists of universal language, was helped and encouraged by another English disciple of Comenius with whom he had a great friendship, Theodore Haak. Comenius himself dedicated his *Via lucis vestigata et vestiganda* to the Royal Society in 1668, in which he stated that the work of Wilkins, published in the same year, represented the realization of his programmes and of his highest aspirations.

In the *Via lucis*, which circulated in manuscript in England from 1641, Comenius had taken up and extended Bacon's observations on 'real characters'. The symbolic characters used by the Chinese, he wrote, allowed men of different languages to understand each other: if such characters seem a good and advantageous thing, should we not dedicate our studies to the discovery of a 'Real Language', to the discovery 'not only of a language, but of thought, and what is more, the truth of things themselves?' If the diversity of languages

> [is the result of] chance, or mere confusion [. . .] why should not a single language be made by a deliberate and reasoned procedure and by a method of rewelding at once elegant and ingenious. For why in this matter should we yield everything to the operation of chance? And if we are free to adjust our concepts of things to the forms of things themselves, why should we not be free to fit language to the more exact expression of more exact concepts?[19]

The problem of universal language is central to Comenius's work: in his philosophy there was undoubtedly a call for greater terminological precision, for a clearer, more accessible and rigorous language. But his project was not motivated simply by methodological considerations; there were underlying religious aspirations, similar to those expressed in Lullist and neoplatonic works of the sixteenth century, together with ideas concerning universal pacification which recalled the utopian visions of pantheists, cabalists and rosicrucians. We should not forget that Comenius's teacher Johann Valentin Andreae had proposed a mystical harmony of nations (the *respublica christianopolitana*) which was to be realized by means of a new universal language, and that Jakob Boehme (with whose works Comenius was familiar) spoke of an originary language of nature (*Natursprache*) which was lost by the confusion of languages and which would be recovered through the salvation of mankind.[20] Comenius believed (like the Lullists and like his teacher Andreae) that the 'real' or 'perfect philosophical' language had two fundamental aims: 1) to put man in renewed contact with the divine harmony of the universe, revealing the full coincidence of the structures of thought and reality, and the correspondence between words and things; and 2) to act as a potential basis for a full reconciliation of humankind, in a stable religious peace.

Comenius saw the multitude and variety of languages as the chief obstacle to the diffusion of the 'light' of Christianity and *pansophia* to all peoples of the world. He believed that when 'an absolutely new language, absolutely clear and rational, a pansophic and universal language', had been constructed, 'then men would all belong to one race and one people'. Before Comenius, Pico, Sabunde, Cusanus, and Guillaume Postel had preached the benefits of a *pax philosophica*, the *concordia mundi*, and the unity of human kind, and Comenius's millenarian hopes recall this religio-philosophical tradition. But the importance and significance of terminological disagreements, the necessity of a common language, and the need to preserve the common elements of faith and abandon vain 'linguistic disputes' had been discussed throughout the Reformation, and in many different intellectual spheres. It is doubtful whether we can hope to do justice to such a complex problem here, but we can perhaps outline a few characteristic positions.

William Bedel (1571–1642), who was one of the major supporters of irenicism and Lutheran–Calvinist reconciliation in England, saw the disagreement between the sects as verbal in character, and no doubt his intense interest in the work of Comenius (and the English Comenians) on projects for a universal language was motivated (at least in part) by this conviction. This religious dimension was, in fact, often foregrounded in the writings of the theorists of universal language. According to Wilkins, the philosophical language would (once it had been perfected and freed from all ambiguity) clarify the nature of religious differences, and reveal them to be inconsistent. Cave Beck also believed that the elimination of linguistic ambiguities would make a substantial contribution to the progress of religion in the world. William Petty, who wanted to translate all of the terms of argumentation into terms which were *signa rerum* (maintaining a distinction between significant and insignificant terms) saw the clarification of the terms of religious life as one of the primary purposes of his dictionary. Determining the exact meanings of God and devil, angel and world, heaven and hell, religion and spirit, Church and Christian, Catholic and pope, he reached the conclusion that the arguments and wars between the various sects had been founded on terminological divergences and he believed that a more effective understanding of concepts and things was possible. In the *Ars signorum* of George Dalgarno we find a similar attempt to achieve perfect communication by means of a complicated system of dichotomies and conventional symbols.[21] In the *History of the Royal Society*, Thomas Sprat spoke of a 'philosophy of humanity' which would overcome religious differences and hostilities: 'for they openly profess, not to lay the Foundation of an *English*, *Scotch*, *Irish*, *Popish* or *Protestant* Philosophy; but a Philosophy of *Mankind*'. The basis of this conviction was not simply a belief that the new 'experimental philosophy' could join men together outside of political and religious convictions, but the hope that the scientific organization itself could become a means of re-establishing the *concordia mundi* – the religious and spiritual unity of humankind. In this, Sprat's vision was close to Bacon's conception of the new science as an instrument of universal redemption from original sin.[22]

While we should guard against the anachronistic projection of our concerns on to those who were writing in the middle of the seventeenth century, we must still give an account of the extent to which the projects for a 'universal' or 'perfect' language (which absorbed the attention of many scholars working at the time) drew nourishment from the cultural climate surrounding the birth of the new science, and the great progress made in physics and mathematics. It is quite clear, however, that these new 'languages' were not intended simply to clarify the semantic problems of natural philosophers, but had much broader and more ambitious aims. They were designed as instruments of total redemption, and a means for deciphering the divine alphabet. The projects for a universal language are connected historically to the dreams of pacification and the millenarian utopias of those authors whose works we have considered in previous chapters.

4 THE CONSTRUCTION OF A PERFECT LANGUAGE

In George Dalgarno's *Ars signorum* and in John Wilkins's *Essay Towards a Real Character* we find discussions of hieroglyphs and alphabets, normal and ciphered writing; there are chapters dedicated to language and logic, grammar and syntax, page after page of minute classifications of the elements, meteors, rocks and metals, plants and animals, the liberal and mechanical arts, together with dictionaries of essential terms from various languages, 'parallel' dictionaries and proposals for an artificial language.[23]

This cluster of topics, which seems so strange and arbitrary to the modern reader, is almost identical to those which we have encountered previously in sixteenth-century encyclopaedias and treatises which, directly or indirectly, dealt with the logical-encyclopaedic themes of Lullism. For the sake of clarity and brevity, and for the ease of the reader, we shall endeavour, in the following pages, to identify and enumerate some of the most important and recurrent themes of the works dealing with the idea of a perfect or universal language. A detailed analysis of these works has shown:

1. The theorists of the 'perfect', 'philosophical' or 'universal' language (assuming the distinction between 'natural' and 'artificial' languages as a given) set out to construct an artificial language or system of signs which will be communicable and comprehensible – and hence applicable to either written or spoken language – regardless of the 'natural' language spoken by the reader. The characters of which the language is composed would be able to be 'effable in a[ny] distinct language'.[24] The rules of the universal languages never coincide with those of natural languages.

2. The artificial language is made possible by the fact that the 'internal notions or apprehension of things' or 'mental images' are common to all men, while the names assigned to these concepts or things in the various natural languages are decided by convention or chance, so that the internal concepts or mental images are expressed differently from language to language. In natural languages then, common expressions do not correspond to common notions: the theorists of universal language set out to artificially create such common means of expression.[25]

3. The artificial language (which endeavours to harmonize the structures of expression and mental images) was seen by its exponents as an effective remedy for the Babelian confusion of languages, and as a means of eliminating the absurdities, difficulties, ambiguities and equivocations of the various 'natural' languages.

The first part of Wilkins's work (i.e. the *Prolegomena*) is dedicated to a close examination of the current state of the various natural languages, identifying their 'changes and corruptions' and 'defects', and considers the problem of the origins of language. Wilkins departs from the commonly held supposition that all natural languages are necessarily imperfect: he believed that every change in the linguistic inheritance coincides with a stage in its 'gradual corruption'. He identified a number of causes of linguistic corruption, including the commerce between different nations through trade, marriages between sovereigns, wars and conquests, and the desire of the learned for elegance (which often leads them to reject the traditional forms of language). He maintained that all languages (with the exception of the original language) were created through *imitation*, and often arrived at arbitrarily, or by chance. In all languages, therefore, there are defects which, with the help of art, it would be possible to eliminate. 'Neither letters nor languages', he observed, had as yet been 'constructed with regularity, according to the rules of art.' Wilkins saw this *non-artificiality* of languages (what we might consider to be their 'spontaneity') as a kind of original sin, the primordial source of an inevitable process of degeneration, and the root of an ever-increasing confusion. In a few hundred years, he argued, some languages could be completely lost, while others would be transformed until they became unintelligible.

Grammar (the only art which can introduce order into language) had arrived too late, and because it was written in the natural languages themselves, it had a limited efficacy because of the bewildering diversity and ambiguity of linguistic meanings. Dalgarno adopted exactly the same position: the art has the task of 'showing a way to remedy the difficulties and absurdities which all languages are clogged with ever since the Confusion, or rather since the Fall, by cutting off all redundancy, rectifying all anomaly, [and] taking away all ambiguity and aequivocation'.[26]

4. The artificial language was presented as an easier and more effective means of communication than any of those actually in use. In the works of Wilkins and Dalgarno we find a reprise of the marvellous promises and expectations which had filled the prefaces of fifteenth- and sixteenth-century Lullian and mnemotechnic works. In the space of two weeks, Dalgarno claimed, men of different languages would be able to learn to communicate in writing and verbally 'in a manner not less intelligible than with their natural languages'. In a month, according to Wilkins, a man of normal intellectual capacities could master the artificial language and express himself in it with the same clarity which one could attain in Latin after forty years of study.[27]

5. The artificial language would, it was believed, have a therapeutic effect on philosophy, curing it of its most pernicious diseases (the use of sophisms and the tendency towards logomachy). The precision of the artificial language would make it a useful instrument for the perfecting of logic: the *Ars signorum*, for example, was presented not only as a remedy for the confusion of languages, and an easier means of communication, but also as a cure for philosophy's ills, through the provision of 'wieldy and manageable instruments of operation for defining, dividing, demonstrating etc'.[28]

6. The adoption of the artificial language would facilitate the transmission of ideas between various nations. The confines of knowledge would be enlarged and the 'general good of mankind' – which is superior to that of any particular nation –

would be able to be pursued with renewed vigour. Ultimately, the new language would make a decisive contribution to the establishment of a true religious peace: 'This design will likewise contribute much to the clearing of our Modern differences in Religion, by unmasking many wild errors, that shelter themselves under the disguise of affected phrases; which being Philosophically unfolded and rendered according to the genuine and natural importance of Words, will appear to be inconsistencies and contradictions.'[29]

7. The signs which make up the universal language are 'real characters' (in the Baconian sense of this term): conventional signs which represent or signify not sounds and words, but concepts and things directly. Following Bacon's theories on real characters, and adapting ideas from contemporary debates on the nature of hieroglyphics, Wilkins distinguished between 'ordinary Letters' (originally invented by Adam), and 'Notes' (i.e. 'notations') which were used 'for *Secrecy* and for *Brevity*'. Examples of the first type include 'that *Mexican* way of writing by Picture' and Egyptian hieroglyphs which were considered to be 'the representation of certain living Creatures, and other Bodies, whereby they were wont to conceal from the vulgar the Mysteries of their religion'; the second type are '*Letters* or *marks*' which can serve as an abbreviated form of writing able to express any given word. The function of the 'universal real character' would be completely different, because it would not 'signifie *words*, but *things* and *notions*, and consequently might be legible by any Nation in their own Tongue'.[30]

All characters, according to Wilkins, signify either 'Naturally' or 'by *Institution*'. Those that signify 'naturally' are 'Pictures of things' or other images or symbolic representations; the others derive their significance from a freely accepted convention. To this last type belong the 'real characters' which ought to be simple, easy to use, clearly distinguishable, with a pleasing sound and a gracious form and, above all, *methodical*: that is to say, they must reveal the presence of correspondences and relations.[31]

8. There is a univocal relation between signs and things, and every sign corresponds to a particular thing or action ('a distinct

mark was assigned to every thing and notion'): the project of a universal language, then, presupposes an encyclopaedia; it presupposes, that is to say, a complete and orderly enumeration and rigorous classification of all those things and concepts which were to correspond to a sign in the perfect language. Since the efficacy of the universal language depends on how much of the field of experience it aims to encompass and describe, it requires a preliminary classification of everything which exists in the universe and all objects of discourse – it requires, in fact, a total encyclopaedia, the construction of 'perfect tables'. In order to facilitate this total classification and reduction of things and concepts into 'tables', a classificatory method needs to be elaborated, based on the division of things into general categories, genera and differences. Only through this encyclopaedic construction can every sign which is employed function as a sign in the perfect language: providing an exact definition of the signified thing or concept. A 'definition' in the universal language is dependent on the sign itself, which reveals the place which the signified thing or action occupies in the universal order of actions and objects, of which the tables are a mirror.

In the early stages of universal language theory (more or less between 1640 and 1657) the constructors of universal languages adopted a slightly different approach: they began with a collection of all the simplest terms (the 'primitive' or 'radical words') of various natural languages in order to construct an essential dictionary. Wilkins adopted this approach in a work written in 1641, which alludes in its title to an expression once used by Comenius: *Mercury or the Secret and Swift Messenger*. Wilkins considered these radical terms to be in a 'less ambiguous relation with things', because they were not 'derived words'.[32] In England, Francis Lodowick and Cave Beck, in their works on perfect language, were also committed to the search for primitive terms (not unlike Bisterfeld's tables of fundamental terms). Beck used the Arabic numerals from 0 to 9 as characters; the combinations of such characters, expressing all the primitive terms of each language, were arranged in progressive order from 1 to 10,000, which Beck considered sufficient to express all the necessary terms in general use. Each number corresponded to a term in the various languages, and once collected formed a 'numerical dictionary' which could also be arranged alphabetically (according to the word-order of various natural languages) into an 'alphabetical dictionary' if required. Each of the two dictionaries was, to some extent, the 'key' to the other.[33]

The adoption of real characters with its dependent project of the construction of 'complete tables' led, then, into a second line of inquiry – the search for 'radical words'. Once these had been established one could proceed to the 'reduction of all things and concepts to tables'. Wilkins believed that this collection was a task which was more appropriate for an academy and an epoch, than for a single person. The principal difficulty was the completeness and systematization which the collection required. The problem of radical or primitive terms could not be avoided – the tables could not actually contain *everything*. The 'regular enumeration and description of [. . .] things and notions' were restricted to those which were to be included in the universal language or those which commonly 'occurred in discourse'.[34]

The completeness of the language depended, then, on the completeness of the tables, which were a mirror of the order of the real world. In order to achieve a realizable completeness Wilkins retracted the initial requirement that the list of radical words should be exhaustive. He decided that the tables need not contain everything, but only those things of 'the simplest nature'; those of 'more mixed and complicated significance' could be reduced to their prime meanings and expressed periphrastically. The English alphabetical dictionary, which Wilkins included as an appendix to his work, was intended to to demonstrate how *all* the terms of the English language could, in some way, be resolved into the terms listed and ordered in his tables.[35]

In order to facilitate the tabulation of all the things and concepts required for the universal language, Wilkins provided a list of forty generic terms, each of which was subdivided according to six categories of difference (with the exception of some of the zoological and botanical classifications). The first six genera included those categories which 'by reason of their Generalness, or in some other respect, are above all those common heads of things called Predicaments.'[36] These were:

1. General transcendence
2. Mixed transcendental relation

3. Transcendental relation of action
4. Discourse
5. God
6. The World.

The other thirty-four genera were ordered into ten predicaments:

Substance
  7. Element
  8. Stone
  9. Metal
10. Leaf
11. Flower   } Plants
12. Seed
13. Shrub
14. Tree
15. Exanguious animals
16. Fish
17. Bird   } Sanguineous animals
18. Beast
19. Peculiar parts
20. General parts   } parts

Quantity
21. Magnitude
22. Space
23. Measure

Quality
24. Natural power
25. Dwelling
26. Customs
27. Sensible qualities
28. Illness

Action
29. Spiritual
30. Corporeal
31. Movement
32. Operation

Relation

33. Oeconomical ⎫
34. Possessions   ⎬ Private
35. Provisions `   ⎭

36. Civil   ⎫
37. Judicial   ⎪
38. Military   ⎬ Public
39. Naval   ⎪
40. Ecclesiastical ⎭

Each of these 40 genera were further subdivided, according to their differences, and then the various species belonging to each of these differences were listed 'following an order and dependence such that they can contribute to a definition of the differences and of the species, determining their primary significance.' The eighth genus (stone), for example, is divided according to six differences as follows:

Stones can be distinguished into:

    I   Vulgar, of no price
    II Middle-prized
        Precious
    III Less Transparent
    IV More transparent

The terrestial concretions are:
    V Dissoluible
    VI Not Dissoluible

Each of the differences is subdivided into various species. The 'vulgar stones' (first difference) includes, for example, eight species which cannot be simply listed (this device is essential to Wilkins's technique), but are variously regrouped according to their greater or lesser magnitude, their uses, the absence or presence of metals, etc.

These tables occupy a little less than thirty densely packed pages of Wilkins's work. By means of this classification of things and concepts which are 'assigned names in accordance with their respective natures,' Wilkins believed it would be possible to realize the *universal philosophy* which would form the basis of the perfect language, by indicating the order, dependence and relations between the concepts and things. Using letters and conventional signs one would be able to create a universal language which would be the complement of the 'universal philosophy'. The genera (restricting ourselves here to the first nine) are denoted as follows:

General transcendence	Bα
Mixed transcendental relation	Ba
Transcendental relation of action	Be
Discourse	Bi
God	Dα
The world	Da
Stone	Di
Metal	Do

The differences are represented by the consonants B, D, G, P, T, C, Z, S, N ; the species are represented by placing the following signs after the consonants which indicate the differences: α, a, e, i, o, ö, v, yi, yö. For example: *Di* signifies 'stone'; *Dib* signifies the first difference, which is 'vulgar stone'; *Diba* indicates the second species which is 'rock'; *De* signifies 'element'; *Deb* signifies the first difference which is 'fire'; *Deb*α denotes the first species which is 'flame', *Det* will be the fifth difference which is 'meteor' and *Det*α the first species of the fifth difference which is 'rainbow'.

Locating the position which a given term occupies in the tables results in a definition, clearly establishing the 'primary significance of things'. Wilkins's tables provide a reasonable amount of information: for example the significance of the term 'diamond', according to the tables is a substance which is a rock, transparent, coloured, hard, and brilliant. But establishing definitions of terms such as 'goodness', 'moderation' or 'fanaticism' would obviously prove more difficult. The formation of plurals, adjectives, prepositions, pronouns etc. allowed Wilkins to construct (albeit very laboriously) a true language. As an example of the use of this language, he offers a translation of the *Pater noster* and the *Credo* – first in the letters of the alphabet, and then in 'real characters'.[37]

George Dalgarno used a similar method to Wilkins in his *Ars signorum, vulgo character universalis et lingua philosophica* in which he presents a logical classification of all ideas and things, dividing them into seventeen supreme classes:

A. Being, things
η. Substances
E. Accidents
I. Concrete beings (composed of substance and accidents)
O. Bodies
v. Spirit
U. Man (composed of Body and Spirit)
M. Mathematical Concretes.
N. Physical concretes
F. Artificial concretes
B. Mathematical accidents
D. General physical accidents
G. Sensible qualities
P. Sensible accidents
T. Rational accidents
K. Political accidents
S. Common accidents

Each of the seventeen supreme classes is subdivided into sub-classes which are distinguished by the variation of the second letter. Take, for example, the subclass of K:

Kα. Relation of office
Kη. Judicial relation
Ke. Judiciary matter
Ki. Role of the parts
Ko. Role of the judge
Kv. Crimes
Ku. War
Ska. Religion

The terms in each of the subclasses are distinguished by the variation of the final letter. In these terms the letter *s* – when it is

not initial – is 'servile' and does not have a fixed logical meaning, *r* indicates opposition, *l* the median between extremes, *v* is
the initial of the names of numbers. From *Ska* (religion), for
example, the following terms are derived:

> Skam: grace
> Skaη: happiness
> Skaf: adoration
> Skab: judgement
> Skad: prayer
> Skag: sacrifice
> Skap: sacrament
> Skat: mystery
> Skak: miracle

By adding the letter *r* the opposites of these terms are derived, in
this case 'nature' as opposed to 'grace'; 'wretchedness' as opposed
to 'happiness'; 'profanation' which is opposed to 'adoration'; and
'praising' which is opposed to 'praying'.

It is not without significance that in the early years of the
eighteenth century (between 1702 and 1704) when Leibniz was
compiling the extensive tables of definitions which formed a
vital part of his project for a universal encyclopaedia, he made
substantial use of Dalgarno's classifications.[38]

9. In the systems of both Wilkins and Dalgarno the effectiveness
of their complex artificial languages is obviously dependent on
the effectiveness of their mechanical classification of things and
concepts. Proponents of the universal language believed that the
encyclopaedia (the classificational tables and the artificial language which is derived from them) was a 'mirror' of the stucture
of reality. The initial classifications had to be based on the order
of the things themselves; terminological relationships reproduced
real relations:

> By learning the *Character* and *Names* of things, [we shall] be
> instructed likewise in their *Natures*, the knowledg of both
> which ought to be conjoyned. For the accurate effecting of
> this, it would be necessary, that the *Theory* it self, upon which

such a design were to be founded, should be exactly *suted to the nature of things.*[39]

It is not surprising that, given this insistence on the coincidence of the naming function and the actuality of things, Wilkins (who devoted a considerable amount of his energies to the problems of language) shared the Baconian 'antipathy' to rhetorical ornamentation, insisting that *'things* are better than words, as real understanding is beyond *elegancy of speech'.*[40]

5 THE MNEMONIC FUNCTION OF UNIVERSAL LANGUAGES: CLASSIFICATORY METHOD IN THE NATURAL SCIENCES

The characters of the perfect or universal language enable us to locate precisely the position which each thing (or action) occupies in the tables, and thus to locate its position in the universal order (which is mirrored by the *universal philosophy* or encyclopaedia). Through this collocation one would theoretically be able to determine the relationship between the thing signified and other things belonging to the same class or species, and the relationship between it and the differences and genera of which it was an element. In order to facilitate this collocation Wilkins devised a series of mnemonic devices which were designed to help one arrive quickly and easily at precise definitions:

> If these *Marks* or *Notes* could be so contrived, as to have such a *dependance* upon, and relation to, one another, as might be sutable to the nature of the things and notions which they represented, and so likewise, if the *Names* of things could be so ordered, as to contain such a kind of *affinity* or *opposition* in their letters and sounds, as might be some way answerable to the nature of the things which they signified; This would yet be a farther advantage superadded: by which, besides the best way of helping the *Memory* by natural Method, the *Understanding* likewise would be highly improved.[41]

In his perceptive account of Wilkins's work on universal language, Benjamin de Mott emphasized this mnemonic facility of Wilkins's system:

It would be easy to recall the 'foreign' word for salmon if one knew that the word must have two syllables and must begin with *Za*, the symbol for the genus Fish . . . Once he recalled the word *Zana*, [the student] would be able, because of his familiarity with the alphabetic progression of the character, to understand the place of salmon within the genus, and ultimately within the whole scheme of creation.[42]

Wilkins's insistence on the mnemonic value of the universal language was not incidental: a language of this kind seemed to fulfil the hopes and realize the aspirations of all those theorists of the artificial memory who wished (to use the words of Giulio Camillo) 'to arrange in an orderly manner . . . enough memory-places to hold in the mind all human concepts and all the things which are in the world'.[43] All the major theorists of the universal language insist on its mnemonic advantages. Cyprian Kinner, who collaborated with Comenius in 1640 and was the first to formulate the project of an artificial language in detail, saw his language not only as a remedy for the 'Babelian confusion of natural languages', but also (and most importantly) as a powerful 'aid to the memory'. He believed that by using his method, scholars of the natural sciences would be able to memorize even the most difficult and complicated concepts: 'which botanist, even the most expert', he asked, 'can memorize the names and properties of every plant, when there are so many conflicting authorities to compare?' By using the artificial language, whose terms would indicate the nature and the qualities of every single plant, and the position which each plant occupies in the classification by genus and species, this seemingly hopeless task would be made not only possible, but easy: 'by means of the artificial language everything can be remembered and recited without interruptions, just as in a golden chain, if one moves the first ring, all the others move, even if we don't want them to.'[44] Lodowick, Edmondson, and Dalgarno also stressed the mnemonic value of the universal language, while Wilkins frequently emphasized the usefulness of his language as an aid to the weakness of natural memory in his *Essay*. The three thousand terms required by Wilkins's universal language are certainly fewer than the number of words usually required to speak effectively in a natural language, but as Wilkins himself pointed out, these three thousand terms were also 'so ordered by the help of natural method that they may be more easily learned and remembred than a thousand words otherwise disposed of'.[45] In a letter written to Robert Boyle in 1663, John Beale, a member of the Royal Society, recommended the use of 'mnemonical characters' (as he called real characters), because of their ability to introduce order into all the possible combinations of letters, syllables and words.[46]

As Kinner realized, the problem of the mnemonic function of artificial languages was closely related to that of the classification of minerals, plants and animals. An interesting discussion on this topic began in 1666: its protagonist was John Ray, the author of the monumental *Historia plantarum generalis* (1686–1704), one of the greatest scientists of the seventeenth century. Ray, together with Francis Willoughby, was an active collaborator in Wilkins's project, and helped to produce a classification of plants which corresponded to the aims and requirements of the universal language.

According to Wilkins, the encyclopaedic tables in the *Essay Towards a Real Character and Philosophical Language* had more than an auxiliary function. In his view the tables ('especially those concerning natural bodies') would help 'promote and facilitate the understanding of nature' contributing, that is, in a direct way to the research of the members of the Royal Society. Addressing himself to the President and the members of the illustrious academy Wilkins affirmed:

> The ranging of these things into such an order as the Society shall approve, would afford a very good method for your *Repository*, both for the *disposal* of what you have already, and the *supplying* of what you want [. . .] so that in a very Short space you would have the most useful *Repository* in the World.[47]

The ambitions of Wilkins must have been disappointed, but it is certain that his attempt at an orderly, complete classification must have greatly interested those working in the natural sciences who were engaged in classifying limited fields of experience. It has been suggested, and not without justification, that Wilkins was proposing to do with words what Linnaeus later did with plants.[48] 'The principal design aimed at in these Tables', Wilkins wrote,

> is to give a sufficient enumeration of all such things and notions, as are to have names assigned to them, and withall so to contrive

these as to their order, that the place of every thing may contribute to a description of the nature of it. Denoting both the *General* and the *Particular head* under which it is placed, and the *Common difference* whereby it is distinguished from other things of the same kind.[49]

This convergence of interests led to the close collaboration between Wilkins, Willoughby and Ray. The classification of animals and plants in Wilkins's *Essay* was, in fact, the work of the two scientists. Wilkins approached them in 1666 because he wanted to include a 'regular enumeration of all the families of plants and animals,' in the finished work.[50] Ray's interest in Wilkins's project was more than casual: which can be attested by the fact that he painstakingly prepared a Latin translation of Wilkin's book with a view to making it more widely accessible to the scientific community.[51] His differences with Wilkins were largely methodological, and concerned the mnemonic aspects of the universal language. 'In the construction of these tables', Ray wrote to Lister,

> I was not asked to follow the commands of nature, but to adapt the plants to the system of the author. I must divide plants into three troops or classes, if possible equal, and then subdivide each class into differences, taking care that the plants ordered within each difference did not exceed a fixed number [. . .] Who could accept such a method as satisfactory? It seems absurd and most imperfect, I must say frankly that it is an absurd method, because I attach more value to the truth than to my personal reputation.[52]

Like Wilkins, Ray accepted that the schemata of the language were designed to correspond exactly with 'the natures of things,' but unlike Wilkins, Ray found it difficult (at least in the field of botany) to reconcile the structural constraints of the alphabet with the order of nature. The difficulties of classifying plants and animals brought the absolute regularity of the tables (which were essential to the functioning of the perfect language) to a crisis point. Each of the forty genera, Wilkins finally conceded,

> may be subdivided by its peculiar *Differences*; which for the better convenience of this institution, I take leave to determine (for

the most part) to the number of six. Unless it be in those numerous tribes of *Herbs, Trees, Exanguious Animals, Fishes* and *Birds*; which are of too great variety to be comprehended in so narrow a compass.[53]

These questions of methodical classification and division had preoccupied theorists of the *ars reminiscendi* for centuries, and led to the construction of those tables, hierarchies, 'theatres', 'trees', ordinations and classifications, which were (as we have seen) essential components of the artificial memory-arts. These historical precedents helped foster the widespread seventeenth-century conception of the *logica memorativa*, which suggested that there was an essential affinity between logic (as the methodical ordering of knowledge) and memory (as a faculty for keeping the system of all sciences in order). In the late sixteenth century, for example, Ramus defined memory in terms of its ordering function, and thus saw it as a part or subdivision of method, while Bacon saw the *ministratio ad memoriam* (which helped to 'eliminate confusion' through the construction of preliminary tables) as an integral part of his new logic. This belief in the affinity of logic and memory was also behind Descartes's understanding of *enumeratio* as a prosthetic for overcoming the natural debility of human memory. In the same years in which Descartes was developing these ideas in France, the German pedagogue Johann Alsted was defining memory as a 'technique for the ordering of notions.' As 'the mother of order,' he argued, memory should be subsumed as a subordinate part of logic – which he understood as the art of classification, as a method for constructing a *systema mnemonicum* or universal encyclopaedia of the sciences.

It was this conception of 'method' which was inherited by seventeenth century natural philosophers who were engaged in the difficult task of creating an exhaustive, ordered and coherent classification of plants, minerals and animals. Classification was seen as the 'methodical division of the different productions of nature into classes, genera, and species', by means of which a nomenclature could be constructed whose terms would signify the relationships between single elements and the genera and species to which they belonged. In this way the place of each element in a larger system could be clearly understood. It was at precisely the same moment in the mid-eighteenth century when the concept of 'method' reached a crisis point, and the traditional modes of classification were being questioned, that we find the first explicit theorizations of the mnemonic function of classifications and method. These theories frequently appeared in the context of polemical attacks on the classificatory methods of the previous century. Buffon, for example, in defending the principle of exact description, and attacking the botanical tradition of the sixteenth and seventeenth centuries, criticized the idea of 'system' itself, vigorously attacking 'all the methods which have been compiled to aid the memory'.[54] Many of the most important botanists of the eighteenth century had argued in favour of this mnemonic function of method: 'The infinite variety of plants has begun to be burdensome to botanists', wrote Adanson in the preface of his *Familles des plantes*, 'Whose memory can possibly deal with all these names? Therefore botanists themselves have devised methods in order to alleviate this burden.'[55] Fontenelle in an elegy addressed to the Academy on the death of Tournefort praised him for having: 'made possible the orderly disposition of the extraordinary number of plants which are scattered higgledy-piggledy over the surface of the earth, and under the sea, and arranged them into different genera and species, which help ease the burden on the botanist's memory which would otherwise collapse under the weight of an infinity of names'.[56]

To ascertain that these are more than offhand remarks, it will suffice to read the article 'Botanique' in the great enlightenment encyclopaedia:

> Method gives us an idea of the essential properties of each object which is classified, and presents the relationships and oppositions which exist between the different productions of nature . . . for the beginner in the study of natural history, method is like a thread which serves to guide them through a complicated labyrinth, for those who are already expert in the sciences it is a sketch which represents all the facts and helps them remember them if they know them already . . . A single method is sufficient for nomenclature: one must construct a kind of artificial memory for oneself, in order to retain the idea and the name of every plant, because the number of plants is too large to dispense with such an aid to memory; for this purpose any method will suffice.[57]

The virulence and vigour of these polemics and refutations are a vivid testimony to the persistence of *the idea of method as a kind of artificial memory* throughout the preceding century. It was this idea which bore the brunt of the encyclopaedist's attacks: 'These methodical divisions', it is written in the entry on *Histoire naturelle*, 'aid the memory and seem to control the chaos formed by the objects of nature [. . .] but one should not forget that these systems are based on arbitrary human conventions, and do not necessarily accord with the invariable laws of nature.'[58] What we have here is not simply a refutation of the idea of 'memory aids' (an idea which, as we have seen, had been theorized and defended by some of the most important exponents of seventeenth-century science and philosophy), but also a resolutely conventionalist attack on the ancient idea of a total correspondence between the terms of the encyclopaedia and the reality of things.

6 Descartes and Leibniz on universal language

Although it is highly likely that Cartesian mathematicism contributed to the creation of an atmosphere favourable to the projects for a universal language, the extent of this influence is nonetheless difficult to determine. In a letter to Mersenne in November 1629, which was published in Paris in the collection of Clerselier (first published in 1657, and reprinted in 1663 and 1667),[59] and could thus (at least hypothetically) have been read by some of the theorists of universal language, Descartes clearly outlined what he saw as the principal characteristics and aims of a philosophical language, but ultimately his statements are rather ambiguous. He obviously considered the idea of a philosophical language to be a theoretical possibility. If one could 'establish an order for all the thoughts of the human spirit, in the same way that there exists a naturally established order of numbers', he suggested, a 'language' composed of easily and quickly understood characters could be constructed. The invention of this language would depend, however, on 'the prior construction of a true philosophy, because otherwise it would be impossible to enumerate all the thoughts of men and put them into their correct order'. A language of this kind, based on the identification of the 'simple ideas which are in the imagination of men and are the basis of all the things which man can think', would be easy to understand and write and, most importantly would help the judgement to represent things so distinctly that it would be impossible to be mistaken about them, whereas the words which we actually use have mostly confused meanings, to which, at length, man's spirit has become accustomed, and so almost nothing is understood perfectly.[60]

But shortly before this, Descartes had published a utopian narrative in which he expressed serious doubts about the practical possibility of realizing a philosophical language of this kind:

> I maintain that this language is possible and that it would be possible to discover the science on which it depends: by means of which the peasant would be able to judge the truth of things as well as the philosophers . . . but you should not hope to see it in use: for that would presuppose great changes in the order of things, and would require the world to be nothing less than an earthly paradise, which can only be found in the countries of romances.[61]

Descartes was clear about one thing: that there was a necessary relationship between the perfect language and the 'true philosophy' upon which it would be based (what Wilkins called 'universal philosophy' or the 'encyclopaedia'). Descartes saw this as a relationship of dependence: without an orderly list of all the possible thoughts of man, from which one would derive the list of the 'simple ideas', the construction of a universal language would be illusory and impossible. Dalgarno and Wilkins had attempted such a total classification of concepts and things. Leibniz, who based his own work on these earlier attempts, explicitly rejected Descartes's position (referring directly to the published letter to Mersenne, which we have just been examining). 'Although this language depends on true philosophy', Leibniz argued,

> it does not depend on its perfection. Let me just say this: this language can be constructed despite the fact that philosophy is not perfect. The language will develop as scientific knowledge develops. While we are waiting, it will be a miraculous aid: to help us understand what we already know, and to describe what we do not know, and help us to find the means to obtain it, but above

all it will help us to eliminate and extinguish the controversial arguments which depend upon reason, because once we have realized this language, calculating and reasoning will be the same thing.[62]

CHAPTER EIGHT
The Sources of Leibniz's Universal Character.

In a letter written from Frankfurt in April 1671 Leibniz enthusiastically acclaimed John Wilkins's book on the universal language: 'I have said little of the *Universal Character* of the learned Wilkins; his tables please me greatly and I wish that he had used diagrams to express those things which cannot be described other than by pictures, as for example, the kinds of animals, plants and instruments. A Latin translation of the work would be a very desirable thing!' In a letter to Henry Oldenburg two years later, Leibniz was still hoping that a translation would soon be published. We have to wait until 1679–80, after the years of his residence in London and Paris, before we find Leibniz expressing any reservations about the work: 'I understand that that famous man [Robert Hooke] shared my good opinion of Bishop Wilkins's "philosophical Character" ', he wrote, 'But I must say, however, that it would be possible to realize something much greater and much more useful – something that would be superior to it in the same way that algebraic characters are superior to the characters of the chemists'.[1]

The comparison between algebraic characters and the notation used by the chemists is very significant. For Leibniz was not only concerned with constructing a language which was able to facilitate communication, but to develop a universal writing which could be used, like algebraic and arithmetical symbols, to *construct demonstrations*. The different opinions expressed by Leibniz in these letters confirms once again (in relation to a particular problem) the validity of those arguments which suggest that Leibniz's sojourn in London and Paris (from March 1672 to October 1676) was a watershed in his thought. In these years Leibniz dedicated himself to the study of mathematics and came into contact with Cartesianism, and other vigorous currents of European thought. A profound interest in the syntactic aspects of language, the discovery of the 'magic of the algorithm' or the 'functionality' of formal procedures, and a belief in the possibility of a general science of forms: these were the themes and discussions which preoccupied Leibniz in his mature years – problems which presuppose a familiarity with the methods of mathematics, algebra and the *combinatoria*.

The Leibnizian project of a universal character was based (as we know) on three principles: 1) that ideas are analysable, and that it would be possible to construct a catalogue or 'alphabet' of simple and primitive notions; 2) that ideas can be represented symbolically, and 3) that it would be possible to represent the relations between ideas and (provided one could find the right rules) to combine them. This project did not originate, however, in the 'algebra' or 'formal logic' of his contemporaries.[2] Willy Kabitz, whilst working in the Hannover Bibliothek, discovered an edition of the works of Johann Heinrich Bisterfeld which had been extensively annotated by Leibniz, and it seems certain that it was from Bisterfeld (rather than from the Lullist tradition in general) that Leibniz derived the idea (which was fundamental to his *combinatorial logic*) of an alphabet of human thoughts, or a catalogue of primitive notions which could be combined to form complex ideas.[3] In a letter, probably written to the Baron of Boineburg, which contains one of the first formulations of his plans for a universal character, Leibniz seems to be proposing a project which does not substantially differ from that of Athanasius Kircher: he believed that the figures of circles, squares and triangles, arranged in various ways, could be used to represent concepts and fundamental notions. By combining these figures in various ways one would be able to express the relations and combinations of ideas. In Leibniz's *Dissertatio de arte combinatoria* of 1666, we find references not only to Bisterfeld and Kircher, but also to Lull, Bruno, Agrippa, Pierre Grégoire, Alsted, Bacon and Hobbes.[4] Leibniz's criticisms of Lull were not directed against the basic principle of the *combinatoria*: he was more concerned about the arbitrariness of Lull's classes and roots, and the insufficiency of his method of combination. He refers to Bacon because he had included an 'inventive logic' among his many lists of *desiderata*; his reference to Hobbes concerns his identification of all mental operations with *computatio*. It would be a mistake to place too much emphasis on this last reference: Leibniz was not in any sense a 'Hobbesian'; his interest in Hobbes is limited to Hobbes's view of logic as a kind of 'calculus', an idea which was also a commonplace found in a wide range of Lullist texts. Hobbes's influence on

Leibniz's universal character (as Louis Couturat has convincingly argued) is very slight, and Leibniz's interpretation of the calculus was very different from that of Hobbes.[5] The most significant sources of Leibniz's ideas are Lullist and encyclopaedic works, especially the influential commentaries of Bruno, Agrippa, and Alsted. In the *Syntaxes* of Grégoire he found a vigorous expression of the search for a general science based on the determination of a limited series of axioms and principles, while many of his ideas on the universal language were derived from Caspar Schott's *Technica curiosa sive mirabilia artis* – one of the most characteristic texts of seventeenth-century Jesuit 'magic'.[6]

The fundamental problem of inventive logic, which is expounded in the *Dissertatio de arte combinatoria*, is that of finding all the possible predicates of a given subject and, given a predicate, finding all its possible subjects. In the interests of economy we will ignore many of the technical complexities of this question, and concentrate instead on an example (taken from Belaval's exposition) of how Leibniz tackled this problem. In order to solve this problem it is necessary to select a series of simple and primitive ideas which can be denoted by conventional signs. These are the terms of the first class: 1) the point, 2) space, 3) interposition, 4) contiguity, . . . 9) part, 10) whole, 11) sameness, 12) difference, 13) the One, 14) number, 15) plurality, 16) distance, 17) the possible, etc. By combining pairs of terms of the first class (*com2natio*) we obtain terms of the second class. For example, quantity (the number of parts) is represented by the formula 14τωv9 (15). By combining the terms in groups of three (*com3natio*) we obtain terms of the third class: for example, *intervallum* is 2.3.10, which is to say that an 'interval' may be defined as 'the space (2) placed within (3) a whole (10)'. And so on for *com4natio*, *com5natio*, etc. In order to find all the predicates of a determinate subject, one must subdivide a term into its prime factors, and then determine all the possible combinations of these factors. The possible predicates of 'interval' are, for example, space (2), interposition (3), the whole (10), these are taken one at a time and subjected to *com2natio*, which gives us 'interposed space' (2.3), 'total space' (2.10), and 'interstitial space' (3.10); finally, through *com3natio*, we produce 2.3.10 which is the definition of 'interval'. To find all the possible subjects of 'interval' (as a predicate) we need to single out all the terms whose definition contains the factors 2.3.10. All the combinations derived from these factors belong necessarily to the classes of complex notions which are above the one to which 'interval' belongs (the third class). 'Line', for example, which is defined as 'an interval between two points,' belongs to the fourth class because one needs the four primitive terms 2, 3, 10 and 1 ('point') in order to define it. Given a number of simple terms n, and the number of prime factors constituting a predicate, k $(n > k)$, there will be 2^{n-k} possible subjects (the tautological proposition of 'an interval is an interval' is obviously included in this number).[7]

Leibniz's character, as Couturat has noted, was not initially conceived as a form of calculus or algebra, but as a universal language or writing.[8] The *ars combinatoria*, as far as Leibniz was concerned, involved the invention of a 'universal writing, intelligible to any trained reader, regardless of their native language'. Among the many texts on universal language written by his contemporaries, Leibniz (following the exposition by Schott) singles out the *Arithemeticus nomenclator mundi*, an anonymous work published in Rome in 1653 in which 'the method was quite ingeniously derived from the nature of things: the author distributed things into various classes, and all the classes were formed from a determinate number of things':[9] to designate any object one simply indicated the number of the class and the number of the object. The other two works which Leibniz mentioned were the *Character pro notitia linguarum universali* of Johann Joachim Becher (Frankfurt, 1661), and the *Polygraphia nova et universalis ex combinatoria arte detecta* of Athanasius Kircher (Rome, 1663). Both of these works outline languages which are based on the construction of a numerical dictionary of the type found in Cave Beck's *Universal Character* (London, 1653).

It has become a commonplace in historical accounts of Leibniz's career to contrast the clear, coherent and 'scientific' plan for a universal language constructed by Leibniz to the 'formless outlines' and 'hazy and confused' projects for a universal language formulated by his 'predecessors'. In reality (when one does not dismiss them as 'predecessors' so as to avoid the trouble of having to read them) things are a little different. When Leibniz first formulated his project for a universal language in the *Dissertatio de arte combinatoria*, he was unfamiliar with the *Ars signorum* of Dalgarno, published in 1661, and, obviously, with the *Essay* of Wilkins (which only came out in 1668). At this time, Leibniz (following Kircher and Bacon) thought that the characters of a universal language ought to be composed of 'geometrical figures and pictures of the type used in the time of the Egyptians, and used today by the Chinese; pictures which cannot be reduced to a fixed alphabet, or to letters, which are a terrible impediment to the memory'.[10] His reservations concerning the work of Becher were very similar to those of Wilkins (which had been formulated independently): he was troubled by the ambiguity of words (which had different meanings in various languages), the lack of exact synonyms, and the diversity of syntactic rules, which made it practically impossible to establish a precise correspondence between words in different languages. He was also concerned by the difficulty of retaining the vast number of numerical characters (which designated not only classes, but the single objects belonging to them) in the memory. A universal language or writing which could avoid these dangers would need to be based on a total analysis of concepts and their reduction to simple terms.[11]

At the beginning of 1671 Leibniz read Wilkins's *Essay on the Real Character* and, probably at around the same time, George Dalgarno's *Ars signorum*. His enthusiasm for the work of Wilkins, and his desire to see the *Essay* translated into Latin so that it would reach a wider European audience, was understandable. He saw in the *Essay* and the *Ars signorum* the realization (at least in part) of that universal language which was both 'artificial' and 'philosophical', which he had inaugurated in his *Dissertatio*: a language which was constructed on the basis of a classification of concepts rather than on a correspondence between dictionaries. Leibniz's criticisms of Dalgarno and Wilkins emerged, as we have seen, during the years of his residence in Paris: in a note written in his copy of the *Ars signorum* and in a letter to Oldenburg (written from Paris) Leibniz criticized the two English authors for having been more concerned with developing a language which would facilitate commerce between nations, than with creating a truly 'philosophical' language which would be able to represent the logical relations between concepts. The convenience of an internationally comprehensible language, Leibniz said, was only one of the peripheral benefits of developing a universal language: it was, first and foremost, an *instrumentum rationis*.[12] But, despite his criticisms of the English writers, Leibniz's conception of the universal language (his use of the term 'real character' is derived from Bacon rather than Wilkins) was in many respects quite traditional, and some of the claims he made about the universal language reveal just how close his own ideas were to those of the English theorists:

1. The universal language or real character is a system of signs which 'represent thoughts directly, rather than words', so that it can be read and understood irrespective of the language which one actually speaks.[13]

2. The construction of a universal language coincides with that of a universal writing: 'It does not matter whether we want to construct only a universal writing or a universal language: it is just as easy, in fact, to devise both at the same time.'[14]

3. Although he claimed to be departing from tradition, Leibniz saw Egyptian hieroglyphs, Chinese writing, and chemical symbols as examples of real characters: 'I consider the hieroglyphs of the Egyptians and the Chinese and, in Europe, the signs used by the chemists to be examples of a real character, as other authors have previously established.'[15]

4. The universal language can be learnt in a very short time (in 'a few weeks', Leibniz says, like Dalgarno before him) and could be used for the propagation of the Christian faith and for the education of people in foreign lands:

> This writing or language . . . can be spread very rapidly through the world, because it can be learnt in a few weeks and gives us a way of communicating wherever we happen to be; for that reason it will be of great importance for spreading the faith and for the instruction of people in distant lands.[16]

5. Learning the universal language would coincide with learning the encyclopaedia, or systematic ordination of fundamental notions. He considered the project of the encylopaedia to be organically linked to that of the universal language and inseparable from it: 'One who learns this language, learns at the same time the encyclopaedia which is the true entrance to the sciences.'[17]

6. The learning of the universal language was, in itself, a remedy for the weakness of the memory: 'Once this language has been learnt no one will forget it, or, having forgotten it, could easily acquire it again simply by relearning the essential words.'[18]

7. The superiority of the universal language to Chinese writing stems from the fact that the connections between the characters would correspond to the order of things, and the connections between them: 'It can be learnt in a few weeks because, unlike Chinese, the characters are linked to each other according to the order and connection of things.'[19]

Leibniz's project differed from those of his predecessors in two fundamental respects:

1. The characters of his universal language would express the relations between thoughts, and (like algebraic and arithmetical notation) could be used for invention and judgement. 'This writing', Leibniz wrote in 1679, 'will be a kind of general algebra and a calculus of reason, so that, instead of disputing, we can say that "we calculate". And we will be able to discover errors in reasoning, just as we can discover errors in particular calculations in arithmetic, by means of proof.' The project of a universal or philosophical language, which Leibniz took up with renewed vigour after reading Wilkins and Dalgarno, was similar in many ways to the combinatorial logic which he developed in his *De arte combinatoria*, which culminated in the construction of an *ars inveniendi* conceived as a kind of calculus.[20]

2. The construction of the universal language was seen not just as a means of communication, but also as a direct contribution to the realization of the *ars inveniendi*. The name (or sign) attributed to a particular object or concept in the universal language not only designated the relations between the thing signified and other things belonging to the same class or species, and identified the 'position' which the object occupied in the scheme of the universe, but also 'indicated the experiments which must be rationally undertaken in order to expand our understanding':

I admit that we cannot extract from the name which we have attributed to gold (for example) those chemical phenomena which are revealed only by time and circumstance, because we cannot derive enough information from a limited number of phenomena to allow us to determine other phenomena. Nonetheless, the name which is given to gold in this language would be the key to everything which can be possibly known about gold, rationally and in an orderly fashion, and would reveal what experiments ought to be rationally undertaken in connection with gold.

In a long fragment entitled *Lingua generalis* (written in February 1678) we find Leibniz's first system of logical calculus, which he saw as the foundation of his project for a universal language.[21] In order to transform the character (composed of numerical symbols) into a language which could be 'spoken', Leibniz had recourse (as Couturat has explained)[22] to the methods developed by Dalgarno and Wilkins, substituting the nine prime consonants (*b, c, d, f, g, h, l, m, n*) for the numbers from 1 to 9, and the five vowels for the decimal units in ascending order (1, 10, 100, 1,000, 10,000). For higher units he allowed the use of diphthongs. Thus the number 81,374 is written and is pronounced *Mubodilefa*. Since every syllable indicates, by means of a vowel, its decimal order, the value of the syllable itself is independent of the place it occupies in the word. The same number can be expressed with the term *Bodifalemu* which signifies 1,000 + 300 + 4 + 70 + 80,000 = 81,374.[23]

This is not the place to attempt a full exposition of Leibniz's theories of rational grammar, or to examine his attempts at simplifying the grammar and syntax of Latin, a project to which he returned (after failed attempts at constructing an artificial language) as a possible 'intermediary' between living languages and the future universal language.[24] It is clear, however, that the problem of compiling a dictionary of primitive terms confronted Leibniz with similar problems to those which had been experienced by many of the English theorists of the perfect language. If the name of every object or notion was to express the definition of the object or notion, so that the words of the artificial language were adequate, and as transparent as those of the Adamic language, it would be necessary to select the prime and simple elements which comprise the 'alphabet' of thought. But to realize this alphabet would require an inventory of all human knowledge, which would be set out in an encyclopaedia in which all notions would be classified according to a unitary system, and reducible to a limited number of fundamental categories:

The character which I am proposing requires a new sort of encyclopaedia. The encyclopaedia is a body in which the most important human notions are placed in systematic order. Once the encyclopaedia is made according to the order which I have proposed, the Character will be virtually finished.[25]

In the numerous outlines, fragments, plans, chapters and sections offered as provisional models (*specimina*) which he addressed to societies and academies, princes and kings, throughout his life, Leibniz presented his project for a universal encyclopaedia not simply as a classification or repository of previously acquired knowledge, but as a 'demonstrative' method, which would be useful in directing scientific research.[26] For evidence concerning the 'sources' of many of these projects we must turn to the testimonies of Leibniz himself. In the *Nova methodus iurisprudentiae*, for example, we find explicit references to Lavinheta, whose collection of fundamental juridical terms Leibniz saw as a potential foundation for an encyclopaedia of law.[27] In a letter written in 1714, Leibniz spoke of the profound influence which Ivo Paris's *Digestum sapientiae* had had upon him as a young man.[28] Leibniz returned many times to the work of Johann Alsted: in the *Dissertatio* of 1666 he discussed his Lullian works, in 1671 he wrote a brief work about perfecting and improving Alsted's encyclopaedia, and was still speaking of him with admiration in 1681.[29] His debt to Comenius is even more significant: at one point he said that his own encyclopaedia 'was not substantially different from that of Comenius', and it was from the works of Comenius that Leibniz derived one of the most important theses of his work: that the universal language and the encylopaedia were coidentical.[30]

As we have already seen in his response to Descartes's letter to Mersenne on the universal language, Leibniz was conscious of the 'parallelism' between the projects for a universal language and the encyclopaedia. In that undated passage, he denied that the universal character was strictly dependent on the encyclopaedia: 'Although this language depends on true philosophy', Leibniz argued, 'it does not depend on its perfection. Let me just say this: this language can be constructed despite the fact that philosophy is not perfect.'[31] Leibniz was not absolutely certain about this point, however, and in a letter to Burnet, dated August 24th 1697 he seems to contradict himself, when he says that 'the characters presuppose the true philosophy and it is only now that I dare to begin its construction'.[32] This difference in viewpoint, Francesco Barone has argued, corresponds to 'the two ways in which Leibniz viewed the universal character, seeing it both as an absolute metaphysical instrument, and as an instrument for the construction of particular deductive systems'.[33]

There is a lot of truth in this observation. The universal character as an instrument, as a calculus modelled on the formalism of algebra, does not require the preliminary foundation of the true philosophy: the universal character and the encyclopaedia merge into each other and proceed together step by step. Continuing, however, to see the universal character as a 'universal key' – as an instrument for revealing essences and deciphering the alphabet of the world which corresponds to the alphabet of thought – Leibniz was forced to confront the same problem which had troubled the English theorists of the perfect language: how to construct a 'universal philosophy' which could be used as a basis and foundation for the philosophical language.

To get some idea of how Leibniz approached this problem, it will be sufficient to examine the extensive encyclopaedic tables which Leibniz composed between 1703 and 1704.[34] After having drafted numerous plans and fragments of encylopaedias, Leibniz turned once again to the method used by Wilkins and Dalgarno. In these pages the encylopaedia takes the form of a logical classification (based on the scholastic distinction between substances and accidents) of the principal concepts of all the sciences (from mathematics to ethics and politics), all natural objects (from minerals to plants and living beings) and all artificial objects (utensils and instruments constructed by man). Leibniz's tables reproduce, with a few negligible differences, the classifications of George Dalgarno's *Ars signorum*:

Things (*Res*):	Accidents (*Accidentia*):
mathematical concrete	common accidents
physical concrete	mathematical accident
artificial concrete	general physical accident
spiritual concrete	sensible qualities
	sensitive accidents
	rational accident
	economic accident
	political accident

Even within the various classes and subclasses Leibniz reproduces Dalgarno's original classification. For both Leibniz and Dalgarno, for example, the class of 'political accidents' comprises: the relation of office, the judiciary relation, judiciary matter, the role of parties, the role of the judge, crimes, war and religion. Even in the list of single terms contained in each class and subclass, Leibniz adhered closely to Dalgarno's scheme.

The important project (in historical terms) of a 'demonstrative' encylopaedia seems here to have been abandoned. The reasons for this change of perspective requires a separate study in itself. I shall restrict myself here to pointing out that the influence of the English theorists of the universal language was not limited to Leibniz's youthful writings.

As we have already noted, the works dedicated to the construction of philosophical or universal languages were all agreed on the mnemonic value of the real character. The numerous references to this issue in the works of Leibniz are extremely significant. Like Descartes and Bacon before him, Leibniz was interested in this problem, which had been extensively debated across Europe, by writers on artificial memory. For Leibniz's interest in the *ars reminiscendi* we need to examine a group of unpublished papers: Phil.VI.19, a collection of notes entitled *mnemonica sive praecepta varia de memoria excolenda*, and Phil.VII.B.III.7 which contains a second collection of notes and epitomes of works on the *ars memorativa*. Towards the beginning of these manuscript notes we find a discussion of a series of mnemonic devices employing a combination of alphabetic letters and numbers:

> *A secret*: From the methods used for memorizing numerical calculations, especially those which are used for chronology, and many other kinds of things, we can deduce an infinite number of other, more advanced methods, so that one can memorize things so that they cannot be forgotten, without overburdening the intellect with the effort of remembering.
>
> If you wish to memorize many numbers without overburdening the intellect or the memory, all the work should be done by using some kind of assistance. Many have attempted various things of this kind without much effect or success, until recently someone invented this method of excogitation, which has been proven by many reasons and by experience.

There are twenty four letters in the alphabet: these are divided into vowels and consonants. These vowels are useful only for substitution, whereas the consonants are of primary importance.

The consonants are: B C D F G K L M N P Q R S T, to which can be added W Z and V. We also have these numbers: 1 2 3 4 5 6 7 8 9 0. Many numbers can be produced using these, so that 1 and 2 together produce the number 12. How this is done is clearly understood.

While it is true that nothing causes so much difficulty for the memory as dealing with things by means of numbers, nevertheless, those who are truly interested in knowing and understanding things by means of the memory will adhere to this method, because using it is conducive to the memory and helps us enhance it.

Reduce the consonants in this way, and treating them as if they were numbers, it will then be easy for you to extricate them [from the memory]:

1 2 3 4 5 6 7 8 9 0
B C F G L M N R S D
P K V
W Q
   Z[35]

The mnemonic use of verses of poetry, which was a commonplace of the mnemotechnical texts of the fifteenth and sixteenth centuries, features in another of these pages of notes, in which Leibniz translates verses 33–42 of Marciano of Eraclea's *Geography* into Latin:

This sight, therefore, should be easily and clearly
ordered in verse, the way comic actors do.
For in this way the memory is helped and the
sensation does not fade away, and a similitude
of life is shown to us. One who wishes to carry
a pile of loose sticks is hindered by difficulty,
But when the cut sticks are bundled together they

are easy to carry. The parts of an oration, flowing
in different directions, are likewise remembered
more faithfully if they are held together in verse.[36]

Before some critical notes on the *Lexicon* of Hoffmann
(Antwerp, 1698), we find further references to the mnemonic uses
of poetry in some brief notes on the grammar of Emmanuel
Alvarez (Dilingae, 1574 and Venice, 1580) and the *Grammatica
philosophica* of Gaspar Schoppe (Amsterdam, 1659):

These things which can be found in the grammar of Emmanuel
Alvarez SJ are praised by Scioppius in his *Grammatica philosophica*,
and he urges us to learn them. He deals with all the rules for
preterite and supine verbs in the well-turned periods of one
hundred and sixty hexametrical verses and the whole method of
Latin prosody in another one hundred and sixty verses.[37]

Hoffmann's *Lexicon universale maxime nominum propriorum utilis
liber*. I have one wish: when an author cannot explain a multitude of things all together, it would be an excellent thing if he
would indicate another author from whom one can get the facts
more quickly.[38]

In some pages headed *Artificium didacticum* and *Exercitia ingenii* we
find other typical precepts of the mnemonic art:

Teaching device. Always mix and blend things which are unknown
with things that are known so that it reduces the amount of
work and trouble. Just as it is easier for us to learn languages in
parallel with a language which we already know, so if we wish to
select a passage for study in order to learn the language, we
choose one from a book which we have already learnt by heart
such as the New Testament. Likewise if we wish to teach a piece
of music, we can refer to the notes of a song written on paper if
we are afraid of forgetting them.[39]

Intellectual exercises. Just as rhetoricians practice their orations, and
grammarians write practise compositions, so I wish to institute
intellectual exercises for children. It requires no more effort to
invent agreeable and effective intellectual exercises than it does

to invent games for them . . . words in a confused order, with the help of mnemonic aids, can be recited from memory, in reverse order as well as section by section, if you wish – stories, such as extemporary descriptions of battles, journey or towns, which have been recited to them by others can be summarized and repeated out loud, and prayers can be composed and ordered so that it teaches them how to resolve the two sides of a debate or construct their own disputations.[40]

A little further on Leibniz makes an extensive and analytical epitome of Adam Bruxius's *Simonides redivivus sive ars memoriae et oblivionis* (Leipzig, 1610),[41] but we also find references, alongside these expositions of traditional mnemonic precepts, to theorists of the geometrical method, whom Leibniz criticises for having neglected the primary propositions which underly all discourse in their investigations:

> I notice that those who deal with the science of geometrical method . . . such as Honoré Fabri, Giovanni Alfonso Borelli, Benedict Spinoza and Rene Descartes, while they tear propositions up into minute fragments, do not give sufficient thought to the primary propositions which underlie these fragments, so that it often makes invention difficult.[42]

We have lingered over these unpublished notes, not because they are of particular interest, but because they reveal how Leibniz's numerous references to memory and mnemotechnics arose not (as has hitherto been believed) from the works of Kircher, but from a detailed knowledge of more specialized mnemotechnical works such as Bruxius's *Simonides redivivus*, which was widely read in the seventeenth century. This conclusion can be confirmed by a cursory examination of the notes contained in the manuscript Phil.VII.B.III.7. In a note dated April 1678, for example, we find, in addition to some rules for the construction of a rational grammar, some observations on mnemotechnics. In these notes we find references to the ancient doctrine of *loci* and *imagines*; the reduction of concepts and ideas to sensible figures; the use of easily memorizable figures such as the names of the patriarchs, the apostles, or Roman emperors; precepts relating to order and the *collocatio in locis*; the use of animal images; and devices relating to words in 'barbarous' languages. It is clear from these notes that Leibniz had read and annotated not only the works of Bruxius, but (as we can see from the first four folios of the manuscript) the works of Schenkel, focusing particularly on those parts of his work which dealt with the learning of Latin, the education of children, rhetoric, and the rules of the *ars reminiscendi*.[43]

These interests were not without influence on Leibniz's approach to more general problems: he saw the art of memory as fulfilling a particular function in the domain of knowledge, and he often compared the mnemotechnical art to logic. In the *Nova methodus discendae docendaeque iurisprudentiae* (1667) he presents mnemonics, topics and analysis as the three parts of *didactica*; in the *Consilium de encyclopaedia nova conscribenda methodo inventoria* (1679), he placed mnemonics between logic and topics; in the *Initia et specimina scientiae novae generalis* 'wisdom' (*sagesse*), or 'the perfect understanding of the principles of all the sciences and the art of applying them' is subdivided into the 'art of reasoning' (*art de bien raisonner*), the 'art of invention' (*art d'inventer*) and the 'art of remembering' (*art de souvenir*). In a letter to Koch in 1708, Leibniz expressed his approval of Ramus's thesis (which had subsequently been taken up by Bacon) that the *ars memoriae* is a part or subsection of logic. Leibniz repeatedly emphasized the mnemonic function of the universal language, the encylopaedia, the tables, and the real character itself: the characters and figures were seen by Leibniz (in accordance with tradition) as a means of strengthening the imagination. Like Bacon, Alsted, Comenius and Wilkins before him, he considered the encyclopaedic tables to be an indispensable aid to the natural debility of the memory:

> *Combinatoria*: those who find it difficult to focus their imagination can be helped by figures and characters; those who who do not have a strong memory, and are not able to retain many things in their memory at the same time can be aided by the use of tables.[44]

In his numerous projects for the real character, universal language, and the encyclopaedia at the end of the seventeenth century, Leibniz gave renewed vigour to the debates on *combinatoria*, the alphabet of thoughts, the universal language and the art of memory which had been initiated by the encyclopaedists of the fifteenth and sixteenth centuries. This inheritance was no negligible part of Leibniz's philosophy. In 1679, thirteen years after the publication of his *Dissertatio de arte combinatoria*, after his sojourns in Paris and London, and his great mathematical 'discoveries', Leibniz spoke again about his invention in tones which are reminiscent of the 'miraculous' and 'magical' claims of the Lullist treatises and mnemotechnical manuals of the sixteenth century:

> My invention contains all the functions of reason: it is a judge for controversies; an interpreter of notions; a scale for weighing probabilities; a compass which guides us through the ocean of experience; an inventory of things; a table of thoughts; a microscope for scrutinizing things close at hand; a telescope for discerning distant things; a general calculus; an innocent magic; a non-chimerical cabala; a writing which everyone can read in his own language; and finally a language which can be learnt in a few weeks, travelling swiftly across the world, carrying the true religion with it, wherever it goes.[45]

These are not words prompted by a desire to be intellectually fashionable, or a cynical appropriation of a contemporary philosophical vocabulary: like the followers of Lull and the theorists of pansophia before him, Leibniz genuinely believed that it was possible to find a method which would be a key to reality; that it was possible to find a general science which would reveal the full correspondence between the original and constitutive forms of reality and the structures of reason or thought. General science, he argued,

> is not only a logic . . . but also an art of invention (*ars inveniendi*) and a method for ordering knowledge (*methodus disponendi*), a synthesis and analysis, a pedagogy (*didactica*) and a science of teaching, it is a noology and an art of memory and mnemonics, an *ars characteristica* or *symbolica*, a philosophical grammar, a Lullian art, a cabala of the wise, and a natural magic.[46]

The set of themes which Leibniz derived from the traditions of Lullist encyclopaedism, pansophia and the universal language were not of secondary importance in his philosophical work. These traditions had a profound influence on one of the central themes of his philosophy: the concept of a 'general science' which is a kind of 'natural magic' (albeit an 'innocent' one), which can reveal the rational processes underlying the cosmos, and clarify the structure of reality. 'The art', Leibniz said in the *Dissertatio*,

> leads the obedient soul through the infinite universe, and brings together the harmony of the world, the innermost constructions of things and the series of forms.[47]

The universal language 'reveals the interior forms of things',[48] and the abstractions of reason have their basis in the ideal fabric of reality: 'If our soul cannot find the *genus* of things . . . God knows it, and the angels can find it, and there is a foundation which pre-exists all these abstractions'.[49] In the *Confessio naturae* of 1668, Leibniz put forward the idea of a universal harmony which originates in the divine spirit,[50] while in a letter of 1704, he explicitly formulated a Platonic-Pythagorean conception of reality:

> What is the cause of the harmony of things? Nothing: for example, one cannot give any reason for the fact that the relation between 2 and 4 is the same as that between 4 and 8, even if you are inspired by the divine will. This fact depends on the essence or idea of things. The essences of things are in fact numbers, and constitute the possibility of entities. They were not created by God, since these possibilities, or ideas of things are coincident with God himself. It is impossible that God, being the most perfect mind, would not love perfect harmony.[51]

Leibniz returned to these themes, and developed them more extensively, in a series of texts written in 1675–6, which Jagodinski collected and published in 1913.[52] These texts seem to confirm Rivaud's claim that

> the principle of harmony was the centre around which all the ideas of Leibniz crystallized, and this same principle appears, from the beginning, to have been not only a simple logical law but an aesthetic and moral necessity.[53]

In the *Elementa philosophiae arcanae*, in which Leibniz states that 'to exist is nothing other than to be harmonious' (*existere nihil aliud esse quam harmonicum esse*), we find an explicit theorization of the logical order of the cosmos: 'what distinguishes one substance from another', he says, 'is its situation in the rational context of the universe.'[54] Leibniz made similar claims in a letter to Frederick, claiming to be able to demonstrate the existence of an 'ultimate order of things, or universal harmony' (*ratio ultima rerum seu harmonia universalis*), and in a letter of 1678 to the Duchess Elizabeth,[55] where he argued that the universal characters and the simple constitutive elements of reality were coidentical:

> The universal character will represent our thoughts truly and distinctly and when a thought is composed of other thoughts, its character will also be composite . . . Simple thoughts are the basic elements of the universal character, and simple forms are the original sources of all things

Appendices

APPENDIX I
THE *LIBER AD MEMORIAM CONFIRMANDAM* OF RAMON LULL

The *Liber ad memoriam confirmandam*, published here for the first time, was composed by Lull between 1307 and 1308. Lull had arrived in Pisa from Genoa in the last months of 1307, after an eventful journey which culminated in a shipwreck, which he described as follows: 'The Saracens permitted him [Lull] to board a ship bound for Genoa, which most fortunately arrived at Pisa Harbour, shortly before it broke into ten thousand pieces, and the Christian [Lull] barely escaped with his skin, and lost all his books and belonging' (*Saraceni ipsum [Lullum] miserunt in quandam navem tendentem Genovam, quae navis cum magna fortuna venit ante Portum Pisanum; et prope ipsum per decem millaria fuit fracta, et Christianus [Lullus] vix quasi nudus evasit, et amisit omnes libros suos et sua bona*).[1] In Pisa Lull completed, amongst other things, a draft of his *Ars magna generalis ultima* which he had begun in Lyon in 1305 and he planned a crusade, hoping to get the backing of the Republic to recommend his scheme to the Pope and the cardinals. In the first months of 1308 (March–April) Lull was back in Genoa, and then went on to Montpellier. The date of the composition given by Salvador Galmés – January 1308 – thus seems extremely probable.[2] It is to Galmés that we also owe a short but accurate biography of Lull, the *Vida compendiosa del Bt. Ramón Lull* (Palma de Mallorca, 1915).

The text of the short Lullian work which follows is preserved in three sixteenth-century manuscripts: Bibliotheca Ambrosiana MS I. 153 inf., ff. 35r.–39v. (indicated by the initial B); Münich Staatsbibliothek MS 10593, ff. 1v.–3v. (indicated by the initial M); and Paris, Bibliotheque Nationale MS 17839, ff. 437r.–444v. (indicated by the initial P). The B manuscript undoubtedly belongs to a different textual tradition than the other two manuscripts which share some common characteristics in relation to B (a different *incipit*, the absence of chapter subdivisions, the same lacunae, different terminology etc.). P has some lacunae which are not present in M. It seems improbable that M was derived from P, or that P was derived from M: the differences between the two manuscripts depend in the majority of cases on different interpretations of abbreviations present in the original text or in a common subarchetype (see for example the variants corresponding to notes 15, 70, 130 and 146).

[B 35r., M 1r., P 437r.] In nomine Sanctissimae Trinitatis incipit liber ad memoriam confirmandam.[1] Ratio quare presentem volumus colligere tractatum est ut memoria hominum[2] quae labilis est et caduca modo rectificetur meliori.[3] Ipsum quidem dividimus in duas partes principales,[4] subsequenter in plures. Prima igitur pars est Alphabetum ideo ut sequitur ipsum diffinimus.[5]

CAP. I[6]

Alphabetum ponimus in hoc tractatu ut per ipsum possimus memoriam diffinire[7] et in certis et[8] terminatis principiis ipsam[9] in duabus ponere potentiis. Primo[10] igitur b. significat memoriam naturalem, c. significat capacitatem, d. significat[11] discretivam. Quid tamen[12] sit naturalis memoria, quid capacitas, quid discretiva, vade ad quintum subiectum[13] per b. c. d. designatum[14] in libro septem[15] planetarum quia ibi tractavimus miraculose et notitiam omnium[16] habebis [P 437v.] entium naturalium, quapropter ipsorum[17] prolixitatem et sermonem[18] declarationis hic ad praesens exprimere praetermitto, cum intellectus[19] per unam literam plura significata habentem sit generalior[20] et possit in memoria plura significata recipere[21] quam per aliam largo modo sumptam.

CAP. II

[B 35v.] Sequitur nunc secunda pars quae memoriam dividit[22] in partes speciales[23] pariter et generales de generali tractans ad specialia[24] postea descendendo. Primo igitur ut laborans in studio[25] faciliter[26] sciat modum scientiam[27] et ne, post amissos quamplurimos labores, scientiae huius[28] operam inutiliter tradidisse[29] noscatur, sed potius labor in requiem et sudor [M 1v.] in gloriam plenarie[30] convertatur, modum scientiae decet pro iuvenibus invenire per quem non tanta gravitate corporis iugiter deprimantur, sed absque nimia vexatione et cum[31] corporis levitate et mentis laetitia ad scientiarum culmina [P 438r.] gradientes[32] equidem[33] propere subeant.[34] Multi enim sunt qui more brutorum literarum studia cum multo et summo labore corporis prosequuntur absque[35] exercitio ingenii artificioso[36] et continuis vigiliis maceratum corpus suum iuxta labores proprios inutiliter exhibentes.(37) Igitur(38) decet(39) modum per quem virtuosus studens thesaurum scientiae leviter valeat invenire et a gravamine tantorum laborum(40) relevari possit.(41) Oportet nos igitur conservare(42) ante omnia quaedam principia et praecepta(43) necessaria et postmodum ad specialia condescendere.(44) Primum ergo oportet praeceptum legis observare, id est diligere Deum eiusque Genitricem beatissimam virginem(45) Mariam. Nam Spiritus Sanctus dat scientiam cum magnitudine ut sit magna, Beata Virgo Maria dat scientiam(46) cum bonitate ut sit bona. Spiritus Sanctus dat scientiam ut charitas duret, Domina nostra beatissima [B 36r.] dat scientiam(47) ut [P 438v.] pietas duret. Spiritus Sanctus dat scientiam cum potestate(48) ut sit fortis, Domina nostra virgo beatissima dat scientiam ut recolatur. Spiritus Sanctus dat scientiam contra infidelitatem, Domina nostra virgo(49) Maria dat scientiam contra peccatum. Spiritus Sanctus dat scientiam cum ratione,(50) Domina nostra(51) pia dat scientiam cum patientia.(52) Spiritus Sanctus dat scientiam cum(53) spe, Domina nostra sanctissima pia Virgo Maria(54) dat scientiam cum(55) pietate. Spiritus Sanctus dat scientiam cui sibi placet, Domina nostra dat scientiam omnibus illis qui ipsam rogant. Spiritus Sanctus dat scientiam ad rogandum, Domina nostra dat scientiam petendi.(56) Spiritus Sanctus dat scientiam divitibus, Domina pia dat scientiam pauperibus. Spiritus Sanctus dat scientiam cum gratia,(57) Domina nostra sacratissima virgo Maria dat scientiam cum petitione.(58) Spiritus Sanctus(59) idiomata dat pariter [P 439r.] et(60) consolationes ab ipso quidem divino(61) Domino nostro Jesu Christo omnia prospere(62) procedunt et conceduntur(63) et sine ipso factum est nihil [M 2r.] et placa(64) ipsum per devotissimas orationes maxime per orationem Sancti spiritus.(65) Secundo est optimum(66) observare modum vivendi in potando et comedendo praecipue ex parte noctis vel etiam in dormiendo quoniam(67) ex superfluitate horum(68) corpus gravitate ponderositatis ultra modum aggravatur et anima, corpori adherens, illius dispositionem sequitur. Nihil enim tam praecipuum scientiam inquirenti(69) ut moderationem ponat ori suo(70) et palpebris suis non concedat multam dormitionem et inordinatam. [B 36v.] Tertium praeceptum invenio(71) quod nunquam(72) deficiat quin(73) maiorem partem sui temporis(74) scientiae operam(75) tribuat cum affectu(76) quoniam(77) ex hoc sequitur capacitas, ex hoc memoria, ex hoc discretio naturalis.

CAP. III

[P 439v.] Sequitur nunc secunda pars ad specialia descendens. In artificioso studendi modo[78] distinguo tres potentias naturales: una est capacitas, alia est memoria, alia est discretio. Prima stat in prima parte capitis quae dicitur phantasia,[79] secunda stat[80] in posteriori, tertia stat[81] in summitate[82] capitis quae aliis velut regina dominatur. Et bonum est habere bonam capacitatem, sed melius est habere bonam memoriam,[83] sed multo melius[84] habere bonam discretionem.[85] Modo restat videre de singulis, et primo videndum[86] est de capacitate,[87] secundo de memoria, tertio de discretione. Si igitur aliquis[88] capacitatem lectionis cuiuscunque facultatis audiendae ambit,[89] regulas quas infra dicam debet diligenter[90] observare, quas si observaverit quod sibi eveniet[91] experientia demonstrabit in brevi tempore.[92] Primo[93] enim, antequam ad scholam accedat, lectionem statim tam de grammatica quam de logica [P 440r.] tam[94] de iure civili quam de iure[95] canonico et ita de omnibus aliis scientiis audiendam,[96] si potest de iure canonico aut civili[97] textum et glossas alias solum textum, et videbit si credit [B 37r.] intelligere; adhuc[98] non confidens de proprio intellectu[99] dabit tibi materiam speculandi,[100] dum legat, utrum bene[101] vel male intellexerit, et postmodum, quando legetur, erit attentus lectioni ut intelligat per alium id quod per se[102] ignorabat.

Item[103] postquam semel in domo viderit, facilius postea intelliget, et tali modo ego[104] scientiam meam multiplicavi, et ita faciet artista meae artis quoniam sic[105] acquiret [M 2v.] scientiam quam voluerit. Item secundo dico quod[106] dum erit in scholiis habeat intellectum[107] ad id quod doctor vel magister tam in sacra pagina quam in artibus dicet, quod si non, faciliter[108] mens eius spargitur et potius videtur esse in loco ubi habet mentem quam in scholiis ubi est tamque frustra.[109] Ex hoc tamen [110] multi perdunt officium capiendi.[111] Item quia dum fuerit casus vel scientia, legere mentaliter in se revolvat et[112] dum questionem secundam vel argumentum[113] cuiuscunque facultatis dicit doctor vel magister vel artista meae artis, primam eodem modo revolvat, et interim quando dicetur tertia[114] reducat ad memoriam secundam[115] et sic de caeteris, et sic habebit intentionem capiendi totam lectionem. Posito quod non, nec[116] partem accipiat quarum[117] paulisper argumentabitur, non autem[118] uno momento poterit habere. Item quando[119] per se vel per alium quis vult habere bonam capacitatem, debet ponere ordinem in legendis.[120] Nam si vult intelligere unam legem vel decretalem vel gramaticae vel logicae lectionem, dividat ipsam in duas [B 37v.] tres quatuor partes secundum quod lectio fuerit parva vel magna quoniam ad capacitatem multum et[121] forsan magis quam aliud[122] operaretur.[123] Et de primo[124] haec sufficiant.

Cap. IV

[P 441r.] Venio igitur ad secundam, scilicet ad memoriam quae quidem[125] secundum antiquos[126] alia est naturalis alia est artificialis.[127] Naturalis est quam quis recipit in creatione vel generatione sua secundum materiam ex qua[128] homo generatur et[129] secundum quod influentia alicuius planetae superioris regnat[130] et secundum hoc videmus quosdam homines meliorem memoriam habentes quam alios sed[131] de ista nihil ad nos quoniam Dei est illud concedere. Alia est memoria artificialis et ista est duplex quia quaedam est in medicinis et emplastris[132] cum[133] quibus habetur et istam reputo valde periculosam quoniam interdum dantur[134] tales medicinae dispositioni hominis contrariae[135] interdum superfluae et in maxima cruditate[136] qua cerebrum[137] ultra modum desiccatur et propter defectum cerebri homo ad dementiam demergitur ut audivimus et vidimus de multis[138] et ista displiciet Deo [P 441v.] quoniam hic non se tenet pro contento[139] de gratia quam sibi Deus contulit unde, posito casu quod ad stultitiam[140] non perveniat,[141] nunquam [M 3r.] vel raro habebit[142] fructum[143] scientiae.[144] Alia est memoria artificialis per alium modum acquirendi nam dum aliquis per capacitatem recipit multum in memoria et in ore revolvat per se ipsum[145] quoniam secundum Alanum[146] in parabolis³ studens est admodum bovis. Bos enim cum maxima velocitate recipit herbas et sine masticatione ad [B 38r.] stomachum remittit quas postmodum remugit et ad finem[147] cum melius est digestum in sanguinem et carnem convertit, ita est de studente qui moribus[148] oblitis capit scientiam sine deliberatione unde ad finem ut duret, debet in ore mentis masticare ut in memoria radicetur et habituetur; quoniam quod[149] leviter capit[150] leviter recedit et ita memoria,[151] ut habetur in libro de memoria et reminiscentia,[152] [P 442r.] per saepissimam reiterationem⁴ firmiter confirmatur.[153] Lectionem igitur diei lunae revolvat die martis et studeat et die martis et[154] die mercurii et sic de caeteris et talia[155] faciendo scientior[156] erit uno anno audiens illo qui sex audierit[157] annis ut artistae hoc consulo meae artis caeterisque addiscere volentibus invenire attingere[158] et habere.

CAP. V

Venio ad tertiam videlicet ad[159] discretivam et dico quod discretio est duplex ut de memoria dixi: alia[160] naturalis, alia[161] artificialis. Naturalis est[162] quam quis habet ex dono Dei[163] et de ista[164] non loquor. Alia est artificiosa et ista acquiritur aliquibus[165] modis. Primo enim acquiritur si ea quae in memoria retinemus diligenter[166] servemus, cum[167] enim aliquid in mente memoramus sive textum sive glosam sive auctoritatem sive rationem per alium [P 442v.] dictam[168] et de illo vel de simili a nobis petatur, per ea quae iam sunt in nostra notitia et memoria radicata[169] faciliter indicabimus cuicumque respondendo, verum[170] et certum est quod melius discernit[171] sciens quam ignarus propter scientiam quam habet[172] iam cum memoria acquisitam.[173]

CAP. VI

[B 38v.] Postquam[174] de memoria et[175] capacitate et discretiva[176] tam in speciali quam in generali pariter et singulari dictum est,[177] nunc videndum est de memoriae recitatione, et ad multa recitanda[178] consideravi ponere quaedam nomina relativa per quae ad omnia possit responderi quoniam quodlibet [M 3v.] eorum[179] erit omnino generale ad omnino speciale et habet scalam ascendendi et descendendi de non omnino generali ad omnino speciale[180] et de non[181] omnino speciali ad omnino generale. Ista enim sunt nomina supra dicta: quid, quare, quantus[182] et quomodo. Per quodlibet istorum poteris recitare viginti rationes in oppositum[183] factas vel quaecunque advenerint tibi recitanda et quam admirabile[184] est quod[185] centum possis[186] [P 443r.] rationes retinere et ipsas, dum locus fuerit[187] bene[188] recitare. Certe hoc auro comparari non debet,[189] ergo qui scientiam habere affectat et universalem ad omnia[190] desiderat, hoc[191] circa ipsum[192] tractatum laboret cum diligentia[193] toto posse quoniam sine dubio scientior erit aliis quia[194] nomina sine speciebus aut[195] sine magistro non possumus recitare ideo[196] ipsas pono: primo enim quid[197] habet tres species quas hic propter earum[198] prolixitatem ponere[199] non curo, sed vade ad quintum subiectum[200] per b. c. d. significatum[201] in libro septem[202] planetarum quoniam[203] ibi videbis miraculose[204] ipsas aliqualiter[205] declarare[206] hic intendo, et sic dictum de primis tribus [B 39r.] ita intelligi potest de aliis[207] sequentibus[208]. Primum igitur per primam speciem nominis quid,[209] poteris certas quaestiones sive rationes sive alia quaecunque volueris recitare[210] evacuando secundam[211] figuram de his quae continet, per secundam vere poteris[212] in duplo[213] respondere seu recitare et[214] hoc per evacuationem tertiae [P 443v.] et multiplicationem primae, et si[215] per primam tu recitas[216] viginti vel triginta nomina seu rationes,[217] per secundam poteris quadraginta vel sexaginta[218] recitare et hoc semper per evacuationem et multiplicationem.[5] Tamen est multum difficile nisi sit homo ingeniosus et intellectu[219] subtilis et non rudalis.[220] Per tertiam vero centum poteris recitare[221] evacuando primam et multiplicando secundam et de aliis poteris sicut de ista cognitionem habere. Quare firmiter et ferventer[222] praedictas stude[223] species in praelibato septem[224] planetarum libro quem nunquam eris studere defessus[225] immo eris gaudio et laetitia plenus; in dicto libro multa[226] sunt studenti[227] necessaria quae si nota essent et bene intellecta non possent ullo modo[228] extimari; ideo consulo cuicumque ut[229] istum habeat prae manibus et prae oculis suae mentis.[230] [P 444r.] Ad laudem et honorem Domini nostri Iesu Christi et publicae utilitati compositus fuit praesens tractatus in civitate Pisana in monasterio sancti Dominici per Raymundum Lullum[231] ut prius dominus Iesus Christus in memoria habeatur et verius recolatur. Amen.

(1) In nomine… confirmandam] Perutilis Raymundi Lulli Tractatus de Memoria B. (2) hominum] *om.* B.] hominis P. (3) meliori] et melioretur B. (4) principales] et *add.* B. (5) diffinimus] definimus M. (6) Cap. I (and all subsequent chapter headings) *om.* MP. (7) diffinire] definire M. (8) et] *om.* B. (9) ipsam] ipsum P. (10) Primo] prima P. (11) significat] *om.* B. (12) tamen] autem B. (13) subiectum] librum B. (14) designatum] *om.* B.] designata M. (15) in libro septem] in libro octavo positum B.] in libro septimo P. (16) omnium] omnem B. (17) ipsorum] ipse MP. (18) sermonem] seriem M.] scientia P. (19) intellectus] generalior sit *add.* MP. (20) per unam literam plura significata habentem sit generalior] pariter in memoria pro litera significata habentem B.] ponit in memoria plura significata P. (21) et possit in memoria plura significata recipere] *om.* BP. (22) quae memoriam dividit] quae est de memoria et dividitur B. (23) speciales] spetiales B. (24) specialia] spetialem B. (25) ut laborans in studio] laboranti in studio virtuose B.] laboranti in studio studiose P. (26) faciliter] facile B. (27) scientiam] scientiae P. (28) huius] huiusmodi M. (29) tradidisse]

credidisse B. (30) plenarie] plenariam M. (31) cum] etiam P. (32) gradientes] gradus BM. (33) equidem] eiusdem B.] eosdem M. (34) propere subeant] properari sublimiter B. (35) absque] nullo *add*. B. (36) artificioso] artificiosi B.] sed *add*. MP. (37) labores proprios inutiliter exhibentes] labores proprios exercentes conservare MP. (38) Igitur] Considerare igitur B. (39) decet] docet P. (40) laborum] aliquando *add*. B. (41) posssit] *om*. MP. (42) Oportet nos igitur conservare] Nos igitur consideramus B. (43) principia et praecepta] praecipitata B. (44) condescendere] condescentia B. (45) beatissimam virginem] perbeatissimam gloriosam B. (46) Maria dat scientiam] *om*. MP. (47) dat scientiam] per sapientiam *add*. B. (48) cum potestate] cum pietate B.] in postestate P. (49) virgo] *om*. B. (50) cum ratione] in ratione P. (51) nostra] Maria B. (52) cum patientia] in patientia P. (53) cum] in P. (54) nostra sanctissima pia Virgo Maria] sacratissima pia virgo B. (55) cum] in P. (56) petendi] poenitenti BP. (57) cum gratia] in gratia P. (58) cum petitione] in petitione P. (59) Sanctus] *om*. MP. (60) et] *om*. B. (61) divino] Deo pio MP. (62) prospere] prospera MP. (63) et conceduntur] *om*. MP. (64) placa] placare B. (65) orationes Sancti Spiritus] orationem spiritus B. (66) Secundo est optimum] Secundum est B. (67) quoniam] cum BM. (68) horum] eorum B. (69) inquirenti] acquirenti B. (70) ut moderationem ponat ori suo] ut ponat custodiam in somno B.] ut moderate ponat ori suo P. (71) invenio] *om*. B. (72) nunquam] nunque B. (73) quin] ut B. (74) temporis] spiritus B. (75) operam] opera M. (76) cum affectu] in affectu P. (77) quoniam] cum M. (78) in artificioso studendi modo] in artificio secundo studendi P. (79) quae dicitur phantasia] *om*. B. (80) stat] *om*. B. (81) stat] *om*. B. (82) summitate] sanitate P. (83) sed melius est habere bonam memoriam] sed multo melius est habere bonam discretionem P. (84) melius] plus B. (85) discretionem] discretivam B. (86) primo videndum] providendum M. (87) de capacitate] de bona capacitate M. (88) aliquis] vult habere bonam *add*. B. (89) ambit] *om*. B. (90) diligenter] diligentia B. (91) evenit] quod *add*. B. (92) tempore] *om*. B. (93) Primo] Secundo B. (94) tam] quam MP. (95) iure] *om*. B. (96) audiendam] auditum M.] audiendum P. (97) civili] simili MP. (98) adhuc] ad hoc MP. (99) de proprio intellectu] proprii intellectus B.] de primo intellectu P. (100) tibi materiam speculandi] et ut viam studendi MP. (101) utrum bene] num vel bene B. (102) per se] per ipsum B. (103) Item] quia *add*. MP. (104) ego] *om*. B.

(105) quoniam sic] cum B.] quoniam P. (106) quod] *om*. B. (107) intellectum] inventionem M. (108) faciliter] facile B.] facilius P. (109) tamque frustra] tamquam frustra B.] *om* P. (110) tamen] tam P. (111) perdunt officium capiendi] per dictum officium capientur B. (112) Item quia dum fuerit casus vel scientia, legere mentaliter in se revolvat et] Item dum sciat causam vel scientiam litere mentaliter inter se revolvat ut B.] Item quod dum fuerit casus vel sententia litterae mentaliter in se revolvat et P. (113) dum questionem secundam vel argumentum] dum questionem vel scientiam vel argumentum B.] dum questionem sciendam vel argumentum P. (114) dicetur tertia] docetur tertia MP. (115) reducat ad memoriam secundam] ducat ad memoriam secundam B.] ducat ad memoriam sciendorum P. (116) nec] nisi B. (117) quarum] quaerere MP. (118) autem] enim *add*. B. (119) quando] si secundo B.] secundo P. (120) legendis] agendis MP. (121) et] est MP. (122) quam aliud] quam quodvis aliud M. (123) operaretur] *om*. MP. (124) primo] priori M. (125) quae quidem] Memoria quidem B. (126) secundum antiquos] in capitulo de memoria *add*. P. (127) artificialis] artificiosa M. (128) secundum materiam ex qua] ex materia qua B. (129) et] etiam MP. (130) secundum quod influentia alicuius planetae superioris regnat] secundum que influentia alicuius planetae inferioris regnat B.] secundum quod influentia actus planetarum superioris regnat M.] secundum quod influentiam accipit planetae superioris regnat P. (131) sed] et MP. (132) emplastris] epistolis M.] eplis P. (133) cum] in P. (134) dantur] dammantur B. (135) dispositioni hominis contrariae] dispositio hominis quae contrariae MP. (136) cruditate] quantitate B.] caliditate P. (137) qua cerebrum] quod certe bene B.] quod cerebrum P. (138) de multis] multos B. (139) tenet pro contento] contentat B. (140) stultitiam] insaniam B. (141) perveniat] deveniat MP. (142) habebit] consequetur B. (143) fructum] fructus B. (144) scientiae] suae *add*. B. (145) Alia est memoria artificialis… revolvat per se ipsum] *om*. B. (146) Alanum] Alonium M.] Aristotelem P. (147) finem] seriem B. (148) moribus] munibus B.] modis M. (149) quod] *om*. B. (150) capit] et *add*. B. (151) et ita memoria] *om*. B. (152) ut habetur in libro de memoria et reminiscentia] *om*. B. (153) firmiter confirmatur] firmiter continetur B.] firmiter confirmiter confirmetur P. (154) studeat et die martis et] *om*. B. (155) talia] taliter B. (156) faciendo scientior] faciendo quis scienter B. (157) illo qui sex audierit] illud quod sex annis audiverit B. (158) attingere]

etiam *add.* M. (159) ad] *om.* BM. (160) alia] est *add.* MP. (161) alia
] est *add.* MP. (162) est] *om.* MP. (163) habet ex dono Dei] debet
dono Dei B. (164) et de ista] de qua B. (165) aliquibus] duobus B.
(166) diligenter] diligentia B. (167) cum] quando P. (168) sive textum sive glosam sive auctoritatem sive rationem per alium dictam]
sine textu sine glossa sine auctoritate sine ratione per aliud dictum
MP. (169) radicata] radicantur B. (170) cuicumque respondendo
verum] cuiuscunque unde B. (171) discernit] discerit B. (172)
propter scientiam quam habet] nam rationem quam habet B. (173)
acquisitam] acquisita M. (174) Postquam] visum est *add.* B. (175) et
] *om.* MP. (176) discretiva] discretione P. (177) dictum est] *om.* B.
(178) recitanda] recitandum B. (179) eorum] illorum B. (180) et
habet scalam… ad omnino speciale] *om.* B. (181) non] *om.* B. (182)
quantus] quotus, totus B.] quatenus M. (183) oppositum] oppositionem P. (184) quam admirabile] quoniam mirabile M.] quam
mirabile P. (185) quod] quia M. (186) possis] possit P. (187) fuerit]
adfuit B. (188) bene] *om.* MP. (189) debet] potest MP. (190) universalem ad omnia] utilis omnia B.] universalis ad omnia M. (191)
hoc] homo esse B. (192) ipsum] istum B. (193) cum diligentia]
eadem diligentia B.] in diligentia P. (194) Quia] quoniam M. (195)
aut] aliquid B. (196) ideo] labore adeo B. (197) Primo enim quid]
primo quo B. (198) earum] illarum B. (199) ponere] *om.* B. (200)
subiectum] librum B. (201) significatum] designatum vel significatum B. (202) septem] septimo P. (203) quoniam] cum B. (204)
miraculose] iam *add.* B. (205) aliqualiter] aliquantum B. (206)
declarare] volo *add.* M. (207) hic intendo… potest de aliis] *om.* MP.
(208) sequentibus] in sequentibus MP. (209) quid] quod B. (210)
recitare] evacuare secundum de his quae continet per scientiam posi-
tis *add.* B. (211) secundam] secundam corrected to primam by a later
hand B. (212) secundam figuram de his quae continet, per secundam
vero poteris] *om.* B. (213) duplo] duo P. (214) seu recitare et] *om.*
B. (215) si] sic P. (216) recitas] duo vel tria nomina seu rationes *add.*
M. duo and tria are later corrections of secunda and tertia. (217) viginti vel triginta nomina seu rationes] *om.* M. (218) vel sexaginta] *om.*
B. (219) intellectu] multum B. (220) rudalis] naturalis B.] non
ruralis M. (221) recitare] *om.* MP. (222) et ferventer] *om.* B. (223)
stude] audire B. (224) quem nunquam eris studere defessus] quem
nunquam eris audire fessus B] quoniam eris studendo defessus M.]
quoniam nunquam eris studere defessus P. (226) multa] nulla B.
(227) studenti] alia evidenter B. (228) ullo modo] modo aliquo B.]

modo P. (229) cuicunque ut] quoscunque quod B. (230) oculis suae
mentis] oculis et suae mentis ferveat B. (231) Lullum] Lulli MP.

APPENDIX II
AN ANONYMOUS VERNACULAR TREATISE OF THE FOURTEENTH
CENTURY

The following anonymous vernacular treatise on artificial memory composed in the fourteenth century comes from Florence, Bibliotheca
Nazionale, MS Palatino 54 (if. 140–2) and MS Conv. Soppr. I. 1. 47.
Contrary to Yates's belief[6] this work cannot be attributed with any certainty to Bartolomeo da San Concordio. This attribution was originally
made by Girolamo Tiraboschi[7] but, as Felice Tocco has noted,[8] the work
contains a reference to the *Rosarum odor vitae* (copies of which are also to
be found in the manuscripts cited above), which was probably composed
in 1373 by Matteo Corsini, prior to the Florentine Republic of 1378.[9]
Even if the year of composition of the *Rosaio* is uncertain the fact remains
that the work was composed by a contemporary of Petrarch.[10] In support
of Tocco's view we should also note that in his reference to the *Rosaio* the
author of the treatise on memory speaks of 84 chapters while both MS
Palat. 54 and MS I.1.47 have 82 chapters. The attribution to San
Concordio seems to have arisen from the fact that in both of the manuscripts Bartolomeo's *Ammaestramenti degli antichi* is preceded by a translation of the chapter on memory from the *Rhetorica ad Herennium* and
followed by a treatise on artificial memory. In Palat. 54 the texts are disposed thus: ff. 29–33v.: *Testus memorie artificiose vulgariter scilicet super quandam partem retorice*; if 44–139v.: *Bartolomeo da S Concordzo gli ammaestramenti
degli antichi*; ff 140–2: *Ars memoriae artificialis*. The translation of the text
from the *Rhetorica ad Herennium* forms the second part or the sixth treatise
of the *Fior di Rettorica* of Bono Giamboni (Magliab. Palch. MS 11, 90,
Riccardiano, 1538. See Tocco, *Le opere latine di G. Bruno*, p. 26). The *Libro
di leggere* which is referred to in the first lines of the treatise could (as
Tocco suggests) be the treatise on pronunciation which is the third book
of the *Fior di Rettorica* in the redactions of Fra Guidotto da Bologna and
Bono Giamboni. The treatise on artificial memory could in all probabil-
ity form part of a redaction of the *Fior di Rettorica*.

The transcription here is from MS Palat. 54, but I have amended it
using the other manuscript versions mentioned above. I have altered some
of the punctuation and orthography of the MS (for example 'nolla' = 'non
l'ha', 'lo' = 'l'ho', 'a' = 'ha' etc).

[140r.] Poi che aviamo fornito il libro di leggere, resta di poter tenere a mente, et però qui di sotto si scrive l'arte della memoria artificiale in si facta forma che non offende la naturale che ha sifatto ordine il libro da sé che con questa memoria si può d'esso grande parte imparare a mente se solamente il libro si legge cinque volte et fra l'una volta et l'altra sia spazio di mezzo di quello che vuoi tenere a mente, et observando le regole di questa memoria non si potrà errare solo in una lettera di tutto questo libro che tutto non si imparasse a mente. La memoria artificiale sta solamente in due cose, cioè ne luoghi e nelle imagini. Luogo non è altro a dire se non come una cosa disposta a potere contenere in sé alcuna altra cosa, sicome una casa, una sala, una camera o simili cose a questa come ab octo dieci anni a te dicte. Le imagini sono il proprio representamento di quelle cose che noi vogliamo tenere a mente. Due sono le maniere de luoghi, cioè naturale e artificiale. Naturale luogo è quello che è facto per mano di natura come e il monte e il piano e gli albori che per sé sono. Artificiale luogo è quello che è facto per mano d'huomo sì come è una camera o un camino, uno versatoio, uno studio, una finestra, una casa, uno cofano et simili luoghi a questi. Non intendere però tutte le masseritie minute de la camera però che non ti riverebbe la ragione, ma vogliono essere masseritie grandi come sono cassoni, soppedani, fortieri, et se pure alcuna masseritia ci vogliamo mettere, conviene che sia molto riconosciuta et stia in luogo continuamente palese, come è una barbuta, uno cappello lavorato, uno elmo da campo o vero cimiero e cose simili a queste. Intorno a luoghi convengono [140v.] piú cose avere. In prima avere dentro molti luoghi, cioè quanti sono i nomi che vogliamo tenere a mente però che ogni luogo ha la sua imagine a pigliare ciascuna imagine e rapresentamento da una cosa sola per sé, et però se aremo a tenere a mente XX nomi si pogniano XX imagini per luogo. Et come dico di XX, cosi si potrebbe fare di cento, CC, CCC, CCCC, pure che luoghi assai aviamo. Non obstante che io dica qui di CC e LII, posto che di questi CCLII viene facta non poca fatica che sono nel libreto dinanzi decto del rosaio odore della vita capitoli LXXXIIII et ad ogni capitolo si possono leggiermente accattare tre nomi sí che tre via LXXXIIII, CCLII. Ma di piú nomi dire qui di sotto piú pienamente. Apresso questo, ci conviene avere e' luoghi ordinati, cioè che per ordine l'uno vada dietro a l'altro. Et se quella persona che vuole usare quella memoria in mancino, cominci e' conti de luoghi a mano mancha et se queste sopra da la directa mano, se a diricta vada sopra la mano diricta, in questo modo: che se in una sala aremo da poter pigliare cinque luoghi, el primo sia uno camino, el secondo un uscio o un armaro da vasi, el quarto una colonna overo uno pilastro, el quinto uno versatoio. Incominciamo dal primo come è il camino, poi il secondo come è un uscio et così per ordine l'uno dopo l'altro et non si dee mai passare niuno luogo se non che si debbono sapergli bene a mente come sono ordinati da sé. A presso si conviene che i luoghi sieno numerati cioè che ogni luogo quinto si segni; cioè a questo modo: che al primo quinto si ponga una mano d'oro che per le cinque dita ripresentino quello luogo essere quinto; poi il secondo quinto, cioè il decimo luogo, ripresenta in questo modo o trovata per sapere subito a quanti nomi sta Piero. Subito puoi avisare se alle due mani sarà il decimo se a due nomi dopo le due mani sarà il duodecimo [141r.] et così seguitando si può sapere di molti. Ma questa regola di queste mani abbi posta qui perché la insegnia Tulio et non vorrei che altri credessi che io non la sapessi, però l'ho posta qui, ma a me pare uno poco faticosa per tale quale persona. Imperò potiamo lasciare andare testé questo affanno delle mani del oro, et fare in questa forma; cioè che i luoghi sempre caggino o in cinque o in dieci; in questa forma che se in una sala sono sei o septe luoghi non tenere a mente se non cinque, et se fussino quattro forzati tanto che sieno cinque che leggiermente viene facto poi che si mette in pratica. Et così similmente vuole andare de decti che se aremo una sala o una camera dove sieno nove luoghi, forzati tanto che ve ne aggiungi un altro si che sieno dieci. Se ce ne fussino da dieci in su sulla sala, non ne tenere a mente se non dieci. Adunque se arai in una tua casa una sala et in questa fussino cinque luoghi, una camera et in questa camera fussino dieci luoghi, uno verone et in questo fussino pure dieci luoghi, un'altra camera et in questa fussino cinque luoghi, uno terrazzo et in questo fussino dieci luoghi, una grotta et in questa fussino dieci luoghi, raccogli tutti questi luoghi et vedi quanti sono, et, quanti sono i luoghi, tanti sono i nomi che puoi tenere a mente. Sí che se i dicti luoghi sono L, et L nomi potrai tenere a mente senza fatica di memoria, et così similmente chi la volessi fare più in grosso, potrebbe avisare dieci case delle dita sue dove trovasse L luoghi ciascuna casa et così la farà di cinquecento et di mille et di diecimila senza fallo, però che troviamo che Seneca fu giovane esso la fe' di dumilia, ritornando alto inanzi et allo indietro, come fanno i fanciulli ad a. b. c. quando la dicono alla dietro. Ancora vogliono essere dieci luoghi noti cioè che bene gli conosciamo etc. Apresso non vogliono essere troppo grandi né troppo piccoli, ma di mezzana fog-[141v.] gia come si richiede alle imagini che qui si pongono. Ancora vogliono essere i luoghi temperati dove non usi troppa gente però che la troppa gente guasta il luogo et la nostra memoria. Ancora vogliono essere né troppo chiare ne troppo obscure però che la troppa chiarezza et la troppa obscurità fa noia agli occhi della mente sí che vedere non possiamo i luoghi. Ancora conviene che i luoghi non si rassomiglino troppo l'uno a l'altro, ma quanto piú sono variati meglio è. Ancora non vogliono essere troppo apresso l'uno a l'altro né troppo di lungi, ma intomo di cinque o di dieci piedi l'una da l'altra. Et questo è tutto quello che bisognia a' luoghi. La imagine non è altro se non, come di sopra è detto, come il proprio representamento di quelle cose le quali vogliamo tenere ad mente. Questa imagine ha due proprietà: cioè che ella ha a ricordare il nome et il sentire. Ricordare il nome è ricordare a mente Piero Giovanni Martino per ordine ciascuno per sé, ricordare sententie è in questo modo che se io mi voglio ricordare come Troia fu presa <dai> Greci con ferro con fuoco con ruina per cagione di Elena, io pongo in uno luogo la imagine di Troia come ardeva e come in lei sieno entrati cavalieri armati. Ancora se io mi volessi ricordare della hedificatione di Cartagine la quale hedificò una donna chiamata Dido, porrò una imagine d'una con molti guatatori di intorno, et cosí va di simile a simile di molte et infinite sententie. Hora d'intorno alle imagini sí come di nomi et di sententie vediamo quante cose sono di necessità. Mostra che sieno sei per ordine. In prima si richiede che le imagini sieno proprie, cioè che se io mi voglio ricordare di Piero solamente ponga in uno luogo la sua propria imagine, et se io voglio tenere a mente Martino, quello medesimo. Ancora conviene che la imagine non sia [142r.] equivoca cioè che rapresenti piú cose di quelle che vogliamo tenere a mente. Ancora conviene che le imagini non sieno troppe, cioè piú che non sieno di bisogno non si pongano nel luogo, che se io voglio tenere a mente Piero, solamente porre una imagine che rapresenti Piero, la quale cosa è contro alla doctrina de Tulio. Ancora conviene che la imagine non sia varia, cioè che abbia alcuna varietà in sé e questa è delle piú utili cose che si possa avere. Questa memoria però sempre ci doviamo studiare di porre imagini di nuove foggie. Ancora conviene che la imagine sia segnata da alcuno segno il quale si convenga a la cosa per la quale è facta, cioè che la imagine del re pare che gli si convenga il segno de la corona, et a' cavalieri il segno dello scudo, al doctore il seguo del vaso et ad cui uno segno ad cui uno altro come la fantasia della memoria comunemente si vuole dotare. Ancora conviene che a la imagine si faccia alcuna cosa cioè la proprino quanto agli acti quelle cose che a loro si convengono, sí come si conviene ad uno lione dare la imagine apta et ardita et alla golpe l'acto sagace et abstuto, al sonatore l'apto di sonare strumento. Adunque veggiano sempre che ne' luoghi si convengono porre le imagini sí come nelle carte si convengono porre le lectere. Qui finisce delle sententie et de' nomi abbreviato. Ancora doviamo tenere questo modo il quale è molto utile: che poi che abbiamo imparato C o CC nomi et recitargli, non per tanto dobbiamo conservargli, piú inanzi ci doviamo studiare piú che possiamo che ci escano di mente e cosi facendo escono di mente e i luoghi rimangono voti per gli altri che volessino imparare. Finis. Deo gratias. Amen.

APPENDIX III
TWO FIFTEENTH-CENTURY MANUSCRIPTS ON THE *ARS MEMORATIVA.*

Bibliotheca Ambrosiano. MS Lat. T. 78 sup. (45 folios.) contains the following works:

ff. 1–21v.: *Tractatus brevis ac solemnis ad sciendam et ad consequendam artem memoriae artificialis ad M. Marchionem Mantuae.* Incipit: 'Iussu tuo princeps illustrissime' [This is a treatise by Jacopo Ragone da Vicenza, written in 1434 and conserved in two examples in different hands also in Bibliotheca Marciana MS CL.VI, 274, ff. 15–34 and 53–66 and in a third version in Bibliotheca Marciana, MS 159 of the same class. The name of the author ('artificialis memoriae regulae per Jacobum Ragonum Vicentium') and the date of composition ('Kal. Nov. 1434') are given in Bibliotheca Marciana, MS 274, ff. 15v. and 53v.].

ff. 22–26: *Tractatus solemnis artis memorativae.* Incipit: 'Artificiosae memoriae egregia quaedam' [This text is transcribed below, omitting the list of *loci* in Italian, ff. 26–7v.] Explicit: 'Trespo da tavola Zovane fameglio'.

ff. 27v.–32v.: *Tractatus artis memorativae eximii doctoris artium et medicinae magistri Girardi*. Incipit: 'Ars commoda naturae confirmat et auget' [In the transcription which follows I have also used MS Angelica 142, which contains the same treatise in ff. 83–7, in a later hand, with the title *Hic traditur preclarus modus conficiende memoriae*. Incipit: 'Ars commoda natura et confirmat et auget'].

ff. 33–40v.: *Excerpta ex libris M. T. Ciceronis de memoria*. Incipit: 'M. T. Ciceronis de oratore haec de memoria scripta sunt' [the *excerpta* in ff. 35v.–40v. are extracts from the *Rhetorica ad Herennium*].

The date of composition of the miscellany is given at the end of the manuscript, f. 45: 'Anno 1466 scriptus pro Raphael de Fuzsy.'

I

[22r.] Tractatus solemnis artis memorativae incipit. Artificiosae memoriae egregia quaedam atque preclarissima praecepta in lucem allaturi, non invanum esse duximus quod ipsa sit primum effingere cum, iuxta Ciceronis sententia in primo De officiis, omnis de quacumque re sumitur disputatio a diffinitione proficisci debeat ut sciri possit quid sit id de quo disputatur. Est igitur artificialis memoria dispositio quaedam imaginaria vel localis vel idealis mente rerum sensibilium super quas naturalis memoria reflexa per ea summovetur atque adiuvatur ut prius memoratorum facilius, distinctius atque divitius denuo valeat reminisci. Vel sit artificialis memoria est decentium imaginum quaedam industriosa collocatio qua eorum quae in his debite applicantur ad tempus memorari valeamus. Tertio vero ex menti Ciceronis, Rhetoricorum tertio, sic eius diffinitionem implecti possumus: memoria artificialis est artificium quoddam quo naturalis memoria praeceptoris voce confirmatur. Differt autem memoria naturalis ab artificiosa. Harum naturalis est una quae nostris animis insita est et simul cum ipsa [22v.] creatione nata. Artificiosa vero est quaedam inductio et praeceptionis ratione confirmatur. Haec autem ars duobus perficitur: locis videlicet et imaginibus, ut Cicero sentit in tertio Rhetoricorum a quo non dissentit beatus Thomas illud addiciens oportere ut ea quae vult quis memoriter tenere ordinata consideratione disponat, ut ex uno memoratu ad aliud facile procedatur. Cicero vero sic inquit: oportet igitur, si multa reminisci volumus, multos locos domus comparare, ut in multis locis multas imagines comprehendere atque amplecti valeamus. Aristoteles vero in eo que de memoria scripsit a locis inquit reminiscimur. Necessarii itaque sunt loci ut res seriatim pronuntiare et memoriter tenere valeamus. Differunt autem loci ab imaginibus quia loci sunt imagines ipsae super quibus tamque super carta imagines delebiles, quasi literae, collocantur. Habeant igitur se loci sicut materia, imagines vero ut forma. Differunt quasi ut fixum et non fixum. Et quoniam haec ars, ut dictum est, duobus absolvitur, locis videlicet et imaginibus, primum locorum praecepta attingenda videntur. Nam cum ars imitetur naturam in quantum potest, volenti autem scribere [23r.] primum carta et cera preparanda est, quibus loci simillimi sunt. Imagines autem literis, dispositio autem et collocatio imaginum scripturae, pronuntiatio autem lectioni comparantur. Illud merito fit ut ex his locis primum diffiniamus. Locus enim, ut quibusdam placet, est spatium quidam domus proportionatum et conditionatum quo conditionari debet; vel melius, secundum Ciceronem, locos appellamus eos qui breviter perfecte et insigniter manu aut natura absoluti sunt ut eos facile naturali memoria comprendere atque amplecti valeamus. Haec autem ars centum locis perficitur quos hoc pacto nobis constituere poterimus si decem domos nobis comparare poterimus in quarum singulis decem loci affigantur in diversis ipsarum domorum parietibus, vel paranda nobis erit una domus quae computatis cameris coquina et scalis constituatur centenus numerus apponendo cuilibet camerae vel scalae quinque locos.

Locorum proprietas multiplex est: primo locorum multitudo, locorum ordinatio, locorum solitudo, locorum meditatio, locorum signatio, locorum dissimilitudo, [23v.] locorum mediocris magnitudo, mediocris lux et distantia. Sequitur de imaginibus. Imagines sunt rerum aut verborum similitudines in mente conceptae. Duplices autem similitudines esse debent, ut ait Cicero, una rerum, alia verborum. Rerum autem similitudines constituuntur cum summatim ipsorum negotiorum imagines comparamus, verborum autem similitudines exprimuntur cum uniuscuiusque vocabuli memoria a nobis imagine notatur. Verborum quidem similitudines aliae sunt notae, aliae ignotae, notabilius aliae animatae, aliae inanimatae. Animatarum quaedam propriae quaedam communes. Propriarum quaedam duplices, quaedam simplices. Communium vero tam animatarum quam inanimatarum quaedam simplices, quaedam ex duabus pluribusne partibus constituuntur, de quibus omnibus dicetur inferius. Et primo videndum est de nominibus propriis simplicibus et duplicibus. Et premicto pro generali regula imaginum collocandarum quod in locis semper collocandae sunt imagines cum motu et acto ridiculoso crudeli admirativo aut turpi vel impossibili sive alio insueto. Talia enim crudelia vel ridiculosa aut insueta sensum immutare solent et melius excitare eo quod animus circa prava multum advertat.

[24r.] Secundo vero noto collocandam circa imaginem ut aliquid agat vel operet circa se vel circa ipsum locum. Si igitur daretur tibi ad memorandum nomen proprium, puta Petrus vel Martinus, debes accipere aliquem Petrum tibi notum ratione amicitiae vel inimicitiae, virtutis vel vituperii vel precellentis pulcritudinis aut nimiae deformitatis, non ociosum sed se exercitantem motu aliquo ridiculoso. Si nomen non adsit tibi notus capias aliquem factum et si non fuerit, recurrendum erit ad regulam dictionum ignotarum. Duplicia vero sunt cum duo ex istis simplicibus sumptis in recto casu quae veniunt ad significationem unius simplicis ut Jacobus Philippus, Johannes Maria. Prenomina vero sunt cum unum preest alteri in unico nomine quae prelatio semper est in obliquo cum dependentia, ut Johannes Andree, Matheus Tomasii. Cognomina autem et agnomina sunt quae parentelae vel ab cunctu [...] faciunt ad singularem notitiam vel alicuius individui: ut Franciscus Barbarus et Scipio Affricanus. Duplicia sic collocanda sunt ut eadem facias etiam ipsam imaginem ordinate operari. Item de prenominibus ita tamen quod [24v.] actus attributus recto habeat se in minus et actus attributus obliquo in maius. Agnomina autem et cognomina secundum primam sui partem ut traditum est de nominibus propriis. Secundum vero secundam sui partem prout tradetur de nominibus ignotis.

Pro clariori doctrina notandum est imagines, ex quibus similitudines capiuntur, formari posse dupliciter: aut ex parte rei, aut ex parte vocis. Si ex parte rei et tunc dupliciter: aut respectu rei propriae in se, aut ex parte methafisicae. Ex parte rei propriae in se similitudo capitur ut rem ipsam formando in propria forma et naturali, et hoc modo in rebus naturalibus maxime convenit. Secundo modo similitudo capitur ex parte rei methafisicae et secundum eius officium quod operatur aut secundum instrumentum cum quo operatur, et isto modo praecipue operamus in rebus invisibilibus. Si igitur rerum invisibilium vis tibi imagines servare, si sint res pertinentes ad virtutes vel vitia duplices possumus similitudines capere scilicet aut capiendo rem in qua est per excellentiam ut pro [25r.]

superbia Luciferum, pro sapientia Salomonem; secundo modo methafisice. Divina autem ut dictum et angelos a pictoribus didicimus collocare. Item de sanctis, ut virtus iustitia angelus anima deus, scilicet Petrus et cetera.

Nominum accidentalium similitudines ita capiuntur indifferenter videlicet ponendo picturam aut similitudinem aut realem rem cuius coloris qua nota collocanda demonstratur. Nota vero dignitatum officiorum et artium mechanicarum sic collocatur, capiendo similitudinem secundum signa et principalia eorum significata demonstrativa et declarativa ipsorum, ut si volumus collocare papam Martinum tibi notum secundum regulam de propriis habentem unam mitriam trium coronarum et sic de singulis secundum signa convenientia suis dignitatibus officiis et artibus.

Si vis memorari inanimatas duobus modis id efficere poteris. Primo modo ipsius rei inanimatae similitudinem capiendo ut aliquid operetur, imaginandus est homo sub concepto naturali non sub spetiali, nota et talis operatio fiat contra locum vel contra se. Secundo modo eligendo ordinem alphabeti et ad unum [25v.] quemque locum ponendo unum hominem tibi notum suprastantem tamque custodem et operarium loci qui operetur quando necesse est cum re inanimata ut dictum est in praecedentibus capitulis. Finalis regula de collocatione prosarum versuum ambasiatarum et ceterorum huiusmodi.

Ad apte figendas certa mente epistulas orationes sermones versus et cetera collocandi ratione potissimum opus esse percipitur, ut videlicet primum res ipsa universa rectissime teneatur ea quae naturali commendata memoriae congrue despiciatur. In primis enim rei totius summa simplici imagine vel nota aut ex pluribus aggregata contineatur quae quidem deinceps partes in suas idonee recitetur. Deinde illae partes in alias subdividere licebit. Finalis tamen divisio loco uno vel multiplicato capiatur. Principales autem divisiones ipsis quinariis applicentur, earum vero partes reliquas in aliorum imaginibus accommodentur. Versus spetialiter vocari possunt si praeter eorum summam figurationem principio annotentur aut spetiali imagine aut sillabis vel litteris.

Historiae vero per actus annotari possunt etiam parte tibi nota.

Rubricae collocari solent aut eorum summas perstringendo imagine accommodata aut per verborum similitudines. [26r.] Ambasiatas vero si commode volueris recordari ipsas, pro quo ambasiata collocanda est, imagines capies sive ipsumet in quo pacta sive promissa repones et ex adversis autem illum cui facienda est ambasiata in illo petita repones, et si sumuntur plures res sive capitula seriatim conclusive per loca dispones.

Argumenta possumus congrue argumentibus applicare quibus absentibus locorum custodibus affigantur. Si enim sologismus fuerit, maiorem dexterae, minorem sinistrae accommodemus, aut potuerimus pro maiori tenere imaginem notatam vel medii aut conclusionis. Si vero fuerit entimema satis erit primam propositionem notare; in iure aut rubricam cum lege aut scilicet cum eius mente notare ut fuerit. Τελοζ.

II

[27v.] Tractatus artis memorative eximii doctoris artium et medicinae magistri Girardi

Ars commoda naturae confirmat et auget, ut inquit egregius Tullius in tertio rhetoricae, cuius experientiam habemus in duplici arte scilicet domificatoria qua artifex finalis per hanc intendit defectui naturae providere; in arte etiam medicatoria minister salutis conatur proposse superflua naturae expellere ac defectus eiusdem restaurare. Que quidem ars minime foret inventa si natura auxilio non egeret. Verum quia anima nostra in principio suae creationis nascitur defectuosa in tribus suis potentiis clarioribus: scilicet memoria, intellectu et voluntate.

Non tamen dico defectuosa sit quod anima nostra in principio creationis suae non habeat omnes potentias sibi concreatas, sed dico defectuosa sit quod in principio nostrae nativitatis anima nostra nequaquam potest per has potentias suos actus exercere. Non igitur parum utilis est artificialis memoria, quae commoda naturae amplificat ratione doctrinae. Huius quippe artis multi fuerunt inventores inter quos quidam nimis occulte, alii nimis confuse eam tradiderunt. Sed ego zelo sapientiae dilatandae [28 r.] hanc artem compendiosis et utilibus verbis declarare intendo, hoc opusculum dividendo per novem capitula.

In capitulo primo ostendetur breviter et succincte quae sint instrumenta quibus utendum est in hac arte.

In secundo tradetur ars memorandi terminos substantiales.

In tertio dabitur ars memorandi terminos accidentales.

In quarto dabitur ars memorandi auctoritates et quascumque orationes simplices.

In quinto tradetur ars memorandi epistolas collectiones et quascumque historias prolixas.

In sexto tradetur ars memorandi argumenta et quascumque orationes sillogisticas.

In septimo tradetur ars memorandi versus.

In octavo tradetur et dabitur ars memorandi dictiones ignotas, puta graecas, hebraicas, sincathagoremata et capita legum.

In nono et ultimo dabuntur secreta huius artis.

Unde versus:

> Sedibus humanis trita stans filia celsi
> Inexculta cibo mens grave tenet in albo
> Sed si concipiat post semen arca volutum
> In varias formas parit similia monstro
> Qui igitur volet perfectam gignere prolem
> Promptam facetam recte natam in ordine membri
> De multis tractum subiectum forbeat haustum.

[Interlineal glosses: *Sedibus humanis*: in corpore humano; *trita*: afflicta; *filia celsi*: scilicet dei; *inexculta*: scilicet impleta; *grave*: graviter; *in albo*: scilicet memoria.]

[28v] Capitulum primum. Pro expeditione primi capituli prenotandum est quod finalis intentio nostra in hac arte est componere librum mentalem qui quid se habeat ad instar libri artificialis. Nam quemadmodum in libro artificiali duo sufficiunt instrumenta duntaxat scilicet carta et scriptura, ita et non aliter in hoc libro mentali quem intendimus per hanc artem conficere duo sufficiunt instrumenta: scilicet loca et rerum similitudines. Unde egregius Tullius in sua rhetorica loca inquit carte simillima, sicut imagines literis. Dispositio vero imaginum in locis lectioni comparatur. Sed quia vari sunt modi accipiendi loca in hac arte, sufficiet ad presens tre modos notare. Primus modus est secundum Tullium, et hic est satis grossus, accipiendo videlicet domum realem vel imaginariam in qua diversa signa notentur inter angulos illius contenta. Secundus modus est servando ordinem scalarum. Tertius est servando ordinem mense vel alium quemvis artificialem huic consimilem. Verum est tamen quod de novo practicantibus in hac arte bonum est in primis modum Tullii imitari ut a facilioribus ad difficiliora facilior sit transitus. Unde versus:

Tipicha fortificat poliniam vallis locorum
[29r.] Hec per ambages deserti querere noli
Que rapuit pacifex iam lux perdit vel atro
Invisaque spernit fugit gravissima quecque
Huius vero plus placuit medios habuisse penatos
Incultos natos diversos noto placentes
In quorum costis fingantur ordine quino
Que fixa maneant signa distantia tractu.

[Interlineal glosses: *Tipicha*: figurata; *poliniam*: memoriam; *vallis locorum*: scilicet ordinatio; *Haec*: loca; *per ambages*: per loca dubia; *pacifex*: scilicet intellectus; *iam lux perdit vel atro*: per nimiam lucem vel obscuritatem; *Invisa*: loca; *gravissima*: dissimillima; *quecque*: loca; *medios habuisse penatos*: scilicet manifestas domos; *Incultos*: non habitatas; *diversos*: scilicet colore vel figura; *noto placentes*: scilicet voluntati; *In quorum*: penatum; *costis:* parietibus; *fixa:* firma.]

Secundum capitulum. Si vis memorari terminos substantiales scire debes quod tales sunt duplices. Quidam sunt proprii et quidam communes. Si igitur vis memorari terminos communes sufficit pro quolibet tali accipere similitudinem agentem aliquid mirabile vel patientem et illam memento in suo loco collocare, praesuppositis his quae dicta sunt de locis in precedenti capitulo. In propriis autem nominibus non sic fit quoniam multorum hominum una est similitudo communis, accipere igitur pro quolibet nomine proprio aliquem tibi notum ratione laudis, vituperii vel conversationis et illum memento in suo loco collocare. Et notatur <quod> dictum est supra quod similitudo rei memorandae debet agere vel pati aliquid mirabile quoniam quanto actio vel passio fuerit mirabilior aut magis ridiculosa tanto diuturnior erit memoria. Unde versus:

Usia post rerum recte ponatur in istis
Cum voles hanc disce viam quae plana patebit
Subiectis propriis proprias est dare figuras
Communes aliis: cythara noscetur Apollo.

[Interlineal glosses: *Usia*: scilicet forma; *recte*: sub ordine; *in istis*: scilicet costis; *Subiectis*: nominibus; *Communes*: similitudines.]

Tertium capitulum. Si vis memorari terminos accidentales, quia accidens non habet esse per se sed totum esse eius dependet a substantia, pro quolibet tali accidente debes accipere substantivum in quo est per excellentiam: ut pro rubeo rosam, pro albo lilium, pro fortitudinem Sansonem, pro sapientia Salomonem. Et nota hic tres regulas solemnes. Prima est quod omne nomen significans substantiam in qua est aliquid accidens per excellentiam significat duo: scilicet substantiam primo et accidens posterius et secundario; et sic monialis significat feminam et castitatem, lupus animal et voracitatem, philomena avem et cantorem. Secunda regula est quod a tali nomine significanti duo descendit nomen adiectivum vel verbum, ut de rosa descendit roseus rosea roseum et roseare quod est rubeum facere. Tertia regula est quod ad commemorandum artificiose derivativa sive fuerint nomina sive verba aut participia [30r.] vel adverbia sufficit habere memoriam primitivi, et ratio est quoniam omnem derivativum virtualiter includitur in primitivo et capit naturam eiusdem. Unde versus:

Quod pendet fixum de se vult capere plenum
Si varias uno profers multis ne licebit
In derivativis quae sit origo notabis.

[Interlineal glosses: *Quod pendet*: illud quod est auribus pendens; *fixum*: subiectum; *de se vult capere plenum*: scilicet in quo est per excellentiam.]

Quartum capitulum. Si vis memoriae auctoritates et quascumque orationes simplices accipe pro qualibet obiectum principale eiusdem et illius memento in suo loco collocare praesuppositis his quae dicta sunt supra. Ratio autem huius est quoniam signum et signatum sunt correlativa. Unde versus:

Complexum si vis obiectum indicat illud.

Quintum capitulum. Si vis memorari epistulas et quascumque historias prolixas divide per suas partes principales et rursus quamlibet per suas partes donec perveneris ad clausulam; quo facto age ut dictum est in capitulo praecedenti de orationibus simplicibus. Et ratio huius est quoniam divisio valet ad tria. Primum animum legentis excitat, secundo intelligentiam confirmat, tertio memoriam artificiose corroborat. Unde versus:

Ut plerique volunt divisio valet

[30v.]   Animum legentis excitat mentem quoque probat
         Intelligentis memoriam roborat atque.

Sextum capitulum. Si vis memorari argumenta et quascumque orationes sillogisticas sufficit pro quolibet argumento habere memoriam medii et ratio est quoniam, ut dicit Aristoteles in primo
priorum, medium est in virtute totus sillogismus. Sed quia difficile
est medium invenire secundum doctrinam quam tradit Aristoteles
in fine primi priorum, sciendum est quod medium in proposito
nihil aliud est quam causa conclusionis, idest illud inferens in quo
virtualiter consistit argumentum. Unde versus:

        Qui nescit causas nihil scit, quia nulla
        Res est nota satis, cuius origo latet.

Septimum capitulum. Si vis memorari versus hoc potest fieri altero
duorum modorum: primo accipiendo a quolibet versu sententiam
meliori via in qua fieri potest et cum versus bis vel ter replicando;
secundo accipiendo duas vel tres dictiones principales cuiuslibet
versus et cum illis ipsum versum bis vel ter repetendo. Sic enim ars
suppedit naturae et ratio huius est quoniam versus ex sua natura
valet ad tria. Unde versus:

        Metra iuvant animos, comprehendunt plurima paucis
        Pristina commemorant quae sunt tria grata legenti.

Octavum capitulum. Si vis memorari dictiones ignotas hoc potest
duobus modis fieri. Primo per viam similitudinis, accipiendo
videlicet pro qualibet dictione ignota dictionem nobis notam
habentem aliquam similitudinem cum tali dictione ignota. Secundo
fiat hoc per viam divisionis sillabarum, dividendo scilicet dictionem
ignotam per suas sillabas, et pro qualibet sillaba accipiendo dictionem tibi notam incipientem ab ea. Unde versus:

        Ignotum memorari si vis barbarum nomen
        Aut summas apparens per partes divide totum.

Ultimum capitulum. Pro expeditione completa huius artis faciendum quod beatus Thomas in secunda secundae, quaestione 49 et
capitulo primo. Ponit quatuor documenta quibus proficimur in

bene memorando. Primus est ut eorum quae vult aliquis memorari quasdam similitudines assumat convenientes nec tantum omnino consuetas, quia et quae sunt inconsueta magis miramur et sic in eis animus magis et vehementius detinetur. Ex quo fit quod eorum quae in pueritia vidimus [31v.] magis memoremur. Ideo autem magis necessaria est huiusmodi similitudinum vel imaginum adinventio, quia intentiones simplices et spirituales facilius ex animo elabuntur nisi quibusdam similitudinibus corporalibus quasi alligentur, quia humana cognitio potentior est circa sensibilia. Unde haec memorativa ponitur in parte sensitiva. Secundo oportet ut homo ea quae memoriter vult tenere sua consideratione ordinate disponat et ex uno memorato facile ad aliud procedat. Unde dixit philosophus in libro de memoria a locis videtur reminisci aliquando, causa autem est quia velocitate ab uno ad aliud veniunt. Tertio oportet quod homo sollicitudinem apponat et affectum adhibeat ad ea quae vult memorari, quia quanto magis aliquid fuerit impressum animo eo minus elabitur. Unde Tullius dixit in sua rhetorica quod sollicitudo conservat integras simulacrorum figuras. Quarto oportet quod ea frequenter meditemur quae volumus memorari. Unde philosophus dixit in libro de memoria quod meditationes servant [32r.] memoriam, quia, ut in eodem libro dicitur, consuetudo est quasi natura. Unde quae multoties intelligimus cito reminiscimur quasi naturali quodam ordine ad uno ad aliud procedentes. Sed quia tota difficultas artis memorativae consistit in difficili et laboriosa locorum acceptione et in illa laboriosa adinventione imaginum convenientium, in hac arte notanda sunt duo pro secretis huius artis. Primo est notandum pro facili et prompta locorum acceptione quod tota perfectio huius artis ex parte locorum consistit in centum locis familiaribus quae pro certa loca habere poterimus duplici via. Primo accipiendo decem domus reales a nobis optime frequentatas in diversibus civitatibus vel in eadem, itaque in qualibet domo notentur decem loca distincta loco situ et figura ac in convenienti ordine et aliqua distantia. Secundo possunt haberi centum loca familiaria accipiendo viginti imagines divisarum rerum quae tamen sint ordinatae secundum ordinem literarum alphabeti: ut pro A accipiamus arietem, pro B bovem, pro C canem, pro D dromedarium, pro E equum, pro F folium, pro G griffonem, pro H hircum, pro I idolum, pro K Katerinam, pro L leonem, pro M monacum, pro N nucem, pro O [32v.] ovem, pro P pastorem, pro Q quiritem, pro R regem, pro S sapientem, pro T turrim, pro V vas olei vel vini. Ita tamen quod in qualibet istarum imaginum notentur quinque determinata signa quae facient quinque loca in qualibet, et hoc quidem facillimum est ut patebit in pratica. Secundo est notandum ex parte imaginum sive similitudinum quod permaxime perficit in memorando artificiose servare imaginibus colligantiam. Talis autem colligantia dupliciter intelligitur. Primo ut quaelibet imago se exercitet aliquo modo cum suo loco. Secundo ut una imago se exercitet cum alia: sic prima cum secunda, tertia cum quarta et sic de aliis. Et est diligenter advertendum in hac arte quod attestatur egregius Tullius in tertio Rhetoricorum videlicet quod artis huius preceptio est infirma nisi diligentia et exercitatio comprobetur. Unde versus:

> Doctrinae pater est usus doctrina scolaris
> Interscissa perit, continuata urget.

Finis.

In addition to the text of his *Phoenix seu artificiosa memoria*, Ravenna included some prefatory letters of privilege in the first printed edition of 1491: from the Comune of Pistoia (12 September 1480); from Bonifacio marchese del Monferrato (24 September 1488); from Eleonora d'Aragona duchessa di Ferrara (10 October 1491). In addition to the letter of Eleonora, we reproduce here the dedicatory verses written by Egidio da Viterbo and some passages from the preface which refer to episodes in Ravenna's life. We have used the copy of the first edition which can be found (together with three other incunabula), in Bibliotheca Marciana, MS Lat. 274, class VI, ff. 82–97v.

I

[82r.] Eleonora de Aragona Ducissa Ferrariae etc. quod ab omnium bonorum datore immortali deo generi humano concessum est plaerique in orbe terrarum a constitutione mundi usque ad hanc aetatem excellentes viri evasere, quos inter nunc adest spectatus miles auratus et insignis utroque iure consultus dominus Petrus

Tomasius Ravennas harum literarum nostrarum exhibitor, qui, praeter alias corporis et animi dotes, ita omni doctrinarum genere et tenacissima memoria refulget ut nedum superiorem, sed etiam in his parem minime habere videatur. Quod quidem nuper latissime re ipsa comprobavit non solum nos, sed etiam omnis haec civitas nostra testimonium perhibere potest. Qua ex re factum est ut eum singulari admiratione precipuaque charitate complexae inter nostros praeter alios familiarem et domesticum habere constituerimus. Quamobrem serenissimos reges, illustres principes, excellentes respublicas et alios quosqunque dominos patres fratres amicos benivolosque nostros precamur et oramus ex animo ut quotienscunque ei contigerit ipsum dominum Petrum [82v] tam optime meritum cum suis famulis et equis usque ad numerum octo cum suis bulgiis forceriis et capsis cum pannis et vestibus suis libris vasis argenteis et aliis cuibuscunque rebus suis ac armis per eorum urbes oppida vicos passus aquas et loca die nocteque liberrime et expeditissime absque alicuius datii gabellae et alius cuiuslibet oneris solutione amoris nostri et potissimum tam maximarum huius hominis virtutum causa transire permittant commendatissimumque ipsum semper habentes ei providere velint de liberrimo expeditissimoque transitu et idonea cohorte ut opus fuerit et ipse requisiverit. Quod quidem nobis iucundissimum semper erit atque gratissimum, paratissimis ad omnia eorum qui sic in eo se habuerint beneplacita. Mandamus autem omnibus et singulis magistratibus quoruncunque locorum nostrorum et potissimum custodibus passuum reliquisque subditis nostris ut praedicta omnia et singula in terris et locis nostris inviolabiliter servent servarique faciant. Sub indignationis nostrae incursu et alia quavis graviori poena pro arbitrio nostro eis imponenda; ad quorum robur et fidem has nostras patentes litteras fieri iussimus et registrari et nostri maiori sigilli munimine roborari. Datas Ferrariae in nostro ducali palatio anno nativitatis dominicae Millesimo quatringentesimo nonagesimo primo, indictione nona, die decimo mensis Octobris. Severius.

II.

[84v.] Paduae Domino Petro memoriae magistro.

Qui modo pyramides, quid iam Babylona canamus
  Quid Iovis et triviae templa superba deae
Non magis immensum mirabimur amphitheatrum

Nam summe facerent hoc quoque semper opes
Scipio non ultra iactet quod fecerat usus
   Agmina qui proprio nomine tota vocat
Petrum fama canat quam nobilis ille Ravennae est
   Gloria, qui plusque docta Minerva potest
Quid magni facere dei mirabile dictu
   Nam retinet quicquid legerit ille semel
Effatur triplici quaecunque orator in hora
   Protinus hic iterum nil minus ore refert
Sic reor hunc genuit doctarum quinta sororum
   Cui pia musa nihil non meminisse dedit.

Frater Egidius Viterbiensis heremita

III

[92v.] Bononiae, Papiae, Ferrariaeque legi et qui me audierunt multa memoriter scire incoeperunt, et quamvis mea artificiosa memoria aliorum auctoritatibus sit comprobata, peccare tamen non puto si acta mea in hoc libello legentur quae ipsam mirabiliter approbabunt. Dum essem iuris auditor, nec vigesimum vidissem annum, in universitate patavina dixi me totum codicem iuris civilis posse recitare; petii namque ut mihi leges aliquae ad arbitrium astantium proponerentur, quibus propositis, summaria Bartoli dicebam, aliqua verba textus recitabam, casum adducebam, tacta per doctores examinabam, lexque ista tot habet glosas dicebam et super quibus verbis erant positae recordabar, [93r.] contraria allegabam et solvebam. Visum est astantibus vidisse miraculum; Alexander Imolensis diu obstupuit, nec fabulam narro: ego palam locutus sum in universitate Paduae ex qua in ore duorum vel trium stat omne verbum; testes huius rei tres habeo: magnificum dominum Ioannem Franciscum Pasqualicum senatorem venetum et iuris utriusque doctorem excellentissimum apud illustrissimum Mediolani ducem nunc legatum, clarissimum doctorem dominum Sigismundum de capitibus listae civem nobilem patavinum cuius predictus Franciscus fuit acutissimi ingenii iuris consultus, spectabilem dominum Monaldinum de Monaldiniis Venetiis commorantem in quo virtus domicilium suum collocavit.

Lectiones etiam Alexandri Imolensis Paduae legentis copiosissimas memoria tenebam et illas ex verbo ad verbum in scriptis redigebam, illas etiam postquam finierat, astante magna auditorum copia, a calce incipiens recitabam ex suisque lectionibus dum in scholis audirem carmina faciebam et omnes earum partes in carminibus positas statim replicabam; et qui hoc viderunt obstupuere : huius rei testes habeo clarissimum equitem et doctorem dominum Sigismundum de capitibus listae et filium Alexandri Imolensis qui nunc est iuris consultus celeberrimus.

Centum et quatraginta quinque auctoritates religiosissimi fratris Michaelis de Mediolano Paduae praedicantis immortalitatem animae probantes, coram eo memoriter et prompte pronunciavi, qui me amplexus est dicens: vive diu, gemma singularis, utinam te religioni dicatum viderem. Testis est tota civitas patavina, sed magnificum dominum Ioannem Franciscum Pasqualicum et dominum Sigismundum de capitibus listae et dominum Monaldinum de Monaldiniis testes habeo. Petii ego doctor [93v.] creatus in universitate patavina, ut mihi in cathedra sedenti, aliquis de universitate auditor unum ex tribus voluminibus digestorum quid eligeret praesentarent locumque in quo legere deberem designaret. Dixi enim supra re proposita innumerabiles leges allegabo. Testes sunt clarissimus iuris utriusque doctor dominus Gaspar Orsatus Paduae iura canonica legens et doctissimus dominus Prosper Cremonensis Paduae commorans [...]

Semel in schachis ludebam et alius taxillos iaciebat aliusque omnes iactus scribebat et ex themate mihi proposito duas [94r.] epistolas dictabam. Postquam finem ludo imposuimus omnes iactus schachorum et taxillorum et epistolarum verba ab ultimis incipiens repetii; haec quatuor per me eodem tempore collocata fuerunt. Testes sunt dominus Petrus de Montagnano et Franciscus Nevolinus nobiles patavini cives.

Dum essem Placentiae monasterium monachorum nigrorum intravi ut illud viderem, in dormitorioque eius comitante monacho quodam bis deambulans monachorum nomina quae in ostiis cellarum erant collocavi; deinde congregatis eis nomine proprio quemlibet salutavi, licet quem nominabam digito demonstrare non potuissem. Mirabantur monachi quo pacto ego peregrinus nomina eorum memoriter proferrem, ipsis mirari non desinentibus, dixi tandem: hoc potuit mea artificiosa memoria, quorum unus dixit ergo hoc Petrus Ravennas facere potuit et non alius.

In capitulo generali canonicorum regularium Paduae, praedicationem domini Deodati Vincentini eo ordine quo ipsam pronunciaverat recitavi astante ipsius praedicationis auctore. Semel me traxit

ad sui contemplationem Cassandra, fidelis veneta virgo excellentis-
sima, quae dum legeret litteras serenissimae coniugis regis
Ferdinandi ad se missas, illas collocavi et recitavi; testis est illa doc-
tissima virgo, dominus Paulus Raimusius doctor excellens arimi-
nensis et Angelus Salernitanus vir clarus [...] [94v.] De mea
artificiosa memoria testis est illustrissimus marchio Bonifacius et
eius pulcherrima uxor quae me egregio munere donavi; testis est
illustrissimus Hercules dux et illustrissima uxor Eleonora; testis est
tota Ferraria duas enim praedicationes celeberrimi verbi dei prae-
conis magistri mariani heremitae recitavi, quo audito obstupuit dic-
tus magister et dixit: illustrissima ducissa hoc est divinum et
miraculosum opus; testis est universitas patavina: omnes enim lectiones meas iuris canonici sine libro quotidie lego ac si librum ante
oculos haberem, textum, et glosas memoriter pronuncio ut nec
etiam minimam syllabam omittere videar. In locis autem meis quae
collocaverim hic scribere statui et quae locis tradidi perpetuo teneo,
in decem et novem litteris alphabeti vigintimilia allegationum iuris
utriusque posui et eodem ordine sacrorum librorum septem milia,
mille Ovidii carmina quae ab eo sapienter dicta continent, ducen-
tas Ciceronis auctoritates, trecenta philosophorum dicta, magnam
Valeri Maximi partem, naturas fere omnium animalium bipedum et
quadrupedem quorum auctoritatem singula verba collocavi, et
quando vires arti- [95r.] ficiosae memoriae experiri cupio, peto ut
mihi una ex litteris illis alphabeti proponantur, super qua proposita
allegationes profero, et ut clare intelligas, exemplum habes:
proposita est mihi nunc littera A in magno doctorum virorum con-
ventu, et statim a iure principium faciens, mille allegationes et
plures proferam de alimentis, de alienatione, de absentia, de arbitris,
de appellationibus et de similibus quae iure nostro habentur incip-
ientibus a dicta littera A; deinde in sacra scriptura de Antichristo,
de adulatione et multas allegationes sacrae scripturae ab illa littera
incipientes pronunciabo, carmina Ovidii, auctoritates Ciceronis et
Valerii non omittam, de asino de aquila de agno de accipitre de
apro de ariete auctoritates allegabo, et quaecumque dixero ab
ultimis incipiens velociter repetam [...]

APPENDIX V
THREE LATE SIXTEENTH-CENTURY MANUSCRIPTS ON THE *ARS*
MEMORATIVA

The mnemotechnical art of Rosselli, who worked primarily within the
'Ciceronian' tradition and had little contact with Lullism, seems in many
ways close to the later sixteenth-century systems of Giordano Bruno.
Throughout the sixteenth century there was no shortage of treatises which
followed the traditional rules of 'classical' mnemotechnics. I give the following account of three manuscript treatises because they are representative of these traditional approaches. In the first of these, Bibliotheca
Nazionale, Florence, MS Palatino 885 (Miscellaneous MSS on paper,
14th–16th centuries, 466 folios), ff. 289r.–313v. (Incipit: 'Queritur primo,
quare, antequam hanc, artificialem memoriam non in aperto tradiderunt'.
Explicit: 'Vox continua est de quantitate continua'.) there is an anonymous
treatise on mnemotechnics written in a sixteenth-century hand in which
one finds a wholly conventional treatment of the doctrine of *loci* and *imagines*. In the second, Bibliotheca Laurenziana, MS Ashburnhamiano 1226
(MS on paper, late sixteenth century, 72 folios) we find again the characteristic transformation from rhetorical treatise to an ordered and systematic classification of notions. The art of memory is not dealt with
explicitly in this work – its mnemonic intentions are made clear in the
tabular arrangement of materials. See f. 1v. for example:

> La Rhetorica è un arte di trovare ciò che in ogni cosa sia acconcio a
> persuadere. Le fedi con le quali si persuade sono: *Dell' arte cotai sono:*
> nella vita e nei costumi dell'Oratore, in mover l'animo del giudice, nel-
> l'oratione quando si prova o par che si prova alcuna cosa. Questa
> maniera di fede si prova e si tratta dall'Oratore. *Fuori dell'arte cotai sono:*
> leggi, patti, testimoni, tormenti, giurí. Quest'altra maniera di fede si
> tratta solamente dall'Oratore.

In the third manuscript, Florence, Bibliotheca Nazionale, MS Magliab.
II, I, 13 (to which Yates refers in her studies on the art of memory),[11] we
know both the author and the date and place of composition. Written by
Fra Agostino Riccio in the Convent of Santa Maria Novella in 1595, the
treatise is addressed 'to the young literary scholars of Florence' (*alla
gioventù fiorentina studiosa di lettere*). Yates describes this work as being 'less
abstract than the treatises of Romberch and Rossellius'.[12] In actual fact
Riccio's short treatise seems wholly conventional, the last echo of a

tradition which had become exhausted. Even in this work, however, there is no lack of novelty regarding its use of classical sources. In order to impress the rules of the art of memory more clearly on the minds of his readers, Riccio uses images and symbols: rather than giving precepts which teach us how to 'arrange' images, we are given explanations in the form of complex images. Bruno's *Explicatio triginta sigillorum* (written twelve years earlier, in 1583) approached the same problem in a similar way.

[1r.] Essendo la memoria madre delle scienze poi che quello che veramente si sa che si ritiene nella memoria impresso, utilissima è l'arte che rende perfetta questa natural potenza. Di essa da molti sono stati scritti vari libri, ma non però ho stimato ch'a me sia negato il formare questo trattato nel quale sotto la similitudine d'un potentissimo Re ch'appresso di sé ha due consiglieri e tre valorosi capitani et un servo che provede ciò che fa di bisogno, brevemente e chiaramente ho ridotto in sette precetti la somma di quest'arte et a voi la dono.

[7r.] Seconda regola o Primo consiglier o luoghi, son nominati da me, ché tutti questi tre nomi significano una cosa medesima come si dichiara per la figura dipinta a uso d'huomo consigliere del Re, ché detto consigliere tiene una mano sopra a un mappamondo dipinto nel quale si vede città, terre, castelli, case, botteghe, cosí anco chiese, palazzi, vie, piazze, conventi di religiosi e a molte altre cose [...]

[17v.] Però io ho fatto molti Alfabeti diversi acciò che tu gli legga e vi facci pratica, un Alfabeto è di fiumi laghi e pesci, un di pietre preziose e tutte l'altre pietre insieme, un d'erbe e piante piccole, un di fiori, un d'alberi e frutti grandi, un d'animali grandi e piccoli ... un di città, un di casati fiorentini, un d'arti meccaniche e liberali o exercitii o servitù che si faccino per guadagnare, un d'huomini honorati [...]

APPENDIX VI
PETRARCH AS TEACHER OF THE ART OF MEMORY

In a work which we have cited frequently in this book,[13] Frances Yates identified a series of texts on the *ars memorativa* which make specific references to Petrarch. In Johannes Romberch's *Congestorium artificiose memorie*, published in Venice in 1520, for example, there are numerous references to Petrarch, crediting him with the invention of many of the 'technical' features of the doctrine of *loci* and *imagines*,[14] and Filippo Maria Gesualdo's *Plutosofia* (1592) refers to Romberch as a follower of 'Petrarchan' mnemotechnics.[15] Tommaso Garzoni's *Piazza universale* (1578) includes Petrarch in a list of the most famous exponents of the art,[16] while Lambert Schenkel in his *Gazophylacium artis memoriae* (1610)[17] after having quoted a long passage from the *Rerum memorandum libri*,[18] says that Petrarch 'ardently supported and diligently improved' (*avide susceptam et diligenter excultam*) the mnemotechnical art.[19]

The scattered references to memory, artificial memory, and famous examples of prodigious memory in the works of Petrarch have been identified, with admirable precision, by Yates. Although there are no specific rules of mnemotechnics, or recommendations of the *ars memoriae* in any of Petrarch's works, he was undoubtedly aware of the art and its popularity: 'Itaque minus miror tanti nature preditum muneribus artificiosam memoriam contempsisse, que tum primum in Grecia reperta, apud nos hodie vulgata est.'[20] The tradition which views Petrarch as a 'classical' writer of the literature on memory did not arise simply out of a desire (widespread amongst authors of these treatises) to invoke ever newer 'authorities'. It has specific origins:

> I think one can see how the tradition about Petrarch as an advocate of the classical mnemonic arose. Everyone knew that the great scholastics in treating memory as a part of prudence had recommended the artificial memory. It was therefore supposed that when Petrarch treated memory as a part of prudence by giving amongst his *exempla* the memories of great classical rhetors in which he made allusions to the classical mnemonic, he thereby meant – though in his own 'humanist' way – to recommend it. And it was probably further supposed that in the description of the memory of his friend he was describing the feats of a modern 'artificial memory' based on the practice of the ancients. This was certainly the assumption made by Lambert Schenkel, in the passage referred to above.[21]

It seems difficult not to agree with Yates's conclusions, even if the only passage which she cites in connection with the emergence of this curious tradition contains statements which only partly corroborate Yates's views:

> Qui autem aequus rerum aestimator, considerans quae ex Francisco Petrarcha hic citata sunt, nempe artificiosam memoriam sua aetate vulgatam fuisse, militem illum amicum ab adolescentia multorum itinerum individuum comitem ipsi fuisse, saepe totos dies et noctes colloquiis traductos, aliasque circumstantias, ac maximam occasionem consequendae huius artis, vel ab ipso, qui eam tali amico, viro tam docto, negare non putuisset, vel ab aliis, iudicet illam ab ipso esse neglectam; praesertim cum memoriae illius excellentia, communi omnium fama, celebretur et a scriptoribus in numerum illorum relatus sit qui admirabili memoria insignes fuerunt, ac scripta facile testentur quantus ille orator, quantus poeta latinus, quodque italorum poetarum princeps habeatur, unde recte colligitur artem memoriae avide ab illo fuisse susceptam et diligenter excultam, atque maximo sibi in studiis omnibus adiumento et ornamento fuisse.[22]

Whatever else happened it seems certain that the tradition of Petrarch as a teacher and theorist of artificial memory continued much longer than Yates suggests (the tradition of associating Petrarch with mnemonics goes on even into the early seventeenth century').[23] In the writings of Jean Belot, published in 1654 and reissued in 1669, 1688 and 1704, for example, the name of Petrarch is included alongside those of Pietro da Ravenna and Giordano Bruno as a theorist of artificial memory.[24] We also find, in a long note added by Diodati to the article on 'Mémoire' in Diderot's encyclopaedia in the late eighteenth century, in addition to the names of Pietro da Ravenna, Jacopo Publicio, Romberch, and Cosma Rosselli, that of Francesco Petrarcha.[25]

APPENDIX VII
AN UNPUBLISHED TEXT BY GIULIO CAMILLO

Eugenio Garin has recently drawn attention to an unpublished work by Camillo of a theological and cabalistic character.[26] Camillo's work begins with a characteristic proem in which, besides other things, he states:

> And since there is no worthier and higher subject than God himself, the present work discusses the interpretation of the Ark of the

Covenant, through which we have true knowledge of the three worlds, that is the supercelestial, the celestial and the inferior [worlds] whence arises true Theological or (as we would say) Divine Understanding, here the Pythagorean six-part canon is explained and cut from the Ternary, that is *Artifex* [Creator], *Exemplar* [Archetype] and *Hyle* [Matter]. Which we interpret as Matter, Form and Privation. Here more obscure and knotty passages of the Sacred Scriptures are made clear. Here you will see how the Pythagorean and Platonic teachings are consonant with our philosophy and theology.

[Et perché né piú degno soggetto, né piú alto si tratta del Sommo Dio, contenendo la presente Opera l'interpretazione dell'Arca del Patto, per la quale si ha la vera Intelligenza delli tre Mundi, cioè Sopra Celeste, Celeste et Inferiore, onde ne risorge la vera Cognitione Theologica, over Divina che dir vogliamo, qui è esponuto il Senario Canone Pitagorico et sforbito dal Ternario, cioè Artifex, Exemplar, Hyle. Qui è dichiarato cos'è Materia, Forma et Privatione. Qui piú luoghi delle Sacre pagine enodati et de oscuri fatti chiari. Qui vedrai accordata la Pitagorica, et Platonica disciplina, con la philosophia et theologia nostra.]

I have found another example of this text in Bibliotheca di Università di Pavia MS Aldino 59 (MS on paper, sixteenth century, 95 numbered folios, bound in paper boards, 185 x 147mm). As in the Neapolitan manuscript, the text in this manuscript is followed by a treatise entitled *De transmutatione*. On f. 40r. it says: 'There are three transmutations: that is divine transmutation, the transmutation of speech and that which pertains to metals. And there is a marvellous correspondence between all three.' (*Tre esser le une transmutationi, cioè: la Divina, quella delle Parole, et quella ch'è pertinente alli Metalli. Et tutte tre fra loro haver una maravigliosa corrispondenza.*) Agrippa and Giovanni da Rupescissa are cited on f. 46r., and ff. 51r. et seq. contain a transcription from the 1548 Venetian edition of *Porte della luce santa*.

Appendix VIII
Memory exercises in seventeenth-century Germany

As we have already seen, the mnemotechnical works of Pietro da Ravenna (and later those of Giordano Bruno) exercised a profound influence on German intellectual circles. The text which follows testifies to the fascination that the 'memory exercises' which had been so fashionable in the sixteenth century (especially in Italy and Germany) continued to exert in German academic circles in the early years of the seventeenth century. Many seventeenth-century emblematists devoted themselves to these kinds of diversions (reciting a list of a hundred or more unusual words or expressions forwards and backwards, for example). As Mario Praz has pointed out, the Jesuit father Menestrier, celebrated author of a hundred emblematic works, displayed his prodigious memory in an audience with Queen Christina of Sweden using exercises of this type.[27] The text which follows is drawn from Joannes Paepp, *Schenkelius detectus seu memoria artificialis hactenus occultata* (Lyons, 1617), pp. 30–9. What is especially interesting in the works of Paepp[28] is his attempt to combine the figures of Lullian *combinatoria* with those used in 'Ciceronian' mnemotechnics. Rudolphus Goclenius, who is named in the text, was a celebrated figure of the time.[29]

Die XXIX Sept., styli veteris anni, MDCII, hora octava matutina convenerunt ad aedes celeberrimi ac magni illius philosophi et professoris D. Rudol. Goclenii, clariss. vir ac D. Henricus Ellenbergerus praeclarus medicinae doctor et professor, D. Mathias à Süchten Dantiscanus Borossus, et M. Christophorus Bauneman Maior stipendiarorum. Petitque Schenkelius a D. Goclenio et D. Ellenbergero dictari XXV sententias, quas ipse calamo excepit, praeposita cuique nota arithmetica, deinde intro vocavit ingenuum ac doctum adolsecentem Dn. Iustum Ingmannum, Cassellanum Hessem iuris ac philosophiae studiosum cui eae omnes ordine prelectae sunt a Schenkelio, singulae bis interiecto aliquantulo more, omnibusque dictis tacitus aliquantisper sedit. Deinde exorsus loqui a prima ad ultimam ordine recto et retrogrado ab hac ad illam sine mora, haesitatione aut errore recitavit. Cum vero bis terve evenisset ut dictionem unam alteri praeponeret, ac bis ut synonymum pro synonymo in quibus facillimus est lapsus ita pro sic, limites pro fines, unico hoc verbo admonitus, dic ordine dixine ita? synonymum ponis: statim et eadem substituit vocabula et suo ordine. Postremo intercalari ordine quolibet expresso numero statim sententiam, aut dicto primo cuiuslibet sententiae vocabulo confestim numerum indicavit. Tum rogavit Dn. Iungmannum Schenkelius an vellet aliquas praeterea sententias adiici. Alacri animo XXV alias addi optavit. Verum Schenkelio respondente nimis multas fore, quindecim petiit; quas arti applicatas eadem dexteritate promptitudine qua superiores quolibet ordine et separatim et cum aliis coniunctim intercalari repetiit. Fuerunt autem sententiae sequentes:

1. Omnia sunt fucata, nihil candoris in aula est.

2. Animus philosophi debet esse in sagina, corpus in macie.

3. Ut planctae saepius translatae raro perveniunt ad frugem, sic et ingenia vagabunda [...]

39. Timiditas ignorantiam audacia temeritatem arguit.

40. Iuvandi non oppugnandi sunt qui nobis iecere fundamenta sapientiae.

Si inter alias a Dominis aliquae dicerentur sententiae paulo tritiores quas coniiciebat D. Iungmannum antea memoriter scire, id sincere Dominis indicavit Schenkelius aliasque illarum loco accepit. Si quoque aliquae iusto breviores videbantur petivit addi aliquid. Ut factum in XXIII et XXIV. Sequenti die XXX Septembris denuo convenerunt supra nominati domini ad aedes D. Mathaei Schrodij pharmacopolae hora nona et ab eisdem dictata sunt quinquaginta vocabula a Schenkelio excepta; et intro vocato Dn. Iungmanno singula semel praelecta, relicto ipsi paululum morae ad cogitandum et applicandum arti, deinde a primo ad ultimum ordine recto ab hoc ad illud retrogrado, postea intercalari quocunque numero dicto subiecit vocabulum, et contra nominato quolibet vocabulo numerum sine mora, haesitatione vel errore. Interrogavit Schenkelius an placeret dominis plura dare. Videlicet: numerum illum duplicatum? Quod desiderabat quidem Dn. Iungmannus, sed responderunt sufficere, nec se dubitare quin possit multo plura eodem modo recitare. Postea Schenkelio conquestus est Dn. Iungmannus dolere se quod non ad quinquaginta sententias et centum vocabula esset processum, haud dubie se optime repetiturum fuisse; fuerunt autem sequentia:

1. Gobius, 2. Peristroma, 3. Ficedula, 4. Ephipium, 5. Phalerae, 6. Canabis [...], 49. Mantica, 50. Locaria.

Rursus oblatis a Schenkelio Dominis ducentis sententiis in quibus se exercuerat, Dn. Iungmannus dum specimini se praepararet, et quas iam memoria tenebat; una cum quadraginta heri pro specimine dictatis, quibus praepositae erant notae arithmeticae. Rogavit ut exprimerent quemlibet numerum et Dn.

Iungmannus statim correspondentem diceret sententiam quod factum est feliciter, non sine praesentium admiratione. Cum praesertim magno id fieret numeri intervallo. E.g. dic 235, dic 27, dic 9, dic 240, dic 228 ... etc. Postremo Dominis sunt oblata 250 vocabula scripta in quibus partim se privatim ad specimen praepararat, partim cum Schenckelio exercuerat ita ut illa quoque memoria teneret; quibus iam eadem hora erant apposita 50 alia, ut cum prioribus trecenta efficerent; et petivit Schenckelius ut Domini quem vellent numerum proferrent. Quod ita ut modo dictum est de sententiis fecerunt et statim Dn. Iungmannus vocabulum quodque reddidit. Si semel aut bis non diceret ipsam sententiam aut vocabulum servato prorsus ordine vocum, monitus rem acu non esse tactam, veram aut sententiam aut vocabulum illico restituit. Die subsequenti primo Octobris interfuit Dn. Iungmannus concioni publicae R. D. Doctoris Winckelmanni Concionatoris ac Professoris celeberrimi quam etiam valde attente audiverunt, ut certius de specimine iudicare possent Eximius Med. Doctor et Professor Ellenbergerus et D. ac M. Christophorus Baunemmannus, qui una cum Schenkelio concione absoluta iverunt recta ad aedes praeclariss. D. Goclenii, ut coram ipsis eam repeteret, quod fecit ita prompte et exacte ut nihil ex tota concione esset praetermissum.

Haec omnia ita ut supra fideliter relata sunt se habere testamur cum ea nobis praesentibus, videntibus sententias et vocabula dictantibus, gesta sint et probata, omni fraude et dolo seclusis. In quorum fidem hoc veritati non minus quam equitati debitum testimonium nominibus nostris subscriptis sigillisque munitum libenter Schenkelio vel non roganti dedimus. Marpurgi Hassorum anno, mense, die suprapositis.

> Rod. Goclenius L. Professor
> Henricus Ellenbergerus Med. Doctor et Professor
> Mathias à Süchten Dantiscanus Borossus
> Cristophorus Bauneman Maior stipend.

Appendix IX
The article on 'L'art mnémonique' from Diderot's encyclopaedia

Commenting on the entry 'Mémoire' in the great Encylopaedia, Diodati lamented that the author of the learned dissertation had not added to his discussion of natural memory an equally extensive and accurate treatment

of the rules of artificial memory.[30] To remedy this defect Diodati added a
section detailing some of the more traditional concepts of 'Ciceronian'
mnemotechnics, and updated Diderot's list of historical figures who possessed prodigious memories: to the names of Pliny, Aulus Gellius, Cineas,
Cyrus, Seneca and Pico, he added that of Antonio Magliabecchi. Diodati
also provided a list of the most celebrated treatise-writers and outlines the
central tenets of both the medicine of memory and the art of local memory.

The oversight which had apparently scandalized Diodati is, however,
illusory. In the first volume of the work (which Diodati had annotated and
published nine years before) there is an entire section of the long article
on 'Art' dedicated to the 'Art mnémonique'. We transcribe here only the
essential parts of this piece which was written by Yvon.[31] In the identification of the mnemonic art with logic, the appeal to clarity and distinction, in the emphasis on the orderly construction of ideas into a chain of
premises and consequences, and in the decisive refutation of every form
of 'artificial memory' as it was traditionally understood, we can see clear
signs of Cartesian influence in this article. The two works which Yvon
cites are Marius d'Assigny's *The Art of Memory* (London, 1697) and
Winkelmann's *Logica mnemonica sive memorativa* (Halle, 1659).[32]

On appelle *art mnemonique* la science des moyens qui peuvent servir
pour perfectionner la mémoire. On admet ordinairement quatre de
ces sortes de moyen: car on peut y employer ou des remedes
physiques, que l'on croit propres à fortifier la masse du cerveau; ou
de certaines figures et *schématismes*, qui font qu'une chose se grave
mieux dans la mémoire; ou des mots techniques, qui rappellent
facilement ce qu'on a appris; ou enfin un certain arrangement
logique des idées, en les plaçant chacune de façon qu'elles se suiv-
ent dans un ordre naturel. Pour ce qui regarde les remedes
physiques, il est indubitable qu'un régime de vie bien observé peut
contribuer beaucoup à la conservation de la mémoire, de même
que les excès dans le vin, dans la nourriture, dans les plaisirs, l'af-
foiblissent. Mais il n'est pas du même des autres remedes que certains auteurs ont recommandés ... qu'on peut voir dans *l'art
mnemonique* de Marius d'Assigny, auteur anglois ... D'autres ont eu
recours aux *schématismes*. On sait que nous retenons une chose plus
facilement quand elle fait sur notre esprit, par les moyens des sens
extérieurs, une impression vive. C'est par cette raison qu'on a tâché
de soulager la mémoire dans ses fonctions, en réprésentant les idées

sous de certaines figures qui les expriment en quelque façon. C'est de cette manière qu'on apprend aux enfans, non seulement à connoître les lettres, mais encore à se rendre familiers les principaux évenemens de l'histoire sainte et profane. Il y a même des auteurs qui, par une prédilection singuliere pour les figures, ont appliqué ces *schématismes* à des sciences philosophiques.

C'est ainsi qu'un certain Allemand, nommé *Winckelmann*, a donné toute la logique d'Aristote en figures … Voici aussi comme il définit la Logique. Aristote est répresenté assis, dans une profonde méditation: ce qui doit signifier que la Logique est un talent de l'esprit et non pas du corps; dans la main droite il tient un clé: c'est-a-dire que la Logique n'est pas un science, mais un clé pour les sciences; dans la main gauche il tient un marteau: cela veut dire que la Logique est une *habitude instrumentale*; et enfin devant lui est un étau sur lequel se trouve un morceau d'or fin et un morceau d'or faux pour indiquer que la fine de la Logique est de distinguer le vrai d'avec le faux.

Puisqu'il est certain que notre imagination est d'un grand secours pour la mémoire, on ne peut pas absolument rejetter la méthode des *schématismes*, pourvû que les images n'ayent rien d'extravagant ni de puérile, et qu'on les applique pas à des choses qui n'en sont point du tout susceptibles. Mais c'est en cela qu'on à manqué en plusieurs façons: car les uns ont voulu désigner par des figures toutes sortes de choses morales et métaphysiques; ce qui est absurde, parce que ces choses ont besoin de tant d'esplications, que le travail de la mémoire en est doublé. Les autres ont donné des images si absurdes et si ridicules, que loin de rendre la science agréable, elles l'ont rendu dégoûtante. Les personnes qui commencent à se servir de leur raison, doivent s'abstenir de cette méthode, et tâcher d'aider la mémoire par le moyen du jugement.

Il faut dire la même chose de la mémoire que l'on appelle *technique*. Quelques-uns ont proposé de s'imaginer une maison ou bien une ville, et de s'y représenter différens endroits dans lesquels on placeroit les choses ou les idées qu'on voudroit se rapeller. D'autres, au lieu d'une maison ou d'une ville, ont choisi certains animaux dont les lettres initiales font un alphabet latin. Ils partagent chaque membre de chacune de ces bêtes en cinq parties, sur lesquelles ils affichent des idées; ce qui leur fournit 150 places bien marquées, pour autant d'idées qu'ils s'y imaginent affichées. Il y en a d'autres qui ont eu recours à certains mots, vers, et autres choses semblables:

par exemple pour retenir les mots d'Alexandre, Romulus, Mercure, Orphée, ils prennent les lettres initiales qui forment le mot *armo*; mot qui doit leur servir à se rappeller les quatres autres. Tout ce que nous pouvons dire là-des-sous c'est que tous ces mots et ces verbes techniques paroissent plus difficiles à retenir que les choses mêmes dont ils doivent faciliter l'étude.

Les moyens les plus sûrs pour perfectionner la mémoire, sont ceux que nous fournit la Logique; plus l'idée que nous avons d'une chose est claire et distincte, plus nous aurons de facilité à la retenir et à la rappeller quand nous en aurons besoin. S'il y a plusieurs idées, on les arrange dans leur ordre naturel de sorte que l'idée principale soit suvie des idées accessoires, comme d'autant de consequences; avec cela on peut pratiquer certains artifices qui ne sont pas sans utilité: par exemple, si l'on compose quelque chose, pour l'apprendre ensuite par coeur, on doit avoir soin d'écrire distinctement, de marquer les différentes parties par de certaines séparations, de se servir des lettres initiales au commencement d'un sens; c'est ce qu'on appelle la *mémoire locale* ...

Les anciens Grecs et Romans parlent en plusieurs endroits de l'*art mnemonique*. Cicéron dit, dans le Liv. II de Orat. c. LXXXVI que Simonide l'a inventé. Ce philosophe étant en Thessalie, fut invité par un nommé *Scopas*; lors qu'il fut à table, deux jeunes gens le firent appeller pour lui parler dans la cour. A peine Simonide fut-il sorti, que la chambre oú les autres étoient restés, tomba et les écrasa tous. Lorsqu'on voulout les enterrer, on ne put les reconnoître, tant ils étoient défigurés. Alors Simonide, se rappellant la place oú chacun avoit été assis, les nomma l'un après l'autre; ce qui fit connoître, dit Cicéron, que l'ordre étoit la principale chose pour aider la mémoire.

APPENDIX X
D'ALEMBERT AND 'REAL CHARACTERS'

The article 'Caractère' in the great Encyclopaedia was produced by various authors in collaboration (Diderot dealt with typographic characters in a separate article on 'Caractères d'imprimerie'). After some brief definitions by Marc Eidous who distinguishes sounds and signs or figures, and traces the origins of characters to the first crude drawings on material bodies, d'Alembert deals briefly with writing in general, postponing a more analytical treatment to the entries on 'Langue' and 'Alphabet'. He deals with Egyptian characters in a few lines, leaving the entries on 'Hiéroglyphe' and 'Symbole' to the celebrated grammarian du Marsais. There then follows a column and a half by d'Alembert dedicated to real characters and to the problem of a universal language; a description of the characters of various alphabets and of signs used in geometry and trigonometry by La Chapelle; a brief entry on 'Characters which are used in the arithmetic of infinites' (*Caractères dont on fait usage dans l'arithmetique des infinis*) also by d'Alembert; and finally a column by Vend on 'Chemical symbols' (*Caractères de la Chimie*).

I wish to draw attention to the second of the three pieces written by d'Alembert. In this passage we find a Baconian opposition between 'real characters' (which do not express sounds or letters, but things) and 'nominal characters' (or normal alphabetic letters). We also find a discussion of the relationship between Chinese ideograms and real characters which can be read and understood independently of the native language of the reader (a theme which is also present in Bacon's *De augmentis* and Wilkins's *Essay*), a brief exposition of the theories of Wilkins, Dalgarno and Lodowick; and finally some of Leibniz's reflections on the characteristic and universal language (significantly, however, these interests are not not mentioned in the article on 'Leibnitianisme on philosophie de Leibniz') which are presented as having been derived from the doctrines of the English authors.

The works of Dalgarno, Wilkins and Lodowick to which d'Alembert refers in the passage are: *Ars signorum, vulgo character universalis et lingua philosophica* (London, 1661); *Essay Towards a Real Character and a Philosophical Language* (London, 1668); *The Groundwork or Foundation Laid (or so Intended) for the Framing of a New Perfect Language* (London, 1652).

Les hommes qui ne formoient d'abord qu'une sociéte unique, et qui n'avoient par conséquent qu'une langue et qu'un alphabet, s'étant extrèmement multipliés, furent forcés de se distribuer, pour ainsi dire, en plusieurs grandes sociétés ou familles, qui séparées par des mers vastes ou par des continens arides, ou par des intérêts differens, n'avoient presque plus rien de commun entr'elles. Ces circonstances occasionnerent les différentes langues et les différens alphabets qui se sont si fort multipliés.

Cette diversité de *caracteres* dont se servent les différentes nations pour exprimer la même idée, est regardée comme un des plus grands obstacles qu'il y ait au progrés des Sciences: aussi quelques auteurs pensant à affranchir le genre humain de cette servitude, ont proposé des plans de *caracteres* qui pussent être universels, et que ces sortes de *caracteres* devroient être *réels* et non *nominaux*, c'est-a-dire exprimer des choses, et non pas, comme les *caracteres* communs, exprimer des lettres ou des sons.

Ainsi chaque nation auroit retenu son propre langage, et cependant auroit été en état d'entendre celui d'unc autre sans l'avoir appris, en voyant simplement un *caractere* réel ou universel, qui auroit la même signification pour tous les peuples, quels que puissent être les sons, dont chaque nation se serviroit pour l'exprimer dans son langage particulier: par exemple, en voyant le *caractere* destiné à signifier *boire*, un Anglois auroit lû *to drink*, un François *boire*, un Latin *bibere*, tin Grec πιυειυ, un Allemand *trincken*, et ainsi des autres; de même qu'en voyant un *cheval*, chaque nation en exprime l'idée à sa maniere. mais toutes entendent le même animal.

Il ne faut pas s'imaginer que ce *caractere* réel soit une chimere. Le Chinois et les Japonois ont déjà, dit-on, quelque chose de semblable: ils on un *caractere* commun que chacun des ces peuples entend de la même maniere dans leur différentes langues, quoiqu' ils le prononcent avec des sons ou des mots tellement différens, qu'ils n'entendent pas la moindre syllabe les uns des autre quand ils parlent.

Les premiers essais, et même les plus considérables que l'on ait fait en Europe pour l'institution d'une langue universelle ou philosophique, sont ceux de l'evêque Wilkins et de Dalgarme: cependant ils sont demeurés sans aucun effet.

M. Leibnitz a eu quelques idées sur le meme sujet. Il pense que Wilkins et Dalgarme n'avoient pas rencontré la vraie méthode. M. Leibnitz convenoit que plusieurs nations pourroient s'entendre avec les *caracteres* de ces deux auteurs; mais, selon lui, ils n'avoient pas attrapé les véritables *caracteres réels* que ce grand philosophe regardoit comme l'instrument le plus fin dont l'esprit humain pût se servir, et qui devoient, dit-il, extrémement faciliter et le raisonnement, et la mémoire, et l'invention des choses.

Suivant l'opinion de M. Leibnitz ces *caracteres* devoient ressembler à ceux dont on se sert en Algebre, qui sont effectivement fort simple, quoique très-expressifs, sans avoir rien de superflu ni d'equivoque, et dont au reste toutes les variétés sont raisonnées.

Le *caractere réel* de l'evêque Wilkins fut bien reçu de quelques savans. M. Hook le recommande après en avoir pris une exacte connoissance, et en avoir fait lui-même l'experience: il en parle

comme du plus excellent plan que l'on puisse se former sur cette
étude. il a eu la complaisance de publier en cette langue quelques-
unes de ses découvertes.

M. Leibnitz dit qu'il avoit en vûe un *alphabet des pensées humaines*,
et même qu'il y travailloit, afin de parvenir à une langue
philosophique: mais la morte de ce grand philosophe empêcha son
projet de venir en maturité.

M. Lodwic nous a communiqué, dans les *transactions
philosophiques*, un plan d'un *alphabet* ou *caractere universel* d'une autre
espece. Il devoit contenir une énumération de tous les sons ou lettres simples, usités dans une langue quelconque; moyennant quoi,
on auroit été en état de prononcer promptement et exactement
toutes sortes de langues; et d'écrire, en les entendant simplement
prononcer, la prononciation d'une langue quelconque, que l'on
auroit articulée; de maniere que les personnes accoutûmées à cette
langue, quoiqu'elles ne l'eussent jamais entendu prononcer par
d'autres, auroient pourtant été en état sur le champ de la prononcer exactement: enfine ce *caractere* auroit servi comme d'étalon ou
de modele pour perpétuer les sons d'une langue quelconque.

After discussing some of the more recent attempts at devising a universal
language,[33] d'Alembert concludes, saying: 'But here the difficulty is less
that of inventing the simplest, easiest and most commodious characters
than of taking account of the usages of different nations; they do not agree
with each other, Fontenelle says, because they do not understand their
common interests.' (*Mais ici la difficulté est bien moins d'inventer les caractères
les plus simples, les plus aisées, et les plus commodes, que d'engager les différentes
nations à en faire usage, elles ne s'accordent, dit M. Fontenelle, qu'à ne pas entendre leurs intérêts communs.*) His distrust of the idea, then, is concerned exclusively with the possibility of its practical realization. The opinions of the
collaborators on the Encyclopaedia on this point vary, however. In order
to give a full account of this one should also compare the article on
'Langage' in which even the theoretical possibility of a universal language
is explicitly rejected: Since the idioms of the different nations arise from
different kinds of peoples, one can see at once that it can never be universal.' (*Puisque du différent génie des peuples naissent les différents idiomes, on
peut d'abord décider qu'il n'en aura jamais d'universel*) with the article on
'Langue' in which a universal language is seen as a practical possibility:
'Mon dessein n'est pas au reste de former un langage universel à l'usage de
plusieurs nations. Cette entreprise ne peut convenir qu'aux académies
savantes que nous avons en Europe, supposé encore qu'elles travaillassent
de concert et sous les auspices des puissances.'

Notes

TRANSLATOR'S INTRODUCTION

1. Henry Percy, ninth Earl of Northumberland, 'The forlorne state of this world', 1594, Petworth House, Sussex, Leconfield MS 24/2, f. 28r. See Stephen Clucas and Gordon R. Batho (eds.), *Henry Percy's Advices to his Son* (London: Roxburghe Club, 2000)
2. Walter Warner, British Library, Additional MS 4394, f. 238 r–v
3. Walter Warner, untitled notebook, Northamptonshire Record Office, Isham-Lamport Papers, MS IL 3422.
4. Isham Lamport papers, MS IL 3422, II, f. 9r.
5. Isham Lamport papers, MS IL 3422, II, f. 18 r.
6. Isham Lamport papers, MS IL 3422, II, f. 19 r.
7. Isham Lamport papers, MS IL 3422, II, f. 2 r.
8. Isham Lamport papers, MS IL 3422, II, f. 4 r.
9. Mary Carruthers, *The Book of Memory. A Study of Memory in Mediaeval Culture* (Cambridge: Cambridge University Press, 1990), p. 8.
10. See p. xxii below.
11. On the logico-encyclopaedic milieu in Germany and central Europe see Howard Hotson, 'Johann Heinrich Alsted: Encyclopaedism, Millenarianism and the Second Reformation in Germany', unpublished D.Phil. dissertation, Oxford 1991, and his forthcoming books *Johann Heinrich Alsted 1588–1638: Between Renaissance, Reformation, and Universal Reform*, Oxford Historical Monographs (Oxford: Clarendon Press, 2000), and *Paradise Postponed: Johann Heinrich Alsted and the Birth of Calvinist Millenarianism,* International Archives of the History of Ideas (Dordrecht: Kluwer, 2000). See also Mark Greengrass, Michael Leslie and Timothy Raylor (eds.), *Samuel Hartlib and Universal Reformation: Studies in Intellectual Communication* (Cambridge: Cambridge University Press, 1994).
12. Rossi, see p. 31 below.
13. Wilhelm Schmidt-Biggemann, *Topica universalis. Eine Modellgeschichte humanistischer und barocker Wissenschaft* (Hamburg: Felix Meiner Verlag, 1983).

14. See esp. Schimdt-Biggemann, *Topica*, pp. 2–21. For a wide-ranging and detailed account of the commonplace tradition see Ann Moss, *Printed Commonplace-Books and the Structuring of Renaissance Thought* (Oxford: Clarendon Press, 1996).

15. See Schmidt-Biggemann, *Topica*, pp. 265–92. On 'polyhistory' see Anthony Grafton, 'The world of the polyhistors: humanism and encyclopaedism', *Central European History*, 18 (1985), pp. 31–47.

16. Schmidt-Biggemann, *Topica*, pp. xiii-xiv.

17. See note 9 above.

18. Mary Carruthers, *The Craft of Thought. Meditation, Rhetoric, and the Making of Images, 400–1200,* Cambridge Studies in Mediaeval Literature, 34 (Cambridge: Cambridge University Press, 1998).

19. See Rossi, p. 76 below and cf. Schmidt-Biggemann, *Topica*, p. 159.

20. Paola Zambelli, *L'apprendista stregone: astrologia, cabala e arte Lulliana in Pico della Mirandola e seguaci* (Venice: Marsilio, 1995).

21. Anthony Bonner (ed and introd.), *Raimundus Lullus opera. Strasbourg 1651 edition with an introduction*, Clavis Pansophiae. Eine Bibliothek der Universalwissenschaften in Renaissance und Barock, 2/1 (Stuttgart–Bad Cannstatt: Frommann–Holzboog, 1996). On the importance of the Zetzner edition see Schmidt-Biggemann, *Topica*, pp. 159–160 and Rossi, pp. 96–97 below.

22. Anthony Bonner (ed. and trans.), *Selected Works of Ramon Llull (1232–1316)*, 2 vols. (Princeton: Princeton University Press, 1985) and Anthony Bonner and Eve Bonner (eds.) *Doctor Illuminatus. A Ramon Llull Reader*, Mythos (Princeton: Princeton University Press, 1993).

23. Wolfgang Neuber and Joerg Jochen Berns, *Ars memorativa: zur kulturgeschichtlichen Bedeutung der Gedächtniskunst 1400–1750*, Frühe Neuzeit, 15 (Tübingen: Niemeyer, 1993).

24. See Neuber and Berns, *Ars memorativa*, p. 4: 'Die innere, psychologische und physiologische Mechanik der Gedächtnis-Kunst sowie die von ihr in dieser Zeit ausgegangene Faszination noch immer einen nur unklar erkannten und irritierenden Faktor in der vom Paradigma der Rationalität bestimmten Rekonstruktion der Frühen neuzeit darstellen.'

25. Gerhard Strasser, *Lingua universalis: Kryptologie und Theorie der Universalsprachen im 16. und 17. Jahrhundert*, Wolfenbütteler Forschungen, 38 (Wiesbaden, 1988).

26. Umberto Eco, *Ricerca della lingua perfetta nella cultura europea* (Rome and Bari: Laterza, 1993), trans. *The Search for the Perfect Language* (Oxford: Blackwell, 1995).

27. Ann Blair, *The Theater of Nature. Jean Bodin and Renaissance Science* (Princeton: Princeton University Press, 1997), p. 4.

28. Blair, *Theater of Nature*, pp. 153–79.

29. Cesare Vasoli, *La dialettica e la retorica dell'umanesimo. 'Invenzione' e 'metodo' nella cultura del XV e XVI secolo*, I fatti e le idee. Saggi e biografie, 174 (Milan: Feltrinelli, 1968).

30. Lisa Jardine, *Francis Bacon: Discovery and the Art of Discourse* (London: Cambridge University Press, 1974).

31. Walter J. Ong, *Ramus, Method, and the Decay of Dialogue. From the Art of Discourse to the Art of Reason* (Harvard University Press: Cambridge, Mass., 1958).

32. Cesare Vasoli, 'Umanesimo e simbologia nei primi scritti Lulliani e mnemotecnici del Bruno', in Enrico Castelli (ed.), *Umanesimo e simbolismo. Atti del IV Convegno Internazionale di Studi Umanistici, Venezia, 19–21 Settembre 1958* (Padua: Centro Internazionale de Studi Umanistici, 1958), pp. 251–304.

33. Leen Spruit, *Il problema della conoscenza in Giordano Bruno*, Saggi Bibliopolis, 29 (Naples: Bibliopolis, 1988).

34. See, in particular, the introduction to Rita Sturlese (ed.), *De umbris idearum* (Florence: Leo. S. Olschki, 1991), and her important article 'Per un interpretazione del *De umbris idearum* di Giordano Bruno', *Annali della scuola normale superiore di Pisa. Classe di lettere e filosofia*, Third Series, 22: 3 (1992), pp. 943–68.

35. Wolfgang Wildgen, *Das kosmische Gedächtnis: Kosmologie, Semiotik und Gedächtnistheorie im Werke Giordano Brunos (1548–1600)* Philosophie und Geschichte der Wissenschaften. Studien und Quellen, 38 (Frankfurt-am-Main: Peter Lang, 1998).

36. Giovanni Crapulli, *Mathesis universalis: genesi di un'idea nel XVI secolo*, Lessico intelletuale europeo, 2 (Rome: Edizioni dell'Ateneo, 1969).

PREFACE

1. Arthur Collier, *Clavis universalis: or, a New Inquiry after Truth. Being a Demonstration of the Non-Existence, or Impossibility of an External World* (London, 1713).

2. William Henry Barber, *Leibniz in France from Arnauld to Voltaire: A Study in French Reactions to Leibnizianism 1670–1760* (Oxford: Clarendon Press, 1955), p. x.

3. Alistair C. Crombie, *Augustine to Galileo: Vol. 1 Science in the Middle*

Ages, Vol. 2 Science in the Later Middle Ages and Early Modern Times XII-XVII Centuries (London: Heinemann, 1952, repr. 1961), II, p. 332.

PREFACE TO THE SECOND EDITION

1. Frances A. Yates, *The Art of Memory* (London: Routledge and Kegan Paul, 1966, repr. Harmondsworth: Peregrine Books, 1978), p. 374.

2. Madeleine V. David, *Le Débat sur les écritures et l'hiéroglyphe aux XVIIe et XVIIIe siècles et l'application de la notion de déchiffrement aux écritures mortes* (Paris: SEVPEN, 1965).

3. James R. Knowlson, 'The idea of gesture as a universal language in the XVIIth and XVIIIth centuries', *Journal of the History of Ideas*, 26:4 (1965), pp. 495–508.

4. Michel Foucault, *Les Mots et les choses* (Paris: Gallimard, 1966), trans. *The Order of Things. An Archaeology of the Human Sciences* (New York: Random House, 1970), p. 157.

5. Foucault, *Order of Things*, pp. 157–8.

6. *L'Arc*, 30 October 1966.

7. Jacques Derrida, *De la grammatologie* (Paris: Editions de Minuit, 1967), trans. Gayatri Chakravorty Spivak, *Of Grammatology* (Baltimore and London: Johns Hopkins University Press, 1974), pp. 269–316.

8. *Encylopaedia Einaudi,* 15 vols. (Turin: Einaudi, 1977–82), VIII, pp. 1068–1109.

9. Eusebio Colomer, *Nikolaus von Kues und Raimund Llull. Aus Handschriften der Kueser Bibliothek,* Quellen und Studien zur Geschichte der Philosophie, 2 (Berlin, 1961).

10. Eberhard Wolfram Platzeck, *Raimund Lull. Sein Leben-seine Werke – die Grundlagen seines Denkens*, Bibliotheca franciscana, 5–6, 2 vols. (Düsseldorf, 1962).

11. Paola Zambelli, 'Il *De auditu kabbalistico* e la tradizione lulliana nel Rinascimento', *Atti dell'Accademia Toscana di scienze e lettere, 'La Colombaria'*, 30 (1965), pp. 115–246. [See also Zambelli's recent study *L'apprendista stregone: astrologia, cabala e arte Lulliana in Pico della Mirandola e seguaci* (Venice: Marsilio, 1995). Trans.]

12. Jocelyn Nigel Hillgarth, *Ramon Lull and Lullism in Fourteenth-Century France* (Oxford, Clarendon Press, 1971).

13. Liselotte Dieckmann, *Hieroglyphics: The History of a Literary Symbol* (St Louis: Washington University Press, 1971).

14. Cesare Vasoli, *La dialettica e la retorica dell'umanesimo. 'Invenzione' e 'metodo' nella cultura del XV e XVI secolo* (Milan: Feltrinelli, 1968).

15. Charles Webster, *Samuel Hartlib and the Advancement of Learning* (Cambridge: Cambridge University Press, 1970)

16. Leroy E. Loemker, 'Leibniz and the Herborn Eencyclopaedists', *Journal for the History of Ideas*, 22 (1961), pp. 323–38.

17. Albert Heinekamp, 'Ars Characteristica und natürliche Sprache bei Leibniz', *Tijdschrift voor filosofie*, 34:3 (1972), pp. 446–88.

18. Massimo Mugnai, *Astrazione e realtà: saggio su Leibniz* (Milan: Feltrinelli, 1976).

19. Lia Formigari, *Linguistica ed empirismo nel seicento inglese* (Bari: Laterza, 1970).

20. Hans Aarsleff, *From Locke to Saussure: Essays on the Study of Language and Intellectual History* (London: Athlone, 1982).

21. David Knight, *Ordering the World: A History of Classifying Man* (London: Burnett/Deutsch, 1981).

22. Paolo Rossi, *Aspetti della rivoluzione scientifica* (Naples: Morano, 1970), pp. 293–370 and 387–410.

23. Paolo Rossi, *Le sterminate antichità: studi vichiani* (Pisa: Nistri-Lischi,1969), pp. 80–131 and 181–4.

24. [This article was published as Paolo Rossi, 'Universal languages, classifications and nomenclatures in the seventeenth century', *History and Philosophy of the Life Sciences*, 6 (1984), pp. 119–132. Trans.]

25. Frances A. Yates, *Lull and Bruno: Collected Essays* (London: Routledge and Kegan Paul, 1982).

26. Yates, *Art of Memory*, p. 13.

27. Paolo Rossi, *Francesco Bacone: dalla magia alla scienza* (Bari: Laterza 1957) trans. Sacha Rabinovitch, *Francis Bacon: From Magic to Science* (London: Routledge and Keegan Paul, 1968).

I The Power of Images and the Places of Memory

1. David Hume, *Enquiries concerning Human Understanding and concerning the Principles of Morals*, ed. L. A. Selby-Bigge (Oxford: Clarendon Press, 1893, repr. and corr. by P. H. Nidditch, 1975), p. 241. On the problem of memory see also *A Treatise of Human Nature*, ed. L. A. Selby-Bigge (Oxford: Clarendon Press 1896, repr. and corr. by P. H. Nidditch, Oxford University Press, 1978), pp. 8–10 (on memory and the imagination); pp 117–18 and notes on pp. 108, 153, 199, 209.

On the absence of all sensation of pleasure or pain in the exercise of memory see Book III, Part III, Section IV.

2. Henricus Cornelius Agrippa, *De incertitudine et vanitate scientiarum* in *Opera*, 2 vols. (Lyon, 1600), II, pp. 32–3.

3. Desiderius Erasmus, *De ratione studii* in *Omnia opera D. Erasmi ... quaecunque ipse auctor pro suis agnovit ... Cum praefatione B. Rhenani Selestadiensis, vitam autoris describente ... Addito indice copiosissimo,* 9 vols. (Basel: Froeben, 1540), I, p. 466.

4. Michel de Montaigne, *Essais,* trans. M. A. Screech, *The Essays of Michel de Montaigne* (Harmondsworth: Allen Lane, The Penguin Press, 1991), I, 9, p. 32 and II, 10, p. 457.

5. Montaigne, *Essays,* I, 25.

6. Montaigne, *Essays,* I, 25. Cf. II, 10.

7. Montaigne, *Essays,* I, 9, p. 32 and III, 9, p. 1090.

8. A. Prall (ed.), *Pädagogische Schriften des Wolfgang Ratichius und seiner Anhänger* (Breslau, 1903). See also Eugenio Garin, *L'educazione in Europa, 1400–1600* (Bari: Laterza, 1957), pp. 234–5.

9. Marius d'Assigny, *The Art of Memory. A Treatise Useful for Such as Are to Speak in Publick* (London, 1697).

10. Luigi Firpo, *Lo stato ideale della controriforma: Ludovico Agostini* (Bari: Laterza, 1957), p. 245.

11. See Robert Klein, 'L'imagination comme vetement de l'ame chez Marsile Ficin et Giordano Bruno', in *Revue de métaphysique et de morale,* 61:1 (1956), pp. 18–38 (esp. pp. 30–1)

12. Ramon Lull, *Beati Raymundi Lulli ... Opera omnia,* 9 vols. (Mainz, 1721–42) III, p. 1: 'Sciendum est ergo, quod ista Ars est et logica et Metaphysica ... Metaphysica considerat res, quae sunt extra animam, prout conveniunt in ratione entis; logica etiam considerat res secundum esse, quod habent in anima ... sed haec Ars tanquam suprema omnium humanarum scientiarum indifferenter respicit ens secundum istum modum et secundum illum.' See also *Opera,* ed. Lazarus Zetzner (Strasburg, 1619), p. 358: 'Logicus tractat de secundariis intentionibus ... sed generalis artista tractat de primis ... Logicus non potest invenire veram legem cum logica: generalis autem artista cum ista arte invenit ... Et plus potest addiscere artista de hac arte uno mense, quam logicus de logica uno anno.'

13. Antonio Corsano, *Il pensiero di G. Bruno nel suo svolgimento storico* (Florence, 1940), p. 41; Felice Tocco, *Le opere latine di G. Bruno, esposte e confrontate con le italiane* (Florence, 1889), p. 37, n. 2.

14. On the links between image and sensation see also *De anima,* III, 8,

423a, 9; *Rhetorica*, I, II, 1370a, 28. For the relationship between memory and imagination see *Posterior Analytics*, II, 19, 99b 36–100; *Metaphysica*, A, I, 980a 27b, 27; *De memoria* I, 450a, 30b, 3. As has been noted the translation of ἀνάμνησις as *reminiscentia*, although corroborated by reference to Plato in *Prior Analytics*, II,21, 67a, 21–1, does not correspond to the meaning which the term has in Aristotle, ἀνάμνησις [*anamnesis*] is a deliberate actualization or reconstruction of a past memory, which is not spontaneous as in remembrance (*De memoria*, 450a 19), but reflexive (452b 7; 453a 9–10) and which is thus characteristic only of man (453a, 8–9). For the *De memoria et reminiscentia* see the translation and commentary of G. R. T. Ross (Cambridge, 1906). The commentary to Tricot's French translation of the *Parva naturalia* (Paris, 1951), pp. 57–75, is also useful. For works on Aristotelian psychology which deal with memory see A. E. Chaichet, *Essai sur la psychologie d'Aristote* (Paris, 1883); Franciscus Johannes Christiaan Jozef Nuyens, *L'Évolution de la psychologie d'Aristote* (Louvain, 1948); Clarence William Shute, *The Psychology of Aristotle: An Analysis of the Living Being*, (New York: Columbia University Press, 1941). On the use of mnemotechnics by the Greeks see the testimony of the *Rhetorica ad Herennium*, III, 23: 'Scio plerosque Graecos, qui de memoria scripserunt.' On the technique of memory in Hippias of Elis see the hypothesis advanced by Otto Apelt, *Beiträge zur Geschichte der griechischen Philosophie* (Leipzig: B. G. Teubner, 1891), p. 381. See also Johann Christian Gottlieb Ernesti, *Lexicon technologiae latinorum rhetoricae* (Leipzig, 1797); Louis Laurand, *Manuel des études grecques et latines*, (Paris, 1933). See esp. Appendix II: 'La mnémotechnie des anciens'.

15. Pseudo-Cicero, *Ad C. Herennium de ratione dicendi* (*Rhetorica ad Herennium*), trans. Harry Kaplan, Loeb Classical Library (London: Heinemann, and Cambridge, Mass.: Harvard University Press, 1954), III, XVI, 28, p. 207: 'Sunt igitur duae memoriae: una naturalis, altera artificiosa. Naturalis est ea quae nostris animis insita est et simul cum cogitatione nata: artificiosa est ea quam confirmant inductio quaedam et ratio praeceptionis.'

16. Pseudo-Cicero, *Rhetorica ad Herennium*, III, XVI, 29, p. 209: 'Aedes, intercolumnium, angulum, fornicem et alia quae his similia sunt.' [I have slightly altered Caplan's translation here Trans.]

17. Pseudo-Cicero, *Rhetorica ad Herennium*, III, XVI, 30, p. 209: 'Quemadmodum igitur qui litteras sciunt possunt id quod dictatur eis scribere et recitare quod scripserunt, item qui mnemonica didicerunt

possunt quod audierunt in locis conlocare et ex his memoriter pronuntiare.' [I have slightly altered Caplan's translation here. He translates 'loci' as 'backgrounds'. Trans.]

18. On the dating of the *Rhetorica ad Herennium* see Friedrich Marx's
introduction to the edition of Leipzig, 1894, p. 1. For the views of
mediaeval scholars on the attribution of the work see ibid., p. 52. The
attribution of the text to Cornificius dates from 1491, see Raphael
Regius, *Utrum ars rhetorica ad H. Ciceroni falso inscribatur* in *Ducenta
problemata in totidem institutionis oratoriae Quintiliani depravationes.*
(Venice, 1491). For Lorenzo Valla's views on the argument see his
Opera (Basel, 1540), p. 510.

19. See Albertus Magnus, *De bono,* ed. Heinrich Kühle in *Sancti doctoris
ecclesiae Alberti Magni … Opera omnia. Ad fidem codicum manuscriptorum
edenda apparatu critico notis prolegomenis indicibus instruenda curavit
Institutum Alberti Magni Coloniense, Bernhardo Geyer praeside,* 37 vols.
(Monasterii Westfaliorum: Aschendorff, 1951), XXVIII, pp. 249 et
seq. For the commentary of Albertus on *De memoria et reminiscentia*
see Auguste Bourgnet (ed.), *B. Alberti Magni Ratisbonensis episcopi,
ordinis Prædicatorum, Opera omnia, ex editione lugdunensi religiose castigata,
et pro auctoritatibus ad fidem vulgatæ versionis accuratiorumque patrologiæ
textuum revocata, auctaque B. Alberti vita ac bibliographia operum a P. P.
Quétif et Echard exaratis, etiam revisa et locupletata, cura ac labore Augusti
Borgnet,* 38 vols. (Paris, 1890–95), IX, pp. 97 et seq. For Aquinas's
commentary see *Doctoris Angelici Divi Thomae Aquinatis … Opera
omnia sive antehac excusa, sive etiam anecdota … notis historicis, criticis,
philosophicis … ornata, studio,* ed. S. E. Fretté, P. Maré et al., 34 vols.
(Paris, 1871–80), XXIV and *S. Thomae Aquinatis … in Aristotelis libros
De sensu et sensato. de memoria et reminiscentia commentarium. Editio III.
ex integro retractata cura et studio P. Fr. Raymundi M. Spiazzi* (Rome:
Taurini, 1949).

20. See Frances A. Yates, 'The Ciceronian Art of Memory', in *Medioevo
e Rinascemento, studi in onore di Bruno Nardi,* Università di Roma.
Istituto di filosofia. Pubblicaziona, 1–2 (Florence: Sansoni, 1955),
pp. 882–3 [See also Frances A. Yates, *The Art of Memory* (London:
Routledge and Kegan Paul, 1966, repr. Harmondsworth: Peregrine
Books, 1978), pp. 67–92. Trans.]

21. Thomas Aquinas, *In Aristotelis libros de sensu et sensato,* p. 371: 'Si ergo
ad bene memorandum vel reminiscendum, ex praemissis quatuor
documenta utilia addiscere possumus. Quorum primum est, ut

studeat quae vult retinere in aliquem ordinem deducere. Secundo ut profunde et intente eis mentem apponat. Tertio ut frequenter meditetur secundum ordinem. Quarto ut incipiat reminisci a principio.'

22. On Alcuin see the *Disputatio de rhetorica et de virtutibus sapientissimi Regis Karli et Albini magistri* in Migne, *Patrologia latina*, 101, cols. 919–50, Karl Halm, *Rhetores latini minores. Ex codicibus maximam partem primum adhibitis emendabat Carolus Halm* (Leipzig, 1863, repr. Frankfurt am Main, Minerva, 1964), pp. 523–50, and the English translation of Wilbur Samuel Howell, *The Rhetoric of Alcuin and Charlemagne* (Princeton: Princeton University Press, 1941). In the treatment of the five parts of rhetoric (which reproduces directly or indirectly that of Cicero) he limits himself to stating that the art of memory is recommended by Cicero. In the *De dialectica* (Migne, *Patrologia latina*, col. 952) logic is divided into two parts: dialectic and rhetoric. While the treatment of dialectic derives from Isidorus, Boethius and the anonymous *Categoriae decem* (believed to be an Augustinian translation of Aristotle's *Categories*) the treatment of rhetoric, based on the partition of the five great arts in the *De inventione* was nearer (as Howells has noted) to the spirit of Cicero. More extensive references to memory appear in Martianus Cappella, book V (where the story of Simonides is recounted) and in the *Novissima rhetorica* of Buoncompagno composed in 1235 where he refers to an 'imaginary alphabet' as an instrument of the art of memory. See the passage from Buoncompagno on memory transcribed by Tocco in *Le opere latine*, p. 25, from Venice, Bibliotheca Marciana, MS Lat. cl. X, 8, f. 29v. See also the section on mediaeval rhetoric in Ernst Robert Curtius, *Europäischer Litteratur und lateinisches Mittelalter,* trans. William R. Trask, *European Literature and the Latin Middle Ages* (London: Routledge and Kegan Paul, 1953, repr. 1979), pp. 62–78.

23. Yates, 'The Ciceronian Memory', p. 887.

24. See the chapter 'Solomon and the *Ars notoria*', in Lynn Thorndike, *History of Magic and Experimental Science*, 8 vols. (New York, 1923–56), II, pp. 279–89.

25. Fra Bartolomeo di San Concordio, *Gli ammaestramenti degli antichi*, dist. 9, cap. 8, 28.

26. The complete text (Appendix I) is from Florence, Bibliotheca Nazionale, Palatina MS 54 and Florence, Bibliotheca Nazionale, MS Conv. Soppr. I, 47. Another commentary on the *Rhetorica ad Herennium* (bk. III, caps. xvi–xxiv) is contained in Pavia, Bibliotheca Universitaria, MS Aldino 441 (fifteenth century, 111 folios). The

Textus de artificiali memoria is ff. 1–20: Inc.: 'Mo passamo al texoro de le cose trovate et de tutte le parte de la Rectorica custedevole Memoria.' Expl.: 'Con le cose premesse cioè con Studio, Fatiga, Ingegno, Diligentia. Finis commenti in particulari.'

27. Florence, Bibliotheca Nazionale, Magliab. MS cl. VI, 5, f. 67v. The date at the end ('Explicit et finitus die X mensis junii millesimo CCCC° XX° Indit. XIII per Petrum quondam Ser Petri de Pragha') refers to the compilation of the miscellany in which the text is contained. Other passages from this same manuscript were transcribed by Tocco, *Le opere latine*, p. 27, n. 4.

28. Lodovico Dolce, *Dialogo di M. Lodovico Dolce nel quale si ragiona del modo di accrescere et conservar la memoria* (Venice, 1582), p. 90. The first edition is 1562.

29. The text of Giovanni Gorini was published in Venice in 1499: *Summa de exemplis et similitudinibus rerum noviter impressa. Incipit summa insignis et perutilis praedictoribus de quacunque materia dicturis fratris Johannis de Sancto Geminiano* (Venice, Johannem et Gregorium de Gregoris, 1499).

30. The expression is taken from Robert of Basevorn, author of a *Forma praedicandi* composed in 1322. The text was published in the appendix of Thomas Marie Charland, *Artes praedicandi, contribution à l'histoire de la rhetorique au Moyen Age* (Paris, 1936), p. 233. See the catalogues of manuscripts compiled by Harry Caplan, *Mediaeval Artes Praedicandi. A Handlist*, Cornell Studies in Classical Philology, 24 (Ithaca, New York: Cornell University Press, 1934), and idem, *Mediaeval Artes Praedicandi: A Supplementary Hand-List*, Cornell Studies in Classical Philology, 25 (Ithaca, New York: Cornell University Press, 1936), and by the same author 'A late mediaeval Tractate on Preaching', in Alexander Magnus Drummond (ed.), *Studies in Rhetoric and Public Speaking in Honour of James Albert Winans, by Pupils and Colleagues* (New York: The Century Co., 1925), pp. 61–91.

31. See Thomas Waleys, *De modo componendi sermones*, cit. Charland, *Artes praedicandi*, p. 370.

32. Ragone's treatise is extant in two different versions (in separate hands) in Venice, Bibliotheca Marciana, MS Lat. cl. VI, 274, ff. 15–34 and 53–66. A third version is in Venice, Bibliotheca Marciana, MS Lat. cl. VI, 159, and a fourth in Milan, Bibliotheca Ambrosiana MS T. 78 sup. There are only minor differences between them. The passages cited here have been transcribed from Bibliotheca Marciana, MS Lat.

cl. VI, 274, ff. 53–66; I have resolved doubtful passages by reference to either the other version contained in the same volume, or to Bibliotheca Ambrosiana, MS T. 78 sup., ff. 1–21v. The text of Ragone is dedicated to the Marchese of Mantua: 'Ad illustrissimum principem et armorum ducem Iohannem Franciscum Marchionem Mantuae. Artificialis memorie regule per Iacobum Ragonam vicentinum.' In the Ambrosian manuscript the title is *Tractatus brevis ac solemnis ad sciendam et ad conseguendam artem memorie artificialis ad M. Marchionem Mantue.*

33. Venice, Bibliotheca Marciana, MS Lat. cl. VI, 274, f. 53r.: 'Iussu tuo, princeps illustrissime, artificialis memorie regulas, quo ordine superioribus diebus una illas exercuimus, hunc in librum reduxi tuoque nomini dicavi, imitatus non modo sententias, verum et plerumque verba ipsa M. Tullii Ciceronis et aliorum dignissimorum philosophorum qui accuratissime de hac arte scripserunt ... Praeceptore Cicerone ac etiam teste sancto Thoma de Aquino, artificialis memoria duobus perficitur: locis videlicet et imaginibus. Locos enim consideraverunt necessarios esse ad res seriatim pronunptiandas et diu memoriter tenendas, unde sanctus Thomas oportere inquit ut ea que quis memoriter vult tenere, illa ordinata consideratione disponat ut ex uno memorato facile ad aliud procedatur. Aristoteles etiam inquit in libro quem de memoria inscripsit: a locis reminiscimur. Necessarii sunt ergo loci ut in illis imagines adaptentur ut statim infra patebit. Sed imagines sumimus ad confirmandum intentiones, unde allegatus Thomas: oportet, ait, ut eorum quae vult homo memorari quasdam assumat similitudines convenientes.'

34. Venice, Bibliotheca Marciana, MS Lat. cl. VI, 274, ff. 53v.–54r.: 'Differunt vero loci ab imaginibus nisi in hoc quod loci sunt non anguli, ut existimant aliqui, sed imagines fixe super quibus, sicut supra carta, alie pinguntur imagines delebiles sicut littere: unde loci sunt sicut materia, imagines vero sicut forma. Differunt igitur sicut fixum et non fixum. Consumitur autem ars ista centum locis, quatenus expedit pro integritate ipsius. Sed, si tue libuerit celsitudini, poteris eodem alios sibi locos invenire faciliter per horum similitudinem. Sed oportet omnino non modo bona, verum etiam optima diligentia ac studio locos ipsos notare et firmiter menti habere, ita ut, modo recto et retrogrado ac iuxta quotationem numerorum, illos prompte recitare queas. Aliter autem frustra temptarentur omnia. Expedit igitur ut locis servetur modus, ne sit inter illos distantia nimis brevis vel nimium remota sed moderata ut puta sex vel octo aut decem pedum vel circa

iuxta magnitudinem camere; nec sit in illis nimia claritas vel obscuritas sed lux mediocris. Et est ratio quia nimium remota vel augusta, nimium clara vel obscura causant moram inquisitionem imaginative virtutis et ex consequenti memoriam retardant dispersione rerum que representande sunt aut earum nimia conculcatione, sicut oculus legentis tedio affligitur si littere sint valde distincte et male composite aut nimus conculcate. Loci vero quantitas non est adeo sumenda modica, ut numero videatur esse capax imaginis, quia violentiam abhorret cogitatio ut si velles pro loco sumere foramen ubi aranea suas contexit tellas et in illo velles equum collocare, non videretur modo aliquo posse equum capere. Sed ipsorum locorum quantitas sumenda est ut statim inferius distincte notatem invenies.'

35. Venice, Bibliotheca Marciana, MS Lat. cl. VI, 274, f. 54r.: 'Oportet etiam ne loci sint in loco nimium usitato sicut sunt plateae et ecclesie, quoniam nimia consuetudo aut aliarum rerum representatio causant perturbationem et non claram imaginum representationem ostendunt sed confusan, quod summopere est cavendum, quia si in foro locum constitueres et in eo rei cuiuspiam simulacrum locares, cum de loco simulacroque velles recordari, additus, redditus meatusque frequens et crebra gentis nugatio conturbaret cogitationem tuam. Studebis ergo habere domum que rebus mobilibus libera sit et vacua omnino, et cave ne assumas cellas fratrum propter nimiam illarum similitudinem, nec hostia domorum pro locis quia cum nulla vel parva tibi sit differentia ideo confusio. Habeas ergo domum in qua sint intra cameras salas coquinas scalas viginti, et quanto in ipsis locis dissimilitudo maior, tanto utilior. Nec sint camere iste et reliquie excessive magne vel parve, et in earum qualibet facies quinque locos iuxta distantiam dictam superius scilicet sex aut octo vel decem pedes. Et incipe taliter ut, a dextris semper ambulando vel a sinistris quocunque altero istorum modorum ex aptitudine domus tibi commodius fuerit, non oporteat te retrocedere. Sed, sicut in re domus procedit, ita continuentur loci tui per ordinem domus, ut sit facilior impressio ex ordine naturali.'

36. The passages which follow here are transcribed from Venice, Bibliotheca Marciana, MS Lat. cl. VI, 274, ff. 41–9 ('Ars memoriae artificialis incipit. Ars memoriae artificialis, pater reverende, est ea qualiter homo ad recordandum de pluribus pervenire potest per memoriam artificialem de quibus recordari non possit, per memoriam naturalem'). I have seen three other versions of this manuscript: Rome, Vaticana, MS Lat. 3678, ff. 2r.–4r. (Incipit: 'Practica super

artificiali memoria. Pater et reverende domine. Quatenus homo ad recordandum') which has only the beginning of the treatise; Rome, Vaticana Lat. 4307, ff. 79–85v. (Incipit: 'Ars memoriae artificialis est qualiter homo ad recordandum de pluribus pervenire possit') which has almost the whole treatise; Rome, Vaticana, MS Lat. 5129, ff. 60–4v. (Incipit: 'Ars memoriae artificialis est qualiter homo') which, like Vaticana, MS Lat. 3678, is interrupted after the first few pages. At f. 68r. the beginning of the treatise is repeated.

37. Bibliotheca Marciana, MS. Lat. cl. VI, 274, ff. 41v.–42v.: '*De ordine locorum*. Circa cognitionem et ordinem locorum debetis scire quod locus in memoria artificialis est sicut carta in scriptura, propterea quod scribitur in carta quando homo vult recordari et non mutatur carta. Ita loca debent esse immobilia, hoc est dicitur quod locus debet semel accipi et nunquam dimitti seu mutari sicut carta. Deinde super talia loca formande sunt imagines illarum rerum vel illorum nominum quorum vultis recordari sicut item scribuntur in carta quando homo recordari vult. *De forma locorum*. Loca debent esse facta et ita formata quod non sint nimis parva nec nimis magna / ut verbi gratia non debes accipere pro uno loco unam domum vel unam terram vel unam schalam, nec etiam, sicut dixi, nimis parvum locum scilicet unum lapidem parvum nec unum foramen vel aliud tale. Et ratio est ista: nam humanus intellectus non circa magnas res nec circa parvas colligitur et imago evanescit; sed debes accipere loca media scilicet terminum clarum et non nimis obscurum, nec enim debes accipere loca in illo loco nimis solitario, sicut in deserto vel in silva, nec in loco nimis usitato, sed in loco medio: scilicet non nimis usitato nec nimis deserto. Et nota quod predicta loca bene scire debes et ante et retro et ipsa adigere per quinarium numerum, videlicet de quinque in quinque. Et debes scire quod loca non debent esse dissimilia, ut puta domus sit primus locus, secundus locus sit porticus, tertius locus sit angulus, quartus locus sit pes schale, quintus locus sit summitas schale. Et nota quod per quintum vel decimum locum debes ponere unam manum auream aut unum imperatorem super quintum vel decimum locum; qui imperator sit bene atque imperialiter indutus vel aliquid aliud mirabile vel deforme, ut possis melius recordari. Et haec sufficiant quantum ad formam locorum. Nunc autem videndum est de imaginibus per predicta loca ponendis. *De imaginibus*. Est enim sciendum quod imagines sunt sicut scriptura et loca sicut carta. Unde notatur quod aut / vis recordari propriorum nominum aut appellativorum aut grechorum aut illorum nominum quorum non intelligis

significata aut ambasiatarum aut argumentorum aut de aliis occuren-
tibus. Ponamus igitur primum quod ego velim recordari nominum
propriorum. Sic enim ponere debes imagines in proprio convenienti
loco et ipso sic facto: cum vis recordari unius divitis qui nominatur
Petrus, immediate ponas unum Petrum quem tu cognoscas qui sit
tuus amicus vel inimicus vel cum quo habuisti aliquam familiaritatem,
qui Petrus faciat aliquid ridiculum in illo loco, vel aliquid inusitatum,
vel simile dicat ... In secundo loco ponas unum Albertum quem tu
cognoscas ut supra licet per alios diversos modos, videlicet quod dic-
tus Albertus velit facere aliquid inusitatum vel deforme scilicet sus-
pendens se et ut supra. In tertio loco, si vis recordari istius nominis
equi, ponas ibi unum equum album, magnum ultra mensuram aliorum, et qui percutiat quenpiam tuum amicum vel inimicum cum cal-
cibus vel pedibus anterioribus, vel aliquid simile faciat ut supra ... '

38. See for example besides the two Ambrosian MSS (T. 78 sup., ff. 22–6
and 27v.-32v., the latter of which is also found in Rome, Bibliotheca
Angelica, MS 142 (B. 5. 12), ff. 83–7) reproduced in our appendices,
Venice, Bibliotheca Marciana, MS Lat. cl. VI, 292 (Incipit: 'De
memoriae locis libellus') and, in Rome, Bibliotheca Casanatense, MS
1193 (E. V. 51), ff. 29–32v. ('Liber seu ars memoriae localis'). A brief
vernacular treatise on the same problems is to be found in Florence,
Bibliotheca Riccardiana, MS 2734, ff. 30–2 (Incipit: 'Appresso io
Michele di Nofri di Michele di Mato del Gioganti ragioniere mostr-
erò il prencipio dello 'nparare l'arte della memoria, la quale mi
mostrò il maestro Niccholo Cieco da Firenze nel 1435, di dicembre,
quando ci venni, cominciando per locar luoghi nella casa mia'.
Explicit: 'E queste sono le otto sopradette fighure della memoria artificiale e tutti i modi, atti e chose che s'appartengono in essi. E matu-
ramente studiare e sapere, e verrai a perfezionare e a notizia vera di
presta scienza').

39. See Milan, Bibliotheca Ambrosiana, MS I. 171 , f. 20v.: 'Regulae
artificialis memoriae. Locorum multitudo; locorum ordinatio; loco-
rum meditatio; locorum solitudo; locorum designatio; locorum dissimilitudo; locorum mediocris magnitudo; locorum mediocris lux;
locorum distantia; locorum fictio. Locorum multiplicatio: addendo
diminuendo per sursum et deorsum, per antrorsum et retrorsum, per
destrorsum et sinistrorsum. Imaginum: alia in toto similis alia in toto
dissimilis: per oppositionem, per diminutionem, per transpositionem
locorum, per alphabetum, per transruptionem locorum, per loquelam.'

See also Milan, Bibliotheca Ambrosiana, MS E. 58 sup., f. 1: 'Ars memoriae. Locorum multitudo, ordinatio, permeditatio, vacuitas sive solitudo, quinti loci signatio, locorum dissimilitudo, mediocris magnitudo, mediocris lux, distantia, fictio. Locus multiplicatur: addendo, diminuendo, mutando (per sursum, deorsum, antrorsum, retrorsum, dextrorsum et sinistrorsum), mensurando (longum, latum, profundum). Idolorum: aliud in toto simile, aliud in toto dissimile per contrarium, per consuetudinem, per transpositionem (per alphabetum, sine alphabeto), aliud parum simile per compositionem, per diminutionem, per transpositionem, per transunptionem (literarum vel sillabarum), per loquelam.' This an another (almost identical) copy of the treatise transcribed in Bibliotheca Ambrosiana, MS E. 58 sup. In Rome, Bibliotheca Casanatense, MS 90, f. 84v. The idea of making the art easy to learn by means of a schema is presented as being closely connected to the idea of a series of verses by means of which it would be possible to memorise the rules of the art. See for example the verses which magister Girardi uses in the treatise contained in Bibliotheca Ambrosiana MS T. 78 sup. and (in another version) in Bibliotheca Angelica MS 142 (see Appendix II), and the *Tractatus de memoria artificiali carmine scriptus* which I have seen in Ambrosiana MS R.50, f. 91 r.

40. Bibliotheca Ambrosiana, MS T. 78 sup. ff. 27v.–32v. Another version is to be found in Bibliotheca Angelica, MS 142 (B.5.12), ff. 83–7.

41. Cf. the previously cited Bibliotheca Marciana, MS Lat. cl. VI, 274, ff. 43r., 44r.: 'De *amabasiatis recordandis*. Si vis recordari unius ambasiate quam facere debes, pone in loco imaginato ut superius scribebam ... Si ambasiata est nimis prolixa, tunc pone unam partem ambasiate in uno loco et aliam partem in uno alio loco ut supra, quia memoria naturalis adiuvabit te. *De argumentis recitandis*. Argumenta si recitare velis ... *De testis recordando*. Si vis recordari unius testis ponas primam particulam in illo loco, primam in primo, tertiam in tertio et sic de aliis successive ... ' But see also Bibliotheca Ambrosiana, MS T. 78 sup. f. 25v.: 'Ambasiatis vero si commode volueris recordari ... ' Most of the treatises dwell on the construction of arguments. See for example Venice, Bibliotheca Marciana, MS Lat. cl. VI, 238, f. 1v.: 'Tractatus de memoria artificiali adipiscenda eaque adhibenda ad argumentandum et respondendum' (Incipit: 'Ne in vobis, fratres, imo fili carissimi opus omittam devotionis').

42. *Congestorius artificiosae memoriae Joannis Romberch de Kryspe, omnium de memoria praeceptione aggregatim complectens. Opus omnibus Theologis, praedictoribus, professoribus, iuristis, iudicibus, procuratoribus, advocatis, notariis,*

medicis, philosophis, artium liberalium professoribus, insuper mercatoribus, nunciis et tabelariis pernecessarium (Venice: Georgii de Rusconibus, 1520).

43. *Phoenix seu artificiosa memoria domini Petri Ravennatis memoriae magistri* (Venice, Bernardinus de Choris de Cremona, 1491). A copy of this original edition edited by the author himself is included, together with two other incunabula, in Bibliotheca Marciana, MS Lat. cl. VI, 274, ff. 82–97v. The citations in the text and the appendices refer to this first edition. The *regulae* of Ravenna's tract (from the first through to the twelfth) are to be found in Rome, Vaticana, MS Lat. 6293, ff. 195–9 (Incipit: 'Fenix domini Petri ravennatis memoriae magistri'. Explicit: 'Finis. Deo gratias matrique Mariae') and are in part reproduced in Pavia, Bibliotheca Universitaria, MS Aldino 167 (sixteenth century, 82 et seq.) ff. 63–6v. (Incipit: 'Magister Petrus de memoria'. Explicit: 'Expliciunt regulae memoriae artis egregii ac memorandi viri Petri Magistri de Memoria'. On Pietro da Ravenna see also Girolamo Tiraboschi, *Storia della letteratura italiana* (Modena, 1787–94), VI, pp. 556 et seq.; Ferrante Bolani Borsetti, *Historia almi Ferrariae Gymnasii*, 2 vols. (Ferrara, 1735), II, pp. 419 et seq. For a biography see Ravenna, Bibliotheca Classense, MS Mob. 3.3.H2.10 which contains a genealogy of the Tommai family. The reasons for the term 'phoenix' in the title are clarified by Pietro himself: 'Et cum una sit Foenix et unus iste libellus, libello si placet Foenicis nomen imponatur.' But other writings also use 'phoenix' in this same sense: see for example Florence, Bibliotheca Nazionale, MS Palatina 885, ff. 314–23v. The *Liber qui dicitur Phoenix super lapidem philosophorum* (Incipit: 'Post diuturnam operis fatigationem'. Explicit: 'de lapide philosophorum natura et compositione sive fixione quae dicta sunt observentur. Deo gratias. Finis').

44. Ravenna, *Phoenix seu artificiosa memoria*, f. 87v.

45. Ravenna, *Phoenix seu artificiosa memoria*, ff. 92v.–94v. (cf. the passages in the appendices). But see also f. 88r.: 'In magna nobilium corona, dum essem adolescens, mihi semel fuit propositum ut aliqua nomina hominum per unum ex astantibus dicenda recitarem. Non negavi. Dicta ergo sunt nomina. In primo loco posui amicum illud nomen habentem in secundo similiter, et sic quot dicta fuerunt, tot collocavi, et collocata recitavi.'

46. The text of the letter of Eleonora d'Aragon is printed in the *Phoenix seu artificiosa memoria*, Venice, Bibliotheca Marciana, MS Lat. cl. VI, 274, ff. 82–2v. (see Appendix IV).

47. The Viennese editions are from 1541 and 1600. The London edition,

which is undated, has been assigned a date of c.1548: the treatise was presented, without the name of the author, by Robert Copland as *The Art of Memory, that otherwise is called the Phenix, a boke very behouefull and profytable to all professours of science, grammaryens, rethoryciens, dialectyks, legystes, phylosophes and theologiens.* Printed by William Middleton it is presented as 'a translation out of french in to englysche'. The date of the Cologne edition is 1608, that of the Vicenza edition 1600. For the reputation of Ravenna in Germany it should be remembered that Agrippa boasted of having had him as a teacher and that a fulsome eulogy to 'Pietro, teacher of memory' is included in Ortwin's *Alphabetum aureum* (Cologne, 1518).

48. Ravenna, *Phoenix seu artificiosa memoria,* ff. 88v., 89r.

49. Rome, Vaticana, MS Urb. Lat. 1743, f. 428r.

50. Bibliotheca Marciana, MS Lat. cl. VI, 274, ff. 41r.–41v. The passages cited here were originally published by Felice Tocco, *Le opere latine,* pp. 29–30, n. 2, which refers to Venice, Bibliotheca Marciana, MS Lat. cl. VI, 226.

51. Tocco has noted the recurrence of Democritus's name as the first inventor of the art in more than one treatise on artificial memory. See, for example, Venice, Bibliotheca Marciana, MS Lat. cl. VI, 274, ff. 1–5: *Tractatus super memoria artificiali, ordinatus ad honorem egregii et famosissimi doctoris nec non et comitis Troili Boncompagni P. F ... Homines enim mortales memoriam labilem conspicientes fuerunt conati quemadmodum fuit Democritus, Simonides et Cicero per artem adiuvare.* But cf. also, in the same manuscript, f. 5, the *Regulae memoriae artificialis ordinatae per religiosum sacrae theologiae professorem magistrum Ludovicum de Pirano ordinis Minorum* (Incipit: 'Democritus atheniensis philosophus, huius artis primus inventor fuit'). The reference to Democritus seems to to be founded, as Tocco explains (p. 30) on the testimony of Aulus Gellius (X, 17), according to whom Democritus removed his eyes in order that he might concentrate better on his thoughts.

52. Venice, Bibliotheca Marciana, MS Lat.cl. VI, 274, ff. 41r.–v.: 'Ars memoriae artificialis, pater reverende, est ea qualiter homo ad recordandum de pluribus pervenire possit per memoriam artificialem de quibus recordari non possit per memoriam naturalem. Debetis enim scire quod sic natura adiuvatur per artem adiunctam sicut sunt navigia ad mare transfretandum quia non potest transfretari per virtutem et viam naturae, sed solum per virtutem et viam artis; unde philosophi vocaverunt artem adiutricem nature. Sicut enim invenerunt homines diversas artes ad iuvandum diversis modis

naturam, sic etiam videntes quod per naturam hominis memoria labilis est, conati sunt invenire artem aliquam ad iuvandum naturam seu memoriam ut homo per virtutem artis recordari possit multarum rerum quarum non poterat recordari aliter per memoriam naturalem et sic adinvenerunt scripturas et viderunt non posse recordari horum quae scripserant. Postea in successione temporis, videntes quod semper non poterant secum portare scripturas, nec semper parati erant ad scribendum, adinvenerunt subtiliorem artem ut sine quacumque scriptura multarum rerum reminisci valerent et hanc vocaverunt memoriam artificialem. Ars ista primum inventa fuit Athenis per Democritum eloquentissimum philosophum. Et licet diversi philosophi conati fuerint hanc artem declarare, tamen melius et subtilius declaravit suprascriptus philosophus Democritus huius artis adinventor. Tulius vero perfectissimus orator in cuius libro Rhetoricorum de hac arte tractavit licet obscuro et subtili modo in tantum quod nemo ipsum intelligere valuit nisi per divinam gratiam et doctorem qui doceret ipsam artem qualiter debere pratichari.'

53. I have used the incunabulum *De nutrienda memoria Dominicis de Carpanis de Neapoli, anno domini 1476, ind. IV, die vero XVI decembris regnante serenissimo et illustrissimo Domino nostro D. Ferdinando Dei gratia rege Sicilie, Hierusalem et Hungarie* in Venice, Bibliotheca Marciana, MS Lat. cl. VI, 274, ff. 97–103v.

54. De Carpanis, *De nutrienda memoria*, f. 97v.: 'Quasi de armario pomorum cibum sumens, verba per dentes ruminantis intellectus emittit.'

55. De Carpanis, *De nutrienda memoria*, ff. 98, 99, 102v.

56. De Carpanis, *De nutrienda memoria*, f. 101r.

57. I have used the incunabulum which can be found (together with works by Pietro da Ravenna and Domenico de Carpanis), in Venice, Bibliotheca Marciana, MS Lat. cl. VI, 274, ff. 69–82: *Iohannis Michaelis Alberti Carrariensis. De omnibus ingeniis augendae memoriae. Ad prestantissimum virum Aloisium Manentem incliti Venetorum Senatus Secretarium. Impressum Bononiae per me Platonem de Benedictis civem bononiensem, regnante inclito principe domino Iohanne Bentivolio, secundo anno incarnationis, dominice 1481 die XXIII Januarii.* The physician Guglielmo Gratarolo, from Bergamo, makes extensive use of Carrara's text, without citing the author, in his *Opuscula* on memory (Basel, 1554). On Carrara see Girolamo Tiraboschi, *Storia della letteratura italiana*, VI, pp. 688–93.

58. Carrara, *De omnibus ingeniis*, f. 72v.: 'Primum est ordo et reminiscibilium consequentia. Cum eam didicimus ex ordine cum

connectione et dependentia si aliquo eorum erimus obliti, facile, repetito ordine, reminisci poterimus. Alterum est ut uno simili in suum simile provehamur: ut si Herodoti obliviscamur de Tito Livio recordati latinae historiae patre, in Grecae historiae patrem Herodotum producemur. Tertium est ut contraria recogitemus ... ut memores Hectoris, reminiscimur Achillis.'

59. Carrara, *De omnibus ingeniis*, f. 73. See Tocco, *Le opere latine di G. Bruno*, p. 34, n. 1.

60. See for example *Tractatus clarissimi philosophi et medici Matheoli perusini de memoria et reminiscentia ac modo studendi tractatus feliciter.* This undated work was probably written at the end of the fifteenth century and deals with the regime necessary for attaining a good memory. On the author see Tiraboschi, *Storia della letteratura italiana*, VI, p. 462 et seq.

61. Averroes Cordubensis, *Compendia librorum Aristotelis qui parva naturalia vocantur*, ed. Aemilia Ledyard Shields in *Corpus commentariorum Averrois in Aristotelem. Versionum latinarum,* Mediaeval Academy of America. Publication no. 54, Corpus philosophorum Medii Aevi (Cambridge, Mass.: Harvard University Press, 1949), VII, pp. 70–1.

62. On these themes see Ernst Cassirer, *Individuo e cosmo nella filosofia del Rinascemento* (Florence, 1935), pp. 119, 149; Philippe Monnier, *Le Quattrocento; essai sur l'histoire littéraire du XVe siècle italien* (Paris, 1901), pp. 127 et seq.; Charles Lemmi, *The Classic Deities in Bacon. A Study in Mythological Symbolism* (Baltimore: Johns Hopkins Press, 1933), pp. 14–19; Paul Oskar Kristeller, *Il pensiero filosofico di Marsilio Ficino* (Florence: Sansoni, 1953), pp. 86 et seq.; Eugenio Garin, *L'umanesimo italiano* (Bari: Laterza, 1952), pp. 120 et seq.; *Medioevo et Rinascimento: studi e ricerche* (Bari: Laterza, 1954), pp, 66–89. Also essential are Jean Seznec, *La Survivance des dieux antiques* (London, 1940), especially the section on iconology, pp. 95–108; Mario Praz, *Studies in Seventeenth-Century Imagery* (London, 1939) and Frances A. Yates, *The French Academies of the Sixteenth Century* (London: Warburg Institute, 1947), p. 132. The art historian Wilhelm Waetzholdt reaches similar conclusions in his work *Dürer and his times*, trans. R. H. Boothroyd (London: Phaidon Press, 1950). See also Robert J. Clements, 'Iconography on the nature and inspiration of poetry in english renaissance emblem literature', *PMLA*, 70:4 (1955), pp. 781–804.

63. Andrea Alciati, *Omnia A. Alciati emblemata* (Antwerp, 1581), pp. 11–13. The first edition was 1531.

64. Cesare Ripa, *Iconologia* (Padua, 1611), titlepage. The first edition of the *Iconologia* was 1503.

65. Ripa, *Iconologia*, p. 335.

66. On Titian's *Allegoria della prudenza* see Erwin Panofsky, *The Meaning of the Visual Arts. Papers on and in Art History* (Garden City, New York: Doubleday, 1955), pp. 146–68. On prudence as 'memory of the past, ordering of the present and contemplation of the future' Panofsky cites, along with a number of less well-known sources, the passages of Albertus Magnus and Thomas Aquinas. But the theme of the connection between memory and prudence in the ancients was probably equally influential on the figurative arts in the renaissance.

67. Publicii Iacobi, *Oratoriae artis epitoma, sive quae ad consumatum spectant oratorem* (Venice, 1482). The work was reprinted in 1485 in Venice, and in Augusta in 1490 and 1498. I have used the incunabulum Rome, Bibliotheca Angelica, 697.

68. Iacobi, *Oratoriae artis epitoma*, sig. d4r.–d4v.

69. Francesco Bianchini, *La istoria universale provata con monumenti e figurata con simboli degli antichi* (Rome, 1697), p. 5.

70. Giambattista Vico, *Opere*, ed. Fausto Nicolini (Milan–Naples: Ricciardi, 1953), p. 367. See also Paolo Rossi, 'Schede Vichiane', *La rassegna della letteratura italiana*, 62:3 (1958), pp. 375–83 (subsequently reprinted as part of my book *Le sterminate antichità*, pp. 181 et seq.).

71. Vico, *Scienza nuova*, p. 699. Thomas Hobbes, *Philosophical Works* (London, 1841), III, p. 9.

II ENCYCLOPAEDISM AND *COMBINATORIA* IN THE SIXTEENTH CENTURY

1. I have used the edition of Lull's works and the Lullian commentaries published in Strasburg by the Zetzner brothers. *Raymundi Lullii Opera ea quae ad inventam ab ipso artem universalem scientiarum artiumque omnium brevi compendio firmaque memoria apprehendendarum locupletissimaque vel oratione ex tempore petractandarum pertinent. Ut et in eandem quorundam interpretum scripti commentarii ... Accessit Valerii de Valeriis patrici veneti aureum in artem Lullii generalem opus* (Strasburg: Lazari Zetzneri, 1617). The first edition of this work was published in 1598. It was reprinted in 1609 and in 1651, and partially reproduced in 1836. The volume contains the following works: Authentic Lullian works: *Logica brevis et nova*, pp. 147–61; *Ars brevis*, pp. 1–42; *Ars magna generalis ultima*, pp. 218–663; *Tractatus de conversione subiecti et praedicati per medium*, pp. 166–77; *Duodecim principia philosophiae*, pp. 112–46.

Apocryphal works and works attributed to Lull: *De auditu kabbalistico seu kabbala*, pp. 43–111; *Oratio exemplaris*, pp. 224–217 (*sic*, error in page numeration); *Liber de venatione medii inter subiectum et praedicatum*, pp. 162–5. Commentaries: Giordano Bruno, *De lulliano specierum scrutinio*, pp. 664–80; *De lampade combinatoria lulliana*, pp. 681–734; *De progressu logicae venationis*, pp. 735–86; Henricus Cornelius Agrippa, *In artem brevem Raymundii Lullii commentaria*, pp. 787–916; Valeriis de Valeriis, *Opus aureum in quo omnia breviter explicantur quae R. Lullus tam in scientiarum arbore quam arte generali tradit,* pp. 969–1109. All further citations of this work will refer simply to 'Zetzner'.

2. On Pedro Dagui who held public lectures on Lullism in the cathedral of Majorca in 1481, and his disciple Janer, and the Platonic philosopher Fernando da Cordoba who defended Dagui against accusations of heterodoxy in a commission appointed by Sextus IV, and on the Lullism of Lefèvre and Bovelles, and the brothers Andres, Pedro and Jaime Canterio see Tomas and Joaquin Carreras y Artau, *Historia de la filosofía española. Filosofia cristiana de los siglos XIII al XIV*, 2 vols. (Madrid, 1939–43), II, pp. 65 et seq., 78, 283 et seq., 201–9, 216 et seq. An important work on the history of Lullism is Elíes Rogant and Estanislau Duràn y Renals, *Bibliografia de las impressions lullianes* (Barcelona, 1927). For the numerous editions of the commentary of Agrippa see Duran y Renals, *Bibliographia*, items 79, 80, 82, 86–8, 103–5, 111, 125, 144, 148, 162, 180. For information on the published and unpublished works and manuscripts of Lull, see *Histoire littéraire de la France ouvrage commencé par des Religieux Bénédictins de la Congrégation de Saint-Maur et continué par des membres de l'institut (Académie des Inscriptions et Belles Lettres)*, 42 vols. (Paris, 1847–), XXIX, pp. 1–386; Ephrem Longpré's article on 'Lull' in A. Vacant et al. (ed.) *Dictionnaire de théologie catholique* 15 vols. (Paris, 1903–50), IX, cols. 1072–1141; Joan Avinyó, *Les obres autentiques del Beat Ramon Lull* (Barcelona, 1935); Carmelo Ottaviano, *L'Ars compendiosa de R. Lulle. Avec une étude sur la bibliographie et le fond* [sic] *Ambrosien de Lulle* (Paris, 1930). For the diffusion of Lullism, particularly in Italy, see the important studies of Miguel Batllori. See esp. his invaluable bibliographical study *Introducción bibliográfica a los estudios lulianos* (Palma de Mallorca: Escuela Lulistica de Mallorca, 1945) and his series of seminal articles: 'El Lulismo en Italia', *Revista. de Filosofia de l'Instituto Lodovico Vives*, 2 (1944), pp. 5–7; 'La obra de R. Lull en Italia' in *Studia* (Palma de Mallorca, 1943); 'Le lullisme de la Renaissance et du Baroque: Padoue et Rome,' in *Actes du XIeme Congrès Internationale de*

Philosophie, Bruxelles, 20–26 août, 1953 14 vols. (Amsterdam: North Holland Publishing Co., 1953), XIII, pp. 7–12. For more complete information on Batllori's work see Giovanni Maria Bertini, *Bibliografia del P. Miguel Batllori S.I.* (Turin: Aresal, 1957).

3. Henricus Cornelius Agrippa, *In artem brevem ... commentaria*, Zetzner, pp. 787–9

4. Henricus Cornelius Agrippa, *De vanitate scientiarum et artium* in *Henrici Cornelii Agrippae ... Opera*, 2 vols. (Lyons, 1600), II, pp. 31 et seq. Chapter IX of the *De vanitate* is entitled 'De arte Lulli', and chapter X 'De arte memorativa'. In Helda Bullotta Barracco's 'Saggio bio-bibliografico su C. Agrippa', *Rassegna di filosofia*, 3 (1957), pp. 222–48, there is no mention of Agrippa's commentary on Lull. The work is not precisely datable. See Gabriel Auguste Prost, *Les Sciences et les arts occultes au XVIe siècle. Corneille Agrippa, sa vie et ses oeuvres*. 2 vols. (Paris, 1881–2) I, p. 35, where a date of 1517 is suggested, although without any supporting evidence. It was certainly written before 1523 (see Claudius Blancheroseus in *Epist.* III, 26, *Opera*, II, p. 802).

5. See Carreras y Artau, *Filosofia cristiana*, II, pp. 10–11.

6. See the introduction to the *Ars demonstrativa* in Lull, *Opera omnia*, III, p. 1. The first three of the eight volumes of the Mainz edition, numbered I–VI and IX–X (volumes VII and VIII were not published) were edited by Ivo Salinger. On Salinger and the Mainz edition see Carreras y Artau, *Filosofia cristiana*, II, pp. 323–53.

7. See *Ars magna generalis ultima*, cap. 101 ('De logica'), in Zetzner, pp. 537–8.

8. Zetzner, p. 663.

9. See Clemens Bäumker, 'Die europäische Philosophie der Mittelalter', in Wilhelm Wundt (ed.), *Allgemeine Geschichte der Philosophie* (Berlin, 1909, repr. 1923), pp. 417–18; Etienne Gilson, 'La philosophie franciscaine', in *Saint François d'Assise* (Paris, 1927), p. 163. An extensive and exact account of Lull's *ars combinatoria* is to be found in Eberhard Wolfram Platzeck, 'La combinatoria Luliana: un nuevo ensayo de exposicion e interpretacion de la misma a la luz de la filosofia general Europea', *Revista de Filosofia*, 12:3 (1953), pp. 575–609 and 13:1 (1954), pp. 125–65 (previously published under the title 'Die Lullische Kombinatorik: ein erneuter Darstellungs- und Deutungsversuch mit Bezug auf die westeuropäische Philosophie', in *Franziskanische Studien*, 34 (1952), pp. 32–60 and 377–407. See also Frances A. Yates, 'The art of Ramon Lull', *Journal of the Warburg and*

Courtauld Institutes, 1–2 (1954), pp. 115–73. In the light of these studies the interpretation and exposition of Karl von Prantl, *Geschichte der Logik im Abendlande*, 4 vols. (Leipzig, 1855–70, repr. 1955), III, pp. 145–77 seems completely insufficient.

10. *Compendium artis demonstrativae*, in Lull, *Opera* (Mainz, 1721–24), III, p. 74.

11. Carreras y Artau, *Filosofía cristiana*, I, p. 484. The Catalan version of the *Arbor scientiae* occupies volumes XI–XIII (1917–26) of the *Obres de Ramon Lull* (Palma de Mallorca, 1901). The most recent Latin editions are Lyons, 1635 and 1637 (the preceding editions are Barcelona, 1482 and 1505 and Lyons, 1505, 1515 and 1605).

12. Yates, 'The art of Ramon Lull'.

13. Paris, Bibliothèque Nationale, Lat. MS 15450 (early fourteenth century). The date of composition is given at the end of the text: 'Anno Domini 1325 per Thomas Migerii. In attrebato.'

14. See Yates, 'The art of Ramon Lull', p. 172.

15. MS Cus. 85, f.. 55v. See Platzeck, 'La combinatoria luliana', p. 135. By the same author see also 'Observaciones del padre Antonio Raimundo Pascual, D. Cista sobre Lulistas Alemanes – Sapientissimi Regis Puerperae. A: El lulismo en las obras del Cardinel Nicolás Krebs de Cusa', *Revista española de teología*, 1:4 (1941), pp. 731–65 and 2:2 (1942), pp. 257–324; 'Los datos lulísticos póstumos del 'Scholae Magister-Fundator' Dr M. Honecker y las glosas del Card. Nic. de Cusa sobre el Arte luliana', *Studia monographica*, rec. 9–10 (1953–4), pp. 1–16; 'Lullische Gedanken bei Nikolaus von Kues', *Trierer theologische Zeitschrift*, 62 (1953), pp. 357–64.

16. See Martin Honecker, 'Ramon Lulls Wahlvorschlag Grundlage des Kaiserwahlplanes bei Nikolaus von Cues?', *Historisches Jahrbuch*, 57:4 (1938), pp. 563–74 (572). On the Lullism of Cusanus see the studies of Franz Xavier Kraus, Jakob Marx, Felice Tocco, and Edmond Vansteenberghe, indicated in the chapter 'Influencias lulianas en Nicolas de Cusa', in Carreras y Artau, *Filosofía cristiana*, II, pp. 178–96. More recently: Maurice de Gandillac, *La Philosophie de Nicolas de Cuse* (Paris: Aubier, Éditions Montaigne, 1941) and Joseph Ehrenfried Hofmann, *Die Quellen der cusanischer Mathematik, I: Ramon Lulls Kreisquadratur (De quadratura et triangulatura circuli)*, Sitzungsberichte der Heidelberger Akademie der Wissenschaften, 4 (Heidelberg, 1942).

17. See Carreras y Artau, *Filosofía cristiana*, II, p. 187.

18. Raimundo Sabund, *Liber creaturarum*, ed. Wolfgang Hoffmannus (Frankfurt-am-Main, 1635), tit. I, p. 8.

19. Milan, Bibliotheca Ambrosiana, MS D. 535 inf., f. 37v. The illustration is reproduced in vol. XIII of the *Obres de Ramon Lull*. The same image is also found in the Latin edition, Lyons 1515, p. 145. The printed edition of the *Arbre de sciencia* which I use here is the Castilian version published in Brussels by Foppens in 1664.

20. I translate here from the first edition, *Raemundi Lullii Eremitae divinitus illuminati in rhetoricam isagoge perspicacibus ingeniis expectata* (Lyons, 1515), unnumbered pages. The quotation is from Remigio Rufo's dedicatory letter. On Rufo see Carreras y Artau, *Filosofia cristiana*, II, pp. 214 et seq. The same work is included in the Zetzner edition, pp. 172–223.

21. Cornelius Gemma, *De arte cyclognomica tomi III doctrinam ordinum universam, unaque philosophiam Hippocratis Platonis Galeni et Aristotelis in unius communissimae et circularis methodi speciem referentes, quae per animorum triplices orbes ad spherae caelestis similitudinem fabricatos, non medicinae tantum arcana pandit mysteria, sed et inveniendis costituendisque artibus ac scientiis caeteris viam compendiosam patefacit* (Antwerp: Christoph Plantin, 1569). Gemma's other works include the *De naturae divinis characterismis, seu raris et admirandis spectaculis, causis, indiciis, proprietatibus rerum in partibus singulis universi, libri III* (Antwerp: Christopher Plantin, 1575) and *De prodigiosa specie naturaque Cometae anno 1577 visa* (Antwerp: Christoph Plantin, 1578). Carreras y Artau misdates Gemma's *De arte cyclognomica* to 1659. This is not simply a printer's error, however, as the authors (who frequently use second- or even third-hand information) deal with Gemma in a chapter dedicated to the development of Lullism in the seventeenth century (See *Filosofia cristiana*, II, p. 304).

22. Gemma, *De arte cyclognomica*, p. 27.

23. Gemma, *De arte cyclognomica*, p. 34.

24. Gemma, *De arte cyclognomica*, p. 105.

25. Gemma, *De arte cyclognomica*, pp. 48–50.

26. Gemma, *De naturae divinis characterismis*, p. 34: 'This therefore is the first foundation of our art' (*Hoc ergo sit primum artis nostrae fundamentum*).

27. Published in Venice by Joh. Dominicum de Imbertis, 1588. The other volume of the work has the title: *Sintaxeon artis mirabilis alter tomus in quo omnium scientiarum et artium tradita est epitome, unde facilius istius artis studiosus de omnibus propositis possit rationes et ornamenta rarissima proferre, ibidem* (Venice, 1588). The work was reprinted by Zetzner in four volumes (Cologne, 1610): *Commentaria in Sintaxes artis mirabilis, per quas de omnibus disputatur habeturque ratio, in quatuor*

tomos ... in quibus plura omnino scitu necessaria ... tractantur. The second
volume was retitled *Sintaxeon artis mirabilis in libros XL digestarum tomi
duo.* In the third and fourth volumes *acutissimae ac sublimes tractiones de
Deo de Angelis et de Immortalitate animae continentur.* The quotations
which follow are from the 1610 edition. For more information on
the author see Carreras y Artau, *Filosofia cristiana,* II, pp. 234 et seq.

28. *Commentaria,* I, pp. 11–12.

29. On de Valeriis see Carreras y Artau, *Filosofia cristiana,* II, pp. 235–7.
    For the first edition of the work see Duran y Renal, *Bibliografia,* item
    138. The quotation is from the *Opus aureum in quo omnia breviter expli-
    cantur quae R. Lullus tam in scientiarum arbore quam arte generali tradit,*
    Zetzner edition, p. 971, fn. 1.

30. De Valeriis, *Opus aureum,* Zetzner, pp. 982, 986, 1009, 1115.

31. Zeztner, pp. 970–1.

32. Zeztner, p. 1026.

33. Ramon Lull, *Liber de nova logica* (Mallorca, 1744), p. 1. See Carreras
    y Artau, *Filosofia cristiana,* II, p. 423.

34. Ramon Lull, *Ars brevis,* VI, 10.

35. On the mnemonic function of the figures and verses see Carreras y
    Artau, *Filosofia cristiana, passim.* For an example of a popular
    mnemonic see the *Logica en rims* or 'new compendium' of the
    Compendium logicae Algazelis lines 6–9 and 1574–80 which are writ-
    ten:

> en rimes e 'n mots qui son plans
> per tal que hom puscha mostrar
> logica e philosophar
> a cels qui no saben lati
> ni arabich ...

> Per affermar e per neguar
> a.b.c. pots aiustar
> mudant subject e predicat
> relativament comparat
> en conseguent antesedent.

> [In rhymes and in words which are plain
> So that man can reveal
> Logic and philosophize
> To those who do not know Latin
> Or Arabic ...

By affirming and by negating
A.B.C. one can combine the propositions,
Changing subject and predicate
Relatively so that one can compare
Each one with its antecedent.]

36. Ramon Lull, 'Aplicaciò de l'art general', in G. Rosello (ed.), *Obras Rimadas ... escritas en idioma Catalan-Provenzal, publicadas por primera vez con un articulo biografico, illustraciones y variantes, y sequidas de un glossario de voces antiguadas* (Palma de Mallorca, 1859), p. 422.

37. Rules for memory can also be found in chapter 161 of Lull's *Liber de contemplaciò*. See Carreras y Artau, *Filosofia cristiana*, I, p. 536.

38. Carreras y Artau, *Filosofia cristiana*, II, pp. 534–9.

39. The *Dictionnaire de théologie catholique* and Littré, *Histoire littéraire de la France*, refer to two manuscripts: Bibliothèque Nationale, Paris, Lat. MS 16116 and Innichen, MS VIII B. 14, ff. 90 et seq. I have found two additional versions in Turin, Nazionale, MS I. V. 47, and Rome, Vaticana, MS Urb. Lat. 852. The Turin manuscript has been destroyed. I have not seen the Innichen MS. The quotations are from Paris, MS Lat. 16116 (fourteenth century), ff. 18v.–23v. (Incipit: 'Per quendam silvam quidam homo ibat'. Explicit: 'Ad gloriam et honorem Dei finivit Raymundus librum memoriae quem diu desideravit ipsum fecisse. Et finivit in Montepessulano in mense februarii anno CCCIIII ab incarnatione Domini Nostri Iesu Christi.').

40. Paris, MS Lat. 16116, f. 23v.

41. Paris MS Lat.16116, ff. 16v.–17r.: 'Per quendam silvam quidam homo ibat considerando quid erat causa quia scientia difficilis est ad acquirendum, facilis vero ad obliviscendum et videbatur ei quod propter defectum memoriae istud erat eo quia sua essentia non bene est cognita atque suae operationes sive condiciones naturales, et ideo proposuit de memoria facere istum librum ad memoriam eaque ei pertinent agnoscendum. Subiectum huius libri est ars generalis, eoque cum suis principiis et regulis memoriam intendimus investigare ... Est autem memoria ens cui proprium et per se est memorari. Dividitur iste liber in tres distinctiones. Prima est de arbore memoriae et de suis conditionibus de principiis artis generalis cum suis diffinitionibus et regulis. Secunda distinctio est de floribus memoriae et de principiis et regulis artis generalis ipsi memoriae applicatis. Tertia distinctio est de quaestionibus de memoria factis et de solutionibus quaestionum. Et primo de prima dicemus. Arbor memoriae dividitur in novem flores ut in se patet.

Primus flos est b et b significat bonitatem [dantem in] <differen-
tiam> memoriam receptivam et utrum; secundus flos est c et c significat magnitudinem concordantiam memoriam remissivam et quid
est; d significat durationem contrarietatem memoriam conservativam
et de quo; e significat potestatem sive principium memoriam activam
et <quare>; f significat sapientiam medium [materiam] memoriam
discretivam et quantum; g significat voluntatem finem memoriam
multiplicativam et quale; h significat virtutem maioritatem memoriam significativam et quando; i significat [veritatem] <virtutem>
aequalitatem memoriam terminativam et ubi; k significat gloriam,
minoritatem memoriam complexionativam et quomodo et cum quo.
In arte ista alphabetum supradictum cordetenus scire oportet.'
[Note: in this passage, the arrow brackets indicate superlineal inser-
tions and the square brackets indicate deletions.]

42. The square brackets in the table indicate words which have been
omitted or altered in the manuscript.

43. See Platzeck, 'La combinatoria luliana'.

44. Paris, Lat. MS 16116, f. 22r.–v.: 'Memoria est in loco ut per regulam
de i in tertia parte. Quod amiserat principium distinctionis signatum
est et est in loco per accidens non per se, hoc est ratione corporis
cum quo est convicta, quoniam memoria per se non est collocabilis
eo quia non habet superficiem sed est in loco in quo corpus est, et
sicut corpus est mutabile de loco in locum, etiam i memoria per
ipsum. Memoria vero mutat obiecta de uno loco in alium non
mutando se, sed mutando suas operationes obiective recipiendo
species quae sunt similitudines locorum cum quibus est discretiva et
multiplicativa et ideo secundum quod ipsa est conditionata cum loco,
debet artista uti ipsa per loca et ideo si vult recordari aliquid traditum
oblivioni, considerat illum locum in quo fuit et primo in genere, sicut
in qua civitate, post in specie, sicut in quo vico, post in particulari,
sicut in qua domo seu in aula seu in coquina et sic de aliis et ideo per
talem discursum memoria multiplicabit se.'

45. On the relationship between Ciceronian mnemotechnics and the
work of Augustine see Yates, 'The Ciceronian art of memory',
pp. 878–81. [See also Yates, *The Art of Memory*, pp. 59–62. Trans.]

46. On this see Paris MS Lat. 16116, f. 23v.: 'Liber iste [the *Liber
memoriae*] valde utilis est et associabilis cum libris Intellectus et
Voluntatis in uno volumine quantum ad invicem sunt se iuvantes ad
attingendum secreta rerum' ('This book is extremely useful and can
be used together with the books of Intellect and Will in one volume,

in as much as they are all equally useful for learning the secrets of things'). On the Lullian art as an image of the Trinity see Yates, 'The art of Ramon Lull', p. 162.

47. Littré, *Histoire littéraire de la France*, xxix, p. 318, refers to Munich, Staatsbibliotek, MS 10517, ff. 22 et seq., Longpré, *Dictionnaire de théologie catholique*, col. 1102, n. 59 (15) mentions, in addition to the Munich manuscript, a version in Rome, Vaticana, MS Ott. Lat. 405, ff. 182 et seq. I have located another version in Milan, Bibliotheca Ambrosiana, MS N. 259 sup., ff. 22 et seq. (Incipit: 'Deus cum tua misericordia incipit liber de tua memoria. Quoniam de divina memoria'. Explicit: 'Ad laudem et honorem Dei finivit Raymundus istum librum in civitate Messanae mense Martii anno 1313').

48. Bibliotheca Ambrosiana, MS N.259, f. 22r.–v.: 'Deus cum tua misericordia incipit liber de tua memoria. Quoniam de divina memoria non habemus tantam notitiam sicut de divino intellectu et voluntate, idcirco intendimus indagare divinam memoriam ut de ipsa tantam notitiam habeamus quantam habemus de divino intellectu et voluntate. Ex hoc habebimus maiorem scientiam de deo ... De divisione huius libri: dividitur iste liber in quinque distinctiones. In prima tractabimus de memoria hominis, in secunda investigabimus memoriam divinam per divinum intellectum, in tertia divinam voluntatem, in quarta divinam trinitatem, in quinta et ultima divinas rationes ... Memoria humana est potentia cum qua homo recolit ea quae sunt praeterita et ad hoc declarandum damus istud exemplum. Potentia imaginativa non habet actum scilicet imaginari in illo tempore in quo potentia sensitiva attingit suum obiectum et de hoc quolibet potest habere experientiam, a simili dum homo attingit obiectum pensatum seu imaginatum in tempore presenti tunc memoria non potest memorari illud obiectum quia intellectus et voluntas hominis impediunt quominus memoria habeat suum actum quia intellectus intelligit ipsum obiectum et voluntas diligit seu odit illud et per hoc ostenditur quia memoria est potentia per se contra illos qui dicunt quod memoria non est potentia per se sed est radicata in intellectu et simul sunt una potentia, quod falsum est ut super declaratum est.'

49. I have seen three examples of this work in the following manuscripts (all sixteenth century): Milan, Bibliotheca Ambrosiana, MS I. 153 inf., ff. 35–39v.; Munich, Staatsbibliotek, MS 10593, ff. 1v.–3v.; Paris, Bibliothèque Nationale, MS Lat. 17839, ff. 437–444r. I have examined Rome, Vaticana, MS Lat. 5437, which has been cited as containing a version of the *Liber ad memoriam confirmandam*, but the

manuscript contains no Lullian works. In my transcription I have
used the three manuscripts indicated above. The folio numbers refer
to the Munich manuscript. For the complete text of the work see
Appendix I.

50. Munich, Staatsbibliotek, MS 10593, f. 1r.–v.: 'Primo igitur ut laborans in studio faciliter sciat modum scientiam invenire et ne, post
amissos quamplurimos labores, scientiae huius operam inutiliter tradidisse noscatur, sed potius labor in requiem et sudor in gloriam plenarie convertatur, modum scientiae decet pro iuvenibus invenire per
quem non tanta gravitate corporis iugiter deprimantur, sed, absque
nimia vexatione et cum corporis levitate et mentis laetitia, ad scientiarum culmina gradientes equidem propere subeant. Multi enim sunt
qui, more brutorum, literarum studia cum multo et summo labore
corporis prosequuntur absque exercitio ingenii artificioso, sed et continuis vigiliis maceratum corpus suum iuxta labores proprios inutiliter
exhibentes. Igitur decet modum per quem virtuosus studens thesaurum scientiae leviter valeat invenire et a gravamine tantorum laborum relevari possit.'

51. Munich, Staatsbibliotek, MS 10593, ff. 2v.–3r. 'Venio igitur ad secundam, scilicet ad memoriam quae quidem, secundum antiquos, alia est
naturalis, alia est artificialis. Naturalis est quam quis recipit in creatione vel generatione sua secundum materiam ex qua homo generatur et secundum quod influentia alicuius planetae superioris regnat:
et secundum hoc videmus quosdam homines meliorem memoriam
habentes quam alios, sed de ista nihil ad nos quoniam Dei est illud
concedere. Alia est memoria artificialis et ista est duplex quia
quaedam est in medicinis et emplastris cum quibus habetur, et istam
reputo valde periculosam quoniam interdum dantur tales medicinae
dispositioni hominis contrariae, interdum superfluae et in maxima
cruditate qua cerebrum ultra modum dessicatur, et propter defectum
cerebri homo ad dementiam demergitur, ut audivimus et vidimus de
multis, et ista displiciet Deo quoniam hic non se tenet pro contento
de gratia quam sibi Deus contulit unde, posito casu quod ad insaniam
non perveniat, nunquam vel raro habebit fructus scientiae. Alia est
memoria artificialis per alium modum acquirendi, nam dum aliquis
per capacitatem recipit multum in memoria et in ore revolvat per
seipsum quoniam secundum Alanum in parabolis studens est
admodum bovis. Bos enim cum maxima velocitate recipit herbas et
sine masticatione ad stomachum remittit quas postmodum remugit et
ad finem, cum melius est digestum, in sanguinem et carnem

convertit: ita est de studente qui moribus oblitis capit scientiam sine deliberatione, unde ad finem ut duret, debet in ore mentis masticare ut in memoria radicetur et habituetur quoniam quod leviter capit leviter recedit et ita memoria, ut habetur in Libro de memoria et reminiscentia, per saepissimam reiterationem firmiter confirmatur.'

52. Munich, Staatsbibliotek, MS 10593, f. 3r.–v.: 'Ad multa recitanda consideravi ponere quaedam nomina relativa per quae ad omnia possit responderi ... Ista enim sunt nomina supra dicta quid, quare, quantus et quomodo. Per quodlibet istorum poteris recitare viginti rationes in oppositum factas vel quaecumque advenerint tibi recitanda et quam admirabile est quod centum possis rationes retinere et ipsas, dum locus fuerit, bene recitare ... Ergo qui scientiam habere affectat et universalem ad omnia desiderat, hoc circa ipsum tractatum laboret cum diligentia toto posse quoniam sine dubio scientior erit aliis ... Primum igitur per primam speciem nominis quid, poteris certas quaestiones sive rationes sive alia quaecunque volueris recitare evacuando secundam figuram de his quae continet, per secundam vero poteris in duplo respondere seu recitare et hoc per evacuationem tertiae figurae et multiplicationem primae.'

53. Vaticana, MS Urb. Lat. 852, paper, 636 folios (sixteenth century). The *Localis memoria per Raimundum Lullum* is to be found in ff. 33r.–38v. Ivo Salzinger, *Catalogus omnium librorum magni operis Raymundi Lulli proxime publico communicandi* (Mainz, 1714), lists an *Ars memorativa* (*Incipit*: 'Ars confirmat et auget utilitates') which can be found in Munich, Staatsbibliotek, MS 10552 (cf. Littré, *Histoire littéraire de la France*, xxix, p. 299). The attribution to Lull was, however, subsequently rejected by Salzinger himself, who omitted the work from the list of Lull's works in the first volume of the Mainz edition of 1721.

54. MS Urb. Lat. 852, ff. 333r.–v., 334v., 338r. and 339v.: 'Localis memoria per Raimundum Lullum. Ars memorativa duobus perficitur modis scilicet locis et imaginibus. Loci non differunt ab imaginibus nisi quia loci non sunt anguli, ut quidam putant, sed imagines quaedam fixae super quas, sicut super cartam, dipinguntur imagines delebiles. Unde loca sunt sicut materia, imagines sicut forma . ... Oportet autem ut locis serbetur modus ne scilicet inter ea sit distantia nimium remota vel nimium brevis, sed moderata ut quinque pedum vel circa; non sit etiam nimia claritas vel nimia obscuritas sed lux mediocris ... Inveni igitur, si poteris, domum distinctam caminis XXII diversis et dissimillibus . ... Habeas semper ista loca fixa ante oculos sicut situata in cameris et scias ante et retro illa recitare per

ordinem etiam scias quis primus, quis secundus, quis tertius et sive de aliis ... Si detur tibi aliud nomen notum, puta Joannis, accipe unum Joannem tibi notum ... et ipsum collocabis in loco.'

55. Bernardo de Lavinheta, *Opera omnia quibus tradidit artis Raymundi Lullii compendiosam explicationem et eiusdem applicationem ad logica rhetorica physica mathematica mechanica medica metaphysica theologica ethica iuridica problematica* (Cologne, 1612).

56. *De necessitate artis.*

57. Lavinheta, *De memoria*, in *Opera*, p. 651.

58. Lavinheta, *Explanatio* in *Opera*, p. 653. Cf. Lull, *Liber ad memoriam confirmandam*, Munich, Staatsbibliotek, MS 10593, f. 2v.: 'There are two kinds [of artificial memory]. The first kind uses medicines and plasters, and I consider this to be extremely dangerous, since occasionally such medicines are given to men with the wrong disposition, and in unnecessarily high dosages, so that the brain becomes too dry, and we have heard of and seen many who, through a weakness in the brain, have become demented, and this is displeasing to God.'

59. Lavinheta, *Explanatio*, in *Opera*, pp. 653–4.

60. Lavinheta, *Explanatio*, in *Opera*, p. 654.

61. Lavinheta, *Explanatio*, in *Opera*, p. 654.

62. Thomas Murner, *Logica memorativa. Chartiludium logicae sive totius dialecticae memoria et novus Petri Hispani textus emendatus, cum jucundo pictasmatis, exercitio* (Brussels: Thomas van der Noot, 1509). See also the *Invectiva contra astrologos* (Salzburg, 1499). I have not been able to see the *Chartiludium institutae summarie doctore Thoma Murner memorante et ludente* (Salzburg: Johannen Priis, 1518) which contains a reduction of Justinian's *Institutions* into synoptic tables constructed on the basis of the armorial bearings and *imprese* of the bishops and imperial princes. In 1515 the University of Trier released a declaration allowing Murner to teach the *Institutions* in the space of four weeks using a method based on artificial memory. On Murner see Carreras y Artau, *Filosofia cristiana*, II, pp. 224–5. On the influence of Lull on Murner see Adam Bernhard Gottron, 'Ein Lullistischer Lehrstuhl in Deutschland um 1600?' in *Estudis Universitaris Catalans*, 7 (1913), pp. 221–3.

63. Prantl, *Geschichte der Logik*, III, p. 294.

64. Francesco Enrico Barone, *Logica formale e logica transcendentale. I: Da Leibniz a Kant* (Turin: Edizioni di Filosofia, 1957, repr. 1964), p. 14.

III THEATRES OF THE WORLD

1. The translations of the works of Machiavelli were published in 1571. On Gohorry see Thorndike, *History of Magic and Experimental Science*, V, pp. 636–40 and Daniel Pickering Walker, *Spiritual and Demonic Magic from Ficino to Campanella*, Studies of the Warburg Institute, 22 (London: Warburg Institute, 1958), pp, 96–106.

2. Stephen Hawes, *The Pastyme of Pleasure,* in William Edward Mead (ed.), *The Pastime of Pleasure. By Stephen Hawes. A literal reprint of the earliest complete copy, 1517, with variant readings from the editions of 1509, 1554, and 1555, together with introduction, notes, glossary and indexes* (London, 1928), p. 52. The first edition is Wynkyn de Worde (London, 1509); further editions were published in 1517, 1554 and 1555. For further information on the author and the printing history of the text see Robert Spindler (ed.), *The Court of Sapience. Spät-mittelenglisches allegorisch-didaktisches Visionsgedicht. Kritische Textausgabe nebst sprachlich-metrischer Einleitung und ausführlichem Glossar*, Beiträge zur englischen Philologie, 6 (Leipzig, 1927), pp. xxix-xli. The passage quoted in the text is cited by William S. Howell, *Logic and Rhetoric in England, 1500–1700* (Princeton: Princeton University Press, 1957), p. 86. I have relied on Howell's book for much of my information on English mnemotechnical texts. For further details on Howell's study see Paolo Rossi, 'Ramismo, logica e retorica nei secoli XVI e XVII', *Rivista critica di storia della filosofia*, 12:3 (1957), pp. 357–65, esp. pp. 361–3.

3. For the text see Edmond Faral, *Les Arts poétiques du XIIe et du XIIe siècle. Recherches et documents sur la technique littéraire du moyen âge*, Bibliothèque de l'École des Hautes Études, 238 (Paris, 1924), pp. 197–262. Cf. Howell, *Logic and Rhetoric*, pp. 75–6.

4. Oliver H. Prior (ed.), *Caxton's Mirror of the World*, Early English Text Society, Extra series 110 (London, 1913). Prior's edition is based on the editions of 1481 and 1491. The treatment of memory (cf. Howell, *Logic and Rhetoric*, pp. 88–9) is taken from the third edition, *The Myrror. Dyscrypcion of the Worlde With Many Marvaylles* (London, c.1527), sigs. D3r–D3v.

5. Leonard Cox, *The Arte or Crafte of Rhetoryke*, ed. Frederic Ives Carpenter (Chicago, 1889).

6. Robert Copland, *An Art of Memory That Otherwise Is Called the Phoenix* (London, c.1548), sig. B3r.

7. Pietro da Ravenna, *Phoenix seu artificiosa memoria*, p. 3r.–v.

8. Thomas Wilson, *The Arte of Rhetorique for the Use of All Suche As Are*

Studious of Eloquence (London, 1553), George Herbert Mair (ed.), *Wilson's Arte of Rhetorique 1560*, Tudor and Stuart Library (Oxford, 1909), p. 215. See Howell, *Logic and Rhetoric*, p. 104.

9. Johannes Romberch de Kyrspe, *Congestorium artificiosae memoriae ... omnium de memoria praeceptiones aggregatim complectens* (Venice, Georgii de Rusconibus, 1520). In 'The Ciceronian art of memory' Frances Yates erroneously assigns a date of 1533 to the first publication of this work. Dolce's translation is *Dialogo di L. Dolce nel quale si ragiona del modo di accrescere et conservar la memoria* (Venice: Giovanbattista Sessa, 1586); the first edition came out in 1562 and the second edition in 1575. Dolce's source was known as early as 1592: see Filippo Gesualdo, *Plutosofia ... nella quale si spiega l'arte della memoria, con altre cose notabili pertinenti, tanto alla memoria naturale, quanto all'artificiale.* (Padua, 1592, repr. Vicenza, 1600), p. 11.

10. Agrippa, *De vanitate scientiarum*, cap. X ('De arte memorativa'), *Opera* (Lyons, 1600), II, p. 32. In this work Agrippa still attributes the *Rhetorica ad Herennium* to Cicero.

11. Philip Melanchthon, *Rhetorices Elementa, autore Philippo Melanchthone* (Venice: Melchior Sessa, 1534), pp. 4v.–5r.

12. Melanchthon, *Rhetorices Elementa*, p. 8. For the identification of topics with the art of memory see also Adrian Barlandum, *Opusculum de amplificatione oratoria seu locorum usu, per Adrianum Barlandum in inclito Lovaniensum gymnasio publicum Rhetoricae professorem* (Louvain: Servatus Zaffenus, 1536).

13. Johannes Spangerbergius, *Artificiosae memoriae libellus in usum studiorum collectus, autore Joanne Spangerbergio Herdesiano apud Northusos verbi ministro* (Wittenberg: Petrum Seitz, 1570). The text was reprinted with the title *Erotemata de arte memoriae seu reminiscentiae* in Lambert Schenkel, *Gazophylacium artis memoriae ... per Lambertum Schenkelium, Dusilivium* (Salzburg, 1610), pp. 339–78.

14. Spangerbergius, *Libellus*, sig. Bv.:

> Omnis *dictio*
> aut est *ignota* aut
>   *nota* aut est res *invisibilis* aut
>   *visibilis* vel est *accidens* vel
>   *substantia*
>   vel est *inanimata*
>   vel *animata*
>   est nomen *commune*
>   vel *proprium*

15. Amongst the different types of *similitudo* Spangerbergius included: '*Effictio corporum*: Vt cum senem facimus tremulum, incuruum, labijs demissis, canum; *Notatio adfectum*: Vt cum dicimus lupum uoracem, lepores timidos. Sic laeta iuuentus, tristis senectus, prodiga adolescentia; *Etymologia*: Vt Philippus amator equorum; *Onomatopoeia*: Quando sumitur cognitio uerbi a sono uocis ut hinnitus equi, rugitus leonum, bombitus apum; *Rerum effectus*: Cum cuilibet mensi officia sua assignamus.' (*Libellus*, sig. Bij v.–Biij r.) Many of the examples appear to have been drawn, directly or indirectly, from a text by Iacobo Publicio, *Oratoriae artis epitomata, sive quae ad consumatum spectant oratorem* (Venice, 1482), sigs. D4 r -D4 v.

16. On Gratarolo see also Tiraboschi, *Storia della letteratura italiana*, VII, pp. 615–16, Frederic C. Church, *The Italian Reformers, 1534–1564* (New York, 1932), pp. 194–201, 211–12, 310–11, 376–8 et *passim* and Thorndike, *History of Magic and Experimental Science*, V, pp. 600–16. There are also references to his writings in Eugenio Garin, 'Note e Notizie', *Giornale critico della filosofia italiana*, Third Series, 11:4 (1957), pp. 535–7. [See also Giovanni Battista Gallizioli, *Della vita, degli studi e degli scritti di Guglielmo Grataroli filosofo e medico* (Bergamo, 1788). Trans.]

17. I have used the 1554 edition, *Guglielmi Grataroli Bergomatis, artium et medicinae doctoris Opuscula, videlicet: De memoria reparanda, augenda confirmandaque ac de reminiscentia: tutiora omnimoda remedia, praeceptiones optimae; De praedictione morum naturarumque hominum cum ex inspectione partium corporis tum aliis modis. De temporum omnimoda mutatione, perpetua et certissima signa et pronostica* (Basel: Nicolaum Episcopum iuniorem, 1554). On the edition of 1553 see p. 3: 'Superiori anno … citius quam voluissem emisi in lucem amicorum ac typographi coactus instantia'. In the third edition Gratarolo included an additional work, the *De literatorum conservanda valetudine liber*.

18. The French translation was Estienne Copé, *Discours notable des moyens pour conserver et augmenter la memoire avec une traité de la physionomie* (Lyons, 1555). On Copé's work, and another edition of the same work with a different title (*Des preceptes et moyens de recouurer, augmenter, & contregarder la Memoire, Auec vn Euure singulier qui demonte à facilement predire, et iuger des meurs & natures des hommes, selon la consideration des parties du corps*) see Thorndike, *History of Magic and Experimental Science*, V, p. 607. The English translation was William Fullwood, *The Castel of Memorie: wherein is conteyned the restoring, augmenting, and conseruing of the Memorye and Remembraunce, with the safest*

remedies, and best preceptes (London, 1562), reprinted in 1563 and 1573.

19. Joannes ab Indagine, *Introductiones apotelesmaticae in physiognomiam ... Quibus ... accessit G. Grataroli ... opuscula de Memoria reparanda, augenda, conservanda: De praedictione morum naturarumque hominum: De mutatione temporum, ejusque signis perpetuis; et P. Gaurici ... Tractatus de symmetriis, lineamentis, et physiognomia* (Ursel, 1603), pp. 179–215.

20. I have used the incunabulum (Bononiae per Platonem de Benedictis, 1491) in Bibliotheca Marciana, MS Lat. cl. VI, 274, ff. 69–82r.

21. The works of Dolce and Romberch are cited by Thorndike, *History of Magic and Experimental Science*, V, p. 607, along with Carrara simply as 'other works on this subject'. Thorndike does not concern himself with mnemotechnics, despite its many links with magic.

22. Giovanni Michele da Carrara, *De omnibus ingeniis augendae memoriae* (1481) in Bibliotheca Marciana, MS Lat. cl. VI, 274, ff. 70r., 73r.

23. Gratarolo, *Opuscula*, pp. 44, 59.

24. Gratarolo, *Opuscula*, p. 2: 'The memory is situated in the brain in what is called the third ventricle or "poop". It would take too long and be superfluous to describe the anatomy of the brain here (where I am trying to be brief) when it can so easily be found in many books, especially that of the most learned and diligent Andreas Vesalius' (*Sedem vero habet memoria in occipitio in tertio vocato ventriculo quem et pupim vocant. Longum esset ac pene superfluum hic (ubi studeo brevitati) cerebri totius anatomen describere, quam in multorum libris videre licet, praesertim doctissimi pariter et diligentissimi Andreae Vesalii*).

25. Giulio Camillo (Delminio), *L'idea del theatro dell' eccelent. M. Giulio Camillo* (Florence, 1550). See also *Di M. Giulio Camillo. Tutte le opere* (Venice: A. Griffo, 1584). On Camillo see Tiraboschi, *Storia della letteratura*, VII, 4, pp. 1520–1532; Benedetto Croce, *Poeti e scrittori del pieno e del tardo Rinascemento*, 3 vols. (Bari: Laterza, 1945–52), III, pp. 111–20; François Secret, 'Les Cheminements de la Kabbale à la Renaissance: le théâtre du monde de Giulio Camillo Delminio et son influence', *Rivista critica della filosofia*, 14:4 (1959), pp. 418–36. On the significance of Camillo's 'planetary rhetoric' and its links with Ficinian ideas on magic and music see Walker, *Spiritual Magic*, chapter 4, section 3, 'Fabio Paolini and the *Accademia degli Uranici*', pp. 126–44.

26. Eugenio Garin, 'Alcuni aspetti delle retoriche rinascementali', in Eugenio Garin, Paolo Rossi and Cesare Vasoli (eds.), *Testi umanistici sulla retorica. Testi editi e inediti su retorica e dialettica di Mario Nizolio,*

Francesco Patrizi e Pietro Ramo (Rome–Milan: Archivio di filosofia, 1953), pp. 32, 36. On the 'worldly' character of humanist dialectic in comparison with Cusanian and Ficinian mysticism see Eugenio Garin, 'La dialettica dal secolo XII ai principi dell' età moderna', *Rivista di filosofia*, 2 (1958), pp. 228–53: 'Humanism operates ... by immobilizing all those symbols which refer to earthly and historical experience and projecting them on to a divine and eternal level.' We can see this 'projection' at work in the Lullian and mnemotechnical works of Camillo, Rosselli and Bruno.

27. See the description of Camillo's work in a letter written in Padua, 28 March 1532, by Viglius Zuichemus to Erasmus in P. S. and H. M. Allen (eds.), *Opus epistolarum des. Erasmi Roterodami denuo recognitum et auctum*, 12 vols. (Oxford: Clarendon Press, 1906–58), IX, p. 475, and X, pp. 28, 54, 96, 124. See also a letter written by Andrea Alciati dated 5 September 1530 in Giovanni Giuseppe Liruti, *Notizie delle vite ed opere scritte da' Letterati del Friuli*, 3 vols. (Venice, 1760–80), II, pp. 69–134, which gives additional information on Camillo's reputation at the court of Francois I.

28. Camillo, *Opere*, II, p. 212 and Johann Sturm, *Libellus de lingua latina resolvenda ratione* (Jena, 1904), p. 5.

29. *L'idea del theatro*, p. 7: 'The most ancient and wisest authors have always been accustomed in their writings to conceal the secrets of God under dark veils so that they will not be understood except by those who (as Christ says) 'have ears to hear', that is to say, those that have been chosen by God to understand his most holy mysteries. And Melissus says that the eyes of the base soul cannot endure the rays of divinity. And this is confirmed by the example of Moses who when he descended from the mountain ... could not be looked upon by the people unless his face was covered with a veil. The Apostles too, when they saw Christ transfigured ... could not look upon him because of their fallen fraility. ... To this we add the words of Hermes Trismegistus who said that religious and godly speech is profaned when it is heard by the vulgar multitude ... A double error is committed when secrets are revealed: one reveals them to a person who is not worthy of them, and one treats things in a base language which ought to be the subject of angelic language ... And in our works we use images to signify things which ought not be profaned ... I cannot remain silent, either, about the Cabalists who say that Maria, the sister of Moses, contracted leprosy for having revealed divine secrets. (*I piu antichi & piu savi scrittori hanno sempre hauuto in costume di*

raccomandare à loro scritti i secreti di Dio sotto oscuri velami acciochè non siano intesi, se non da coloro, i quali (come dice Christo) hanno orecchie da vdire, cio è che da Dio sono eletti ad intendere i suoi santissimi misteri. Et Melisso dice che gli occhi delle anime volgari non possono sofferire i raggi della diuinità. Et ciò si conferma con lo esempio di Mose, il quale scendendo dal monte ... non poteua esser guardato dal popolo, se egli il viso col velo non si nascondeua. Et gli Apostoli anchora veduto Christo trasfigurato ... non sufficienti a riguardarlo per la debolezza cadderono ... A questo habbiamo da aggiunger che Mercurio Trismegisto dice che il parlar religioso & pien di Dio viene ad esser violato quando gli soprauiene moltitudine volgare ... I segreti reuelando doppio error si viene à commettere. Et cio è discoprirgli à persone non degne, & di trattargli con questa nostra bassa lingua, essendo quello il suggetto delle lingue de gli angeli ... Et noi nelle cose nostre ci seruiamo delle imagini, come de significatrici di quelle cose che non si debbon profanare ... Né tacerò io, che i ... Cabalisti tengono che Maria sorella di Mose fosse dalla lebbra oppressa per hauer reuelate le cose secrete della diuinità.)

30. *L'idea del teatro*, pp. 9, 11: 'Salomone al nono de Proverbi dice la sapienza hauersi edificato casa, & hauerla fondata sopra sette colonne. Queste colonne significanti stabilissima eternità habbiamo da intender che siano le sette saphiroth del sopraceleste mondo, che sono le sette misure della fabbrica del celeste e dell'inferiore nelle quali sono comprese le Idee di tutte le cose al celeste & all'inferiore appartenenti ... L'alta adunque fatica nostra è stata di trouare ordine in queste sette misure, capace, bastante, distinto, & che tenga sempre il senso suegliato, & la memoria percossa ... Questa alta & incomparibile collocatione fa non solamente officio di conseruarci le affidate cose parole, & arte ... ma ci da anchor la vera sapienza nei Fonti de quella venendo noi in cognition delle cose dalle cagioni, & non da gli effetti.'

31. *L'idea del teatro*, pp. 10–11: 'Or se gli antichi oratori volendo collocar di giorno in giorno le parti delle orationi che haueuano à recitare, le affidauano à luoghi caduchi, come cose caduche, ragione è, che volendo noi raccomandar eternalmente gli eterni di tutte le cose ... trouiamo à loro luoghi eterni. L'alta adunque fatica nostra è stata di trouare ordine in queste sette misure ... Ma considerando che se volessimo metter altrui dauanti queste altissime misure, & si lontane dalla nostra cognitione, che solamente da propheti sono state anchor nascostamente tocche, questo sarebbe vn metter mano à cosa troppo malageuole. Per tanto ... le vseremo, che non ce le propogniamo come termini fuor de quali non habbiamo ad vscire, ma come quelli

che alla menti de saui sempre rappresentino le sette sopracelesti misure.'

32. Girolamo Ruscelli, *Trattato del modo di comporre versi in lingua italiana*
(Venice, 1594), p. 14.

33. Giovanni Pico della Mirandola, *Apologia tredecim quaestionum* in
Commentationes J. Pici Mirandulae (Bologna, 1496), quaestio V, sig.
[Eevi]r.: 'De magia naturali et cabala hebreorum': 'This is the first and
true cabala which, I believe, I am the first Latin author to refer to
explicitly ... This method of handing things down through tradition
which is called "cabalistical" seems to be suited to singular, secret and
mystical things, hence it is the custom of the Hebrews to call "cabala"
any knowledge which is secret or hidden, and any knowledge which
they have by means of any occult method they say is had by means of
the "cabalistical method". In general two kinds of knowledge are
honoured with this name: the first is what is called the combinatorial art, which is a method for extending and advancing knowledge,
which is similar to what we call the *ars Raymundi*, although it works
in a very different way. The other concerns the powers of supercelestial things and is the supreme part of natural magic.' (*Haec est prima et
uera cabala de qua credo me primum apud latinos explicitam fecisse mentionem
... Quia iste modus tradendi per successionem qui dicitur cabalisticus uidetur
conuenire unicuique rei secrete et mistice hinc est quod usurparunt hebrei ut
unamquamque scientiam quae apud eos habeatur pro secreta et abscondita
cabalam uocent et unumquodque scibile quod per uiam occultam alicunde
habeatur dicatur haberi per uiam cabalae. In universali autem duas scientias
hoc etiam nomine honorificarunt: unam quae dicitur ... ars combinandi et est
modus quidam procedendi in scientis et est simile quid sicut apud nostros dicitur ars Raymundi licet forte diuerso modo procedant. Aliam quae est de uir-
tutibus rerum superiorum quae sunt supra lunam et est pars magiae naturalis
suprema.*) On the function of letters and names in the cabala, and its
relation to allegorism and mystical exemplarism see Chapter 6 of
Gerschom Scholem, *Major Trends in Jewish Mysticism* (Jerusalem:
Schocken Publishing House, 1941, rev. and repr. New York:
Schocken Books, 1995), pp. 205–43. See also Gerschom Scholem,
'Zur Geschichte der Anfänge der Christlichen Kabbala' in *Essays
Presented to Leo Baeck on the Occasion of his Eightieth Birthday* (London:
East and West Library, 1954), pp. 158–93. An important document of
the cross-fertilization between Renaissance cabala and Lullism is the
pseudo-Lullian *De auditu kabalistico sive ad omnes scientias introductiorum*,
first published in Venice in 1518 and 1533, the work came to be

attributed to Lull and was included as such in the Strasbourg edition of 1617 (Zetzner, pp. 43–111). On the cabala and Lullism in Pico see Marcelino Menéndez y Pelayo, *Historia de los heterodoxos españoles,* 3 vols. (Madrid, 1880–2), I, pp. 464 and 525, and Eugenio Garin, *Giovanni Pico della Mirandola, vita e dottrina* (Florence, 1937), pp. 90–105, 146–54 and François Secret, 'Pico della Mirandola e gli inizi della cabala cristiana', *Convivium,* 25:1 (1957), pp. 31–47. Additional information can be found in George Sarton, *Introduction to the History of Science,* 3 vols, Carnegie Institution Publication 376 (Washington, 1927–48), II, pp. 901–2. Joseph Leon Blau's *The Christian Interpretation of the Cabala in the Renaissance* (New York: Columbia University Press, 1944) is completely unreliable.

34. On the question of the relationship between Christianity and the Cabala in the Renaissance, in addition to the works on Pico cited in the previous note, see the important studies of François Secret: 'L'astrologie et les Kabbalistes chrétiens à la Renaissance', in *La Tour Saint-Jacques,* 2 (1956); 'Les débuts du Kabbalisme chrétien en Espagne et son histoire à la Renaissance', *Sefarad,* 17:1 (1957), pp. 36–48; 'Les domenicains et la kabbale chrétienne à la Renaissance', *Archivium franciscianum praedicatorum,* 27 (1957); 'Le symbolisme de la kabbale chrétienne dans la *Scechina* de Egidio da Viterbo', in Enrico Castelli (ed.), *Umanesimo e simbolismo, Atti del IV convegno internazionale di studi umanistici* (Padua: Casa Editrice Dott. Antonio Milani, 1958), pp. 131–51; 'Les jésuites et le kabbalisme chrétien à la Renaissance', *Bibliothéque d'humanisme et Renaissance. Travauxs et documents,* 20:3 (1958), pp. 542–55. But see also Jose M. Millas Vallicrosa, 'Algunas relaciones entre la doctrina luliana y la cabala', *Sefarad,* 18:2 (1958), pp. 241–53.

35. Paul Scalichius de Lika (Paul Skalich), *Encyclopaediae seu orbis disciplinarum tam sacrarum quam prophanarum epistemon* (Basel, Oporinus, 1559). On Skalich see Gerta Krabbel, *Paul Skalich: ein Lebensbild aus dem 16 Jahrhunderts,* Geschichtliche Darstellungen und Quellen, 1 (Münster, 1915); Thorndike, *History of Magic and Experimental Science,* V, pp. 455 et seq. and François Secret, 'La tradition du De omni scibili à la Renaissance: l'oeuvre de Paul Scaliger', *Convivium,* 23:4 (1955), pp. 492–7.

36. For the work of Dolce, see note 9 above and Tiraboschi, *Storia della letteratura italiana,* VII, pp. 1028–9. On the work of Orazio Toscanella's *Retorica di M. Tullio Cicerone … ridotta in alberi* (Venice, 1561), see Tiraboschi, *Storia,* VII, p. 1156. On the partitions of

rhetoric see *La retorica di Bartolomeo Cavalcanti ... divisa in sette libri, dove si contiene tutto quello che appartiene all'arte oratoria* (Venice: Gabriel Giolito de Ferrari, 1559), pp. 24–5. For a clearer understanding of the reasons for the diffusion of memorative techniques in the rhetorical manuals of the period see Georgius Trapezuntius (George of Trebizond), *Rhetoricum libri quinque* (Lyons: Seb. Gryphium, 1547), pp. 355–60.

37. The quotations are taken from *L'arte de ricordare del signor Gio. Battista Porta Napoletano* (Naples: Mattio Cancer, 1566) translated from Latin into Italian by M. Dorandino Falcone da Gioia. Francesco Fiorentino in his *Studi e ritratti della Rinascenza* (Bari, 1911), pp. 268–9, wrongly assigns the date of 1602 to the first edition of the *Ars reminiscendi*.

38. On the writing of the Egyptians see cap. XIX. On gestures see cap. XX: 'We can likewise express the meanings of some words with gestures ... Mutes express what they wish to say with gestures, using their hands instead of their tongues.'

39. On sixteenth- and seventeenth-century interpretations of hieroglyphs see Daniel Georg Morhof, *Polyhistor literarius, philosophicus et practicus, cum accessionibus*, 3 vols. (Lübeck, 1732), II, pp. 167 et seq. On the connection between Egyptomania and emblematism see Erwin Panofsky, 'Titian's Allegory of Prudence', in *Meaning in the Visual Arts*, pp. 158–62, Mario Praz, *Studi sul concettismo* (Milan, 1934, repr. Florence: Sansoni, 1946), pp. 17 et seq., and vol. II of his *Studies in Seventeenth Century Imagery*, 2 vols., Studies of the Warburg Institute, 3 (London [Bruges]: Warburg Institute, 1939). Further information on the Renaissance literature on hieroglyphs can be found in Ludwig Volkmann, *Bilderschriften der Renaissance, Hieroglyphik und Problematik in ihren Beziehungen und Fortwirkungen* (Leipzig, 1923) and Thorndike, *History of Magic and Experimental Science*, V, pp. 446 et seq.

40. Cosma Rosselli, *Thesaurus artificiosae memoriae ... authore P. F. Cosma Rossellio florentino* (Venice: Antonium Paduanium, 1579).

41. Rosselli, *Thesaurus*, p. 117v.

42. Jean Bodin, *Universae naturae theatrum in quo rerum omnium effectrices causae et fines contemplantur, et continuae series quinque libris discutiuntur* (Lyons: Jacobum Roussin, 1596). The first edition was published in 1590.

43. Bodin, *Universae naturae theatrum*, 'Propositio totius operis', pp. 1, 6.

44. See Kenneth D. McRae, 'Ramist tendencies in the thought of Jean Bodin', *Journal of the History of Ideas*, 16:3 (1955), pp. 306–23.

45. This new approach can be seen at work, for example, in Jacopo

Mazzoni da Cesena's *De triplici vita*, (Rome, 1576) – which reworks the *Ars predicandi* of Francesco Panigarola. See Panigarola, *L'Art de prescher et bien faire un sermon avec la mémoire locale et artificielle, ensemble l'art de mémoire de H. Marafiote*, trans. G. Chappuis (Paris, 1604). On Panigarola, see Tiraboschi, *Storia della letteratura italiana*, VII, pp. 1602–9.

IV THE IMAGINATIVE LOGIC OF GIORDANO BRUNO

1. See Leo Olschki, *Giordano Bruno* (Bari, 1927); Guido De Ruggiero, *Storia della filosofia. Rinascimento riforma e controriforma* (Bari, 1930), p. 166; Dorothea W. Singer, *Giordano Bruno, His Life and Thought with Annotated Translation of his Work on the Infinite Universe and Worlds* (New York: Henry Schuman, 1950).
2. See Felice Tocco, *Le opere latine di G. Bruno esposte e confrontate con le italiane* (Florence, 1889): on the mnemotechnic tradition see esp. pp. 21–43. On the importance of Bruno's mnemonic works see p. 94, and on the rigid distinction between Lullian and mnemotechnic works see pp. 94 et seq. For Bruno's relationship to Lullism and to Cusanus see also 'Le fonti piú recenti della filosofia di Giordano Bruno', *Rendiconti dell' Accademia dei Lincei*, 5:1 (1892), pp. 503–37; 585–622. In Christian Bartholomess, *Jordano Bruno*, 2 vols. (Paris, 1847), II, pp. 158 et seq., all the mnemotechnical works are erroneously identified as Lullist, and Pietro da Ravenna is mistaken for a follower of Lull. For a critique of Tocco's distinction see Erminio Troilo, *La filosofia di Giordano Bruno*, 2 vols. (Rome, 1914), II, pp. 55–103.
3. See Frances A. Yates, 'Giordano Bruno's conflict with Oxford', *Journal of the Warburg and Courtauld Institute*, 2 (1938–9), pp. 227–42; *The French Academies in the Sixteenth Century*, Studies of the Warburg Institute, 15 (London: Warburg Institute, 1947); 'The Art of Ramon Lull', *Journal of the Warburg and Courtauld Institute*, 17 (1954), pp. 115–73; 'The Ciceronian art of memory', in *Medioevo e Rinascemento*, pp. 54–104; Eugenio Garin, *La filosofia*, Storia dei generi letterari italiani, 2 vols. (Milan, 1947), II, pp. 149–154; Cesare Vasoli, 'Umanesimo e simbologia nei primi scritti Lulliani e mnemotecnici del Bruno', in Castelli, *Umanesimo e simbolismo*, pp. 251–304.
4. Vasoli, 'Umanesimo e simbologia', pp. 243–54.

5. Felice Tocco et al. (eds.), *Iordani Bruni Nolani opere latine conscripta publicis sumptibus edita* (Naples–Florence, 1879–91), II, 2, p. 130: 'Hoc modica favilla fuit, quae iugi meditatione progrediens in vasti aggeris irrepsit accensionem, e cuius flammiferis ignibus plurimae hinc inde emicant favillae, quarum quae bene dispositam materiam attingerit, similia maioraque flagrantia lumina potuerunt excitare.' All further references to this work will be abbreviated to '*Op. Lat.*'. On the significance of this passage, previously noted by Felice Tocco in *Le opere latine*, p. 37, n. 2, see Antonio Corsano *Il Pensiero di G. Bruno* (Florence, 1940), p. 41, and Vasoli, 'Umanesimo e simbologia', pp. 254, 277 *et passim*.

6. 'Stupidi est discursus velle sensibilia ad eandem conditionem cognitionis revocare, in qua ratiocinabilia et intelligibilia cernuntur. Sensibilia quippe vera sunt non iuxta communem aliquam et universalem mensuram, sed iuxta homogeneam, particularem, propriam, mutabilem atque variabilem mensuram. De sensibilibus ergo, qua sensibilia sunt, universaliter velle definire, in aequo est atque de intelligibilia vice versa sensibiliter.'

7. Yates, *French Academies*, pp. 77–94, 95–151. On Lullism in France see T. and J. Carreras y Artau, *Historia de la Filosofía Española. Filosofía cristiana de los siglos XIII al XV*, 2 vols. (Madrid: 1939–43), II, pp. 207 et seq.; Augustin Renaudet, *Préréforme et humanisme à Paris pendant les premières guerres d'Italie, 1494–1517* (Paris, 1916, repr. 1953), pp. 378 et seq.

8. Prior to this, in 1583, Alexander Dicson published his *De umbra rationis et iudicii sive de artificiosa memoria quam publice profitetur vanitate*, which was printed by Thomas Vautrollier, and dedicated to the Earl of Leicester, in which he makes reference to Bruno's *De umbris*. Dicson, who appears as a character in Bruno's *De la causa principio et uno* (see *Dialoghi italiani*, ed. Giovanni Gentile and Giovanni Aquilecchia, Florence, 1958, p. 225 *et passim*) received a polemical response from 'G. P.' (William Perkins), author of *Antidicsonus cuiusdam Cantabrigensis G. P. Accessit libellus in quo dilucide explicatur impia Dicsoni artificiosa memoria* (London, 1584): in his dedicatory epistle he refers to Metrodorus, Rosselli, Bruno and Dicson. Thomas Watson also refers to Bruno's *Sigillus* in his *Compendium memoriae localis*, probably printed in London in 1585. Perkins was also the author of a Ramist critique of the *ars memoriae* entitled *Prophetica, sive de sacra et unica ratione concionandi* (Cambridge, 1592), which was translated into English in 1606. The text of the Bohemian student Johann â Nostitz,

who heard Bruno's lectures on mnemotechnics in Paris, has been lost. In this work the names of Aristotle, Lull, Ramus and Bruno were linked in a significant fashion: *Artificium Aristotelico-Lullio-Rameum in quo per artem intelligendi Logicam, Artem agendi Practicam, Artis loquendi partem de inventione Topicam methodo et terminis Aristotelico-Rameis circulis modo Lulliano inclusis via plura quam centies mille argumenta de quovis themate inveniendi cum usu conveniens ostenditur, ductu Io. a Nostitz, Jordani Bruni genuini discipuli elaboratum a Conrado Bergio* (Brega, 1615). The title was recorded in Johann Ludolph Bünemann's *Catalogvs msstorvm membranaceorvm et chartaceorvm, item librorvm ab inventa typographia vsqve ad ann. MD. et inde vsqve ad ann. MDLX et vlterivs impressorvm rarissimorum cvm mvltis aliis eximiis operibvs pro adsignato pretio venalivm apvd Ioannem Lvdolphvm Bünemannvm* (Minden, 1732), pp. 117–18. Nostitz's letter to the reader is published in Singer, *Giordano Bruno*, pp. 19–20. On the author, who died in 1619, whose family library was conserved intact in Prague until 1938, see pp. 20 and 188.

9. See Vasoli, 'Umanesimo e simbologia', p. 272.
10. *Op. Lat.* II, 1, pp. 23–4, 47: 'Cum vero in rebus omnibus ordo sit atque connexio … ut unum sit universi entis corpus, unus ordo, una gubernatio, unum principium, unus finis, unum primum … illud obnixe nobis est intentandum, ut pro egregiis animi operationis naturae schalam ante oculos habentes, semper a motu et multitudine ad statum et unitatem per intrinsecas operationes tendere contendamus … Talem quidem progressum tunc te vere facere comperies et experieris, cum a confusa pluralitate ad distinctam unitatem per te fiat accessio; id enim non est universalia logica conflare, quae ex distinctis infimis speciebus, confusas medias, exque iis confusiores suprema captant. Sed quasi ex informibus partibus et pluribus formatum totum et unum aptare sibi … ita cum de partibus et universi speciebus, nil sit seorsum positum et exemptum ab ordine (qui simplicissimus, perfectissimus et citra numerum est in prima mente) si alias aliis connextendo, et pro ratione uniendo concipimus: quid est quod non possumus intelligere memorari et agere? Unum est quod omnia definit. Unus est pulchritudinis splendor in omnibus. Unus e multitudine specierum fulgor emicat.'
11. *Op. Lat.*, II, I, p. 66: 'Scriptura etiam habet subiectum primum chartam tanquam locum: habet subiectum proximum minimum, et habet pro forma ipsos characterum tractus.'
12. See pp. 57–8, and also Paolo Rossi, 'La costruzione delle immagini

nei trattati di memoria artificiale del Rinascemento', in Castelli, *Umanesimo e simbolismo*, pp. 161–8. For Bruno's 'rules' on the construction of memory places see *Op. Lat.* II, 1, pp. 69–71. Tocco's view in *Le opere latine*, p. 51, was reprised in Vasoli, 'Umanesimo e simbologia', p. 276. For the text of Carrara, already cited above, cf. 'Guido pater meus ex animalibus cepit locos suos et eorum ordine ex alphabeto deduxit ... asinus, basiliscus, canis, draco ... haec singula in quinque locos dividebat ... Nam hunc ordinem ipsa natura porrexit neque confundi in eis enumerandis ingenium potest'.

13. See Tocco, *Le opere latine*, pp. 63–6; *Op. Lat.* II, 2, pp. 69–119.

14. *Op. Lat.* II, I, p. 215: 'Intentio nostra est, divino annuente numine, artificiosam metodicamque prosequi viam: ad corrigendum defectum, roborandam infirmitatem, et sublevandum virtutem memoriae naturalis: quatenus qualibet (dummodo sit rationis compos, et mediocris particeps iudicii) proficere possit in ea, adeo ut nemo talis existentibus conditionibus, ab ademptione huius artis excludatur. Quod quidem ars non habet a seipsa, neque ex eorum qui praecesserunt industria, a quorum inventionibus excitati, promoti sumus diuturnam cogitationem ad addendum, tum eis quae faciunt ad facilitatem negotii atque certitudinem, tum etiam ad brevitatem.'

15. *Op. Lat.* II, I, p. 216: 'Hortatur enim Plato in Euthidemo ut res celeberrimae atque archanae habeantur a philosophis apud se et paucis atque dignis communicentur ... Idem omnibus iis, in quorum manus ista devenerint, consulimus: ne abutantur gratia et dono eisdem elargito. Et considerent quod figuratum est in Prometheo qui cum deorum ignem hominibus exhibuisset, ipsorum incurrit indignationem.'

16. *Op. Lat.* II, 1, pp. 221–4: 'Forma sumitur ... secundum rationem logicam non quidem rationalem, sed phantasticam (quatenus nomen logices amplius accipitur).'

17. Tocco, *Le opere latine*, p. 93.

18. *Op. Lat.* II, 1, p. 81: 'Opus est non ita adiecta subiectis applicari, quasi ea casu ut accidit proiiciantur ... ita adeoque invicem connexa, ut nullo ab invicem discuti possint turbine.'

19. On the application of Babylonian zodiacal images to the art see Vasoli, 'Umanesimo e simbologia', pp. 281, 291.

20. See *Op. Lat.* II, 1, pp. 107–15

21. *Op. Lat.* II, 1, p. 56: 'Habitus quidam ratiocinantis animae, ab eo quod est mundi vitae principio, ad omnium atque singulorum se exporrigens vitae principium.'

22. See pp. 32-44.

23. *Op. Lat.* II, 2, pp. 12, 41–9.

24. Tocco, *Le opere latine*, p. 15.
25. See *Op.Lat.* II, 3, pp. 12–13.
26. See pp. 32-34.
27. See Vasoli, 'Umanesimo e simbologia', pp. 293 et seq.
28. *Op. Lat.* II, 2, pp. 327, 235.
29. *Op. Lat.* II, 2, p. 234: 'Hic super illius adinventionem excolendam elaboravimus, cuius genium summi philosophorum principes habiti admirantur, persequuntur, imitantur; unde Scotigena theologicam metaphysicam (quam scholasticam appellant) theologiam, cum subtilibus aliis extrassisse constat; a quo admirandum illud vestratis Cusani quanto profundius atque divinius, tanto paucioribus pervium minusque notum ingenium, mysteriorum, quae in multiplici suae doctrinae torrente delitescunt, fontes hausisse fatetur; a quo novus ille medicorum princeps Paracelsus.'
30. *Op. Lat.* II, 1, p. 62: 'Quaedam vero adeo arti videntur appropriata, ut in eiusdem videatur naturalibus omnino suffragari: haec sunt Signa, Notae, Characteres et Sigilli: in quibus tantum potest ut videatur agere praeter naturam, supra naturam, et, si negotium requirat, contra naturam.'
31. *Op. Lat.* III, pp. 412–13 (*De magia*): 'Cum certo numinum genere non nisi per definita quaedam signa, sigilla, figuras, characteres, gestus et alias ceremonias, nulla potest esse participato.'
32. See Vasoli, 'Umanesimo e simbologia', p. 303. *Op. Lat.* III, 393–454, 455–91, 494–506.
33. *Op. Lat.* II, 2, p. 179: 'Una lux illuminat omnia, una vita viuificat omnia ... Atque altius conscendentibus non solum conspicua erit una omnium vita, unum in omnibus lumen, una bonitas, et quod omnes sensus sunt unus sensus, omnes notitiae sunt una notitia, sed et quod omnia tandem, utpote notitia, sensus, lumen, vita sunt una essentia, una virtus et una operatio.'
34. *Op. Lat.* II, ii, p. 133: 'Ideoque philosophi sunt quodammodo pictores atque poëtae, poëtae pictores et philosophi, pictores philosophi et poëtae, mutuoque veri poëtae, veri pictores et veri philosophi se diligunt et admirantur; non est enim philosophus, nisi qui fingit et pingit.' Cf. Corsano, *Il pensiero di G. Bruno*, p. 97.
35. Johann Paepp, *Artificiosae memoriae fundamenta ex Aristotele, Cicerone, Thoma Aquinate, aliisque praestantissimis doctoribus petita, figuris, interrogationibus ac responsionibus clarius quam unquam antehac demonstrata* (Lyon: Bartholomeum Vincentium, 1619); *Eisagoge seu introductio facilis in praxin artificiosae memoriae* (Lyon: Bartholomeum Vincentium,

1619); *Schenkelius detectus, seu memoria artificialis hactenus occultata* (Lyon: Bartholomeum Vincentium, 1617).

36. 'Sed miror cur eidem [the opponents of the art] non et logicam artificialem nigro calculo notent. Ut enim logica artificiosa intellectui rerum cognitionem secutius venatur, sic artificiosa memoria acquisitam ac comparatam cognitionem tenacius conservat ac tuetur naturali; quare Alstedius non minus hanc ad omnes artes et disciplinas, quam istam as nonullas necessarium probat.' (*Artificiosae memoriae fundamenta*, p. 10.)

37. On the function of the 'circles' see *Artificiosae memoriae fundamenta*, pp. 13, 49, 52. On the secret writing used in teaching the art see pp. 99–102, where two fundamental rules are set out: '1) Legendum more hebraico, puta ordine retrogrado; 2) Alpha et omega sunt otiosa id est primae et ultimae literae non habetur ratio'; *osras* means *ars*, *codrot* is *ordo* and *bogamir* is *imago* etc.

38. See *Eisagoge seu introductio*, p. 1.

39. For the relationship between Paepp and Bruno see Nicola Badaloni, 'Appunti intorno alla fama del Bruno nel secoli XVII e XVIII', *Società*, 14 (1953), pp. 517–18, n. 3. For the use of images of the ancient gods in Paepp, see *Artificiosae memoriae fundamenta*, pp. 86, 89.

40. See *Artificiosae memoriae fundamenta*, pp. 55–6 and esp. *Schenkelius detectata*, pp. 31–9.

41. For the encyclopaedia depicted on walls and for the facility of learning the sciences see *La città del sole* in Luigi Firpo (ed.) *Scritti scelti di Giordano Bruno e Tommaso Campanella* (Turin: Unione, 1949), pp. 412–15, 419.

42. Tommaso Campanella, *F. Thomae Campanellae De sensu rerum et magia, libri quatuor* (Frankfurt, 1620) ed. by Antonio Bruers, *Del senso delle cose e della magia. Testo inedito italiano con le varianti dei codici e delle due edizioni latine*, Classici della filosofia moderna, 24 (Bari, 1925), pp. 98–100.

43. See Joannes Magirus, *De memoria artificiosa liber singularis* (Frankfurt, 1600); Filippo Gesualdo, *Plutosofia ... nella quale si spiega l'arte della memoria* (Vicenza, 1600); Girolamo Marafioto, *Nova inventione et arte del ricordare per luoghi et imagini et figure poste nelle mani* (Venice, 1605). Translated into Latin as *De arte reminiscentiae per loca et imagines ac per notas et figuras in manibus positas*, Marafioto's work was included in Lambert Schenkel's *Gazophylacium artis memoriae* (Strasburg, 1610), pp. 273–338. This work also includes Johannes Austriacus's *De memoria artificiosa libellus*, pp. 183–272. The most significant of the many

commentaries on Schenkelius's *De memoria* (first published in 1595) are Adamus Bruxius, *Simonides redivivus sive ars memoriae et oblivionis ... tabulis expressa ... cui accessit Nomenclator mnemonicus* (Leipzig, 1610), Francesco Martino Ravelli, *Ars memoriae ... in gratiam et usum iuventutis explicata* (Frankfurt, 1617) and Martin Sommer, *Gazophylacium artis memoriae ... nunc vero a Martino Sommero traditum et illustratum* (Venice, 1619). Morhof claimed (*Polyhistor*, I, p. 374) that 'Martin Sommer' was a pseudonym for Schenkel himself. An anonymous Leipzig professor published *Ars memoriae localis plenius et luculentis exposita ... cum applicatione eiusdem ad singulas disciplinas et facultates* (Leipzig, 1620). I have not be able to see this work, nor Juan Velasquez de Azevedo's *El fenix de Minerva y arte de memoria que ensena sin maestro a aprender y retenir* (Madrid, 1620), whose title is reminiscent of Pietro da Ravenna's *Phoenix seu artificiosa memoria*. In Leipzig–Frankfurt, in 1678, a collection of mnemotechnical writings including works by Schenkel, Ravelli, Paepp, Austriacus, Marafioto, and Spangerbergius was published, with the title *Variorum de arte memoriae tractatus selecti*. Schenkel, whose work was briefly discussed by Descartes, is a particularly interesting figure: a successful teacher and popularizer of the *ars mnemonica* in France, Italy and Germany ('artem hanc', wrote Morhof, I, 374, 'magno cum successu suo nec sine insigni suo lucro exercuit'), he was accused of witchcraft during a sojourn at the University of Louvain, but managed to obtain the protection and support of the theology faculty at Douai. The first edition of his work, subsequently reprinted many times, is that of 1595: *De memoria liber secundus in quo est ars memoriae* (Liège, 1595). Together with the three small works of Austriacus, Marafioto and Spangerberg, mentioned above, it was reprinted with the title *Gazophylacium artis memoriae* (1610). Among the writings which comprised his *Apologia pro rege catholico in calvinistam* (Antwerp, 1589) was a collection of *Flores et sententiae insigniores ex libris de Constantia Justi Lipsii* (n.p., 1615), which was reprinted in a modern edition, with the Latin text and a German translation by Johann Ludwig Klüber in his *Compendium der Mnemonik oder Erinnerungswissenschaft aus dem Anfänge des siebenzehnten Jahrhunderts von L. Schenckel und M. Sommer. Aus dem Lateinischen mit Vorrede und Anmerkungen* (Erlangen, 1804). Schenkel's teachings are also handled in the curious encyclopaedia of Adrian le Cuirot, *Le Magazin des sciences, ou vrai art de mémoire découvert par Schenkelius, traduit et augmenté de l'alphabet de Trithemius* (Paris, 1623), which makes significant additions to the original text.

44. Wolfgang Hildebrand, *Magia naturalis, das ist, Kunst und Wunderbuch, darinnen begriffen Wunderbare Secreta, Geheimnüsse und Kunststücke, wie man nemlich mit dem gantzen Menschlichen Cörper, fast unerhörte wunderbarliche Sachen, verrichten … kan … zusammen getragen* (Leipzig, 1610).

45. See Pierre Morestel, *Enciclopaedia sive artificiosa ratio et via circularis ad artem magnam R. Lullii per quam de omnibus disputatur habeturque cognitio* (n.p., 1646); *La philosophie occulte des devanciers d'Aristote et de Platon, en forme de dialogue, contenant presque tous les préceptes de la philosophie morale extraite des fables anciennes* (Paris, 1607); *Les secrets de la nature … contenant presque tous les préceptes de la philosophie naturelle extraite des fables anciennes* (Paris, 1607) *Artis kabbalisticae sive sapientiae divinae academia* (Paris, 1621); *Regina omnium scientiarum qua duce ad omnes scientias et artes, qui literis delectantur facile conscendent* (Tremona, 1664) – the first edition of this work was Rothomagi, 1632. The definition of the art of Lull in these texts is outlined according to conventional schemes: 'Ars R. Lullii non vulgaris, non trivialis, non circa unum aliquod obiectum occupata, sed ars omnium artium regina … Huius artis ea est excellentia praestantiaque, ea generalitas ac certitudo, ut se sola sufficiente, nulla alia praesupposita … cum omni securitate et certitudine. .. de omni re scibili veritatem ac scientiam non difficulter invenire faciat.' Significantly, Morestel perceives the *ars combinatoria* as a mnemonic art: 'Artificium igitur memoriae, a veteribus traditum, locis constabat et imaginibus; quidni igitur dabitur aliqua ars memoriae quae terminis constabit? Talis est ars Lullii, cuius termini generales patefaciunt aditum non solum ad inventiones plurimas … sed etiam maxime faciunt ad memoriam, cum sint quasi via artificiosa et methodica ad corrigendum defectum, roborandum infirmitatem et sublevandam virtutem memoriae naturalis.' (Cf. *Regina scientiarum*, pp. 19, 318.)

46. See Lazare Meyssonnier, *Pentagonum philosophicum-medicum sive Ars nova reminiscentiae cum institutionibus philosophiae naturalis et medicinae sublimioris et secretioris … clave omnium arcanorum naturalium Macrocosmi et Microcosmi* (Lyons, 1639); *La Belle Magie ou science de l'esprit contenant les fondemens des subtilitez et de plus curieuses et secrètes connoissances de ce temps* (Lyons, 1669). Meyssonnier also testifies to his astrological skills: 'Apres avoir durant vingt-cinq ans examiné soigneusement les écrits et les observations de ceux qui ont traité de l'astronomie et de l'astrologie, dressé et jugé plus de deux milles figures de nativité, qu'on nomme vulgairement horoscopes.' Cf. *Aphorismes d'astrologie tirée de Ptolomée, Hermes, Cardan, Munfredus et plusieurs autres, traduit en françois*

par A. C. (Lyons, 1657), p. 1. The theory of *conarium* held by Meyssonnier in his *Pentagonum* and *Belle Magie* must be studied in the light of the attitude of Descartes towards this eccentric character. For the contacts between Meyssonnier and Mersenne and Descartes see the letter of Meyssonnier to Mersenne, 25 January 1639, in Adam and Tannery, *Correspondence*, III, p. 17. The first letter to Descartes has been lost, and also the reply to Descartes's letter of 29 January 1640 (Adam and Tannery, *Correspondence*, III, p. 18). See also the letters of Descartes to Mersenne of 29 January 1640, 1 April 1640 and 30 July 1640 (Adam and Tannery, *Correspondence*, III, pp. 15, 47, 120).

47. See Jean d'Aubry, *Le Triomphe de archée et la merveille du monde, ou la medicine universelle et veritable pour toutes sortes de maladies les plus deses-perées ... etablie par raisons necessaires et demonstrations infaillibles* (Paris, 1661). The quotation is from a public advertisement, with unnumbered pages. Included in this French edition, which followed a Latin edition of 1660 – *Triumphus archei et mundi miraculum sive medicina universalis* (Frankfurt, 1660) – is an appendix, *Apologie contre certains docteurs en médicine ... respondant à leurs calomnies que l'autheur a guéry par art magique beaucoup de maladies incurables et abandonées* which he had previously published in Paris in 1638. Among the writings more particularly dedicated to Lull see the translation of the *Blanquerna* (*Le Triomphe de l'amour et l'eschelle de la gloire, ou la médicine universelle des ames, ou Blanquerne de l'amy et de l'aimé* (Paris, n.d.) the *Abregé de l'ordre admirables des connoissances et des beaux secrets de saint Raymund Lulle martyr* (n.d.) and *Le firmament de la vérité contenant le nombre de cent demonstrations ... qui preuvent que tous les prestres ... abbés, commandataires, prédicateurs et bernabites doivent etre damnés éternellement s'ils ne vont prescher l'Evangile aux Turcs, Arabes, Mores, Perses, Musulmans et Mahométans* (Grenoble, 1642). But see pp. 155–61 of the *Apologie* (ed. 1661) for the eight reasons why the books of Lull 'should be treated in the same way as those of a Church Father' (*doivent estre receus de mesme que ceux d'un Père de l'Eglise*).

48. Robert Fludd, *Tomus secundus de supernaturali, naturali, praeternaturali et contranaturali Microcosmi historia* (Oppenheim, Hieronimi Galleri, 1619), pp. 47–70.

49. See *Les Oeuvres de Jean Belot ... contenant la chiromance, physionomie, l'art de mémoire de Raymond Lulle, traité des devinations, augures et songes, les sciences steganographiques, paulines et almadelles et Lullistes* (Lyon, 1654), pp. 329–45. There was another edition of this work published in Rouen in 1688, which was reprinted in Liège in 1704. On the 'arts paulines et almadelles', see Lynn Thorndike, 'Alfodhol and

Almadel: hitherto unnoted books of magic in Florentine manuscripts', in *Speculum*, 2:3 (1927), pp. 326–31. I would have discussed
the works of Belot (which were favourable to the Copernican theory,
and mention the 'vortices of matter' (*tourbillons de matière*) as early as
1603) in greater detail, if it had not already been done by Thorndike
(see *History of Magic and Experimental Science,* VI, pp. 360–2, 507–10).
Belot's works also show clear signs of Ramist influence: see esp.
pp. 52, 56 of the edition of 1654, and pp. 62–3, 67–8 of the edition
of 1688. Belot frequently refers to Bruno as one of the greatest exponents of the art: see Paolo Rossi, 'Note bruniane', *Rivista critica di storia della filosofia,* 14:2 (1959), pp. 197–203.

50. Belot, *Oeuvres*, pp. 330–4. For the connection between chiromancy
and the mnemonic art see the work of Marafioto, cited in note 42
above.

51. See Belot, *Oeuvres*, second part, p. 1.

52. Belot, *Oeuvres*, Preface: 'Ce que l'antiquité a recherché avec beaucoup de labeur toutesfois sans en avoir acquis la parfaite connoissance,
je te le donne tout entier: c'est ce qu'ont voulou acquerir les
Prophetes, Mages, Rabins, Cabalistes et Massorets, et depuis eux le
docte H. C. Agrippa.'

53. Belot, *Oeuvres*, second part, p. 3: 'Pour les parties, elles reçoivent
toutes les cinq pour bonnes et utiles, mais il y en a cinq autres parti-
culieres aussi: car pour la memoire, elle a l'Art notoire; pour l'action
ou pronunciation, l'art Paulin et pour les autres parties, a pour l'elocution l'art d'Almadel; pour la disposition la seconde partie de la
Theurgie et pour l'invention l'arts des revelations, que Tritheme dit
venir d'Ophiel, esprit Mercurial.'

V Artificial Memory and the New Scientific Method: Ramus, Bacon, Descartes

1. I have not seen the work of Campanus, which is described at length
by Morhof; I have seen the Parisian 1520 edition of the *Ars memoratiua Guglielmi Leporei Avallonensis.*

2. For a bibliography of Ramus see Paolo Rossi, 'Ramismo, logica e
retorica nei secoli XVI e XVII', *Rivista critica di storia della filosofia,* 3,
(1957), pp. 359–61. In addition to the studies cited in my article see
Michel Dassonville, 'La genèse et les principes de la Dialectique de
Petrus Ramus', *Revue de l'Université d'Ottawa,* (1953), pp. 322–55 and
idem, 'La dialectique de Petrus Ramus', *Revue de l'Université de Laval*

(1952–3), pp. 608–16; Paul Dibon, 'L'influence de Ramus aux universités néerlandaises du XVII siècle', in *Actes du XIe Congr. Int. de Philosophie* (Louvain 1953), 14, pp. 307–11 and Rosemond Tuve, 'Imagery and logic: Ramus and metaphysical poetics', *Journal of the History of Ideas*, 3:4 (1942), pp. 365–400.

3. Petrus Ramus, *Scholae in liberales artes* (Basel, 1569), pp. 157–8.

4. Ramus, *Scholae*, p. 63.

5. See Petrus Ramus, *Oratio de studiis philosophiae et eloquentiae coniungendis Lutetiae habita anno 1546*, reprinted in Petrus Ramus, *Brutinae quaestiones in Oratorem Ciceronis* (Paris, 1547), p. 45r.

6. See Petrus Ramus, *Dialectique de Pierre de La Ramée, à Charles de Lorraine, cardinal, son Mécène* (Paris, 1555), pp. 3–4.

7. See Petrus Ramus, *Rhetoricae distinctiones in Quintilianum* (Paris, 1559), p. 18; *Ciceronianus et brutinae quaestiones* (Basel, 1577), p. 329; *Rhetoricae distinctiones*, p. 43: 'Duae sunt universae et generales homini dotes a natura tributae: ratio et oratio; illius doctrina dialectica est, huius grammatica et rhetorica. Dialectica igitur generales humane rationis vires in cogitandis et disponendis rebus persequatur; grammatica orationis puritatem in etymologia et sintaxi ad recte loquendum vel scribendum interpretetur. Rhetorica orationis ornatum tum in tropis et figuris, tum in actionis dignitate demonstret. Ab his deinde generalibus et universis, velut instrumentis, aliae artes sunt effectae ... Aristoteles summae confusionis author fuit: inventionem rhetoricae partem primam facit, falso ut antea docui, quia dialecticae propria est; sed tamen rhetoricae partem facit et eius multiplices artes primo artis universae loco conturbat in probationibus ... Quintilianus concludit materiam rhetorices esse res omnes quae ad dicendum subiectae sunt ... Dividitur rhetorica in quinque partes: inventionem, dispositionem, elocutionem, memoriam et actionem. In qua partitione nihil iam miror Quintilianum dialectica tam nudum esse, qui dialecticam ipsam cum rhetorica hic confusum non potuerit agnoscere, cum dialecticae sunt inventio, dispositio, memoria; rhetorica tantum elocutio et actio.'

8. Petrus Ramus, *Scholae in tres primas liberales artes* (Frankfurt, 1581), p. 31: 'Non potest ... sine numeris Geometria, Musica, Astrologia consistere: an propterea hae artes numeros explicare et suae professioni subiicere debebunt. Usus artium, ut iam toties dici, copulatus est persaepe. Praecepta tamen confundenda non sunt, sed propriis et separatis studiis declaranda.'

9. Petrus Ramus, *Animadversionum aristotelicarum libri XX* (Paris,

1553–60), II, preface to books IX–XX, p. 1; *Institutionum dialecticarum libri tres* (Paris, 1543), II, pp. 2, 3, 77: 'Duae partes sunt artis logicae: topica in inventione argumentorum, id est mediorum principiorum elementorum (sic enim nominatur in *Organo*) et analytica in eorum dispositione ... Dispositio est apta rerum inventarum collocatio ... Atque haec pars est quae iudicium proprie nominatur, quia sillogismus de omnis iudicandis communis regula est ... Dialecticae artis partes duae sunt: inventio et dispositio. Posita enim quaestione in qua disserendum sit, probationes et argumenta quaerantur; deinde, iis via et ordine dispositis, quaestio ipsa explicatur.'

10. Petrus Ramus, *Ciceronianus et Brutinae quaestiones*, p. 8v.: 'Dicis oratori tria esse videnda: quid dicat, quo quidque loco, et quomodo: primo membro inventionem, secundo collocationem, tertio elocutionem et actionem comprehendis. Memoria igitur ubi est? Communis est – ais – multarum artium, propterea omittitur. Enimvero, inquam, inventionem et dispositionem communes cum multis esse (ais), cur igitur haec recensentur, illa contemnitur?'

11. Petrus Ramus, *Scholae in tres primas liberales artes*, pp. 14–46; *Dialecticae institutiones*, cit., p. 19v.: 'Dialectico inventionem, dispositionem, elocutionem, memoriam merito assignamus; elocutionem et actionem oratori relinquamus ... Iudicium definiamus doctrinam res inventas collocandi, et ea collocandi, et ea collocatione de re proposita iudicandi: quae certe doctrina itidem memoriae (si tamen eius esse disciplina ulla potest), verissima certissimaque doctrina est, ut una eademque sit instituto duarum maximarum animi virtutum: iudicii et memoriae ... Rationis duae partes sunt: *inventio* consiliorum et argumentorum, eorumque iudicium in dispositione ... dispositionis umbra quaedam est memoria ... Tres itaque partes illae, inventio inquam dispositio memoria, dialecticae artis sunto.'

12. Phillip Melanchthon, *Erotemata dialecticae*, in Carl Gottlieb Bretschneider et al. (eds.), *Corpus reformatorum* (Halle, 1834–), XIII, col. 573: 'Habitus videlicet scientia, seu ars, viam faciens certa ratione, id est, quae quasi per loca invia et obsita sensibus, per rerum confusionem, viam invenit et aperit, et res, ad propositum pertinentes, eruit ac ordine promit.'

13. Petrus Ramus and Audomarus Talaeus, *Petri Rami professoris regi et Audomari Talaei collectanae prefationes, epistolae, orationes* (Marburg, 1559), p. 15.

14. Pierre Gassendi, *De logicae origine et varietate,* cap. IX ('Logica Rami') in *Opera omnia in sex tomos divisa* (Florence, 1727), I, p. 52: 'Cum observasset enim quinque vulgo fieri partes Rhetoricae, inventionem,

dispositionem, elocutionem, memoriam et pronunciationem, censuit ex ipsis duas solum pertinere ad rhetoricam: elocutionem puta et pronunciationem seu actionem; duas artes esse proprias Logicae: inventionem puta et dispositionem, quibus, quia memoria iuvatur, posse illam eodem cum ipsis spectare. Quare et Logicam seu Dialecticam ... in duas partes distribuit: inventionem et iudicium (sic enim potius dicere quam dispositionem maluit ...) atque idcirco artem totam duobus libris complexus est.'

15. Quotes from the texts of Descartes and Bacon will be from *Oeuvres de Descartes*, ed. Charles Adam and Paul Tannery, 11 vols. (Paris, 1897–1909) and *The Works of Francis Bacon*, ed. J. Spedding, R. L. Ellis, D. D. Heath, 7 vols. (London, 1887–92) respectively, henceforth referred to as *Oeuvres* and *Works*.

16. Descartes to Beeckmann, 29th April 1619; *Oeuvres*, X, pp. 164–5; *Discours* (ed. Gilson), p. 17: 'Repperi nudius tertius eruditum virum in Diversorio Dordracensi, cum quo de Lulli arte parva sum loquutus ... Senex erat, aliquantulum loquax, et cuius eruditio, utpote a libris hausta, in extremis labris potius quam in cerebro versabatur ... Quod illum certe dixisse suspicor, ut admirationem captaret ignorantis, potius quam ut vere loqueretur.' 'Je pris garde que, pour la logique, ses syllogismes et la plupart de ses autres instructions servent plutôt à expliquer à autrui les choses qu'on sait, ou même, comme l'art de Lulle, à parler, sans jugement, de celles qu'on ignore, qu'à les apprendre.'

17. Bacon, *De augmentis*, VI, 2, in *Works*, I, p. 669: 'Neque tamen illud praetermittendum, quod nonnulli viri, magis tumidi quam docti insudarunt circa Methodum quandam, legitimae methodi nomine haud dignam; cum potius sit methodus imposturae, quae tamen quibusdam ardelionibus acceptissima procul dubio fuit. Haec methodus ita scientiae alicuius guttulas aspergit, ut quid sciolus specie nonnulla eruditionis ad ostentationem possit abuti. Talis fuit Ars Lullii; talis Typocosmia a nonnullis exarata; quae nihil aliud fuerunt quam vocabulorum artis cuiusque massa et acervus; ad hoc, ut qui voces artis habeant in promptu, etiam artes ipsas perdidicisse existimentur. Huius generis collectanea officinam referunt veteramentarium, ubi praesegmina multa reperiuntur, sed nihil quod alicuius sit pretii.'

18. Agrippa, *Opera* (1600), II, pp. 31–2: 'Hoc autem admonere vos oportet: hanc artem ad pompam ingenii et doctrinae ostentationem potius quam ad comparandam eruditionem valere, ac longe plus habere audaciae quam efficaciae.'

19. See Schenkel, *De memoria liber* (Liège, 1595) reprinted in *Gazophylacium artis memoriae* (Strasburg, 1616). On Schenkel's work and his links to Leibniz see *infra*, pp. 189–90.

20. Descartes, *Oeuvres*, X, p. 230.

21. Bacon, *Works*, I, pp. 647–8: 'Verum est tamen inter methodos et syntaxes locorum communium quas nobis adhuc videre contigit, nullam reperiri quae alicuius sit pretii; quandoquidem in titulis suis faciem prorsus exhibeant magis scholae quam mundi; vulgares et pedogogicas adhibentes divisiones, non autem eas quae ad rerum medullas et interiora quovis modo penetrent.'

22. Bacon, *Works*, I, pp. 647–8

23. Bacon, *Works*, I, p. 647.

24. For the difference between ordinary logic and the new logic see Bacon, *Partis instaurationis secundae delineato et argumentum* in *Works*, III, pp. 547 et seq.; *Distributio operis* in *Works*, I, pp. 135–7; *Praefatio generalis*, in *Works*, I, p. 129; *Novum organum*, I, pp. 26, 29.

25. See Bacon, *Advancement of Learning*, in *Works*, III, p. 399; *De augmentis* in *Works*, I, pp. 648–9, 651–3.

26. See *L'arte del ricordare del Signor Gio. Battista Porta Napoletano, tradotta da latino in volgare per M. Dorandino Falcone da Gioia* (Naples, 1566). On the writing of the Egyptians see cap. XIX, on gestures see cap. XX; C. Rossellius, *Thesaurus artificiosae memoriae* (Venice, 1579), p. 117v.; Johannes Austriacus, *De memoria artificiosa libellus* (Strasburg, 1610), p. 215. On Egyptomania and the fashion for emblems in the sixteenth and seventeenth centuries see pp. 78–9 above and the works cited in note 39, p. 278.

27. For Bacon's opinions on Lull see *De augmentis*, in *Works*, I, p. 699; on the *prima philosophia* see *De augmentis* in *Works*, I, pp. 540–4. On the distinction between the Baconian *prima philosophia* and traditional metaphysics see Fulton H. Anderson, *The Philosophy of Francis Bacon* (Chicago: University of Chicago Press, 1948), pp. 214–15.

28. See Henri Gouhier, 'Le refus du symbolisme dans l'humanisme cartesien', in Castelli, *Umanesimo e simbolismo*, p. 67; Marcel de Corte 'La dialectique poètique de Descartes', *Archives de philosophie*, 13:2 (1937), 'Autour du Discours de la Méthode', pp. 106–7; Pierre Mesnard, 'L'arbre de sagesse', in *Cahiers de Royaumont philosophie. No.II: Descartes,* The Philosophy of Descartes, 10 (Paris, 1957, repr. London and New York, Garland, 1987), pp. 336 et seq. In the same volume see also Theodor Spoerri, 'La puissance metaphorique de Descartes'. For a fuller examination see Henri Gouhier, *Les Premières*

Pensées de Descartes, contribution à l'histoire de l'anti-Renaissance (Paris: Vrin, 1958).

29. Descartes, *Oeuvres*, X, p. 230. On writing and the other aids to memory see *Entretiens avec Burman* (Paris, 1937), pp. 8, 16.

30. Descartes, *Oeuvres*, X, pp. 217–18, 'Ut imaginatio figuris ad corpora concipienda, ita intellectus utitur quibusdam corporibus sensibilibus ad spiritualia figuranda, ut vento, lumine: unde altius philosophantes mentem cognitione possumus in sublime tollere … Sensibilia apta concipiendis Olympicis: ventus spiritum significat, motus cum tempore vitam, calor amorem, activitas istantanea creationem.'

31. 'Mirum videri possit, quare graves sententiae in scriptis poetarum magis quam philosophorum. Ratio est quod poetae per enthusiasmum et vim imaginationis scripsere: sunt in nobis semina scientiae, ut in silice, quae per rationem a philosophis educuntur, per imaginationem a poetis excutiuntur magisque elucent.' (Descartes, *Oeuvres*, X, p. 217). 'On peut faire un jardin des ombres qui representent diverses figures, telles que les arbres et les autres … dans un chambre faire [que] les rayons du soleil, passant pour certaines ouvertures, representent diverses chiffres ou figures.' (Descartes, *Oeuvres*, X, p. 215). 'Inquiribam autem diligentius utrum ars illa non consisteret in quodam ordine locorum dialecticorum unde rationes desumuntur.' (Descartes, *Oeuvres*, X, p. 165).

32. Descartes, *Oeuvres*, X, p. 218.

33. *Descartes à Mersennes* (1639) in Descartes, *Oeuvres, Supplément*, pp. 97–8: 'Quemadmodum Deus est unus et creavit naturam unam, simplicem, continuam, ubique sibi cohaerentem et respondentem, paucissimis, constantem principiis elementisque ex quibus infinitas propemodum res, sed in tria regna minerale, vegetale et animale certo inter se ordine gradibusque distincta perduxit; ita et harum rerum cognitionem esse oportet, ad similitudinem unius Creatoris et unius Naturae, unicam simplicem, continuam, non interruptam, paucis constantem principiis (imo unico Principio principali) unde caetera omnia ad specialissima usque individuo nexu et sapientissimo ordine deducat permanent, ut ita nostra de rebus universis et singulis contemplatio similis est picturae vel speculo universi et singularum eiusdem partium imaginem exactissime repraesentanti.' The letter was first published in Jan Kvacala (ed.), *Korrespondence. Listy Komenského a vrstevníků jeho*, 2 vols. (Prague, 1897–1902), I, p. 83. The 'book' which Descartes referred to in a letter of 1639 (Descartes, *Oeuvres*, II, pp. 345–8: 'j'ai lû soigneusement le livre que vous avez pris la peine

de m'envoyer') was the *Pansophiae prodromus* of Comenius (cf. Descartes, *Oeuvres Supplément*, pp. 99–100 where there is a letter from Mersenne to Theodore Haak in which Descartes is singled out as one of the philosophers most competent to speak of the work of Comenius).

34. Descartes, *Oeuvres*, X, p. 215: 'Larvatae nunc scientiae sunt: quae, larvis sublatus, pulcherrimae apparerent. Catenam scientiarum pervidenti, non difficilius videbitur eas animo retinere, quam seriem numerorum.' On this passage see Raymond Klibansky, 'The philosophic character of history', in Raymond Klibansky and H. J. Paton (eds.), *Philosophy and History: Essays Presented to Ernst Cassirer* (Oxford: Clarendon Press, 1936), pp. 323–37.

35. Nicholas J. Poisson, *Commentaire ou remarques sur la Methode de R. Descartes* (Vandosme, 1670), Part II, observation 6, p. 73: 'Il regne je ne sçai quelle liason, qui fait qu'une verité fait découvrir l'autre, et qu'il ne faut que trouver le bon but du fil, pour aller jusqu'à l'autre sans l'interruption. Ce sont à peu-près les paroles de M. Descartes que j'ay leües dans un de ses fragmens manuscrits: Quippe sunt concatenatae omnes scientiae, nec una perfecta haberi potest quin aliae sponte sequantur, et tota simul encyclopaedia apprehendatur.' (Cf. Descartes, *Oeuvres*, X, p. 255.)

36. Descartes, *Oeuvres*, X, p. 261: 'Credendum est, ita omnes [scientias] inter se esse connexas, ut longe facilius sit cunctas simul addiscere, quam unicam ab aliis separare. Si quis igitur serio rerum veritatem investigare vult, non singularem aliquam debet optare scientiam: sunt enim omnes inter se coniunctas et ab invicem depedentes.'

37. Jean d'Aubry *Le Triumphe de l'archée et la merveille du monde*, (Paris, 1661 – first edition 1638), *Apologie contre certains docteurs*, etc. in appendix with unnumbered pages: 'Qui doute que les parties de la doctrine (que les sots et les ignorants appellent sciences, comme s'il y en avoit plusieurs) ne se trouvent enchaînées l'une avec l'autre, qu'il est impossible d'estre entendu en la moindre sans avoir une pleine connoissance du toutes; l'Eptaple de Pic de la Mirande sur les jours de la création et l'armonie di monde de Paul Venitien vous le montrent.'

38. See Descartes, *Oeuvres*, X, p. 157.

39. See for example Jean Laporte, *La Rationalisme de Descartes* (Paris: Presses universitaires de France, 1945, repr. 1950), pp. 8–10. For a more exact assessment see Augusto del Noce, *Meditazioni metafisiche ed estratti dalle obbiezioni e risposte / Renato Descartes* (Padua: CEDAM, 1940, repr. 1949), pp. xxiii–xxiv.

40. Bacon, *De augmentis*, III, 1 in *Works*, I, pp. 540–1: 'Quoniam autem partitiones scientiarum non sunt lineis diversis similes, quae coeunt ad unum angulum; sed potius ramis arborum qui continguntur in uno trunco (qui etiam truncus ad spatium nonnullum integer est et continuus, antequam se partiatur in ramos); idcirco postulat res ut priusquam prioris partitionis membra persequamur, constituatur una Scientia universalis, quae sit mater reliquarum et habetur in progressu doctrinarum tanquam portio viae communis antequam viae se separent et disiungant. Hanc Scientiam Philosophiae primae, sive etiam Sapientiae … nomine insignimus.'

41. Descartes, *Regulae*, IV, and preface to the *Principes*, in Descartes, *Oeuvres*, X, pp. 373–4: 'Quicumque tamen attente respexerit ad meum sensum facile percipiet me nihil minus quam de vulgari Mathematica hic cogitare, sed quamdam aliam me exponere disciplinam, cuius integumentum sit potius quam partes. Haec enim prima rationis humanae rudimenta continere, et ad veritates ex quovis subiecto eliciendas se extendere debet; atque, ut libere loquar, hanc omni alia nobis humanitus tradita cognitione potiorem, utpote aliarum omnium fontem, esse mihi persuadeo … Ainsi toute la philosophie est comme un arbre, dont les racines sont la méthaphysique, le tronc est la physique, et les branches qui sortent de ce tronc sont toutes les autres sciences.'

42. Bacon, *Advancement of Learning*, in *Works*, III, pp. 383–4; *De augmentis*, in *Works*, I, p. 616.

43. Bacon, *Advancement*, in *Works*, III, p. 389.

44. Bacon, *Partis restaurationis secundae delineato*, in *Works*, III, p. 552: 'Ministratio ad memoriam hoc officium praestat ut ex turba rerum particularium, et naturalis historiae generalis acervo, particularis historia excerpatur, atque disponatur eo ordine, ut iudicium in eam agere, et opus suum exercere possint … Primo docebimus qualia sint ea, quae circa subiectum datum sive propositum inquiri debeant, quod est instar topicae. Secundo, quo ordine illa disponi oporteat, et in tabulas digeri … Tertio itaque ostendemus quo modo et quo tempore inquisitio sit reintegranda, et chartae sive tabulae praecedentes in chartas novellas transportandae … Itaque ministratio ad memoriam in tribus (ut diximus) doctrinis absolvitur: de locis inveniendis, de methodo contabulandi, et de modo instaurandi inquisitionem.'

45. 'Admonet ubi quaerenda sit materia aut certe quid ex magno acervo eligendum et quo ordine distribuendum sit. Nam loci inventionis tum apud dialecticos tum apud rhetores non conducunt ad inveniendam

materiam, quam ad eligendam postquam acervus aliquis … oblatus fuerit.'

46. *Novum organum*, II, 10: 'Historia vero naturalis et experimentalis tam varia est et sparsa, ut intellectum confundat et disgreget, nisi sisatur et compareat ordine idoneo. Itaque formandae sunt tabulae et coordinationes instantiarum, tali modo et instructione, ut in eas agere possit intellectus.'

47. Bacon, *Works*, III, p. 619.

48. *Commentarius solutus*, in Bacon, *Works*, III, pp. 626–8: 'Tria motuum genera imperceptibilia, ob tarditatem, ut in digito horologii; ob minutias, ut liquor seu aqua corrumpitur et congelatur etc.; ob tenuitatem, ut omnifaria aeris, venti, spiritus … Nodi et globi motuum, and how they concur and how they succeed and interchange in things most frequent. The times and moments wherein motions work, and which is the more swift and which is the more slow'.

49. The three works are respectively in Bacon, *Works*, III, pp. 623–40, 644–52; 657–80.

50. Bacon, *Inquisitio legitima de motu* in *Works*, III, pp. 637–8.

51. Bacon, *Praefatio generalis* in *Works*, I, p. 129.

52. Bacon, *Delineatio* in Works, III, p. 553. See also *Novum organum*, II, 20.

53. Bacon, *Novum Organum*, II, 18: 'Neque enim tabulas conficimus perfectas, sed exempla tantum.'

54. On the significance of the final paragraph of Book I of the *Novum organum* see Benjamin Farrington, *Francis Bacon: Philosopher of Industrial Science* (London: Lawrence & Wishart, 1951), pp. 114–24.

55. On this see Paolo Rossi, *Francesco Bacone: dalla magia alla scienza*, revised edition (Turin: Einaudi, 1974), chapter 6.

56. Descartes, *Regulae* in *Oeuvres*, X, p. 454: 'Operae pretium est omnes alias [dimensiones] ita retinere, ut facile occurrant quoties usus exigit; in quem finem memoria videtur a natura instituta. Sed quia haec saepe labilis est … aptissime scribendi usum ars adinvenit; cuius ope freti … quaecumque erunt retinenda in charta pingemus.'

57. Anonymous, sixteenth century, Bibliotheca Marciana, MS Lat. cl. VI, 274, f. 41r.: 'Sicut enim invenerunt homines diversas artes ad iuvandum diversis modis naturam, sic enim videntes quod per naturam memoria hominis labilis est, conati sunt invenire artem aliquam ad iuvandum naturam seu memoriam … et sic adinvenerunt scripturam.'

58. Bacon, *Works*, I, p. 647: 'Adminiculum memoriae plane scripto est, atque omnino monendum quod memoria, sine hoc adminiculo,

rebus prolixioribus impar sit, neque ullo modo nisi de scripto recipi debeat.'

59. Descartes, *Oeuvres*, X, pp. 458, 454.

60. The problem of notation or the use of algebraic symbols is even more clearly linked, in the text of the *Discours de la méthode* (cf. Descartes, *Oeuvres*, VII, p. 20), to the problem of retention and memory: 'Je pensai que, pour les considérer mieux en particulier [he is referring to relations and proportions], je les devais supposer en des lignes, à cause que je ne trouvais rien de plus simple, ni que je puisse plus distinctement représenter à mon imagination et à mes sens; mais que, pour les retenir ou les comprendre plusieurs ensemble, il fallait que je les expliquasse par quelques chiffres, les plus courts qu'il serait possible.' The term *chiffres* is translated in the Latin edition as 'characteribus sive quibusdam notis' (cf. Descartes, *Oeuvres*, VI, p. 551).

61. See the title of *Regulae* XII: 'It is necessary to make use of … aids to the memory.'

62. Descartes, *Oeuvres*, X, p. 369: 'At vero haec intuitus evidentia et certitudo, non ad solas enuntiationes, sed etiam ad quoslibet discursus requiritur. Nam; exempli gratia, sit haec consequentia: 2 & 2 efficiunt idem quod 3 & 1; non modo intuendum est 2 & 2 efficere 4, et 3 & 1 efficere quoque 4, sed insuper ex his duabus propositionibus tertiam illam necessario concludi.'

63. Descartes, *Oeuvres*, X, pp. 369–70. 'Hinc iam dubium esse potest, quare, praeter, intuitum, hic alium adiuniximus cognoscendi modum, qui sit per deductionem: per quam intelligimus, illud omne quod ex quibusdam aliis certo cognitis necessario concluditur. Sed hoc ita faciendum fuit, quia plurimae res certo sciuntur, quamvis non ipsae sint evidentes, modo tantum a veris cognitisque principiis deducantur per continuum et nullibi interruptum cogitationis motum singula perspicue intuentis: non aliter quam longae alicuius catenae extremum annulum cum primo connecti cognoscimus, etiamsi uno eodemque oculorum intuitu non omnes intermedios, a quibus dependet illa connexio, contemplemur, modo illos perlustraverimus successive, et singulos proximis a primo ad ultimum adhaerere recordemur. Hic igitur mentis intuitum a deductione certa distinguimus ex eo, quod in hac motus sive successio quaedam concipiatur, in illo non item; et praeterea, quia ad hanc non necessaria est praesens evidentia, qualis ad intuitum, sed potius a memoria suam certitudinem quodammodo mutuatur' (see also rule XI, Descartes, *Oeuvres,* X, pp. 408–9).

64. Descartes, *Oeuvres*, X, p. 387: 'Hoc enim sit interdum per tam longum consequentiarum contextum, ut, cum ad illas devenimus, non facile recordemur totius itineris quod nos eo usque perduxit; ideoque memoriae infirmitati continuo quodam cogitationis motu succurendum esse dicimus.'

65. Descartes, *Oeuvres*, X, pp. 387–8: 'Si igitur, ex gr., per diversas operationes cognoverim primo, qualis sit habitudo inter magnitudines A & B, deinde inter B & C, tum inter C & D, ac denique inter D & E: non idcirco video qualis sit inter A & E, nec possum intelligere praecise ex iam cognitis, nisi omnium recorder. Quamobrem illas continuo quodam imaginationis motu singula intuentis simul et ad alia transeuntis aliquoties percurram, donec a prima ad ultimam tam celeriter transire didicerim, ut fere nullas memoriae partes relinquendo, rem totam simul videar intueri; hoc enim pacto, dum memoriae subvenitur, ingenii etiam tarditas emendatur, eiusque capicitas quadam ratione extenditur.'

66. Leslie J. Beck, *The Method of Descartes, a Study of the Regulae* (Oxford: Clarendon Press, 1952), p. 143, but see also pp. 111–46. On Descartes's 'enumeration', see René Hubert, 'La théorie cartésienne de l'énumération' in *Revue de metaphysique et de morale*, 23:3 (1916), pp. 489–516; J. Sirven, *Les Années d'apprentissage de Descartes (1596–1628). Thèse pour le doctorat ès lettres présentée à la Faculté des lettres de l'Université de Paris [Texte imprimé], par J. Sirven* (Paris, 1928, repr. New York, Garland, 1987), pp. 210–13; Norman Kemp-Smith, *New Studies in the Philosophy of Descartes. Descartes as Pioneer* (London: Macmillan, 1952), pp. 70–7, 144–9, and 150–9.

67. Descartes, *Oeuvres*, VI, p. 550.

68. Descartes, *Oeuvres*, X, p. 388: 'Est igitur haec enumeratio sive inductio, eorum omnium quae ad propositam aliquam quaestionem spectant, tam diligens et accurata perquisitio, ut ex illa certo evidenterque concludamus, nihil a nobis perperam fuisse praetermissum.'

69. Beck, *The Method of Descartes*, p. 130.

70. While Beck and Gouhier have a detailed understanding of the Cartesian texts, they do not seem to be familiar with other philosophical and non-philosophical texts circulating in French and European culture in the seventeenth century. See, for example, the way in which Gouhier (in his book *Les Premières Penseés de Descartes*) disposes of the relationship between Descartes and the Lullist tradition in two lines, without having seen the only study on the subject, and without mentioning that Descartes's opinion of Lull ('parler sans

jugement des choses qu'on ignores') is simply the repetition of a commonplace, to be found in the philosophical texts of Agrippa and Bacon (see p. XX, n. 55). Even the Cartesian expression 'in quodam ordine locorum dialecticorum unde rationes desumuntur' refers, contrary to what Gouhier believes, to a particular type of literature. Likewise, the affirmation 'una est rebus activa vis etc.' and the proposed use of 'sensible things' to represent 'spiritual things' and the image of the *catena scientiarum* become completely incomprehensible (even if one takes them as elegant speculations), if they are not understood in relation to a tradition or background. Descartes, who had read Schenkel, did not need to turn to Kepler for the idea of corporeal things serving as symbols of the spiritual. In the passage where Descartes refers to Schenkel's *ars memoriae*, Gouhier omits the second half (which makes it difficult to understand for anyone who has not seen Schenkel's text) without explaining what the 'new procedure' is which Descartes believes he has invented (see Gouhier, *Les Premières Penseés de Descartes*, pp. 27–8, 69, 82–4, 92).

71. See note 44 above.
72. Descartes, *Oeuvres*, X, pp. 390–1.

VI Encyclopaedism and Pansophia

1. For the relationship between the encyclopaedia and educational curricula see Eugenio Garin, *L'educazione in Europa: 1400–1600. Problemi e programmi* (Bari, 1957), pp. 235–9. On Alsted's Lullism see Carreras y Artau, *Filosofia cristiana* (Madrid, 1939–43), II, pp. 239–49; Jean Michel Alfred Vacant et al., *Dictionnaire de théologie catholique*, 15 vols. (Paris, 1899–1950), I, col. 923–4, and for many unpublished works see Jean Pierre Niceron, *Mémoires pour servir à l'histoire des hommes illustres dans la Republique des Lettres avec un catalogue raisonné de leurs ouvrages* , 43 vols. (Paris, 1729–45), pp. 298–311.

2. See Johann Alsted, *Clavis artis lullianae et verae logices duos in libellus tributa id est solida dilucidatio artis magnae, generalis et ultimae quam Raymundus Lullus invenit ... edita in usum et gratiam eorum, qui impendio delectantur compendiis et confusionem sciolorum qui iuventutem fatigant dispendiis* (Strasburg, 1609), Preface. The *Clavis* was reprinted in 1633 and 1651.

3. Johann Alsted, *Panacea philosophica seu encyclopaediae universa discendi methodus. De armonia philosophiae aristotelicae lullianae et rameae* (Herborn, 1610).

4. Alsted, *Clavis artis lullianae*, pp. 9–14 (19): 'Tantum de Rameis restant philosophi in Germania, minus celebres Lullisti. In Germania, dico quia in Hispaniis, Galliis et Italia sunt quamplurimi de hoc grege, et nominatim quidem in Italia sunt speculatores … qui huic arti sunt deditissimi … Haec duo sectae, Peripatetica dico et Ramaea in prae- sentiarum sunt florentissimae, superest tertia, puta Lullistarum, quae hodie ferme "Multis pro vili, sub pedibus iacet".' His judgement on the commentators was particularly harsh: 'Moreover these commen- tators of Lull (would that they had simply been his recommenders) darkened the face of his divine works with shadows and clouds rather than illuminating them, thrusting them down rather than raising them up into the light. They mixed his works with their own fan- tasies, or explained his obscure words with obscure words of their own.' (*Nam commentatores (utinam fuissent commendatores) Lulliani, tene- bras potius et nebula offunderunt quam lucem attulerunt, aut facem prae- tulerunt divino operi. Aut enim sua somnia immiscuerunt, aut obscura per aeque obscura explicarunt.*) The aim of the divine art of Lull was 'talem invenire scientiam, qua cognita, reliquae quoque sine difficultate ulla laboreque magno cognoscerentur, et ad quam, tamquam lydiam lapi- dem, filum Thesei et Cynosuram omne scibile examinaretur'. The closeness of the Lullian art to the cabala is a persistent theme in the work of Alsted. See, for example, the *Tabula ad artis brevis cabalae trac- tatus et artis magnae primum caput pertinens* and the judgement on Lull: 'Quum Lullius fuerit mathematicus et kabbalista, impendio delecta- tus est methodo docendi mathematica et kabbalista, ideoque circulus adhibuit, quos non nemo concinne vocavit magistros scientiarum. Et huc facit tritus versiculus: Omnia dant mundo Crux, Globus atque Cubus.' It is interesting to note that among the cultivators of the art, Alsted also referred to Poliziano 'qui, opino per hanc artem, se dis- putare posse de omnibus pollicebantur', p. 14. For Alsted's reference to Bruno see Paolo Rossi, 'Note bruniane', *Rivista critica di storia della filosofia*, II, 1959, pp. 198–9.

5. Johann Alsted, *Systema mnemonicum duplex … in quo artis memorativae praecepta plene et methodice traduntur: et tota simul ratio docendi, discendi, Scholas aperiendi, adeoque modus studendi solide explicatur et a pseudo- memoristarum, pseudo-Lullistarum, pseudo-cabbalistarum imposturis discer- nitur atque vindicatur* (Frankfurt, 1610), p. 5.

6. Alsted, *Systema mnemonicum duplex*, p. 105: 'Logicae duplex est finis et duplex obiectum: primus est directio intellectus, secundus est memoriae confirmatio.'

7. Alsted, *Systema mnemonicum duplex*, pp. 106–7: 'Prima lex est lex homogeniae ... secunda lex dicitur coordinationis ... tertia lex dicitur transitionis.'

8. Following a tradition which began in Lavinheta, Alsted likens the circles of the Lullian art to the *loci* of Ciceronian mnemotechnics, *Clavis artis lullianae*, p. 25: 'Circulus in arte Lulliana est locus et quoddam quasi domicilium in quo instrumenta inventionis collocantur.' But see also: *Artium liberalium, ac facultatem omnium systema mnemonicum de modo discendi, in libros septem digestum et congestum* (Prostat, 1610), *Encyclopaedia septem tomis distincta* (Herborn, 1630). Amongst his pedagogical and religious works are: *Theatrum scholasticum* (Herborn, 1610) (which contains a *Gymnasium mnemonicum*); *Trigae canonicae* (Frankfurt, 1611) (which contains an *Artis mnemologicae explicatio*); the *Dissertatio de manducatione spirituali, transubstantiatione, sacrificio missae, de natura et privilegiis ecclesiae* (Geneva, 1630). For his classification of the mathematical sciences see *Methodus admirandorum mathematicorum novem libris exhibens universam mathesin* (Herborn 1623): 'Mathematics is the part of the philosophical encyclopaedia which deals with quantity in general terms ... This is the way in which the mathematical sciences are arranged. The mathematical sciences are either pure or mixed. The pure sciences are those which are concerned with quantity alone: these are arithmetic and geometry. The mixed sciences are those which concern the quantity which is inherent in physical bodies: such as cosmography, uranoscopy and geography; or those which deal with qualities such as optics, music and architectonics.' (*Mathesis est pars encyclopaediae philosophicae tractans de quantitate communiter ... Ordo scientiarum mathematicarum hic est. Scientiae mathematicae sunt purae vel mediae. Purae sunt quae occupantur circa solam quantitatem: quales sunt arithmetica et geometria. Mediae sunt quae occupantur circa quantitatem haerentem in corpore: ut cosmographia, uranoscopia, geographia; vel in qualitate ut in optica, musica et architectonica.*)

9. Pierre Bayle, *Dictionnaire historique et critique* (Amsterdam 1740), pp. 165–6.

10. Comenius's *Janua linguarum* was eventually translated into Arabic and Persian and by this means the pansophic ideal eventually spread as far as the Far East.

11. On the origins of pansophia see Will-Erich Peuckert, *Pansophie. Ein Versuch der Geschichte der weissen und schwarzen Magie* (Stuttgart, 1936). On his pedagogical ideals see Jan Kvacala, *J. A. Comenio* (Berlin, 1914) and Eugenio Garin, *L'educazione in Europa*, pp. 241–52. For

some brief remarks on Comenius's Lullism see Carreras y Artau, *Filosofia cristiana*, cit., II, p. 299.

12. See Jan Amos Comenius, *Philosophiae prodromus et conatuum pansophicorum dilucidatio. Accedunt didactica dissertatio de sermonis latini studio perfecte absolvendo, aliaque eiusdem* (Leiden, 1644), pp. 120–2. The first edition of this work was published in London in 1639. I have also seen an edition published in 1644 in the Bibliotheca Angelica (SS.10.90) which is bound together with the *Faber fortunae sive ars consulendi sibi ipsi itemque regulae vitae sapientis* (Amsterdam, 1657).

13. Jan Amos Comenius, *Orbis sensualis picti pars prima. Hoc est: omnium principalium in mundo rerum et in vita actionum pictura et nomenclatura, cum titulorum iuxta atque vocabulorum indice* (Nuremberg, 1746; first edition, 1658). See esp. the preface.

14. See Comenius, *Orbis sensualis*, preface and pp. 4–5.

15. The text of the *Dissertatio didactica de sermonis latini studio* in *Pansophiae prodromus*, pp. 173–224. For the temple of Christian *pansophia* see pp. 122–65: 'Pansophiae christianae templum ad ipsius supremi Architecti Onnipotentis Dei ideas, normas, legesque istruendum, et usibus Catholicae Iesu Christi Ecclesiae, ex omnibus gentibus, tribubus, populis et linguis collectae et colligendae consecrandum.' Cf. also Jan Amos Comenius, *Pansophiae Diatyposis iconographica* (Amsterdam 1654).

16. See Comenius, *Pansophiae prodromus*, pp. 132–6, and Eugenio Garin, *L'educazione in Europa*, p. 249.

17. See Comenius, *Pansophiae prodromus*, p. 41: 'Quas adhuc vidi Encyclopaedias etiam ordinatissimas similiores visae sunt catenae annulis multis eleganter contextae, quam automato rotulis artificiose ad motum compositio et seipsum circumagente; et lignorum strui, magna quadam cura et ordine eleganti dispositae similiores, quam arbori e radicibus propriis assurgenti spiritus innati virtute se in ramos et frondes explicanti, et fructus edenti.'

18. Comenius, *Pansophiae prodromus*, pp. 21, 41–2, 136.

19. Comenius, *Pansophiae prodromus*, pp. 4, 24–5, 78, 85. On the coincidence of the *Janua linguarum* and the encyclopaedia see J. A. Comenius, *Janua linguarum reserata aurea* (London, 1640, first edition London, 1631), preface to the *Eruditionis scholasticae artium rerum et linguarum ornamenta exhibens* (Nuremburg, 1659), p. 5.

20. Comenius, *Pansophiae prodromus*, p. 67: 'Eadem proinde sunt rerum rationes, nec differunt, nisi existendi forma: quia in Deo sunt ut in Archetypo, in natura ut in Ectypo, in arte ut in Antitypo.'

21. Comenius, *Pansophiae prodromus*, p. 86.

22. Comenius, *Pansophiae prodromus*, pp. 67, 55–6. But see also Jan Amos Comenius, *Janua rerum reserata hoc est sapientia prima (quam vulgo metaphysicam vocant) ita mentibus hominum adaptata ut per eam in totum rerum ambitum omnemque interiorem rerum ordinem et in omnes intimas rebus coeternas veritates prospectus pateas catholicus simulque et eadem omnium humanarum cogitationum, sermonum, operum fons et scaturigo, formaque et norma esse appareat* (1681).

23. Comenius, *Pansophiae prodromus*, p. 44: 'Cederent etiam non invitae tam claro lumini errorum tenebrae et hominibus facilius cessarent dissidia, lites, bella quibus se nunc conficit mundus.'

24. R. L. Sieur de Vassi, *Le Fondement de l'artifice universel … sur lequel on peut appuyer le moyen de pervenir à l'Encyclopedie ou universalité des sciences par un ordre méthodique beaucoup plus prompte et vrayment plus facile qu'aucun autre qui soit communement receu* (Paris: Antoine Champenois, 1632).

25. The work was published in Paris by D. Langleus in 1628. I have used the edition of 1647. Also by Frey are the *Compendium medicinae* published in 1646 and the *Omnis homo item amor et amicus, item physiognomia chiromantia oneiromantia* (Paris, 1630). For these last two writings and the panegyric composed by Gaffarel (*Lacrimae sacrae in obitum Iani Caecilii Frey medici*, Paris 1631) see Thorndike, *History of Magic and Experimental Science*, VIII, pp. 456–7, 472–3. See also the *Universae philosophiae compendium luculentissimum, ad mentem et methodum Aristotelis concinnatum* (Paris 1633).

26. Janius Caecilius Frey, *Opera quae reperiri potuerunt in unum corpus collecta*, 2 vols. (Paris: J. Gesslin, 1645–6).

27. Frey, *Opera*, p. 527. For his treatment of the traditional motifs of Ciceronian mnemotechnics see pp. 443–50.

28. Ivo de Paris's *Digestum sapientiae, in quo habetur scientiarum omnium rerum divinarum atque humanarum nexus et ad prima principia reductio*, was published in Paris in 1648 and 1650. Another, better known, edition was published in Lyons in 1672. See Carreras y Artau, *Filosofia cristiana*, II, pp. 297–8. Julius Pacius, *L'Art de Raymond Lullius esclaircy … divisé en IV livres ou est enseigné une méthode qui fournit grand nombre de termes universels d'attributs, de propositions et d'argumens par le moyen desquels on peut discourir sur tous sujets* (Paris, 1619); *Artis lullianae emendatae libri IV* (Naples, 1631). On the great Aristotelian commentary – *In Porphyrii Isagogen et Aristotelis Organum commentarius analyticus* (Orleans, 1605), see Giorgio Colli *Organon / Aristotele; introduzione,*

traduzione e note di Giorgio Colli, Classici della filosofia, 1 (Turin: Einaudi, 1955), p. xxv.

29. P. Sebastian Izquierdo, *Pharus scientiarum ubi quidquid ad cognitionem humanum humanitus acquisibilem pertinet, ubertim iuxta atque succincte pertractatur* (Lyons, 1659).

30. On Kircher see Carreras y Artau, *Filosofía cristiana,* II, p. 309–13; Thorndike, *History of Magic and Experimental Science,* VII, pp. 567–8; Louis Couturat, *La Logique du Leibniz* (Paris: Felix Alcan, 1901), pp. 541–3; Paul Friedlander, 'Athanasius Kircher und Leibniz. Ein Beitrag zur Geschichte der Polyhistorie im XVII Jahrhunderts', in *Atti della Pontifica Accademmia romana di archeologia* (Rendiconti, 1937), pp. 229–247.

31. Athanasius Kircher, *Mundus subterraneus in XII libros digestus, quo divinum subterrestris mundi opificium ... universae denique naturae majestas et divitiae summa rerum varietate exponuntur,* 2 vols. (Amsterdam, Joannnem Janssonium et Elizeum Weyerstraten, 1664–5); *Arithmologia sive de abditis numerorum mysteriis* (Rome, 1665).

32. Athanasius Kircher, *Ars magna sciendi in XII libros digesta, qua nova et universali methodo per artificiosum combinationum contextum de omni re proposita plurimis et prope infinitis rationibus disputari omniumque summaria quaedam cognitio comparari potest,* 2 vols. (Amsterdam, 1669).

33. On the hypothesis that the Jesuits took a position in favour of magic rather than accept the new science, see Thorndike, *History of Magic and Experimental Science,* VII, pp. 577–8.

34. Caspar Knittel SJ, *Via regia ad omnes scientias et artes, hoc est ars universalis scientiarum omnium artiumque arcana facilius penetrandi et de quocunque proposito themate expeditius disserendi* (Prague, 1687), but see also the *Cosmographia elementaris* (Nuremberg, 1674).

35. Morhof, *Polyhistor literarius,* I, p. 358.

36. I have used two volumes of this work: *Bisterfeldus redivivus seu operum Joh. H. Bisterfieldi ... tomus primus-secundus* (The Hague: A. Vlacq, 1661). The first volume contains: *Alphabeti philosophici libri tres* (pp. 1–132); *Aphorismi physici* (pp. 133–190); *Sciagraphia Analyseos* (pp. 191–211); *Parallelismus analyseos grammaticae et logicae* (pp. 212–43); *Artificium definendi catholicum* (pp. 1–104); *Sciagraphia symbioticae* (pp. 3–144). The second volume contains *Logica disputandi* (pp. 1–451); *De puritate, ornatu et copia linguae latinae* (pp. 1–26); *Ars disputandi* (pp. 27–33); *Ars combinatoria* (pp. 34–6); *Ars reducendorum terminorum ad disciplinas liberales technologia* (pp. 37–41); *Ars seu canones de reductione ad praedicamenta* (pp. 42–6); *Denarius didacticus seu decem aphorismi bene*

discendi (pp. 47–9); *Didactica sacra* (pp. 50–3); *Usus lexici* (pp. 54–64). I have also used *Phosphorus catholicus, seu ars meditandi epitome cui subjunctum est consilium de studiis feliciter instituendis* (Leiden: H. Verbiest, 1657).

37. Bisterfeld, *Alphabeti philosophici libri tres*, I, p. 1

38. See *Alphabeti philosophici libri tres*, I, p. 53: 'Termini transcendentales sunt primae universae encyclopaedia radices'; *Sciagraphia analyseos*, I, p. 191: 'Analysis est accuratum de textu seu dissertatione in sua principia resoluto iudicium. Totuplex sit analysis quotuplex in textu adhibita fuit genesis, idque ordine retrogrado. Analysis autem utpote praxis frugalem compendiorum ac tabularum cognitionem praesupponit'; *Alphabeti philosophici*, I, p. 110: 'Praxis logica est vel simplicium combinatio vocaturque Genesis, vel combinatorum reductio vocaturque analysis, vel denique mixta estque vel Genesis-analysis vel Analysis-genesis cuius varietas est infinita'; *Artificium definiendi*, I, pp. 1–2: 'Artificium definiendi catholicum est quod docet modum omnium encyclopaediae terminorum definitiones accurate inveniendi ac diiudicandi … Scopus huius artificii est foelix id est facilis, solida ac practica, et quoad in hac vita fieri potest, certa perfectaque universa encyclopaediae cognitio … Definitiones sunt omnis geneseos et analyseos claves et normae. Omnis enim mentis et entis, cum reductionem tum deductionem complectuntur, si singula definitionum verba in primos terminos per scalam descendentem et ascendentem resolvantur, sic enim erunt omnigenae reductionis claves, argumentorum compendia, propositionum fontes, syllogismorum et methodorum lumina.'

39. On the definitions see *Artificium*, I, esp. pp. 3–6. On the tables see pp. 11–12, 15: 'Tabulae fundamentales (quae sunt certae terminorum homogeanorum subordinationes et coordinationes) sunt faciles, sed accuratae totius mundi totiusque encyclopaediae repraesentationes … Universa illa inductio ac structura tabularum nititur panharmonia tum rerum tum disciplinarum … Tabula primitiva et prima simplicissima universalissima adeoque brevissima totius mundi totiusque encyclopaediae repraesentatio … eam vocabimus catholicam.'

40. *Logica*, II, p. 325.

41. *Artificium definiendi*, p. 1; *Alphabetici philosophici libri tres*, I, p. 110; *Logica*, II, pp. 330–1.

VII The Construction of a Universal Language

1. John Wilkins, *An Essay Towards a Real Character and a Philosophical Language. (An alphabetical dictionary, wherein all English words ... are either referred to their places in the Philosophical tables, or explained by such words as are in those Tables)* (London, 1668), p. 13. On John Wilkins, Bishop of Chester and member of the Royal Society, author of the celebrated *The Discovery of a World in the Moone* (1638) see Niceron, *Mémoires*, IV, pp. 129–34. Amongst the most important studies are: Patrick Arkley Wright Henderson, *The Life and Times of John Wilkins, Warden of Wadham College* (London, 1910), Dorothy Stimson, 'Dr Wilkins and the Royal Society', *Journal of Modern History*, 1931, pp. 539–63; Richard Foster Jones, 'Science and language in England of the mid-seventeenth century', *Journal of English and Germanic Philology*, 31:3 (1932), pp. 315–21, later reprinted in Richard Foster-Jones *et al.*, *The Seventeenth Century. Studies in the History of English Renaissance Thought and Literature from Bacon to Pope* (Stanford: Stanford University Press, 1951), pp. 143–60; E. N. da C. Andrade, 'The Real Character of Bishop Wilkins', *Annals of Science*, 1:1 (1936), pp. 4–12; Francis Christensen, 'John Wilkins and the Royal Society's reform of prose style', *Modern Language Quarterly*, 7:2–3 (1946) pp. 179–87 and 279–90; Rosemary Hildegarde Syfret, 'The origins of the Royal Society', in *Notes and Records of the Royal Society of London*, 5:1 (1948), pp. 75–137; Clark Emery, 'John Wilkins' universal language', *Isis*, 38:3 (1948), pp. 174–85; Benjamin de Mott, 'Comenius and the Real Character in England', *Proceedings of the Modern Language Association of America*, 70:5 (1955), pp. 1068–81; 'Science versus mnemonics: notes on John Ray, and on John Wilkins' *Essay towards a Real Character, and a Philosophical Language*', *Isis*, 48:1 (1957), pp. 1–12; There are also a few interesting observations in Charles Kay Ogden and Ivor Armstrong Richards's *The Meaning of Meaning: A Study of the Influence of Language upon Thought and Science* (London, 1923, repr. 1948), pp. 40–4. Extracts from Wilkins's Essay were printed in Friedrich Heinrich Hermann Techmer, *Beiträge zur Geschichte der französischen und englischen Phonetik und Phonographie* (Heilbronn, 1889).

2. See Francis Bacon, *The Works of Francis Bacon*, ed. James Spedding, Robert Leslie Ellis and Douglas Denon Heath, 14 vols. (London, 1857–74), *De dignitate et augmentis scientiarum*, I, pp. 651–3; *Advancement of Learning*, III, 399–400.

3. On universal languages in seventeenth-century England see Otto Viktor Conrad Wilhelm Funke, *Zum Weltsprachenproblem in England im 17 Jahrhunderts: George Dalgarno's 'Ars Signorum', 1661, und J. Wilkins 'Essay towards a Real Character and a Philosophical Language', 1668* (Heidelberg, 1929) and Louis Couturat and Léopold Leau, *Histoire de la langue universelle* (Paris 1907), pp. 11–28.

4. See also Richard Foster Jones, 'Science and English prose-style in the third quarter of the seventeenth century', *Proceedings of the Modern Language Association of America*, 45:4 (1930), pp. 978–1009, and 'Science and criticism in the neoclassical age of English literature', *Journal of the History of Ideas*, 1:4 (1940), pp. 381–412, reprinted in Jones, *The Seventeenth Century*, pp. 41–74 and 75–110.

5. Francis Bacon, *Redargutio philosophiarum*, in *Works*, III, p. 581. On the 'idols of the marketplace' (*idola fori*) see *The Advancement of Learning*, III, pp. 396–7, *Cogitata et visa*, III, p. 599 and the *Novum organum*, I, pp. 159–160, 164, 170–171.

6. See Morris William Croll, '"Attic prose" in the seventeenth century', *Studies in Philology*, 18:2 (1921), pp. 79–128; 'Attic Prose: Lipsius, Montaigne, Bacon', in *Schelling Anniversary Papers. By his former pupils* (New York, 1923) and 'The Baroque Style of Prose', in Kemp Malone and Martin B. Ruud (eds.), *Studies in English Philology: A Miscellany in Honour of F. Klaeber* (Minneapolis, 1929).

7. John Webster, *Academiarum Examen: or, the Examination of Academies: Wherein is discussed and examined the matter, method, and customes of academick and scholastick learning, and the insufficiency thereof discovered and laid open; as also some expedients proposed for the reforming of schools, etc.* (London, 1654), pp. 21–2, 24, 88, cit. Jones, *The Seventeenth Century*, pp. 82, 147–8.

8. Thomas Birch (ed.), *The Works of the Honourable Robert Boyle ... to which is prefixed the life of the author*, 6 vols. (London, 1772), I, pp. 11, 29–30; II, 92, 136; III, pp. 2, 512; IV, p. 365; V, pp. 54, 229.

9. Joshua Childrey, *Britannia Baconica, or The Natural Rarities of England, Scotland, & Wales. According as they are to be found in every Shire. Historically related, according to the Precepts of the Lord Bacon* (London, 1669), 'The Preface to the Reader', sig. B3v.

10. Thomas Sprat, *The History of the Royal Society* of London (London, 1667), pp. 95–115. See Harold Fisch and Harold W. Jones, 'Bacon's influence on Sprat's *History of the Royal Society*', *Modern Language Quarterly*, 12:4 (1951), pp. 399–406.

11. George Thomson, Μισοκυμίαζ ελεγοζ *or a Check Given to the*

Insolent Garrulity of H. Stubbe: in Vindication of my Lord Bacon and the author, with an assertion of experimental philosophy (London, 1671), pp. 31, 40–41, cit. Jones, *The Seventeenth Century*, p. 145.

12. Sprat, *History of the Royal Society*, p. 113.

13. Seth Ward, *Vindiciae Academiarum. Containing, some briefe animadversiones upon Mr Websters book, stiled, the Examination of Academies* (Oxford, 1654), pp. 20–1, cit. Jones, *The Seventeenth Century*, p. 151–3.

14. *The Petty Papers. Some unpublished writings ... edited from the Bowood Papers by the Marquis of Landsdowne*, 2 vols. (London, 1927), I, pp. 150–1 and *Petty-Southwell Correspondence: 1676–1687*, edited from the Bowood Papers by the Marquis of Landsdowne (London, 1928), p. 324. But see also the *Advice to Hartlib* (London, 1648), pp. 5 et seq. in which he deals with the question of real characters.

15. Robert Boyle to Samuel Hartlib, 19 March 1647, *Works*, I, p. 22.

16. The *De algebra tractatus historicus et practicus eiusdem origines et progressus varios ostendens* is contained in the second volume of Wallis's *Opera mathematica*, 3 vols., (Oxford, 1695). On the characters of Viète and Oughtred see vol. II, pp. 69–73. For the references to writing in the *Mathesis universalis, sive arithmeticum opus integrum tum philologice tum mathematice traditum* see vol. I, pp. 47 et seq. For the attack on Hobbes see vol. I, p. 361 (on this and other anti-Hobbesian writings by Wallis see Gaston Sortais, *La Philosophie moderne depuis Bacon jusqu'à Leibniz*, Etudes historiques, 2 vols. (Paris, 1922), II, pp. 289–92.). On memory see the chapter of *De algebra* (II, pp. 448–50) entitled 'De viribus memoriae satis intentae, experimentum'. The first edition of the *Grammatica linguae anglicanae cui praefigitur de loquela sive sonorum formatione tractatus grammatico-physicus* is that of 1653. I have seen the fourth edition (Oxford, 1674). On Wallis as a mathematician see esp. Joseph Frederick Scott, *The Mathematical Work of John Wallis* (London, 1938), his work on grammar has been studied by Martin Lehnert, *Die Grammatik des englischen Sprachmeisters John Wallis, 1616–1703* (Breslau, 1936).

17. See Dorothy L. Stimson, 'Comenius and the Invisible College', *Isis*, 23:2 (1935), pp. 373–88, and idem, *Scientists and Amateurs. A History of the Royal Society* (New York: Henry Schumann, 1948); Benjamin de Mott, 'Comenius and the real character in England' and Matthew Spinka, *John Amos Comenius, that Incomparable Moravian* (Chicago, 1943), pp. 72–5

18. Henry Edmundson, *Lingua Linguarum. The natural language of languages, in a vocabulary ... contrived and built upon analogy* (London, 1655).

19. Jan Amos Comenius, *Vita lucis*, trans. Ernest Trafford Campagnac, *The Way of Light of Comenius* (London, 1938), cap XIX, sections 16 and 19, pp. 186, 189.

20. See Johann Valentine Andreae, *Fama fraternitatis* (Frankfurt-am-Main, 1616), pp. 3, 12–13. See Benjamin de Mott, 'Comenius and the real character', p. 1070 and Jakob Boehme's *Sämmtliche Werke*, ed. K. W. Scheibler, 6 vols. (Leipzig, 1831–46, repr. 1922), IV, pp. 83 et seq.

21. *The Petty Papers*, I, p. 150. George Dalgarno, *Ars signorum* in Thomas Maitland (ed.), *The Works of George Dalgarno of Aberdeen* (Edinburgh, 1834), pp. 22–3.

22. For the passage of Sprat cited in the text see *History of the Royal Society*, p. 63. Samuel Hartlib also saw religious unity as one of the primary objectives of scientific organization. On this see George Henry Turnbull, *Samuel Hartlib: A Sketch of his Life and his Relations to J. A. Comenius* (London, 1920), *passim*, and idem, *Hartlib, Dury, Comenius. Gleanings from Hartlib's Papers* (Liverpool: Liverpool University Press, 1947), p. 75.

23. Wilkins's *Essay* is divided into four parts: *Prolegomena*; *Universal Philosophy*; *Philosophycal grammar*; *Real character and philosophical language*. The full title of Dalgarno's work is: *Ars signorum: vulgo character universalis et lingua philosophica, qua potuerunt homines diversissimorum idiomatum spatio duarum septimanarum omnia animi sua sensa non minus intelligibiliter, sive scrivendo sive loquendo, mutuo communicare, quam linguis propriis vernaculis. Praeterea hinc etiam potuerunt iuvenes philosophiae principia et veram logices praxin citius et facilius multo imbibere quam ex vulgaribus philosophorum scriptis* (London, 1661).

24. Wilkins, *Essay*, 'To the Reader', and p. 414.

25. Wilkins, *Essay*, p. 20: 'As men do generally agree in the same Principle of Reason, so do they likewise agree in the same *Internal Notion* or *Apprehension of things*. The *External Expression* of these Mental notions, whereby men communicate their thoughts to one another, is either to the *Ear*, or to the *Eye*. To the *Ear* by *Sounds*, and more particularly by Articulate *Voice* and *Words*. To the *Eye* by any thing that is *visible*, Motion, Light, Colour, Figure; and more particularly by *Writing*. That *conceit* which men have in their minds concerning a Horse or Tree, is the Notion or *mental Image* of that Beast, or natural thing, of such a nature, shape and use. The *Names* given to these in several Languages, are such arbitrary *sounds* or *words*, as Nations of men have agreed upon, either casually or designedly, to express their Mental notions of them. The *Written word* is the figure

or picture of that Sound. So that if men should generally consent upon the same way or manner of expression, as they do agree in the same *Notion*, we should then be freed from that Curse in the Confusion of Tongues, with all the unhappy consequences of it.' (The emphases are in the original text.)

26. On this see Wilkins, *Essay*, pp. 2–3, 6–9, 17. On grammar see p. 19: '[The] very Art by which Language should be regulated, viz. *Grammar*, is of much *later* invention *then Languages themselves*, being adapted to what was already in being, rather then the rule of making it so.' For the quotation from Dalgarno see *Didascalcophus, or Deaf and Dumb Man's Tutor to which is added a Discourse on the Nature and number of Double Consonants* (Oxford, 1680), preface, cit. Funke, *Weltsprachenproblem*, p. 16.

27. Wilkins, *Essay*, p. 454.

28. Dalgarno, *Ars signorum*, p. 45.

29. Wilkins, *Essay*, 'Epistle dedicatory', sig. br.

30. On 'Notes' and Egyptian hieroglyphs see Wilkins, *Essay*, pp. 12–13. Wilkins alludes to Bacon's discussion of real characters, when he observes 'that such a Real character is possible hath been reckoned by Learned men amongst the *Desiderata*', and also makes reference to Bacon and Isaac Vossius's discussions of Chinese characters: 'The Inhabitants of that large Kingdom, many of them of different Tongues, do communicate with one another, every one understanding this common Character, and reading in his own Language.'

31. On the alphabets, see Wilkins, *Essay*, pp. 12–15, and on the differentiation of characters and their functions see pp. 385–6.

32. John Wilkins, *Mercury or the Secret and Swift Messenger: Shewing, How a Man may with Privacy and Speed communicate His Thoughts to a Friend at any Distance* (London, 1641), pp. 109 et seq.

33. Emery, 'Wilkins' universal language', p. 175.

34. Wilkins, *Essay*, pp. 20–2 and the 'Epistle Dedicatory', *passim*.

35. Wilkins, *Essay*, pp. 455 et seq.: 'An Alphabetical Dictionary, Wherein all English words According to their various significations, Are either referred to their Places in the Philosophical Tables, Or explained by such Words as are in those Tables.'

36. Wilkins, *Essay*, pp. 23–4. For the exposition which follows see also pp. 60 et seq., pp. 415 et seq. and the summary of the various parts of the work, pp. 1 et seq.

37. Wilkins, *Essay*, pp. 395–413.

38. Louis Couturat, *Opuscules et fragments inédits de Leibniz* (Paris, 1903), pp. 437–510.

39. Wilkins, *Essay*, p. 21.
40. Wilkins, *Essay*, 'Epistle dedicatory', sig. [a2]r.
41. Wilkins, *Essay*, p. 21.
42. De Mott, 'Science versus mnemonics', pp. 8–9.
43. See Giulio Camillo detto Delmineo, *Tutte le opere*, 2 vols. (Venice, 1584), II, p. 212.
44. 'Quotus quisque enim est exercitatissimorum Botanicorum; qui omnes vires est appellationes, in tanta Authorum de singulis istis discrepantia, cognitas habeat; aut vulgata ediscentia imprimere memoria, inque ea conservare queat? ... [Q]uorum ope quidvis ... recordari et successive recitare liceat: perinde, uti catena aurea, aliquot mille articulis constante, moto, primo articulo una moventur caeteri omnes; etiamsi vel nolimus caeteros commoveri.' Cyprian Kinner to Samuel Hartlib, 27 June 1647, cit. Benjamin de Mott, 'The sources and development of John Wilkins' Philosophical Language', *Journal of English and German Philology*, 57:1 (1958), pp. 1–13 (11–13).
45. Wilkins, *Essay*, pp. 31, 385, 453–4.
46. Birch, *Works of the Honourable Robert Boyle*, VI, p. 339.
47. Wilkins, *Essay*, 'The epistle dedicatory', sig. av.
48. Emery, 'John Wilkins' universal language', p. 176.
49. Wilkins, *Essay*, p. 289.
50. See the letter of John Wilkins to Francis Willoughby in William Derham (ed.), *Philosophical Letters between ... Mr Ray and several of his ... Correspondents* (London, 1718), p. 366. The Wilkins project for a universal language was circulating from about 1647. On the first contacts of Wilkins with Ray and Willoughby see de Mott, 'Science versus mnemonics', p. 4. On the scientific work of John Ray (1628–1705) who was known as the 'English Pliny' and was the first to use the term 'species' in botanical classification see Emile Guyénot, *Les Sciences de la vie au XVIIe and XVIIIe siècle. L'ideé d'évolution* (Paris, 1941), pp. 359 et seq., and Charles Earle Raven, *John Ray, Naturalist* (Cambridge: Cambridge University Press, 1942), and George Louis Buffon, *Storia naturale: primo discorso: sulla maniera di studiare la storia naturale: secondo discorso: storia e teoria della terra*, ed. and trans. Marcella Renzoni (Turin: P. Boringhieri, 1959), pp. 479, 483, 490. Ray's famous classificatory system presented in his *Methodus plantarum nova* (1682), is an elaborate reworking of the basic methodical classification which was published in Wilkins's Essay. On the joint work of Ray and Francis Willoughby (1635–72) author of *Ornithologia* (1657), *Historia piscium* (1686) and *Historia insectorum* (1710), see Emile

Guyénot, 'Biologie humaine et animale', in René Taton (ed.), *Histoire générale des sciences*, 3 vols. (Paris: Presses Universitaires de France, 1957–64), II, p. 362.

51. Ray's translation was finished but not published. See George Scott (ed.), *Select Remains of the Learned John Ray by the Late William Derham* (London, 1760), p. 23.

52. John Ray to Dr Lister, 7 May 1669, in Edwin Lankester (ed.), *The Correspondence of John Ray, consisting of selections from the philosophical letters published by Dr Derham, and original letters of J. Ray, in the collection of the British Museum* (London, 1848), pp. 41–2: 'Praeterea in iis ordinandis coactus sum non naturae ductum sequi, sed ad autoris methodum praescriptum plantas accommodare, quae exegit ut herbas in tres turmas seu tria genera quamproxime aequalia distribuerem, singulas deinde turmas in novem differentias illi dictas h. e. genera subalterna dividerem, ita tamen ut singulis differentiis subordinatae plantae certum numerum non excederunt … Quae jam spes est methodum hanc absolutam fore et non potius imperfectissimam et absurdam? qualem eam ipse libenter et ingenue agnosco, non tam existimationi meae quam veritati studens.' On the significance of these reservations see de Mott, 'Science versus mnemonics', pp. 5 et seq.

53. Wilkins, *Essay*, p. 22.

54. Renzoni (ed.), *Storia naturale*, pp. 22–3.

55. Michel Adanson, *Familles des plantes,* 2 vols, (Paris, 1763), I, p. xcv.

56. Bernard de Fontenelle, *Eloge de Tournefort* (Paris, 1708) p. 147, cit., Renzoni, *Storia naturale*, pp. 478, 483.

57. Denis Diderot and Jean le Rond d'Alembert, *Encyclopédie, ou Dictionnaire raisonné des sciences, des arts et des metiers, par une societé de gens de lettres*, 17 vols. (Paris, 1751–65), II, 'Botanique', pp. 340–5 (342): 'Une seule méthod suffisoit pour la nomenclature; il ne s'agit que de se faire une sorte de mémoire artificielle pour retenir l'ideé & le nom de chaque plante, parce que leur nombre est trop grand pour se passer de ce secours: pour cela toute méthode est bonne.'

58. Diderot and d'Alembert, *Encyclopédie*, VII, 'Histoire naturelle', pp. 225–30 (230): 'Ces divisions méthodiques soulagent la mémoire, & semblent debrouiller le cahos que forment les objets de la nature, lorsqu'on les regarde confusement: mais il ne faut jamais oublier que ces systèmes ne sont fondés que sur les conventions arbitraires des hommes; qu'ils ne sont pas d'accord avec les lois invariables de la nature.'

59. René Descartes to Marin Mersenne, 20 November 1629 published in

Claude Clerselier (ed.), *Lettres de Mr Descartes. Où sont traittées les plus belles questions de la morale, de la physique, de la médecine, & des mathematiques*, 3 vols. (Paris, 1657), I, pp. 498–502, reprinted in Paul Tannery and Cornelis de Waard (eds.), *Correspondance du P. Marin Mersenne, religieux minime* (Paris: Press Universitaires de France, 1945–), II, pp. 323–9.

60. *Correspondance du Marin Mersenne*, I, p. 328: 'et ce qui est le principal, qui aideroit au jugement, luy representant si distinctement toutes choses, qu'il luy seroit presque impossible de se tromper; au lieu que tout au rebours, les mots que nous avons n'ont quasi que des significations confuses, ausquelles l'esprit des hommes s'estant accoutumé de longue main, cela est cause qu'il n'entend presque rien parfaitement.'

61. Descartes, *Oeuvres*, I, pp. 80–2.

62. Couturat, *Opuscules et fragments inédits de Leibniz*, pp. 27–8.

VIII THE SOURCES OF LEIBNIZ'S UNIVERSAL CHARACTER

1. Carl Immanuel Gerhardt, *Die philosophischen Schriften von G. G. Leibniz*, 7 vols. (Berlin, 1875–90), VII, pp. 5–6, 9, 16–17 (this edition will hereafter be referred to as G immediately followed by the number of the volume and the pages).

2. For his relationship with Bisterfeld and the presence of mystical-Pythagorean ideas in Leibniz's work see Willy Kabitz, *Die Philosophie der jungen Leibniz. Untersuchungen zur Entwicklungsgeschichte seines Systems* (Heidelberg, 1909); for his relations to pansophia see: *Leibniz' Verhältnis zur Renaissance im allgemeinen und zu Nizolius im besonderen* (Bonn, 1912); for his relations with Alsted and Henry More see Dietrich Mahnke, 'Leibnizens Synthese von Universalmathematik und Individual Metaphysik', *Jahrbuch für Philosophie und phänomenologische Forschung* (1925), pp. 305–612; Walter Feilchenfeld, *Leibniz und Henry More* (Berlin, 1923).

3. G. VII, 11; Louis Couturat, *Opuscules et fragments inédits de Leibniz* (Paris, 1903), pp. 430, 435 (hereafter we will refer to this work with the abbreviation *Op.* followed by the page number); Gottfried Wilhelm Leibniz, *Textes inédites publiés et annotés par Gaston Grua*, 2 vols. (Paris, 1948), pp. 542–5 (hereafter we will refer to this work with the abbreviation *Grua* followed by the page number).

4. See *Op.* 29–30; 536–7; G, IV, 62, 64, 70.

5. Louis Couturat, *La Logique de Leibniz d'après des documents inédits*

(Paris, 1901), Appendix II and see esp. pp. 458–9 (hereafter refered to by the abbreviation 'Couturat').

6. Caspar Schott, *Technica curiosa, sive mirabilia artis* (Nuremberg, 1664).

7. G. IV, 70–1 and cf. Yvon Belaval, *Pour connaître la pensée de Leibniz* (Paris: Bordas, 1952), pp. 41–2; Couturat, pp. 35–40; for a fuller exposition see Francesco Barone, *Logica formale e logica transcendentale da Leibniz a Kant* (Turin, 1957), pp. 5 et seq.

8. Couturat, p. 51.

9. G. IV, 72 and see Schott, *Technica curiosa,* cit., pp. 484–505. The author of *Arithmeticus nomenclator mundi* has now been identified as the Jesuit Pedro Bermundo or Vermundo (see Albert Heinekamp, 'Ars Characteristica und natürliche Sprache bei Leibniz', *Tijdschrift voor filosofie,* 34:3 (1972), pp. 446–88).

10. G. IV, 73.

11. G. IV, 72–3.

12. G. VII, 12; Couturat, note III.

13. G. VII, 21, 204.

14. G. VII, 13.

15. G. VII, 25.

16. G.VII, 26

17. G.VII, 13.

18. G. VII, 13.

19. G. VII, 26.

20. G. VII, 23, 205 and cf. Grua, pp. 263–4.

21. G. VII, 13; *Op.* 277–9.

22. Couturat, pp. 62–3.

23. *Op.* 278.

24. On these arguments see Couturat, pp. 66 et seq., and by the same author, *Histoire de la langue universelle* (Paris, 1907), pp. 11–28. For a reprisal of these Leibnizian themes by Couturat see 'Des rapports de la logique et de la linguistique dans le problème de la langue internationale', in *Atti del IV Congresso internazionale di filosofia* (Bologna, 1911), II.

25. G. VII, 40.

26. On the demonstrative character of the Leibnizian encyclopaedia see the useful account of Robert McRae, 'Unity of the sciences: Bacon, Descartes, Leibniz', *Journal of the History of Ideas,* 18:1 (1957), pp. 27–48.

27. Louis Dutens, *G. G. Leibnitii Opera omnia,* 6 vols. (Geneva, 1768), III, pp. 156 et seq.

28. *Op.* 561 and see Carreras y Artau, *Filosofia cristiana,* II, p. 321.

29. G. IV, 62; G. VII, 67; *Cogitata quaedam de ratione perficiendi et emendandi Encyclopaediam Alstedii* in Dutens, *Leibnitii Opera*, V, p. 183, cf. *Op.* 354–5.
30. See Carrera y Artau, *Filosofía cristiana*, II, p. 320; Couturat, pp. 571–3; *Iudicium de scriptis comenianis* in Dutens, *Leibnitii Opera*, V, pp. 181–2.
31. *Op.* 27–8.
32. G. III, 216.
33. Barone, *Logica formale e logica transcendentale*, p. 24.
34. *Op.* 437–510.
35. Hannover, MS Phil. VI.19, ff. 5r.–v.: '*Arcanum*: qua ratione omnes et singulos numeros, praesertim eos quorum usus est in chronologia, atque aliorum infinitorum usus est in chronologia, atque aliorum infinitorum, memoriae mandare, eorum citra omnem ingenii cruciatum recordari, ac nunquam oblivisci possis, ne dicam, ulteriora et infinita queas deducere. Si quis multos numeros citra cruciatum memoriae atque ingenii memoriae cupit, omnino opus est ut subsidio aliquo utaris. Sunt qui varie rem tentarunt, absque tamen singulari effectu ac successu, donec non adeo pridem hunc modum quispiam excogitando invenerit, multis rationibus ipsaque experientia reddiderit probatum. Alphabeti elementa sunt XXIV: haec dividuntur in vocales et consonantes. Vocales hac in re vicariam nobis tantum praebent utilitatem, consonantes vero primariam./ Consonantes autem sunt hae: B C D F G K L M N P Q R S T, his adiungatur W Z V. Numeros habemus hos: 1 2 3 4 5 6 7 8 9 0. Si plures dantur numeri, ex hisce componuntur, ut ex 1 et 2 fiunt 12 quemadmodum res est plana. Iam vero nihil memoriam adeo torquet quam res referta numeris, quos tamen scire memoriaque comprehendere maximi interest itaque hocce subsidii, ut utaris, valde prodest et conducit memoriam. Reduc consonantes istas ita, et puta quod sint numeri, sic facile te extricabis:

   1 2 3 4 5 6 7 8 9 0
   B C F G L M N R S D
   P K V
   W Q
     Z'

36. Hannover, MS Phil. VI. 19, f. 7r.:

   Haec ergo visum est explicare carmine
   facili atque claro, quali utuntur comici.

Nam sic iuvatur memoria nec sensus perit
et simile quiddam vita nobis exhibet.
Qui vult solutam ferre lignorum struem
prohibebit aegre ne quid illi decidat
sed colligatam facile fasciculo geret.
Oratio soluta pariter diffluit
comprehensa versu mens fidelius tenet.

Cf. *Geographi graeci minores*, I, pp. 155 et seq.

37. Hannover, MS Phil. VI. 19, f. 8r.: 'Eos quos in grammatica sua habet
Emmanuel Alvarez Societatis Iesu, ipse Scioppius in Grammatica
philosophica laudat et disci suadet. Ait eum centum et sexaginta
versibus hexametris feliciter complexum omnes regulae de verborum
praeteritis et supinis et omnem prosodiae latinae rationem centum
sexaginta aliis versibus.'

38. Hannover, MS Phil. VI. 19, f. 9r.: 'Hofmani lexicon universale
maxime nominum propriorum utilis liber. Unum desidero: cum non
posset autor ob rerum multitudinem cuncta plenis edisserere, prae-
clare fecisset si ubique indicasset autorem aliquem unde celerior in
studio peti possit.'

39. Hannover, MS Phil. VI. 19, f. 10r.: '*Artificium didacticum.* Semper cognita incognitis miscenda et temperanda sunt ut labor et molestia min-
uantur. Ita optime discimus linguas per parallelismum cum linguis
nobis notis, ita scriptum non satis cognitae lecturae, discendae linguae
causa, sumamus librum familiarem nobis cuius sensa pene memoriter
tenemus ut Novum Testamentum. Hinc etiam si cui musicam docere
possem aut vellem, monstrarem cantiunculas sibi notas posset in
charta exprimere si vereretur oblivisci.'

40. Hannover, MS Phil. VI. 19, f. 11r.: '*Exercitia ingenii.* Ut Rhetores
exercitia habent orationis, Grammatici exercitia styli, ita ego in pueris
exercitia ingenii institui desidero. Exercitia ingenii nec gratiora nec
efficaciora reperiri posse nititur quam ludos ... verba quo ordine tur-
bato iterum recitare ope mnemonices cuiquam facilis, inverso etiam
si placet aut per saltus, historias ab aliis recitatas iterum recitare,
extempore describere proelia, itinera, urbes quorum ipsis via ante
audita, historias ab aliis recitatas resumere et denuo recitare, fingere
preces et iubere ut quis ex duorum disputationibus et concertation-
ibus patrias causas cuiquam implicatas discat facere aut solvere.'

41. Hannover, MS Phil. VI. 19, f. 16r.–v.

42. Hannover, MS Phil. VI. 19, f. 13r.: 'Video eos qui geometrica methodo tractare ... scientias, ut P. Fabrius, Joh. Alph. Borellus, Benedictus Spinosa, R. des Cartes, dum omnia in propositiones minutas divellunt, efficere ut primarias propostiones lateant inter illas minutiores, nec satis animadvertantur, unde saepe quod quaeris difficulter invenies.' Honoré Fabri was a Jesuit father, an anti-Copernican and author of the *Dialoghi physici* (Lyon, 1665). Borelli was a mathematician whose *Euclides restitutus sive prisca geometriae elementa* was published in Rome in 1658.

43. On Schenkel see note 43 in chapter 4.

44. For these references to artificial memory see Dutens, *Leibnitii Opera*, III, pp. 150 et seq.; *Op.* 37; *G.* VII, 82, 84, 476–7. On the mnemonic use of classifications see also the letter to Wagner in *G.* VII, 516–17 and, on his 'palpable' and 'sensible' characters, Grua, pp. 548–9.

45. Gottfried Wilhelm Leibniz, ed. Paul Ritter *et al.*, *Sämtliche Schriften und Briefe herausgegeben von der Preussischen Akademie der Wissenschaften* (Darmstadt, 1923–), I, ii, pp. 167–9.

46. *Introductio ad encyclopaediam arcanam*, in *Op.* 511.

47. *G.* IV, 56. The passage has been emphasized by Kabitz in his *Die philosophie der jungen Leibniz*, cit. p. 26.

48. *G.* VII, 13.

49. *G.* VII, 61,70.

50. Leibniz, *Sämtliche Schriften und Briefe*, VI, i, p. 492.

51. On this passage see Kabitz, *Die philosophie der jungen Leibniz*, p. 36, and Barone, *Logica formale e transcendentale*, p. 8. The letter was published by Trendelenburg in *Historischen Beiträge zur Philosophie*, II, 1855, p. 190.

52. Ivan Jagodinski, *Leibniziana: elementa philosophiae arcanae. De summa rerum* (Kasan, 1913); by the same author see *Leibniziana inedita: confessio philosophi* (Kasan, 1915), Latin text with a facing-page Russian translation.

53. Albert Rivaud, 'Textes inédits de Leibniz publiés par M. Ivan Jagodinsky', *Revue de metaphysique et de morale*, 22:1 (1914), pp. 93–120.

54. Jagodinski, *Leibniziana*, pp. 32, 220.

55. See *G.* I, 61 and *Sämtliche Schriften und Briefe*, II, i, p. 438. On the metaphysical motifs underlying Leibniz's panlogism see Bogumil Jasinowski, *Die analytische Urteilslehre Leibnizens in ihrem Verhältnis zu seiner Metaphysik* (Vienna, 1918). Although he derives most of his ideas from the work of Couturat and Russell, Giulio Preti's *Il*

cristanesimo universale di G. G .Leibniz (Milan: Fratelli Bocca, 1953) reaches some interesting conclusions: 'Leibniz never fully realized his logic, and it remained entangled in serious difficulties because he was unable to completely abandon his original Platonism. The criteria of evidence (immediate intuition of ideas), logical realism (which insists on the actual existence of 'primitive' or 'composite' ideas), and his belief in a formal symbolism which would reproduce the eternal relations which subsist between the ideas in the mind of God, prevented Leibniz from developing his logical intuitions, however congenial they were to him, and despite their subsequent success. In reality, Leibniz created a logic which was always preoccupied with creating an ontology and a metaphysics; but in order to create modern logic, it was necessary to free oneself of all ontological and metaphysical preoccupations and follow a gnoseology (a process which began with Hume and culminated in the neopositivism of the Vienna and Chicago Schools), a path which Leibniz never pursued.' Francesco Barone came to similar conclusions to Preti in his *Logica formali e logica transcendentale*, pp. 8 et seq., where he spoke of a 'fundamental difference' between modern formal logic and the logic of Leibniz, whose work was, he said, 'permeated and underpinned – even in the most modern of his technical inquiries – by the metaphysical ideal of pansophia'. Preti also emphasized the 'Platonic-Pythagorean conception of forms which is the basis of [Leibniz's] logical schemes'. Antonio Corsano in his *G. W. Leibniz* (Naples: Libreria Scientifica Editrice, 1952) reached very different conclusions: examining the influence of Suarez on Leibniz Corsano argued that Leibniz's works were primarily inspired by a 'profound and almost total adherence to nominalism'. I find it difficult to agree with this argument, because I do not share Corsano's belief that Leibniz's use of 'the archaic and decrepit motifs of Platonic-Pythagorean mysticism' was solely due to Leibniz being 'constrained to bow down in homage to the opinions of his masters and to speak in a language which was accessible to the backward scientific and philosophical culture of the German baroque'. See Antonio Corsano, in 'Schede', *Rivista critica di storia della filosofia*, 12:4 (1957), pp. 493–5, 495. I hope that this chapter has demonstrated that the persistence of these 'archaic' ideas into the seventeenth century exerted a considerable influence on Leibniz's work, and are in no way reducible to a kind of academic expedience.

APPENDICES

1. Ramon Lull, *Disputatio Raymundi Christiani et Hamar Saraceni*, 4 vols (Margonza, 1729), IV, p. 45
2. Salvadore Galmés, *Dinamisme de R. Lull* (Mallorca, 1935), p. 47
3. See Alanus, *Doctrinale minus, alias Liber parabolarum magistri Alani* (one of the *auctores octo*) in Migné, *Patrologia Latina*, 210, col. 585 (425D): 'Dentibus atritas bos rursus ruminat herbas/ Ut toties tritae sint alimenta sibi/ Sic documenta tui si vis retinere magistri/ Saepe recorderis quod semel aure capis.'
4. Aristotle, *De memoria et reminscentia*, II, 452a, 28–9
5. On the *multiplicatio et evacuatio figurarum* (multiplication and evacuation of the figures) see *Ars brevis* and *Ars Magna*, ed. Zetzner, pp. 15–16, 278–9.
6. Yates, 'Ciceronian art of memory', p. 888.
7. Tiraboschi, *Storia della letteratura italiana*, V, p. 242.
8. Tocco, *Le opere latine di G. Bruno*, p. 26.
9. See Filippo Luigi Polidori (ed.), *Rosaio della vita. Trattato morale attribuito a Matteo de Corsini e composto nel MCCCLXXIII, ora per la prima volta pubblicato* (Firenze, 1845).
10. Polidori, *Rosaio della vita*, p. 96.
11. Yates,'The Ciceronian art of memory'.
12. Yates,'The Ciceronian art of memory', p. 899.
13. Yates, 'The Ciceronian art of memory', pp. 889–94.
14. Romberch, *Congestum*, pp. 20r., 28r., 29r.
15. Filippo Maria Gesualdo, *Plutosofia* (Padua, 1592), p. 14r.
16. Tommaso Garzoni, *Piazza universale* (Venice, 1578), disc. LX.
17. Lambert Schenkel, *Gazophylacium artis memoriae* (Strasburg, 1610), pp. 26–8.
18. Francesco Petrarca, *Rerum memorandum libri,* ed. G. Billanovich (Florence, 1943), pp. 46, 48.
19. Schenkel, *Gazophylacium*, p. 28.
20. Petrarca, *Rerum memorandum libri*, p. 46.
21. Yates, 'The Ciceronian art of memory', pp. 893–4.
22. Schenkel, *Gazophylacium*, p. 28.
23. Yates, 'The Ciceronian art of memory', p. 890.
24. Jean Belot, *Les Oeuvres de M. Jean Belot contenant la chiromancie, physionomie, l'art de memoire de Raymond Lulle* (Lyons, 1654), p. 334.
25. Denis Diderot and Jean le Rond d'Alembert, *Encyclopédie, ou Dictionnaire raisonné des sciences, des arts et des metiers, par une societé de gens de lettres*, 17 vols. (Paris, 1751–65).

26. Naples, Bibliotheca Oratoriana, MS. Phil. XV, n. 11, (16th century, 55 unnumbered folios). See Eugenio Garin, 'Note e Notizie', *Giornale critico della filosofia italiana*, Third Series, 13:1 (1959), p. 159 and Enrico Mandarini, *I codici manoscritti della Biblioteca oratoriana di Napoli; illustrati da Enrico Mandarini* ... *Opera premiata dalla R. Accademia di archeologia, lettere e belle arti di Napoli*. (Naples, 1897), p. 122.

27. Praz, *Studi del concettismo*, p. 233.

28. See also *Artificiosae memoriae fundamenta ex Aristotele, Cicerone, Thoma Aquinate* (Lyons, 1619), and *Introductio facilis in praxin artificiosae memoriae* (Lyons, 1619).

29. See Morhof, *Polyhistor literarius*, II, p. 455 and Thorndike, *History of Magic and Experimental Science*, V, p. 326 and VI, pp. 137, 368, 485 and 506.

30. Diderot, *Encyclopedie* (Lucca, 1767), X, pp. 263–4.

31. On Yvon and his intellectual position see Franco Venturi, *Le origini dell'Enciclopedia (L'Illuminismo politico in Francia)* (Rome: Edizioni U, 1946), pp. 40–8.

32. 'Winkelmann' was the pseudonym of Stanislaus Mink von Venusheim.

33. The *Journal littéraire* of 1720, on which see Couturat and Leau, *Histoire de la langue universelle*, pp. 29 et seq.

Index